PSYCHOLOGICAL METHODS IN CRIMINAL INVESTIGATION AND EVIDENCE

David C. Raskin, Ph.D.
Editor

SPRINGER PUBLISHING COMPANY
New York

Copyright © 1989 by Springer Publishing Company, Inc.

All rights reserved

No part of this publication may be reproduced, stored in a retrieval system, or transmitted in any form or by any means, electronic, mechanical, photocopying, recording or otherwise, without the prior permission of Springer Publishing Company, Inc.

Springer Publishing Company, Inc.
536 Broadway
New York, NY 10012

89 90 91 92 93 / 5 4 3 2 1

Library of Congress Cataloging-in-Publication Data

Psychological methods in criminal investigation and evidence / edited by David C. Raskin.
   p.   cm.
  Bibliography
  Includes index.
  ISBN 0-8261-6450-1
  1. Evidence (Law)—United States. 2. Witnesses—United States.
3. Psychology, Forensic. I. Raskin, David C.
KF9660.P87 1989
345.73'06—dc19   89-4301
[347.3056]   CIP

Printed in the United States of America

In Memory of

Robbi Morris
Scholar, Colleague, and Friend

Contents

Introduction　　vii

Contributors　　xiii

PART I　ISSUES IN EYEWITNESS PERFORMANCE　　1

1　The Psychology of Eyewitness Testimony　　3
　Elizabeth F. Loftus, Edith L. Greene, and *James M. Doyle*

2　Procedures for Obtaining Identification Evidence　　47
　Brian R. Clifford and *Graham Davies*

3　Field Studies of Eyewitness Memory of Actual Crimes　　97
　Judith Cutshall and *John C. Yuille*

4　Legal Issues in Eyewitness Evidence　　125
　James M. Doyle

PART II　INTERVIEWING AND ASSESSING WITNESSES, VICTIMS, AND SUSPECTS　　149

5　Investigative Hypnosis　　151
　Martin Reiser

6	The Cognitive Interview Technique for Victims and Witnesses of Crime	191
	R. Edward Geiselman and *Ronald P. Fisher*	
7	Criteria-Based Statement Analysis	217
	Max Steller and *Guenter Koehnken*	
8	Polygraph Techniques for the Detection of Deception	247
	David C. Raskin	
9	Hazards in Detecting Deceit	297
	Paul Ekman and *Maureen O'Sullivan*	
10	The Admissibility of Evidence Derived from Hypnosis and Polygraphy	333
	Roberta A. Morris	

Index 379

Introduction

During the last 20 years there has been a dramatic increase in the use of investigative methods that involve psychological techniques and expertise. This has been accompanied by a growing realization by law enforcement personnel, judges, and attorneys that many traditional investigative methods are highly dependent on psychological processes for their effectiveness. Furthermore, it has become clear that a variety of factors can affect the outcomes of investigative procedures and alter the testimony of witnesses. As a result, psychologists have become heavily involved in research to increase our understanding of these processes so that their effectiveness can be improved and problems in their applications can be avoided.

This book provides the scientific and professional communities with current psychological knowledge, and the current legal status, of major methods used for investigation and evidence in law enforcement and other legal situations, many of which are complex and controversial. It includes in-depth summaries and analyses of the scientific literature on topics such as eyewitness perception and memory, identification procedures, interview techniques, and credibility assessment. In addition, there are thorough and up-to-date summaries of the legal issues surrounding the use of some of these methods and information for evidentiary purposes.

The first section of the book is devoted to processes and issues in eyewitness performance. The first chapter, by Loftus, Doyle, and Greene, describes the basic processes of human perception and memory as they relate to the abilities of eyewitnesses to perceive and accurately recall events that they have observed. They provide the necessary background for understanding the limits of human perception and memory and the many difficulties that can arise when investigators attempt to gather information and identifications concerning an event of interest.

Clifford and Davies present a detailed description of the various methods employed by investigators for obtaining eyewitness descriptions and identifications. They review the literature pertaining to these methods and describe research and development efforts to improve the use of techniques for obtaining composite descriptions of suspects and identifications from photo spreads, lineups, and voice samples. These analyses will greatly assist those whose task is to obtain information and identifications, as well as those who must look for weaknesses in the procedures that were employed in specific cases.

The chapter by Cutshall and Yuille presents a series of studies of eyewitness performance and memory in criminal cases that brings together knowledge from laboratory studies of witness behavior and data gathered from police and psychologist interviews of witnesses to actual crimes. These data represent the first extensive study of witness performance and memory derived from police investigations of serious crime. Interestingly, their results reinforce many of the findings and conclusions derived from laboratory simulation research, while challenging the common laboratory finding that witness memories are relatively short-lived.

The legal perspective on eyewitness evidence and the controversial use of expert testimony concerning that evidence is explored by James Doyle. He provides an overview of the evidentiary and legal issues relating to eyewitness testimony and discusses the problems surrounding the use of psychologists as expert witnesses to educate judges and jurors about the strengths and weaknesses of eyewitness performance as they relate to deciding the guilt or innocence of criminal defendants. This rapidly developing area of professional and legal controversy is thoroughly explored, to meet the needs of lawyers and psychologists.

The next section of the book deals with important techniques for interviewing and assessing witnesses, victims, and accused persons. These chapters not only review relevant scientific literatures, but they also present detailed descriptions of techniques and procedures that will be of great value to the professional practitioner and investigator.

This section begins with Reiser's thorough exposition and analysis of the use of hypnosis to assist witnesses to recall information, describe events, and provide identifications. In this very controversial area, his presentation explores the various issues from scientific and applied perspectives. He provides the reader with a detailed picture of the use of hypnosis interviews in investigation, including a comprehensive discussion of the data that bear on the controversy concerning its effectiveness in criminal investigation and the appropriateness of testimony from witnesses who have undergone such interviews.

Geiselman and Fisher present the methods of the cognitive interview technique that they developed. In response to the criticisms and limitations placed by courts on the use of hypnosis interviews, they embarked on a project to construct an interview protocol using principles derived from cognitive psychology that would enhance witness recall and performance without incorporating the problems and pitfalls of hypnosis procedure. They describe the psychological rationale of the cognitive interview, describe its procedures, and present the scientific evidence concerning the procedures' effectiveness. They also compare the cognitive interview to hypnosis and demonstrate its utility and desirability in criminal investigation.

The chapter by Steller and Koehnken presents for the first time in the English language literature a description of assessment procedures developed in Germany for use with child witnesses in sexual abuse cases. The problem of evaluating children's statements concerning sexual abuse has grown to enormous proportions in the United States, but the Germans developed and implemented special methods to deal with this problem more than 30 years ago. This chapter provides a detailed description of the method of content analysis used by German psychologists to distinguish between descriptions of events that were actually experienced and those that were invented by a child. This is an extremely valuable approach that should be of great interest to psychologists, investigators, and case workers who must deal effectively with this important social problem.

The chapter by Raskin on polygraph techniques provides an analysis of the psychological basis for the use of physiological methods for detection of deception. It also presents detailed descriptions and analyses of the major polygraph techniques and the scientific literature concerning their accuracies in investigative applications. Many of the controversial aspects of these techniques are thoroughly explored from a scientific as well as practical point of view. Since these methods are frequently discussed and misunderstood by members of the scientific and legal communities, this exposition is designed to foster better understanding among psychologists, investigators, attorneys, and judges.

Attempting to detect deception is most frequently performed without the aid of instruments, and Ekman and O'Sullivan provide an exposition of some of the basic principles and problems that must be considered by those whose task includes the assessment of credibility. They discuss basic psychological processes involved in deception, along with factors that may affect the likelihood of success on the part of both the deceiver and the person whose task it is to detect the deception. Many of the characteristics of deceptive contexts and motives for deception and detection are analyzed, and the authors present a method by which those who attempt to assess credibility may avoid some of the pitfalls of detecting deception.

The final chapter is by Roberta Morris, to whom this book is dedicated. Just before her untimely death, she provided us with the most extensive legal analysis yet performed on the issues surrounding the uses of evidence obtained from hypnosis

Introduction

interviews and polygraph examinations. The fruits of this monumental effort constitute a presentation of the scientific and legal issues raised against the admissibility of such evidence and a comprehensive treatment of the legal status of the evidence in the federal and state courts. This information will be especially useful to those who employ such methods and to those who must contend with problems regarding their evidentiary value.

Contributors

Brian R. Clifford is Reader in the Psychology Department of North East London Polytechnic. He received his B.A. and his Ph.D. from London University. He also has an M.Sc. in artificial intelligence from Brunel University. He has published two books and some 45 papers in the area of eyewitness testimony. In addition, he has acted as an expert witness in several major criminal cases in the United Kingdom.

Judith Cutshall received her M.A. in cognitive psychology from the University of British Columbia in 1985. She is currently completing work on her Ph.D. in clinical psychology. Her interests include the application of psychological research to forensic and clinical settings.

Graham Davies is Professor of Psychology and Head of the Psychology Department, North East London Polytechnic. He obtained his B.A. and Ph.D. from the University of Hull. Much of the research on composite systems described in Chapter 2 was conducted at Aberdeen University in association with Hadyn Ellis and John Shepherd, for the British Home Office. His research interests remain focused on the accuracy and reliability of eyewitness testimony, and he is currently involved in research on children's credibility and suggestibility.

James M. Doyle is a senior trial counsel with the Committee for Public Counsel Services, the public defender in Boston, Massachusetts. He graduated from Trinity College in 1972 with a B.A. in English and political science. In 1975 he received a J.D. from the Northwestern

University School of Law. He was awarded an E. Barrett Prettyman Fellowship at Georgetown University Law Center in 1975 and completed the Legal Internship Program with an LL.M. degree in 1979. He received a Deutscher Akademischer Austauschdienst Fellowship from the German government in 1982 and an Interdisciplinary Criminal Justice Fellowship from the Law Enforcement Assistance Administration in 1974. He is active in both the trial representation of indigent defendants in serious felony cases and in postconviction representation of capital defendants and is also the author of several articles on legal aspects of eyewitness identification testimony and the coauthor, with Elizabeth Loftus, of *Eyewitness Testimony: Civil and Criminal.*

Paul Ekman was an undergraduate at the University of Chicago and New York University. He received his Ph.D. in clinical psychology at Adelphi University in 1958, after a year's internship at the Langley Porter Neuropsychiatric Institute. After 2 years as a Clinical Psychology Officer in the U.S. Army, he returned to Langley Porter in 1960, where he has been ever since. His research on facial expression and body movement began in 1954 and served as the subject of his Master's thesis in 1955 and of his first publication in 1957. In addition to his basic research on emotion and its expression, he has, for the last 20 years, also been studying deceit.

Currently he is Professor of Psychology and Director of the Human Interaction Laboratory the University of California, San Francisco. In 1971 he received a Research Scientist Award from the National Institute of Mental Health that award was renewed in 1976, 1981, and 1987.

Ekman is a coauthor of *Emotion in the Human Face* (1971), *Unmasking the Face* (1975), and *Facial Action Coding System* (1978); the editor of *Darwin and Facial Expression* (1973); a co-editor of *Handbook of Methods in Nonverbal Behavior Research* (1982) and *Approaches to Emotion* (1984); and the author of *Face of Man* (1980) and *Telling Lies* (1985, paperback, 1986). His next book will be entitled *Why Kids Lie.*

Ronald P. Fisher is Associate Professor of Psychology at Florida International University. He holds a Ph.D. in experimental psychology from Ohio State University and has contributed articles on memory theory and retrieval processes to several scientific journals. He is a member of the American Psychological Association and the Psychonomic Society.

R. Edward Geiselman is Associate Professor of Psychology at the University of California at Los Angeles. He received his Ph.D. in experimental psychology from Ohio State University and has contributed articles on memory theory and applied psychology to several scientific journals. He is a member of the American Psychological Association and the Psychonomic Society.

Edith L. Greene is Assistant Professor of Psychology at the University of Colorado in Colorado Springs. She earned her B.A. in 1975 at Stanford University, her M.A. in 1977 at the University of Colorado, and her Ph.D. in 1983 at the University of Washington.

Guenter Koehnken received his Ph.D. in psychology at the University of Kiel in 1982, where he is currently Lecturer in Psychology. His publications have dealt with the areas of psychology and law, clinical psychology, and organizational psychology.

Elizabeth F. Loftus is Professor of Psychology and Adjunct Professor of Law at the University of Washington. She received her B.A. from the University of California at Los Angeles in 1966, and her M.A. and Ph.D. from Stanford University in 1967 and 1970, respectively.

Roberta A. Morris received her J.D. and Ph.D. in social psychology from the University of Nebraska at Lincoln in 1982 and 1987, respectively. After serving several years as Assistant Professor in the Psychology Department at the University of Nebraska at Lincoln, she became a practicing attorney at Banta, Hoyt, Banta, Greene, Hannen & Everall, P.C., in Englewood, Colorado. She was a member of the Disability Law Committee of the Colorado Bar Association, Chair of the Behavioral Sciences Committee in the Section of Science and Technology of the American Bar Association, and Adjunct Assistant Professor in the Psychology Department of the University of Nebraska at Lincoln.

David C. Raskin received his Ph.D. in experimental psychology at the University of California at Los Angeles (UCLA) in 1963. He has served on the faculties of UCLA and Michigan State University and is currently Professor of Psychology at the University of Utah. Dr. Raskin has conducted extensive scientific research in psychophysiology and has been deeply involved in detection of deception research and applications of polygraph techniques and other methods for assessment of credibility. He is a past president of the Rocky Mountain Psychological Association, a fellow of the Division on Psychology and Law of the American Psychological Association, and has testified on polygraph techniques and credibility assessment before committees of the U.S.

Senate, the British House of Commons, the Israeli Supreme Court, and federal and state courts all over North America.

Martin Reiser is Director of Behavioral Science Services for the Los Angeles Police Department. He received his Ed.D. in Clinical and School Psychology from Temple University in 1961. A diplomate in clinical psychology, he is also a Fellow of the American Psychological Association and of the American College of Forensic Psychology. A past president of the Los Angeles County Psychological Association, he is the author of 90 articles and four books: *The Police Department Psychologist,* 1972; *Practical Psychology for Police Officers,* 1973; *Handbook of Investigative Hypnosis,* 1980; *Police Psychology—Collected Papers,* 1982.

Max Steller received his Ph.D. at the University of Kiel in 1974 and is currently Professor for Forensic Psychology at the Free University of Berlin. His publications have been devoted to the areas of forensic and criminal psychology, clinical psychology, and psychodiagnostics, and include a training program for prison staff and books on behavior modification with juvenile delinquents, psychological problems of offender therapy, and psychophysiological methods of detection of deception. He is the coauthor of a forthcoming book on interview and assessment techniques in cases of child sexual abuse.

Maureen O'Sullivan received her Ph.D. in psychometrics at the University of Southern California under Dr. J. P. Guilford. From 1966 to 1972 she was Senior Psychologist at the Langley Porter Neuropsychiatric Institute and Professor of Medical Psychology at the University of California, San Francisco. Since 1972 she has been at the University of San Francisco, where she is currently Professor and Chair of the Department of Psychology. Her research interests are in social intelligence, nonverbal communication, individual differences in emotional expressiveness, and psychological factors in detecting deceit.

John C. Yuille received his Ph.D. from the University of Western Ontario in 1967. He is currently Professor of Psychology at the University of British Columbia. His research interests include human memory, cognition, and forensic psychology.

Issues in Eyewitness Performance

I

The Psychology of Eyewitness Testimony

1

Elizabeth F. Loftus, Edith L. Greene, and James M. Doyle

In July 1977, *Flying Magazine* reported the fatal crash of a small plane that killed all eight people aboard and one person who was on the ground. Sixty eyewitnesses were interviewed, although only a few appeared at a hearing to investigate the accident. Two of these people had actually seen the airplane just before impact, and 1 of them was certain that "it was heading right toward the ground—straight down." This witness apparently did not know that several photographs of the crash site made it absolutely clear that the airplane hit flat and at a low enough angle to skid for almost 1,000 ft.

This example points to the serious problems posed by evidence provided by eyewitnesses, due to the influence of memory processes that normally occur whenever human beings acquire, retain, and attempt to retrieve information. These processes hamper the efforts of scientific and legal institutions in attaining their shared goal of discovering the truth about past events.

Psychologists have become interested in eyewitness testimony for a variety of reasons, although no reason is likely to be stranger than that of Australian psychologist Donald Thomson.

Thomson found his interest in the topic fueled after he became a victim of mistaken identification (Baddeley, 1982). Thomson had taken part in a televised discussion of the topic of eyewitness testimony. Within a short time of his television appearance, he was arrested and accused of rape. Much to his shock, the rape victim identified him from a lineup. He pressed the police for details of the rape and discovered that it had occurred at precisely the same time as his television appearance. He explained that he had an excellent alibi, as he had been on television with the Australian Civil Rights Committee and an assistant commissioner of police. Further investigation into the case showed that the woman had been raped while watching the television program, and that she had apparently merged her image of Thomson's face with her memory of this tragic episode.

Thomson's experience is certainly unusual, but it has features common to many other known cases. It is a clear-cut instance of mistaken identification. The tip of the iceberg of mistaken identification has been revealed dramatically in newspaper stories over the years. The *New York Post* (December 30, 1980) reported that "an innocent South Carolina man, charged with the murder of [a police officer] expressed a sigh of relief yesterday when told he was cleared." Three eyewitnesses searching police mugshot files had picked out this man, but he had been able to prove that he had been at work that day.

The *Seattle Times* ran this headline on November 25, 1980: "Five years in prison, innocent man home." The story was about a former Baptist Sunday school teacher who had been convicted of two rapes that prosecutors now know he did not do. Two women had identified him in a police lineup as the man who raped them, but another man eventually confessed to the crimes.

From the *San Francisco Chronicle* of March 5, 1981, we learned that "the wrong man spent nine years in prison." Aaron Lee Owens of Oakland, California, was convicted of double murder after several eyewitnesses positively identified him. New evidence that eventually freed Owens took many years to uncover.

This chapter explores the factors that may contribute to such tragedies as these and how psychologists have contributed to their prevention. First, it is important to understand why people misidentify others. Researchers have uncovered a number of factors that influence how people attempt to identify or recognize persons they have seen in the past. We know, for example, that variables inherent in the criminal act itself, including its duration, violence level, lighting conditions, and the type of facts involved, can affect a witness's memory. Variables inherent in the witness, including stress level, gender, age, expectations, previous training prior to recognition attempts, and physiological state, also may have a role in influencing a person's ability to attend to the details of a scene. During the retention interval, the witness may simply forget details of the event or may be influenced by postevent information. Researchers have demonstrated that the effects of postevent information can be mitigated through the use of warnings and nonleading questions, but in practice these optimal conditions are rare. Finally, psychologists and other have recently focused much attention on attempts to ameliorate the identification process at the time of retrieval. Their studies have focused on varying methods of asking questions and on using techniques such as context reinstatement, hypnosis, and cognitive interviews to improve the conditions surrounding retrieval.

We will never know how many people have been mistakenly identified and, like Donald Thomson, Aaron Lee Owens, the South Carolina man, and the Baptist Sunday school teacher, deserve to have newspaper stories written about their plights. However, psychologists have amassed a sizeable body of scientific knowledge that has advanced our understanding of the cognitive and social processes that underlie eyewitness memory. This chapter presents an overview of that work.

GENERAL THEORY OF PERCEPTION AND MEMORY

Over a period of decades, a number of investigators have established that our experiences of important events are not simply recorded in memory like a videotape. Rather, most theoretical analyses divide the memory process into three major stages. First, the event is perceived by a witness, and information is entered into the memory system. This is called *the acquisition stage*. Next, time passes before a witness attempts to remember the event; this is called *the retention stage*. Finally, the witness tries to recall the stored information; this is called *the retrieval stage*. This three-stage analysis is central to the concept of human memory, and psychologists try to identify and study the important factors in each of the three stages. The numerous factors now known to affect the accuracy and completeness of an eyewitness account will be discussed in detail in succeeding sections.

ACQUIRING INFORMATION IN MEMORY

During the acquisition stage, information about an event is perceived by the witness. The event may last a few seconds or several hours. Many factors influence the quality of information that is stored in memory at this time. It is customary to divide these acquisition factors into two major classes. First, there are factors inherent in the event itself, such as the lighting conditions and duration of the event, and its factual features. Second, there are factors inherent in the witness, among them age and gender.

Event Factors

Lighting Conditions

Many crimes and accidents occur at night. In fact, more than half of all traffic deaths occur at night, even though we drive less at night than during the day (Leibowitz & Owens, 1986). Under the best of conditions, (high beams, no glare from oncoming traffic, a pedestrian dressed in white) a driver can see a pedestrian from about 300 ft, and it takes the average driver 317 ft to stop a car traveling 55 mph. Under less than ideal conditions (low beams, dark clothing) visibility drops to less than 100 ft. This poor visibility means that even drivers who are traveling at reasonable speeds cannot see pedestrians in time to avoid hitting them.

The commonsense notions that people see better in good light than in poor light and better during the day than at night were tested in a recent study by Yarmey (1986) that evaluated verbal, visual, and voice identifications of a rape suspect under different levels of illumination. Participants in this study viewed a color slide sequence depicting an assault and an implied rape under one of four simulated illumination conditions: daylight, start of twilight, end of twilight, and night. Free reports of assailant and victim characteristics and identifications from lineups were more accurate when made under the first two lighting conditions than under the latter two. Discrepancies between subjective estimates of accuracy and the completeness of recall were most apparent in the night-viewing condition, where subjects recalled only 0.06% of the assailant characteristics, although they claimed to be 74% accurate and 65% complete in their reports. Apparently, subjects were confident of their witnessing abilities even under conditions of poor illumination and poor performance.

Dark adaptation. Abrupt changes in lighting conditions can also result in poor visual sensitivity. When illumination decreases to a level of darkness, the witness will undoubtedly have difficulty seeing. The ability to adapt to the dark can take up to 30 min, depending on the intensity and duration of the light to which the person was previously exposed.

Dark adaptation can be explained by the differential functions of the two major types of retinal cells, rods and cones. Rods mediate nighttime or low-illumination vision. Cones mediate daytime or high-illumination vision and are primarily responsible for color vision. Thus, we see little color by moonlight because there is not enough light to stimulate the cones, but we can see shades of light and dark because moonlight is intense enough to stimulate the rods. Since rods provide a much less sharp image than do cones, dimly lit objects often appear coarse and ill defined.

Light adaptation. A person who goes suddenly from darkness into light typically experiences a moment of visual discomfort, but recovery of visual sensitivity takes place relatively quickly, when compared to dark adaptation. Light adaptation is mostly complete in a matter of a few seconds. However, there is some residual recovery of sensitivity over a period of approximately 15 sec, during which time the cones complete their recovery of sensitivity (Sekular & Blake, 1985). Eyewitnesses who experience an abrupt change from one lighting condition to another during the event may have difficulty accurately seeing what occurs.

Duration of Event

It seems obvious that the longer a person looks at something, the better the memory of it will be. Less obvious is what happens when people recall an event and try to estimate how long it lasted. It is of interest to know the accuracy of the duration estimates routinely given by eyewitnesses in court. In terms of fast-moving, complex events, people tend to overestimate duration. For example, Marshall (1966) asked subjects to watch a 42-sec film in which a young man rocked a baby carriage and then fled when a woman approached him. A week later, subjects were asked to estimate the duration of the film. The subjects thought it had lasted about 90 sec.

In another study, subjects witnessed a staged assault on a university campus. The entire event was recorded on videotape and lasted 34 sec. Later, subjects were asked questions, including the duration of the incident. The average estimated duration was 81 sec, more than double the actual duration (Buckhout, 1977).

Sometimes the estimate of time is extremely exaggerated. In one study (Loftus, Schooler, Boone, & Kline, 1986), subjects viewed a 30-sec simulated bank robbery on videotape. Two days later they were asked questions about the tape, including how long it lasted. The average estimate of duration was 152 sec. Very few people (6% of men and less than 1% of women) estimated a duration that was equal to or less than the true value of 30 sec.

Taken together, the literature paints a clear picture of witness overestimation of time, indicating that time estimates produced by witnesses should be only cautiously accepted. This observation about time estimation can also help one to understand time overestimation in the real world. In one study of actual crime victims (Schneider, Griffith, Sumi, & Burcart, 1978), over 200 reports of crime incidents from a Portland, Oregon, survey were matched with official crime reports of the same incidents. Among other facts, victims were asked to estimate the amount of time it took before the police arrived on the scene. Only two victims estimated the time to be shorter than that indicated by the police records. Almost half of the victims estimated the time within 15 min of the time given on the police report, and the other half said that the time was at least 15 min longer than indicated by the police report. Most dramatic were the estimates, amounting to 10% of the total, that differed from the police estimate by over 2 hr. Although the police may have underestimated the time, the possibility of such a large discrepancy is remote because recordings were routinely made of the victim's call to the police, the dispatcher's call to the officer, and the officer's call upon arrival at the scene. Thus, it is highly likely that the victims overestimated, sometimes quite dramatically.

Type of Fact

Witnesses to crimes and accidents are typically asked about a variety of facts, some of which may be crucial to the resolution of the case. In a criminal case, important facts often concern the height, weight, and hair color of the perpetrator of the crime. In cases involving auto accidents, the witness might be asked about the speed of the vehicles involved in the accident. These different types of facts are not equally easy to perceive and recall, and it is important to know about the errors that people make.

Speed and distance. Accurate judgments of speed and distance are difficult. In one early study, Cattell (1895) asked students to estimate the distance between two buildings on the college grounds. The actual distance was 310 ft, and the average estimate was 356 ft.

Estimating speed is of greater concern because it is often a crucial fact in accident cases. There can be large variations from one witness to another as to how fast a vehicle was actually traveling. In one test administered to U.S. Air Force personnel who knew in advance that they would be questioned about the speed of a moving automobile, estimates ranged from 10 to 50 mph for a car that was actually going only 12 mph (Marshall, 1966).

Speed estimates are influenced by some interesting perceptual errors, as Leibowitz (1985) found in his study of collisions at railroad crossings. Leibowitz began his investigation by riding in the cab of a locomotive that retraced the route on which an accident had occurred earlier. Surprisingly, he saw that many drivers drove around the crossing gates and crossed the tracks in front of an oncoming train.

To attempt to determine why people risk their lives in this way, Leibowitz (1985) relied on estimates that had shown that the size of an object influences its apparent speed. Large objects appear to be moving more slowly than small objects, even when they are moving at the same speed. Thus, the great bulk of most trains can cause their speed to be seriously underestimated. This in turn causes people to overestimate the time the train will take to reach the crossing, so that they think they have enough time to dash across ahead of the train.

Color vision. Because the retina's rods cannot convey information about the different wavelengths of light under conditions of dim illumination, we see only variations in intensity in the dark. Despite this general law, it is important to realize that even during daylight, not everyone's experience of color is the same. Most striking are the perceptions of people whose color vision differs markedly from normal.

There are different types of color blindness. A few people have monochromatic, or total, color blindness (Sekular & Blake, 1985). They see the world in shades of gray. A more common type of deficiency is dichromatic color blindness. These people lack one of the three visual pigments typically found in the cones. Most dichromats are red-green blind; they see everything in shades of blue and yellow. Less common are people who are blue-yellow blind; they see the world in shades of red and green. The incidence of color blindness is much higher in males than females (Hurvich, 1981).

Many types of color blindness are genetic in origin, but some are caused by certain diseases (Adams, Zisman, Rodic, & Cavender, 1982). Alcoholism occasionally causes color disturbances, such that reds look darker than they actually are. Certain toxins, such as the carbon disulfide used in insecticides, can cause color disturbances. In fact, the presence of abnormal color vision can often serve as an early warning of a health threat (Sekular & Blake, 1985).

Even normal aging can affect color vision. After approximately the age of 50, changes occur in the lens of the eye, causing blues to look darker and be more readily confused with greens (Weale, 1982). This problem is sufficiently pervasive to have caused researchers to worry that it could cause an elderly person to mistake one type of medicine capsule for another (Hurd & Blevins, 1984). The same problem can cause an elderly person to mistake a car of one color for another and give erroneous testimony in a hit-and-run accident case. In short, whenever color perception is crucial, these potential color abnormalities should be explored.

Violence of an Event

An important question concerns the extent to which people are capable of reporting the details of a violent event. To study this issue, Clifford and Hollin (1981) asked witnesses to watch a videotape that showed a woman walking, alone, toward the camera. In the violent version, a man grabbed her arm, forced her back against a wall, and then pulled her bag from her grasp. He then ran away, leaving the woman alone and sobbing. In the nonviolent version, the man approached the woman and asked for directions. After viewing the tape, the subjects were asked to recall the incident and to identify the man from a set of photographs. The results showed that accuracy of testimony was consistently poorer in the violent condition, replicating earlier work (Clifford & Scott, 1978).

These results suggest that the violence of an event can hamper witnesses' ability to perceive and remember it. Further research suggests that the violence of an event can also distort the perceptions that occurred prior to the outbreak of violence.

Loftus and Burns (1982) showed witnesses a short film of a shocking event that ended when a young boy was violently shot in the face. Compared to other witnesses who saw a nonviolent version of the same film, those who saw the shocking version showed poorer retention of details. The impairment in memory occurred not only for items seen immediately prior to the critical incident but also for items that occurred nearly 2 min earlier. One explanation for these memory deficits is that mental shock disrupts the subsequent processing necessary for full storage of information in memory. Whatever the exact reason for the poorer performance in the case of the violent incident, it is clear that testimony about an emotionally loaded incident should be treated with a degree of caution.

Another source of information about people's memories for emotional events comes from studies that compared survey reports of crime incidents with actual police records. In one study, interviews were conducted with people who were known to have been victims of crimes during the 12-month period preceding the interview (*San Jose Methods Test*, 1972). Information obtained from each respondent during the interview was compared with data in police files. About 74% of all incidents, and 84% of property crimes for which the victim was interviewed, were mentioned to the survey interviewer. Thus, people seem reasonably good at remembering that the crime did happen, at least if they were asked within a year of its occurrence. However, their ability to recall certain details, such as the dollar loss or the month of occurrence, was not particularly good.

There are several explanations for these memory deficits. Emotional events cause people to become more self-preoccupied, more worried, or more distracted (Eysenck, 1983; Sarason, 1975). However, some aspects of emotional events are well remembered, whereas other aspects suffer. One theoretical perspective that seems to deal with that observation is that of Easterbrook (1959), who emphasized the effects of emotionality on the selectivity of attention. According to this view, a highly emotional event is accompanied by attentional narrowing. This restricted range of viewing induced by the emotional event means that fewer details are noticed. The process of attentional selectivity could conceivably improve memory for the main theme of the event and some of the central details, but the encoding of peripheral details will consequently suffer.

An event that is sufficiently emotional to cause a person to focus on the main theme of the event and a few of the outstanding details is likely to be rehearsed, either overtly or covertly. Accurate rehearsal would be expected to improve the persistence of the information initially extracted. The most vivid memories, such as of injuries or accidents, tend to be rehearsed (Rubin & Kozin, 1984). This rehearsal can freeze certain accurately rehearsed details, but it can also freeze the inaccurately rehearsed details.

Recent research (Christianson & Loftus, 1986) supports the hypothesis that people are better able to recall the occurrence of an emotional event as compared to a nonemotional event and to recall aspects of the emotional event that were focused on and accurately rehearsed. At the same time, the more peripheral details of the event were not rehearsed and were recalled less well.

Witness Factors

The lighting, duration, factual features, and violence of an event are factors inherent in the event itself. In addition to these, there are many significant factors inherent in the witness. For example, the amount of stress or fear that a witness experienced during the acquisition stage will influence the quality of information that is stored in memory. We now consider some of these witness factors.

Stress and Fear

A vivid description of the effects of stress was published over 80 years ago (Mosso, 1896, cited in Idzikowski & Baddeley, 1983):

> Never shall I forget that evening. From behind the curtains of the glass door I peered into the large amphitheatre crowded with

people. It was my first appearance as a lecturer, and most humbly did I repent having undertaken to try my powers in the same hall in which my most celebrated teachers had so often spoken. . . . As the hour grew nearer, stronger waxed within me the fear that I should become confused, lose myself, and finally stand gaping, speechless before my audience. My heart beat violently, its very strings seemed to tighten, and my breast [*sic*] came and went as when one looks down into a yawning abyss. . . . As I cast the last glance at my notes, I became aware, to my horror, that the chain of ideas was broken and the links lost beyond recall. (pp. 123–124)

Mosso's experience is not uncommon; the same symptoms can be experienced by witnesses to accidents and crimes. Even in the absence of obvious physical symptoms, many people experience a high degree of arousal as a result of witnessing such traumatic events. An important question concerns the possible effects of arousal on witness accuracy.

The role that stress plays at the time a witness experiences a complex event can be captured in the Yerkes-Dodson Law (Yerkes & Dodson, 1908), which suggests that the level of performance will sometimes be improved and sometimes be lowered by increases in stress. As a general rule, there seems to be an optimal level of stress at which performance is at its best. Stress levels lower or higher than this optimal level will interfere with performance.

The Yerkes-Dodson Law also states that the optimal level of stress and the shape of the curve relating stress to performance may be different with different tasks. A simple, well learned habit is much less susceptible to disruption by emotional arousal than a more complex response. In a moment of intense fear, people would probably still be able to spell their names, but the ability to play a good game of chess would be seriously impaired.

Researchers have learned about the effects of stress by watching people perform in stressful circumstances. In one case, stress was induced in army recruits on a simulated tactical exercise. The recruits were made anxious by being told either that they were being shelled with live ammunition by mistake or that they had mistakenly been put in an area subject to intense, accidental atomic radiation. After an army recruit had been sufficiently stressed, he was required to contact headquarters by radio. The radio, however, was broken. In order to repair it, he had to follow complicated instructions. The study showed that simulated danger situations produced a good deal of anxiety that tended to hinder the ability to remember or follow detailed instructions (Berkun, Bialek, Kern, & Yagi, 1962).

In his review of the literature on arousal and eyewitness memory, Deffenbacher (1983) described 11 studies that suggest that higher arousal levels decrease eyewitness accuracy and 10 studies that suggest that they do not. Deffenbacher argued that the former group of studies seemed to have tapped arousal levels more similar to those that occur in the crimes of assault, homicide, rape, and robbery.

Studies have shown that inferior eyewitness memory under stressful conditions involves either experimentally manipulated arousal or high, individually assessed arousal levels. An example of the former is Loftus and Burns's (1982) study, in which witnesses saw either a violent or nonviolent version of a filmed bank robbery. Subjects who saw the violent version showed poorer recall and recognition of details in the film.

Individually assessed arousal levels were used in a study by Buckhout, Alper, Chern, Silverberg, and Slomovits (1974). Unsuspecting subjects witnessed a purse-snatching incident, and immediately after the incident they indicated on a 7-point scale how much stress they experienced. Subjects who felt relatively little stress at the scene of the "crime" were more accurate at recognizing the culprit from a subsequent videotaped lineup than were witnesses who reported higher levels of arousal at the scene. In a similar vein, Peters (1988) reported that only 31% of persons who responded to an inoculation with high physiological arousal were able to identify from a photospread the nurse who injected them, whereas 59% of those who responded with lower physiological arousal were able to do so.

Some recent field research questions these findings. Yuille and Cutshall (1986) interviewed 13 witnesses to a homicide in which a gun thief was shot and a store owner seriously injured. The witnesses were interviewed immediately after the incident and again 4 to 5 months later. At the second interview, they were questioned about the degree of stress they experienced at the time of the incident. The degree of reported stress was unrelated to the witness's accuracy. The overall mean accuracy level (as measured by correct action details, person descriptions, and object descriptions) in the second interview was 88% for people who reported high levels of arousal and 76% for those who reported more moderate levels of arousal. Yuille and Cutshall suggested that subjects who experienced heightened arousal were more directly involved in the event and may have had better viewing positions. In this instance, stress does not appear to have negatively affected memory. These conflicting findings suggest that laboratory studies may not generalize to the criminal justice system and that further field and archival research evaluating the effects of arousal on actual witnesses' memory is needed.

Weapon focus. One apparent effect of stress is a narrowing of attention, such that people concentrate on certain features of their environment and consequently pay less attention to other features. The term *weapon focus* refers to the concentration of a witness's attention on a weapon—the barrel of a gun or the blade of a knife—and the resultant reduction in ability to remember other details of the crime. Evidence for the existence of weapon focus stems from diverse sources. In the traditional perception literature, there are experiments in which eye movements have been monitored while people observe complex scenes. This work shows that people fixate faster, more often, and for longer durations on unusual or highly informative objects (Loftus & Mackworth, 1978). It is generally agreed by eye movement researchers that eye fixation data provide a valid measure of where and to what an individual is attending.

More conclusive evidence comes from a study in which eye movements were monitored while subjects watched one of two versions of an event that began with a customer going through a cafeteria line in a fast-food restaurant (Loftus, Loftus, & Messo, 1987). In the weapon version, the customer pointed a gun at the cashier, and she handed him some money. In the no-weapon version, the customer handed the cashier a check, and she returned some money. The events are identical except for the presence of the weapon in one case and the check in the other. Eye movements were recorded during the viewing of the event. The results of the study showed that subjects made more eye fixations on the weapon than on the check and that these eye fixations were of longer duration than fixations on the check. Moreover, the subjects who saw the weapon had poorer memory for other details of the event. They were also less able to recognize the culprit from a 12-person photospread.

Another recent study assessed the possibility of weapon focus (Tooley, Brigham, Maass, & Bothwell, 1987). Subjects played a bogus visual discrimination game in which they viewed 24 target photos. Half of the targets were holding an automatic pistol or machete in their hands, and the other half were holding similarly sized objects that were not weapons. A signal detection analysis assessed identification accuracy from a photospread, and the data showed a significant weapon focus effect. Subjects were better at identifying photographs of targets not holding weapons than targets who were holding weapons, even in situations where they were instructed to focus on the target's face.

In a real-life crime situation, weapon focus could be interwoven with high arousal caused by the crime itself and intensified by the presence of a weapon. The high stress itself could be expected to lead to a narrowing of the range of perceptual focus. In the studies of weapon focus, we have shown that such narrowing of perceptual focus can occur in response to a weapon, even when the events are not especially stressful. (See also Kramer, 1984, for additional evidence for weapon focus.)

Chronic Stress

Another kind of stress that is important to consider is general anxiety caused by stressful life events. This is different from the stress or anxiety produced by the crime or accident itself. It has been shown that people who have undergone a number of recent negative life changes, such as the death of a close friend or loss of a job, show small deficits in memory (Siegel & Loftus, 1978).

Chronic stress seems to cause preoccupation, so that individuals do not pay adequate attention to important cues in their environment. Thus, they may miss information that is crucial for accurate memory.

Expectations

The powerful effect of prior expectations on perception was demonstrated by Peterson (1976). In this study, witnesses watched a videotaped disturbance and fight that lasted about 7 min. The incident involved several main actors who started fighting at a forum organized for the purpose of considering the proposed impeachment of President Richard Nixon. Prior to viewing the tape, witnesses were provided with one of two explanations for the motives of the actors involved in the incident. One group of witnesses was led to believe that the actors were angry radicals who intended to prevent a speaker from completing a controversial talk. The other group of witnesses was led to believe that the actors were concerned about free speech and wanted to be sure that both sides of the controversial subject would be heard.

After seeing the tape, all witnesses answered questions about what had happened. Witnesses who were led to believe the angry-radical motivation remembered a larger proportion of details that were consistent with the conclusion that the actors wanted to prevent one side from speaking or wanted to attack or harm the speaker. They were less likely to remember facts that showed good behavior on the part of the radicals, such as that one of them said "Excuse me" to the speaker.

The biases created in this study are temporary biases. They are created a short time prior to some critical event. However, cultural expectations or biases can also affect the way we perceive and remember. In one study, subjects were exposed to an event in which a Black man and a white man were apparently arguing. The white man was holding a razor. Using a serial reproduction technique, in which one subject described the scene to a second who described it to a third, and so on, investigators found that in successive descriptions the razor often migrated from the hand of the white man into the hand of the Black man (Allport & Postman, 1947). This result was due to cultural biases or stereotypes.

Age

Researchers have recently become interested in the extent to which the age of a witness can affect the reliability of testimony. Some of these studies compare children to young adults, and some compare the elderly to young adults. In brief, psychological research seems to indicate that young children may be poorer eyewitnesses than young adults. Elderly individuals are also less proficient than young adults on some kinds of memory tasks.

The child witness. Over the years there has persisted a firm belief that children are not only inaccurate as witnesses but also highly suggestible. This view was stated most strongly by Brown (1926), who said, "Create, if you will, an idea of what the child is to hear or see, and the child is very likely to hear or see what you desire" (p. 133).

An accurate description of children's eyewitness memory is actually more complex than this. Children often report more limited information than adults, but what they report is not always less accurate. Two variables, the age of the child and the type of questioning used to evaluate the child's memory, are crucial to deciphering some conflicting results.

In several studies (Ceci, Ross, & Toglia, 1987; Goodman & Reed, 1985; King, 1984), very young children (3-year-olds) were found to be more suggestible than older children or adults. For example, Ceci et al. presented an illustrated story to children aged approximately 3, 5, 7, and 10. One day later, an experimenter met with each child and presented either biased or unbiased information about events in the story. When the children were instructed 2 days later to select a picture that accompanied the original story, the youngest children were more likely than the two older groups to select the suggested picture. Interestingly, studies that failed to find developmental differences in suggestibility involved children no younger than 5 years old (Duncan, Whitney, & Kunen, 1982; Marin, Holmes, Guth, & Kovac, 1979), so concern about suggestibility may be relevant only to very young children.

The type of question used to compare the memories of children and adults is crucial. Goodman and Reed (1985) tested 3-year-olds, 6-year-olds, and adults 4 or 5 days after they had interacted with an unfamiliar adult. Although the 3-year-olds were inferior to the other two groups in free recall, recognition, and answering objective and suggestive questions, the 6-year-olds were deficient on some measures and not others. They were comparable to adults in answering objective questions and recognizing the target in a photospread, but they recalled less than adults and were more suggestible. These data suggest that children's eyewitness abilities are not uniformly less reliable than adults. Rather, the age of the child and the ways in which the child is questioned are crucial mediating variables.

The elderly witness. In the last few years, interest in the elderly has intensified because people are living longer, and more crimes, accidents, and other legally important events are being witnessed by elderly people.

Researchers have attempted to identify specific memory processes that are affected by aging. It seems clear that performance in some kinds of memory situations, such as tasks involving hand-eye coordination, does weaken with age (Baltes & Schaie, 1976), but other cognitive functions are fully maintained with advancing age (Craik, 1977; Schaie, 1984). Even though performance may weaken, it is only the performance of the average older person compared to the performance of the average younger person. One person may show decline with advancing age whereas another shows no decline.

A few studies have examined how the elderly fare when it comes to the specific task of observing a complex event and remembering it later. In one study (Farrimond, 1968), men between the ages of 23 and 79 were shown scenes recorded on silent film. One scene showed a 4-sec clip of a young boy inflating a bicycle tire, and another showed a man winding up a watch. To conceal the purpose of the study, subjects were told to try to read the lips of a commentator after each scene was presented. This also ensured that they would pay attention to each of the scenes. Finally, a surprise memory test was given. The results showed that for men of both high and low intelligence, recall declined with advancing age and those in their mid-40s performed best.

In a study by Yarmey and Rashid (1981, reported in Yarmey, 1984), elderly and young adults viewed a simulated assault and robbery of a young man by either 1, 3, or 5 male assailants. A young adult male bystander appeared near the scene. Subjects were shown two photo lineups; one contained the assailants and the other contained a picture of the bystander. Results of this study showed that although the elderly and the young were equally accurate in recognizing the assailants in the lineup, the elderly showed deficits in facial recognition in the three and five-assailant conditions and were more likely than the young to identify the bystander as the criminal suspect.

Studies such as these lead to the conclusion that elderly witnesses are not as able as young adults to describe or identify people whom they have previously seen. Yarmey (1984) believes that these problems may be exacerbated when the observational conditions are ambiguous and brief. Thus, we must treat the testimony of the elderly with some degree of caution. Of course, this is not to say that elderly witnesses are of no value; it is only on the average that elderly witnesses perform less well than young adults.

Gender

Studies evaluating potential differences between men and women in eyewitness abilities have found equivocal results. Some studies have shown that women perform better than men (e.g., Ellis, Shepherd, & Bruce, 1973; Lipton, 1977). Other studies have shown that women perform worse (e.g., Trankell, 1972), or that there are no differences in the accuracy of women and men (Bird, 1927; Cady, 1924; Geiselman, Fisher, MacKinnon, & Holland, 1985).

A few studies have produced rather complicated results. For example, Clifford and Scott (1978) reported that men and women were equally accurate in recalling details of a nonviolent event, but men were better at recalling the details of a violent one. Yarmey and Jones (1983) reported that men and women were generally equivalent in their ability to recall details of a simulated assault and to recognize people previously seen. However, women showed a greater tendency to report that they had not seen an individual when they had. However, a close examination of the data reveals an interesting trend. The event that was shown was a simulated assault and rape. Subjects later tried to identify the suspect and the victim. When given a test that did not contain the correct individuals, women made more false identifications and fewer correct rejections with respect to the suspect, and men made more errors on the victim. This suggests that men and women may pay attention to different aspects of a criminal incident.

Some research suggests that women and men pay more attention to items that catch their interest and consequently store better information about those items. If a subsequent test asks about female-oriented items, women outperform men. The converse is true if the testing concerns male-oriented details (Powers, Andriks, & Loftus, 1979). In this research, subjects saw a simulated incident, and some were later exposed to misleading information about four critical items. Two critical items were male oriented, and two were female oriented. Results indicated that men were more accurate and less suggestible about the male-oriented items and women were more accurate and less suggestible about the female-oriented items.

One consequence of this differential interest is a difference in the effects of misleading information about these specific items on men and women. Eagly (1978) pointed out that "individuals are more readily influenced to the extent that they lack information about a topic or regard it as trivial and unimportant" (p. 96). The specific items are critical. One could select a set that would favor women or a set that would favor men. Thus, a piece of research could show men to be more accurate than women, or vice versa, depending on the specific items.

Training

One question concerns the extent to which some people, by virtue of their occupations, experience, or training, may be better witnesses. There are two ways that training or experience could help a witness's memory. First, the training could increase the likelihood that a witness would make a deliberate effort during the event itself to pay attention to details and explicitly try to remember them. With stressful crimes and accidents, witnesses without training may not think to do this. Training could also teach specific strategies for trying to remember details, such as to look for distinctive features of people or cars. The use of these specific strategies could lead to better memory over and above any benefits arising from the emphasis on good attention.

There is evidence that training can help people to notice certain kinds of special details, but it is questionable that training helps a person to remember ordinary descriptive details. Criminal justice specialists have suggested that police should receive training to look for both physical and behavioral clues that might escape the notice of a layperson (Silberman, 1978). For example, a jacket worn on a warm day might suggest a concealed weapon; a late-model car that has been repainted or a license plate that is too clean and shiny may suggest a stolen car. These are some of the signals to which some police are alert. Yet, trained law enforcement personnel may not be better at ordinary details. Evidence for this conclusion can be seen in research that compared trained arson investigators to students in terms of their ability to remember the details of a 24-min traumatic film depicting a large hospital fire (Keating & Loftus, 1981). The subjects were students and arson investigators from a large metropolitan area. They saw an extremely upsetting film in which numerous people were burned to death. Following the film, each subject answered 50 questions about the film. The trained arson investigators were no more accurate than the student population on nontechnical matters, but they were more accurate on items that specifically related to fire fighting, such as the number of water hoses the chief had ordered inside and outside of the building. This result constitutes additional evidence that new information is easier to assimilate when it relates to a familiar body of knowledge.

Additional studies of ability to remember details and to recognize the faces of strangers compared police or other specially trained people with laypersons. In one study on memory for details (Tinkner & Poulton, 1975), subjects watched a film that depicted a street scene. The subjects were police officers and civilians, and they were asked to watch for particular people in the film and to report instances of crimes, such as petty theft. The researchers found that the officers reported more false detections of thefts than the civilians, but the civilians did just as well in detecting actual crimes. This kind of result is partially responsible for Clifford's (1976) conclusion that the police perform poorer than laypersons due to their biased interpretation of events.

On the positive side, Yuille (1984) showed police trainees and university students a simulated auto accident. Yuille found that the police surpassed the students in recall of descriptive facts and had a lower percentage of errors in their recall. The students performed as well on questions about sequential information. Yuille thus demonstrated a positive effect of police training. In a subsequent experiment, Yuille tested police officers who had not only been trained but also had an average of 8 years of experience. When he compared them to another group who had finished training but had had very little experience, he found no difference in memory performance. This led him to conclude that experience is not as critical as training.

In sum, as far as recollection of descriptive facts is concerned, many issues about the effects of training are unsettled. Certain unique details are remembered more readily by trained persons. However, most of the studies show that mundane facts are not better remembered by those with special training.

When a witness sees a crime, an accident, or other legally important event, some information about the event is stored in memory. This constitutes the first stage of the process and is called the acquisition stage. In the acquisition stage numerous factors affect the accuracy of the initial perception. Some of these factors, such as how long the event lasted or how violent it was, are inherent in the event itself. Other factors, such as the degree of stress or fear that the witness felt, are inherent in the witness. Both event factors and witness factors are important for understanding the likely reliability of eyewitness testimony.

Once the crucial event is over, the information that has entered the witness's memory resides there for some period before it is retrieved. If the event is an accident, it may be several minutes before help arrives and the witness tells a version of the events. It may be several more minutes before the police arrive and even more information is given. It can be months or years before the witness tells the story in court. While information resides in memory (the retention stage) and when it is eventually reported (the retrieval stage), new factors come into play. The next few sections discuss these stages and factors.

RETAINING EVENTS IN MEMORY

In this section, we review literature pertaining to the effects on memory of information that the witness receives subsequent to an event.

Forgetting

The problem of forgetting has captured the attention of psychologists for at least a century. The first major experimental investigation of forgetting was conducted by Ebbinghaus (1885/1964). Ebbinghaus decided to study forgetting in its purest possible form, unaffected by any previous learning or emotional factors. To do this, he used nonsense syllables like *dax, col,* or *fup.* In one of his experiments, Ebbinghaus learned a list of syllables to a criterion of mastery and recorded the time it took to do this. After an interval during which forgetting could take place, he learned the list a second time, keeping track of the time required. The difference between the amount of time it took to learn the list the first and second times was his measure of forgetting.

Ebbinghaus (1885) worked with many different lists, which he relearned after varying intervals. These studies resulted in his famous forgetting curve, which showed that we forget a good deal of new information soon after we learn it and that forgetting then becomes more gradual.

Similar forgetting curves have been reproduced by other researchers using a variety of other materials. For example, Shepard (1967) tested clerical workers for recognition of pictures after intervals of 2 hr, 3 days, 1 week, or about 4 months. Shepard found that the retention of the picture material dropped from almost 100% correct recognition after a 2-hr delay to only chance after 4 months.

A clear instance of forgetting can also be seen in a study conducted to evaluate motor vehicle accidents (Cash & Moss, 1972). The study consisted of interviews with nearly 600 persons known to have been in injury-producing accidents during the 12-month period preceding the interview. Information obtained from each respondent during the interview was compared with data on the official report filed at the time of the accident. Of those interviewed, approximately 14% did not report the accident. When the relationship between likelihood of report and length of time since the accident was examined, a typical forgetting curve could be seen. The percentage of people who reported the accident dropped with the passage of time. Of those interviewed, 97% reported the accident if they were asked within 3 months, but only 70% reported the accident if they were asked between 9 and 12 months after the accident.

Although the forgetting curves obtained in many studies routinely show decline in recall with the passage of time, not all forgetting curves have precisely the same shape. Severe losses developed quickly for Ebbinghaus (1885), but for other researchers the losses have not been as severe and quick. For example, Linton (1979) studied her own memory every day for 6 years, beginning in 1972. She wrote down individual events such as "I have dinner at the Canton Kitchen." By 1977 she had written down descriptions of more than 5,000 items. Every month she tested her memory, and she discovered that she seemed to forget things at a fairly steady rate, with the numbers of forgotten items usually increasing from year to year. Thus, the precise shape of forgetting curves depends on the type of material to be remembered as well as on many other factors.

Forgetting after very long intervals. Studies using different types of procedures can involve retention intervals that are somewhat longer than those used by Ebbinghaus (1885/1964) and Shepard (1967). Linton (1979) made the decision to record her memories for several years, and her results tell us something about forgetting after long intervals. However, she recorded mostly ordinary events, not crimes or accidents of a traumatic nature, and so her results may be only indirectly relevant to eyewitnesses.

One study that may have a bearing on eyewitness ability after very long periods of time is that of Bahrick (1983). He looked at memory for faces encountered over an academic term. His subjects were professors who had taught a class of approximately 40 students either 2 weeks, 1 year, 4 years, or 8 years previously. He created a recognition memory test where chance accuracy was 20% and found that accuracy of identification was 69% after 2 weeks, 48% after 1 year, 31% after 4 years, and close to chance at 26% after 8 years. Even though these students had been seen several times a week for a period of 10 weeks, the facial memory trace was extremely weak after 4 to 8 years. With a single encounter lasting a brief period, the trace has been estimated to be effectively gone in less than a year (Shepherd, Ellis, & Davies, 1982).

Causes of forgetting. One reason that we fail to recall is that we never stored the information we want to remember. Even in cases where we have seen something quite clearly, we are sometimes unable to remember it later. Psychologists have advanced a number of reasons for this.

One reason why people forget is that other information prevents the original information from being remembered. In other words, events interfere with each other in memory. Occasionally, we deliberately forget because we want to forget.

People who gamble are prone to remember the times they won and to forget the times they lost.

Motivated forgetting could be a cause of Edward Kennedy's poor memory of the events of Chappaquiddick (Dunn, 1979). That summer weekend in 1969, Kennedy joined a group of campaign workers at a reunion cookout in a small cottage on Chappaquiddick Island. Sometime after 11:00 PM, Kennedy slipped away from the group in order to catch the last ferry; Mary Jo Kopechne was with him. Kennedy missed the correct road and instead turned down a dirt lane. Crossing a narrow wooden bridge, Kennedy's car flipped over into the water. Kennedy managed to swim to safety, but his companion did not survive. For years afterward, the press hounded Kennedy for information. Five years after the incident, he told reporters, "I wish I could help you. . . . I don't recall that. . . . I have no recollection" (Dunn, cited in Loftus (1980) p. 73). After an enormously stressful experience such as this one, many individuals wish to forget, and often their wish is granted.

New experiences are undoubtedly forgotten for all of these reasons. But another constructive force is also at work. People seem to be able to take bits and pieces of their experience and integrate them to construct objects and events that never really happened. These forces may help to explain why some individuals perceive things that others do not, and why some individuals perceive things that never happened at all.

Postevent Information

As the notion of interference suggests, time alone is not responsible for the loss of memory. Forgetting is caused in part by what goes on during the retention interval. After witnessing important events, witnesses are often exposed to new information. Evidence has been accumulating that postevent experiences can affect the memory of the original event.

Basic findings. The malleability of memory has been observed in many experiments (for a review of this work, see Loftus, 1983). Consider a typical experiment in which students were presented with a film of an automobile accident and immediately afterward asked a series of questions about the accident. Some of the questions were designed to present misleading information that suggested the existence of an object that did not exist. Half of the subjects were asked, "How fast was the white sports car going when it passed the barn while traveling along the country road?" In fact, no barn existed. The remaining subjects were asked, "How fast was the white sports car going while traveling along the country road?" When asked a week later if they had seen a barn, more than 17% of those exposed to the false information about a barn said they had seen one.

Apparently, the assumption of a barn during the initial questioning caused many subjects to incorporate the nonexistent barn into their recollections of the event. Moreover, a subsequent experiment showed that simply asking people whether they had seen a barn, a question to which they usually answered no, was enough to increase the likelihood that they would later instate a barn into their memories of the accident. It seems that the false information had become integrated into the person's recollection of the event, thereby supplementing memory.

New information can do more than simply supplement a memory. Apparently, it can alter or transform the memory. In another study (Loftus, Miller, & Burns, 1978), subjects saw slides of a simulated accident involving an auto and a pedestrian. A red Datsun was traveling toward an intersection at which a stop sign was seen by half of the subjects and a yield sign by the other half. After stopping at the intersection, the Datsun turned right and knocked down a pedestrian.

Immediately after viewing the accident, subjects answered a number of questions. One question presupposed the existence of either a stop sign or a yield sign. For half of the subjects, the presupposed sign was consistent with what they had actually seen; for the other half, it was inconsistent. Subjects were then given another test. One of the test items required them to report whether they had actually seen a stop or a yield sign. Of the subjects who had earlier received consistent information, 75% picked the correct traffic sign. Of those who had earlier received inconsistent information, only 41% picked the correct traffic sign. This experiment suggests that presuppositions are capable of transforming a person's recollection as well as merely supplementing it.

These experiments and many others that used similar procedures confirm the plasticity of memory. False information can be introduced into a person's recollection, and later this information is reported as if it had actually occurred. False information can supplement the previously acquired memory (as in the case of the barn), or it can transform the recollection (as in the case of the stop sign and yield sign).

Witnesses pick up new information when they talk to other witnesses, are asked questions by authorities, read newspaper accounts, or see television coverage of events they have witnessed. In all of these ways, there is a potential for new information to contaminate recollection.

The fate of memory. There is now little doubt that a person's recollection can easily be altered by exposure to new information. However, there is still a question of why. The postevent information is remembered instead of what was originally experienced. A further question concerns whether the underlying memory traces have truly been updated or altered by the postevent information, so that the original traces could not be recovered in the future. This *alteration position* suggests that the original memory representations are altered by postevent information that is different from what was originally experienced (Loftus et al., 1978).

An alternative view is the *coexistence* position, which assumes that the original and postevent information coexist in memory (Bekerian & Bowers, 1983). The introduction of postevent information is thought to make the original memories simply less accessible but still potentially recoverable at some future time. There is a third, *nonimpairment position* that postevent information does not affect the underlying memory traces but only what the subject reports (McCloskey & Zaragoza, 1985).

The fate of the underlying memory traces is important both from a theoretical and a practical standpoint. Speaking practically, the distinctions drawn here have implications for attempts that one might make to correct a memory after it has been biased by postevent suggestions. Under the coexistence and the nonimpairment views, but perhaps not under the alteration view, it makes sense to vigorously use retrieval techniques, such as hypnosis and reinstating the context of the event, that might access the original information in memory. Under the alteration view, one's efforts would be placed elsewhere, because it is likely that the only way to return to the original information is by a realteration of memory.

The argument about the fate of memory bears on one of the most fundamental questions about the human mind, the question of the permanence of memory traces. The coexistence view is consistent with the idea that once it is stored in memory, all information remains there more or less permanently. The alteration view implies a true loss of information from memory due to the updating, substitution, or blending of new inputs. Whatever the ultimate answer to the permanence question, it is fruitful to ask about the various conditions that either encourage distortion in recollection or seem to minimize it.

Factors Affecting Memory Distortion

Time intervals. The intervals of time between viewing an initial event, encountering a subsequent misleading message, and engaging in a final act of recollection can affect memory change. The number of people whose recollection is distorted increases with longer intervals between an event and the misleading message and with shorter intervals between the message and a subsequent recollection. In other words, acceptance of the misleading information appears to be enhanced by the fading of the original memory with the passage of time (Loftus et al., 1978).

Form of the postevent information. The syntax of a postevent message influences the likelihood of its acceptance. A question such as "Was the moustache worn by the tall intruder light or dark brown?" causes fewer people to accept the false premise of a moustache than does the question "Did the intruder who was tall and had a moustache say anything?" This seems to occur because, in the latter case, less attention is given to the misinformation, since it is embedded in a minor clause. Thus, the misinformation is casually or unintentionally assimilated into the memory. On the other hand, when placed at the focus of the question, the misinformation seems to be given more direct and critical attention, and the likelihood of its rejection is enhanced (Loftus & Greene, 1980).

Warnings. The alteration of recollection can often be minimized if witnesses are warned that a postevent message that they are about to receive might contain misinformation. However, the immediacy of the warning appears to be critical. To be effective, the warning should be given just before the presentation of the misleading message. With a warning, witnesses are able to scrutinize the postevent information more carefully, and this enhances the likelihood that it will be rejected in favor of the witness's original memory (Greene, Flynn, & Loftus, 1982).

In sum, several variables influence the alteration of recollection. In all of these cases, the witness's detection of discrepancies or failure to detect discrepancies between the original memory and the postevent message appears to be a crucial factor. With a long interval between the event and misinformation and with misinformation that is subtly embedded, the ability of people to detect a discrepancy between the event information and the postevent information is minimized. Conversely, when people are warned about the likelihood of incorrect information, they scrutinize the postevent information, and the likelihood of detecting a discrepancy is enhanced. The general principle is that change in memory for an event is more likely to occur if discrepancies between the original event and postevent information are not initially detected.

Real and unreal memories. We have attempted to find ways to distinguish between a memory that results from a true perceptual experience and one that results from postevent suggestions (Schooler, Gerhard, & Loftus, 1986). To do so, we showed people a simulated accident in which a car went through an intersection that had a yield sign. Other people saw the car go through an intersection that did not have a yield sign, but they later received a suggestion that there had been a yield sign. All subjects were later asked whether they had seen the yield sign, and if so, to describe it. The real and the fabricated descriptions are virtually indistinguishable. Consider these examples:

1. "I saw the sign as the Datsun pulled up toward it."
2. "When the Datsun pulled up to the yield sign, it was there on the right corner. It was a red and white triangle, not yellow."
3. "The yield sign was on the right of the road before the Datsun turned the corner. It had nothing to do with the accident but was there so the Datsun wouldn't go into the traffic and possibly get hit by the bus that came by."
4. "It was on the corner on the right of the street."

In reality, the first two descriptions came from people who saw the sign, and the last two came from people who had created it in their minds.

It is difficult to assess the authenticity of an individual description. However, when descriptions from people who actually saw the sign were compared with descriptions from people who did not, some interesting differences emerged. People who did not actually see the sign generally used more words to describe what they had "seen." A second difference concerns the content of the descriptions. People who actually saw the sign were more likely to say something about its specific features, such as "It was a red and white triangle, not yellow." People who did not see it were more likely to describe their own thought processes or the sign's function, such as "It . . . was there so the Datsun wouldn't go into the traffic and possibly get hit by the bus." Despite this initial success in distinguishing real from unreal memories, it should be noted that there was tremendous variability in the length and the content of the descriptions. Thus, it will remain very difficult to tell whether a real world recollection is based on a true perception or was created after the fact.

There is little doubt that human recollection can be supplemented, partly restructured, and even completely altered by postevent inputs. There is still dispute about the mechanisms by which these changes occur and the fate of underlying memory traces. Perhaps some memory traces are modified by subsequent inputs, and others are not. If that is so, a major question for psychologists is to determine when one process or the other occurs. For situations in which original memories remain intact, it makes sense to develop techniques that can be used to facilitate retrieval. However, we cannot ignore the possibility that some memories may undergo transformation due to postevent suggestion, and that no technique, no matter how powerful, would result in successful retrieval.

RETRIEVING EVENTS FROM MEMORY

Witnesses to crimes and accidents retrieve information from memory in numerous ways. Sometimes they are asked open-ended questions, to which they report any details that come to mind. They may be asked very specific questions requiring short answers, and sometimes they are presented with objects, such as people or cars or guns, for purposes of identification. There is substantial agreement that eyewitness reports can be biased or distorted at the retrieval stage. How the information is elicited from a witness is critical.

Method of Questioning

The task of eliciting information from a witness can be thought of as helping the witness to accurately reconstruct past events. In order to do this effectively, an interviewer must be aware of the ways in which a witness's recollection is likely to be affected by different methods of elicitation. A large body of research has shown that when witnesses are allowed to report freely rather than being required to answer specific questions, they produce the most accurate but the least complete initial recall (e.g., Lipton, 1977). Researchers have suggested that optimal results will be achieved by an interviewing strategy that first allows the witness to report freely and then requires the witness to answer specific questions to fill in gaps in the recollection (see Yarmey, 1979, for a review of research bearing on this issue). However, one must pay careful attention to the wording of specific questions.

Question Wording

Lawyers and social scientists are aware that the answer one receives depends on the question one asks, but very few people are fully aware of the subtle influences of questions. In a very early study, Muscio (1916) presented motion pictures to his subjects and later asked people about objects or events in the film. Muscio found that the most reliable type of question explicitly mentioned the actual seeing of an event ("Did you see a gun?" rather than "Was there a gun?"). More reliable questions were ones that did not use either a definite article (e.g., "Did you see the gun?") or a negative construction (e.g., "Didn't you see a gun?").

Contemporary researchers have confirmed these early results by demonstrating that small changes in question wording can result in dramatically different answers. In one study, people viewed a simulated accident and later answered some questions (Loftus & Zanni, 1975). The question "Did you see the broken headlight?" led to more erroneous yes responses than the question "Did you see a broken headlight?" More recent research has shown that leading questions decrease witness accuracy only when the questioner is assumed to be knowledgeable about the crime (Smith & Ellsworth, 1987). These experiments show that in a variety of situations the wording of a question concerning an event can influence the answer.

The legal system's partial recognition of this situation has resulted in rules indicating when leading questions are allowed (*Federal Rules of Evidence*, 1975). Although the rules of evidence and other safeguards provide protection in the courtroom, they are absent in the interview room of the precinct station and in the telephone conversation between a witness and a lawyer who represents one of the parties. The protection offered in the courtroom is obviated if it is applied only after information has already been obtained by improper questioning techniques.

Confidence

Intuition suggests that a witness is more likely to be correct if the witness is certain rather than less certain. This intuition must be explained empirically, because it has important practical significance since jurors tend to be very impressed by witnesses who are confident (Wells, Ferguson, & Lindsay, 1981). Moreover, the U.S. Supreme Court has formally endorsed the idea of using eyewitness confidence as an indication of eyewitness accuracy (*Neil v. Biggers,* 1972). A number of literature reviews bear on the relationship between witness confidence and accuracy (Deffenbacher, 1980; Wells & Lindsay, 1985; Wells & Murray, 1984). The consensus seems to be that eyewitness confidence does not assure accuracy but may indicate only that the identified person resembled the perpetrator (Lindsay, 1986).

Despite this pessimistic summary, it is important to distinguish the types of situations that tend to lead to significant confidence/accuracy correlations and the types of situations that do not lead to significant correlations. There is evidence that under relatively poor viewing conditions, the confidence/accuracy relationship suffers most (Deffenbacher, 1980). Witnesses who saw an accident occur on a dark and stormy night from quite a distance would be expected to show a weaker relationship than would witnesses who saw an accident in daylight from a closer distance. Similarly, longer observation times result in greater correspondence between accuracy and confidence (Bothwell, Deffenbacher, & Brigham, 1987). Other work has shown that when witnesses believe that their recollections have some important consequences, the confidence/accuracy correlation is lower than when witnesses do not believe their recollections will have important consequences (Wells & Lindsay, 1985). Research has also shown that briefing eyewitnesses after their initial recollection regarding the type of questions they might be asked under cross-examination serves to inflate confidence, and this briefing further reduces the small confidence/accuracy correlation that might otherwise be observed (Wells & Lindsay, 1985).

Finally, it has been shown that when witnesses watch a videotape of themselves making an eyewitness identification and then rate their confidence in the identification, the confidence/accuracy relationship is enhanced (Kassin, 1985). This finding suggests that law enforcement officials might videotape witnesses as they make their identifications. This could be done prior to assessing their degree of certainty and their willingness to testify. Although the procedure may seem somewhat radical, Kassin pointed out that videotape technology has already been accepted for several evidentiary purposes, such as recording undercover operations, confessions, and deposition testimony.

Before leaving the subject of confidence, another form of the correlation between confidence and accuracy should be described. The confidence/accuracy relationship is usually evaluated across a number of different witnesses. Even though witness A is confident and witness B is not, the data reported above suggest that witness A may be no more accurate than witness B. Another form of the relationship involves a within-individual correlation (Stephenson, 1984). It provides information about what happens when a single witness's testimony is partly confident and partly tentative and whether less weight should be given to tentative testimony than to the confidently delivered testimony. The available evidence suggests that within-individual confidence/accuracy relationships are generally positive. That is, witnesses are somewhat more likely to be correct when they are confident than when they express doubt.

Improving Retrieval

After a critical event has transpired, the only hope for maximizing the accuracy of memory is in the use of retrieval strategies. Thus, investigators, law enforcement personnel, and others have a strong common interest in finding retrieval techniques that can aid memory.

Context reinstatement. Some encouraging research has tried to improve memory by reinstating the context of the original event. In one study, subjects viewed a staged but unexpected vandalism (Malpass & Devine, 1981). Five months later, subjects were given an opportunity to attempt to identify the suspect in a photographic lineup. One might expect that a 5-month delay would result in substantial fading of memory. Indeed, of the subjects who were asked simply to identify the suspect, only 40% were able to do so. By comparison, prior to attempting identification, other subjects were asked to recall each sequence of actions and objects that constituted the original event. Their rehearsal was guided and entailed a vivid reconstruction of the event. Sixty percent correctly identified the suspect from a lineup, a significantly better performance than was obtained without guided rehearsal.

More recently, Davies, Ellis, and Shepherd (1985) examined the phenomenon of context reinstatement and found that both mental guidance and physical reinstatement of the event can produce small improvements in the quality of postevent composites. In their study, witnesses came to an untidy office, ostensibly to complete some personality tests. An intruder interrupted and began ransacking the room looking for a missing calculator. One week later, the witnesses returned and tried to construct a composite picture of the intruder. Those who worked in the room where the incident had occurred produced better composites than those who worked in a different, bare room. However, if the witnesses in the bare room first reminisced about the original incident and their own reactions to it, they were as accurate as those who had been taken to the original room.

Other studies have also demonstrated successful context reinstatement. Bekerian and Bowers (1983) showed that ordering the test questions to recreate the temporal order of an event can lead to better memory. Krafka and Penrod (1985) showed that providing some details about an event can lead to better memory for other details.

Attempts to obtain better memory with the use of context reinstatement have not always led to the sought-after improvement (Fernandez & Glenberg, 1985; McCloskey & Zaragoza, 1985) and have sometimes made matters even worse (Loftus, Manber, & Keating, 1983). Thus, the use of context reinstatement can be somewhat unpredictable.

There are factors that influence the accuracy and completeness of retrieval that come into play in this final stage. The method of questioning and in particular the way questions are asked can be crucial. New research is being done to devise ways of interviewing witnesses so as to maximize the accuracy of the resulting information. Although success rates have not been uniformly high, initial results look promising. (See Chapter 5 for a detailed treatment of the investigative use of hypnosis and Chapter 6 for a comprehensive description of the cognitive interview.)

This chapter has summarized a portion of the research on the factors that affect the reliability of eyewitness testimony. Much recent work has focused on ways that the identification process can be improved. The following chapter describes some the procedures frequently used to obtain identification evidence.

REFERENCES

Adams, A. J., Zisman, F., Rodic, R., & Cavender, J. (1982). Chromaticity and luminosity changes in glaucoma and diabetes. In G. Verriest (Ed.), *Colour vision deficiencies. Proceedings of the Sixth Symposium of the International Research Group on Colour Vision Deficiencies* (pp. 413–416). The Hague: W. Junk.

Allport, G. W. & Postman, L. J. (1947). *The psychology of rumor.* New York: Henry Holt & Co.

Baddeley, A. (1982). *Your memory: A user's guide.* New York: Macmillan.

Bahrick, H. P. (1983). Memory for people. In J. Harris (Ed.), *Everyday memory, actions, and absentmindedness* (pp. 19–34). London: Academic Press.

Baltes, P. B., & Schaie, K. W. (1976). On the plasticity of intelligence in adulthood and old age: Where Horn and Donaldson fall. *American Psychologist, 31,* 720–25.

Bekerian, D. A., & Bowers, J. M. (1983). Eyewitness testimony: Were we misled? *Journal of Experimental Psychology: Learning, Memory, and Cognition, 9,* 139–145.

Berkun, M. M., Bialek, H. M., Kern, R. P., & Yagi, K. (1962). Experimental studies of psychological stress in man. *Psychological Monographs, 76*, No. 15.

Bird, C. (1927). The influence of the press upon the accuracy of report. *Journal of Abnormal and Social Psychology, 22*, 123–129.

Bothwell, R. K., Deffenbacher, K. A., & Brigham, J. C. (1987). Correlation of eyewitness accuracy and confidence: Optimality hypothesis revisited. *Journal of Applied Psychology, 72*, 691–695.

Brown, M. R. (1926). *Legal psychology.* Indianapolis: Bobbs-Merrill.

Buckhout, R. (1977). Eyewitness identification and psychology in the courtroom. *Criminal Defense, 4*, 5–10.

Buckhout, R., Alper, A., Chern, S., Silverberg, G., & Slomovits, M. (1974). Determinant of eyewitness performance in a lineup. *Bulletin of the Psychonomic Society, 4*, 191–192.

Cady, H. M. (1924). On the psychology of testimony. *American Journal of Psychology, 35*, 110–112.

Cash, W. S., & Moss, A. J. (1972). Optimum recall period for reporting persons injured in motor vehicle accidents. (*DHEW-HSM Publication No. 72-1050.*) Washington DC: U.S. Government Printing Office.

Cattell, J. M. (1895). Measurements of the accuracy of recollection. *Science, 2*, 61–66.

Ceci, S. J., Ross, D. F., & Toglia, M. P. (1987). Suggestibility of children's memory: Psycholegal implications. *Journal of Experimental Psychology: General, 116*, 38–49.

Christianson, S. A., & Loftus, E. F. (1986). *Memory for traumatic events.* Unpublished manuscript, University of Washington, Seattle.

Clifford, B. R. (1976). Police as eyewitnesses. *New Society, 36*, 176–177.

Clifford, B. R., & Hollin, C. R. (1981). Effects of the type of incident and the number of perpetrators on eyewitness memory. *Journal of Applied Psychology, 66*, 364–370.

Clifford, B. R., & Scott, J. (1978). Individual and situational factors in eyewitness testimony. *Journal of Applied Psychology, 63*, 352–359.

Craik, F. I. M. (1977). Age differences in human memory. In J. E. Birren and K. W. Schaie (Eds.), *Handbook of the psychology of aging* (pp. 384–420). New York: Van Nostrand Co.

Davies, G., Ellis, H., & Shepherd, J. (1985, May). Wanted—faces that fit the bill. *New Scientist*, pp. 26–29.

Deffenbacher, K. A. (1980). Eyewitness accuracy and confidence: Can we infer anything about their relationship? *Law and Human Behavior, 4*, 243–260.

Deffenbacher, K. A. (1983). The influence of arousal on reliability of testimony. In S. Lloyd-Bostock & B. R. Clifford (Eds.), *Evaluating witness evidence* (pp. 235-251). New York: John Wiley.

Duncan, E. M., Whitney, P., & Kunen, S. (1982). Integration of visual and verbal information in children's memory. *Child Development, 83,* 1215-1223.

Dunn, J. G. (1979, December 3). On the matter of Chappaquiddick. *New West.* Cited in Loftus, E. F. (1980). *Memory.* Menlo Park, CA.: Addison-Wesley.

Eagly, A. H. (1978). Sex differences in influenceability. *Psychological Bulletin, 85,* 86-116.

Easterbrook, J. A. (1959). The effect of emotion on the utilization and organization of behavior. *Psychological Review, 66,* 183-201.

Ebbinghaus, H. E. (1964). *Memory: A contribution to experimental psychology.* New York: Dover. (Original work published 1885.)

Ellis, H., Shepherd, J., & Bruce, A. (1973). The effect of age and sex upon adolescents' recognition of faces. *Journal of Genetic Psychology, 123,* 173-174.

Eysenck, M. W. (1983). Anxiety and individual differences. In G. R. J. Hockey (Ed.), *Stress and fatigue in human performance,* (pp. 273-298). Chichester: John Wiley.

Farrimond, T. (1968). Retention and recall: Incidental learning of visual and auditory material. *Journal of Genetic Psychology, 113,* 155-165.

Federal Rules of Evidence for United States Courts and Magistrates (1975). St. Paul, MN: West Publishing.

Fernandez, A., & Glenberg, A. M. (1985). Changing environmental context does not reliably affect memory. *Memory & Cognition, 13,* 333-345.

Geiselman, R. E., Fisher, R. P., MacKinnon, D. P., & Holland, H. L. (1985). Eyewitness memory enhancement in the police interview: Cognitive retrieval mnemonics versus hypnosis. *Journal of Applied Psychology, 70,* 401-412.

Goodman, G. S., & Reed, R. (1985). Age differences in eyewitness testimony. *Law & Human Behavior, 10,* 317-332.

Greene, E., Flynn, M. B., & Loftus, E. F. (1982). Inducing resistance to misleading information. *Journal of Verbal Learning & Verbal Behavior, 21,* 207-219.

Hurd, P. D., & Blevins, J. (1984). Aging and the color of pills. *New England Journal of Medicine, 310,* 302.

Hurvich, L. M. (1981). *Color vision.* Sunderland, MA: Sinaver Assoc.

Idzikowski, C., & Baddeley, A. D. (1983). Fear and dangerous environments. In R. Hockey (Ed.), *Stress and fatigue in human performance*. Chichester: Wiley.

Kassin, S. M. (1985). Eyewitness identification: Retrospective self-awareness and the accuracy-confidence correlation. *Journal of Personality and Social Psychology, 49*, 878–893.

King, M. A. (1984). *An investigation of the eyewitness abilities of children*. Unpublished doctoral dissertation, University of British Columbia, Vancouver.

Keating, J. P., & Loftus, E. F. (1981, June). The logic of fire escape. *Psychology Today*, pp. 14–19.

Krafka, C., & Penrod, S. (1985). Reinstatement of context in a field experiment on eyewitness identification. *Journal of Personality and Social Psychology, 49*, 58–69.

Kramer, T. H. (1984). *The effects of weapon focus and arousal of eyewitness recall*. Unpublished doctoral dissertation, City University of New York.

Leibowitz, H. W. (1985). Grade crossing accidents and human factors engineering. *American Scientist, 73*, 558–562.

Leibowitz, H. W., & Owens, A. (1986, January). We drive by night. *Psychology Today*, pp. 55–58.

Lindsay, R. C. L. (1986). Confidence and accuracy of eyewitness identifications from lineups. *Law & Human Behavior, 10*, 229–240.

Linton, M. (1979, July). I remember it well. *Psychology Today*, pp. 81–86.

Lipton, J. P. (1977). On the psychology of eyewitness testimony. *Journal of Applied Psychology, 62*, 90–93.

Loftus, E. F. (1983). Misfortunes of memory. *Philosophical Transactions of the Royal Society, 302*, 413–421.

Loftus, E. F., & Burns, T. E. (1982). Mental shock can produce retrograde amnesia. *Memory and Cognition, 19*, 318–323.

Loftus, E. F., & Greene, E. (1980). Warning: Even memory for faces may be contagious. *Law & Human Behavior, 4*, 323–334.

Loftus, E. F., Loftus, G. R., & Messo, J. (1987). Some facts about "weapon focus." *Law and Human Behavior, 11*, 55–62.

Loftus, E. F., Manber, M., & Keating, J. P. (1983). Recollection of naturalistic events: Context enhancement versus negative cueing. *Human Learning, 2*, 83–92.

Loftus, E. F., Miller, D. G., & Burns, H. J. (1978). Semantic integration of verbal information into a visual memory. *Journal of Experimental Psychology: Human Learning & Memory, 4*, 19–31.

Loftus, E. F., Schooler, J. W., Boone, S. M., & Kline, D. (1986). *Time went by so slowly: Overestimation of event duration by males and females.* Unpublished manuscript, University of Washington, Seattle.
Loftus, E. F., & Zanni, G. (1975). Eyewitness testimony: The influence of the wording of a question. *Bulletin of the Psychonomic Society, 5,* 86–88.
Loftus, G. R., & Mackworth, N. H. (1978). Cognitive determinants of fixation location during picture viewing. *Journal of Experimental Psychology: Human Perception and Performance, 4,* 565–572.
Malpass, R. S., & Devine, P. G. (1981). Guided memory in eyewitness identification. *Journal of Applied Psychology, 66,* 343–350.
Marin, B. V., Holmes, D. L., Guth, M., & Kovac, P. (1979). The potential of children as eyewitnesses. *Law & Human Behavior, 3,* 295–305.
Marshall, J. (1966). *Law and psychology in conflict.* New York: Bobbs-Merrill.
McCloskey, M., & Zaragoza, M. (1985). Misleading postevent information and memory for events: Arguments and evidence against memory impairment hypotheses. *Journal of Experimental Psychology: General, 114,* 1–16.
Muscio, B. (1916). The influence of the form of a question. *British Journal of Psychology, 8,* 351–389.
Neil v. Biggers, 409 U.S. 188 (1972).
Peters, D. (1988). Eyewitness memory and arousal in a natural setting. In M. M. Gruneberg, P. E Morris & R. N. Sykes (Eds.), *Practical aspects of memory: current research and issues* (pp. 89–94). London: Academic Press.
Peterson, M. A. (1976). *Witnesses: Memory of social events.* Unpublished doctoral dissertation, University of California at Los Angeles.
Powers, P. A., Andriks, J. L., & Loftus, E. G. (1979). Eyewitness accounts of females and males. *Journal of Applied Psychology, 64,* 339–347.
Rubin, D. C., & Kozin, M. (1984). Vivid memories. *Cognition, 16,* 81–95.
San Jose Methods Test of Known Crime Victims (1972). Washington, DC: U.S. Department of Justice.
Sarason, I. G. (1975). Anxiety and self-preoccupation. In I. G. Sarason, & C. D. Spielberger (Eds.), *Stress and anxiety* (Vol. 2, pp. 27–44). Washington, D.C.: Hemisphere Press.

Schaie, K. W. (1984). The Seattle longitudinal: A 21 year exploration in the development of psychometric intelligence. In K. W. Schaie (Ed.), *Longitudinal studies of adult psychological development*. New York: Guilford.

Schneider, A. L., Griffith, W. R., Sumi, D. H., & Burcart, J. M. (1978). *Portland forward records check of crime victims*. Washington, DC: U.S. Department of Justice.

Schooler, J. W., Gerhard, D., & Loftus, E. F. (1986). Qualities of the unreal. *Journal of Experimental Psychology: Learning, Memory, and Cognition, 12,* 171–181.

Sekular, R., & Blake, R. (1985). *Perception*. New York: Random House.

Shepherd, J. W., Ellis, H. D., & Davis, G. M. (1982). *Identification evidence: A psychological evaluation*. Aberdeen, Scotland: Aberdeen University Press.

Shepard, R. N. (1967). Recognition memory for words, sentences and pictures. *Journal of Verbal Learning and Verbal Behavior, 6,* 156–163.

Siegel, J. M., & Loftus, E. F. (1978). Impact of anxiety and life stress upon eyewitness testimony. *Bulletin of the Psychonomic Society, 12,* 479–480.

Silberman, C. F. (1978). *Criminal violence, criminal justice*. New York: Random House.

Smith, V. L. & Ellsworth, P. C. (1987). The social psychology of eyewitness accuracy: Misleading question and communicator expertise. *Journal of Applied Psychology, 72,* 294–300.

Stephenson, G. M. (1984). Accuracy and confidence in testimony: A critical review and some fresh evidence. In D. J. Muller, D. E. Blackman, & A. J. Chapman (Eds.), *Psychology and law* (pp. 229–248). London: John Wiley.

Tinkner, A. H., & Poulton, E. C. (1975). Watching for people and actions. *Ergonomics, 18,* 35–51.

Tooley, V., Brigham, J. C., Maass, A., & Bothwell, R. K. (1987). Facial recognition: Weapon effect and attentional focus. *Journal of Applied Social Psychology, 17,* 845–859.

Trankell, A. (1972). *Reliability of evidence: Methods for analyzing and assessing witness statements*. Stockholm: Beckmans.

Weale, R. A. (1982). *The biography of the eye*. London: Lewis.

Wells, G. L., Ferguson, T. J. & Lindsay, R. C. L. (1981). The tractability of eyewitness confidence and its implications for triers of fact. *Journal of Applied Psychology, 66,* 688–696.

Wells, G. L., & Lindsay, R. C. L. (1985). Methodological notes on the accuracy-confidence relation in eyewitness identifications. *Journal of Applied Psychology, 70,* 413–419.

Wells, G. L., & Murray, D. M. (1984). Eyewitness confidence. In G. L. Wells & E. F. Loftus (Eds.), *Eyewitness testimony: Psychological perspectives* (pp. 155–170). Cambridge: Cambridge University Press.

Yarmey, A. D. (1979). *The psychology of eyewitness testimony.* New York: Free Press.

Yarmey, A. D. (1984). Age as a factor in eyewitness memory. In G. L. Wells & E. F. Loftus, (Eds.), *Eyewitness testimony: Psychological perspectives* (pp. 142–154). Cambridge: Cambridge University Press.

Yarmey, A. D. (1986). Verbal, visual, and voice identification of a rape suspect under different levels of illumination. *Journal of Applied Psychology, 71,* 363–370.

Yarmey, A. D., & Jones, H. P. T. (1983). Accuracy of memory of male and female eyewitnesses to a criminal assault and rape. *Bulletin of the Psychonomic Society, 21,* 89–92.

Yerkes, R. M., & Dodson, J. D. (1908). The relation of strength of stimulus to rapidity of habit formation. *Journal of Comparative Neurology & Psychology, 18,* 459–482.

Yuille, J. C. (1984). Research and teaching with police: A Canadian example. *International Review of Applied Psychology, 33,* 5–24.

Yuille, J. C., & Cutshall, J. L. (1986). A case study of eyewitness memory of a crime. *Journal of Applied Psychology, 71,* 291–301.

Procedures for Obtaining Identification Evidence

2

Brian R. Clifford and Graham Davies

On April 16, 1985, Mr. and Mrs. Peters, together with their mentally handicapped son, set out from their home in Cumberland, England, to attend an antiques fair. On a road not far from their home, their car was rammed by another car containing three masked men, who attacked them with staffs and truncheons. The Peterses put up a fight; Mr. Peters thought he might have cut one of the men with a penknife, and Mrs. Peters ripped off the mask of another. Nevertheless, the men got away with over £28,000 in cash and antique jewelry.

All three of the victims provided descriptions of their attackers, and Mrs. Peters worked with a police artist to produce a likeness of the face of one of the robbers who had lost his mask in the fight. Armed with this information, the police visited local hotelkeepers to see whether anyone recalled the gang. The staff of one hotel thought they recognized the impression as one of three men who had stayed the previous night and left early. Using this new information and the descriptions, the police made a tentative identification of a gang of three experienced thieves working out of nearby Manchester.

The police eventually arrested three men who were identified by the hotel staff. Mrs. Peters was able to identify one man but not a second. One proved to have a knife injury on his neck consistent with Mrs. Peters's account. At the trial, the prosecution relied upon some strong circumstantial evidence, but Mrs. Peters's identification was the key feature of the case. The defense argued that her identification was unreliable and pointed to her failure to identify the second man. After a 4-hr deliberation, the jury found all three men guilty of robbery with violence.

This brief account, taken from an actual case, illustrates the three major phases at which identification evidence is employed by the police. The *descriptive phase* involves eliciting identity information from the eyewitness, either as a verbal description, a pictorial likeness, or both. The *search phase* involves relating the obtained information to criminal records or the recollections of other witnesses to establish a tentative identification of the subject. The *identification phase* involves evaluating the hypothesis that the suspect is the perpetrator by asking the witness to attempt to select the perpetrator from an identification parade, or *lineup*.

PHASE ONE: ELICITING DESCRIPTIONS

Verbal Descriptions

"What did the person look like?" This question is the starting point for all police investigations. Descriptions can be elicited in a number of ways. A *free description* is the simplest and merely invites the witness to provide a description of the person. A *cued description* requires the witness to respond to a series of specific questions ("How old?" "How tall?" etc.); a *prompted description* offers the witness a range of alternative descriptions from which to choose the most appropriate one ("Were his eyes close together? Wide apart? Deep Set? Protruding?").

Laboratory research suggests that the initial free descriptions are likely to be generally accurate but incomplete (Deffenbacher & Horney, 1981). In one study, normally articulate college faculty members averaged fewer than six adjectives when requested to describe the face of a familiar colleague. Information on a range of basic parameters is required in order to conduct a systematic search of police crime files, usually making prompting of witnesses essential. For instance, police in Seattle, Washington, routinely request information regarding race, sex, age, height, weight, build, complexion, hair, and eye color. Kuehn (1974) examined 100 statements collected by the Seattle Police Department from victims of assault and found that information was provided for at least six of these nine categories, on the average. White witnesses reported more details than black witnesses, women more than men, and victims of robbery more than victims of assault. The two latter results were confirmed in a parallel analysis conducted on 200 statements made to the Aberdeen Police in Scotland (Macleod & Shepherd, 1986). Bystanders as well as victims were included in the sample, and the investigators reported that the latter produced appreciably greater amounts of information.

The research by Kuehn (1974) and Macleod and Shepherd (1986) was conducted with victims of real crimes, and there was no way to establish the accuracy of the information they volunteered. Accuracy may also be assessed under the more artificial but controlled conditions of a laboratory experiment. Wogalter (1987), for instance, showed a series of six photographs of unknown men to student observers, who were required to compile a description immediately following the presentation of each face. Descriptions were based either on cued recall for six major facial features (hair, eyes, nose, mouth, chin, and eyebrows) or on prompted descriptions where subjects selected an appropriate adjective to describe each feature from a range of 10 alternatives. In addition, half of the subjects were instructed to maintain a mental image as they worked, whereas the remainder received no special instructions. Wogalter then assessed the quality of the descriptions by asking other students to match them to the appropriate target. Higher accuracy was achieved with the cued than with the prompted description method, and the poorest performance occurred when prompting was not accompanied by instructions to use imagery. This surprising finding seems to suggest that witnesses' powers of description are constrained and impaired by a multiple-choice format. If the same result can be replicated with a less verbally fluent sample, then it suggests that widespread use of multiple-alternative description forms by police personnel should be discouraged.

The descriptions in Wogalter's study were obtained immediately after presentation and not after the extensive delays that are more typical of real criminal incidents. Ellis, Shepherd, and Davies (1980) examined the accuracy and completeness of facial descriptions made 1 hr, 1 day, and 1 week after exposure to a photograph. Accuracy and completeness showed a steady deterioration over time, with a 15% fall over the extended interval. Recently, Yuille and Cutshall (1986) have challenged the generalizability of such findings to forensic settings by arguing that in actual cases involving trauma and excitement, descriptive material will be better remembered than under the less realistic conditions of a laboratory test. In support of their contention, they cited follow-up interviews of 13 persons who were witnesses to a shooting incident outside a downtown gun shop in Vancouver, British Columbia. Comparison of statements made to the police shortly after the shooting and those given to researchers 4 to 5 months later showed little or no decline either in accuracy or completeness. The witnesses showed an overall accuracy of 76% in their person descriptions, but errors in estimates of height, weight, and age were particularly prevalent (see Chapter 3 for a detailed description of their research). Similar inaccuracies in the reporting of these basic parameters also emerge from field studies where members of the public have made estimates in the context of noncriminal incidents (Flin & Shepherd, 1986).

An important question concerns the aspects of the face that witnesses are likely to attend to and report. Data on the description of facial features show a surprising consistency across laboratories, according to the findings of Laughery, Duval, and Wogalter (1986). They analyzed the range of descriptions provided by volunteers who had taken part in an Identikit or police artist interview, and their findings were very similar to data obtained by Ellis et al. (1980) from witnesses who described photographs. The concordance between the two studies was very high.

Hair emerged as the most frequently mentioned feature, followed by the nose, the eyes, and the eyebrows. There were few spontaneous mentions of the chin, the lips, and the mouth. The dominance in reporting of upper as compared to lower features also emerged from a rather different recall method explored by Ellis (1986). Subjects were asked to imagine well known faces and to rate the strength of their mental image for different aspects of the face. Hair, age, and facial shape emerged as the most frequently recalled features.

The existing research suggests that most credence should be attached to the immediate, spontaneous statements of witnesses. Where supplementary questioning is necessary, it is better done by cuing than by prompting with multiple-alternative questions. The typical selective recall of facial information should be taken as a reflection of selective attention that limits the amount of information that a witness can recall. It should not be taken as the occasion for further, probably counterproductive, questioning.

Visual Representations

Verbal descriptions of suspects are frequently supplemented by portraits of their faces based on descriptions given by the witness. The use of portraits and composites as aids to detection has a long history. Colonel Griffiths, in his book entitled *Mysteries of Police and Crime* (1908), referred as early as 1828 to the publication of "rough but often life-like woodcuts" of wanted persons (p. 13). However, there is no generally accepted technique for producing a finished portrait, and different police forces utilize artists in different ways (Davies, 1986a).

Police Artists

In the United States, artists are employed by only 200 of 2,000 police departments. Most are police officers who have shown an interest in this form of work. A recent survey suggested that only 20% of the police artists in the United States had received any extended training, although 76% claimed to be amateur artists in their spare time (Domingo, 1984). The normal mode of these artist's operation is to interact directly with the witness, gradually producing a portrait in their presence. Training courses and instruction manuals have begun to appear (Cormack, 1979; Homa, 1983), but there is little consistency in the methods they advocate and empirical data concerning their success rate are not available.

Homa (1983) and Cormack (1979) both suggest that interviews by the artist should begin by eliciting a verbal description from the witness. The artist then attempts to establish more precisely the type of feature described, directing the witness's attention to reference material, such as photographs of representative faces (Homa) or freehand drawings of the ranges of a given facial feature (Cormack). Only at this point is a preliminary sketch improvised, either using a graticule indicating the approximate position of the main features (Homa) or freehand (Cormack). After an approximate facial structure has been negotiated, hair, scars, and similar details are added to provide the finished portrait.

Not all police forces advocate direct interaction between the witness and artist. For instance, the Federal Bureau of Investigation employs a small number of highly trained artists at their headquarters in Washington, DC. All interviews are conducted by agents in the field, who carry a set of some 2,000 reference photographs that are also kept in the Washington office. Details are provided to the artists by telephone and form the basis of a sketch that is quickly transmitted from the headquarters to the field agent by facsimile. Using the telephone, the witness may then suggest necessary modifications to the artist, who then transmits the final drawing. No systematic assessments have been made of this procedure, but a 35% clearance rate has been claimed (R. S. Gast II, personal communication, March 12, 1986).

Composite Systems

Few police departments can justify the cost of employing a full-time police artist, and many rely upon commercially manufactured kits of facial components. The American Identikit and the British Photofit are the best known (see Davies, 1981, and Allison, 1973, for detailed treatments of alternative systems).

Most composite systems advocate an initial interview with the witness, during which a detailed verbal description is elicited. The attention of the witness is then directed to facial components that seem most relevant to the description provided, and the witness is asked to select the most appropriate components. The number of alternative features from which the witness selects varies greatly among the available systems. For example, Photofit contains 562 individual components, among which there are 195 hairstyles, 99 eyes and eyebrows, 89 noses, 105 mouths, and 74 chin and cheek pieces. These facial features are supplemented with such accessories as hats, scars, and eyeglasses. After the witness has made a selection of relevant components, the operator synthesizes these into a total "face" that can be shown to the witness for comment. Amendments can then be made, either by exchanging features or by modifying their appearance through the use of a wax pencil applied to the surface of the composite. Penciled amendments to the hair components are frequently necessary because of the rapid evolutions in styling for both men and women. Kit manufacturers attempt to cope with the problem by issuing periodic supplements.

The aim of many police artists is to produce a finished and lifelike portrait (Cormack, 1979). However, the philosophy underlying the original Identikit and such successors as the Field Identification System (Laughery, Smith, & Yount, 1980) is to produce a schematic line drawing that illustrates a general facial type. On the other hand, Photofit and the new Identikit II strive for a realistic impression by using components derived from photographs of actual facial features. This search for realism has been carried a stage further by the introduction of color in some of the more recent systems. The prototype Magnaface system assembles a composite picture from colored photographs of facial features that are blended together by the use of a special form of transparent overlay, where the Videofit uses the facilities of the Quantel Paintbox computer graphics package to color up a standard monochrome composite picture and to remove intrusive boundary lines between features (see Davies, 1986b).

Given the widespread use of these and similar systems in police investigations, it is surprising that little information exists on their operational effectiveness, in absolute terms or compared to that of the police artist. There are wide variations in the frequency with which different police forces utilize artists (Domingo, 1984) and composite technicians (Kitson, Darnbrough, & Shields, 1978), which seem to be based on the particular experience and preferences of the investigating officers (Bennett, 1986).

The British Home Office study conducted in 1977 is the most systematic survey to date (Darnbrough, 1977). Follow-up questionnaires were distributed to investigating officers in 729 cases where Photofit composites had been produced, of which 140 had been successfully resolved after 2 months of investigation. Officers estimated that among these 140 cases, composites had been "entirely responsible" (5%) or "very useful" (17%) for solving the case. However, these figures must be interpreted in light of the 20% of cases in which the composites had been "no use at all." To judge from a more recent survey summarized by Bennett (1986), Photofit has not greatly improved the clearance rates for cases. This later survey was confined to a series of 360 cases investigated by the London Metropolitan Police, of which only 14 had resulted in arrests. The composites in these cases were judged to be "good" likenesses of the suspect in 7 cases, "fair" in 3 cases, and "poor" in 4 cases. These results were based on the use of Photofit, but there is no reason to believe that they are unrepresentative of composite systems as a whole (Davies, 1981). It is of interest to explain the apparent ineffectiveness of such devices.

Improving composite performance. The simplest explanation for the poor performance of subjects who used Photofit is that witnesses are not particularly good at remembering faces. Although recall of facial detail is indeed poor, this seems insufficient to explain the difficulties of producing accurate composites, since subjects are reasonably competent at recognizing faces under laboratory conditions (Ellis, 1984). This suggests that certain facial information has been internalized, and

Christie and Ellis (1981) demonstrated that the initial verbal descriptions provided by witnesses under laboratory conditions proved to be a better guide to likeness than the subsequent Photofit pictures themselves. In addition, they found no relationship between the accuracy of the description provided by witnesses and the quality of their composites. Both results have since been replicated using samples of juvenile witnesses (Flin, Markham, & Davies, in press). It appears that composite kits such as Photofit fail to transmit existing information effectively from the witness to the user of the created composite.

A second possibility is that existing composite systems are basically sound but are not being used effectively. Composite technicians and artists receive little in the way of formal training (Domingo, 1984; Kitson et al., 1978). A study that compared a novice to a highly experienced composite operator suggested that the quality of the likeness achieved by the latter was significantly higher and resulted from differences in the techniques used to elicit information (Davies, Milne, & Shepherd, 1983). The experienced operator took much longer to establish the initial description and showed the witness a smaller range of features. Both strategies were associated with better composite quality (Laughery et al., 1986). Using information derived from this and other laboratory studies of the Photofit, psychologists at the University of Aberdeen worked with experienced police officers to conduct a number of week-long courses for composite technicians. Although postcourse questionnaires demonstrated a high degree of acceptance and approval of the course by police trainees, there has been no objective demonstration of improvement in composite quality as a result of such training (Davies, Shepherd, Shepherd, Flin, & Ellis, 1986).

Another avenue of research to improving existing systems might increase the representativeness of features by more satisfactorily echoing the range of human physiognomy. As noted earlier, kits vary widely in the number and distribution of their facial components. Multidimensional scaling of the different features in the Photofit has revealed a degree of omission and duplication among the Caucasian features (Davies et al., 1982). Sorting procedures revealed that a number of the female features were sufficiently androgenous to be assimilated into the male kit without difficulty. This had the effect of increasing the number of young-looking features and of hairstyles more typical of the modern urban offender. The features were also rearranged and labeled so as to be more compatible with the intuitive groupings and classifications employed by witnesses. A laboratory comparison of the existing Photofit kit and this enhanced, enlarged kit and revised indexing system showed a significant advantage for the latter, in terms of both overall composite quality and production time (Davies et al., 1982). The resulting enlarged kit and Aberdeen Index to Photofit is now in regular operational use by police forces in the United Kingdom.

There is clearly room for improvement in existing equipment, and there is also a need for a more fundamental analysis of the problem of facial recall. Existing systems appear to be based on a logical rather than a psychological analysis of the process of composition of faces, and it is important to more clearly align any new system with the dynamics of facial perception and memory as revealed by experimental research. Some insight into these issues can be gained by consideration of some of the areas of conflict and controversy in the design and development of aids to recall of faces.

Type likeness versus realistic portrait. One source of controversy for both artist and composite technician is the optimal level of realism to be attained. The debate between advocates of the schematic Identikit and the photograph-based Photofit is paralleled by the debate between artists who opt for a three-dimensional portrait appearance and those who advocate two-dimensional sketches. At one extreme, unaccented and unshaded line drawings of the kind typified by the Identikit are extremely difficult to recognize, even when the face represented is a very familiar one. Faces of celebrities presented in photographs are four times as likely to be recognized as the same pictures transcribed into line form (Davies, Ellis, & Shepherd, 1978b). Even the use of a professional caricature is not sufficient to rival the superiority of a monochrome photograph (Tverskey & Baratz, 1985).

It could be argued that photographs are veridical portraits, and it is of interest to determine whether they have advantages over the approximate likenesses more typically represented by police composites. Davies (1986a) identified two groups of Photofit pictures generated by volunteers in a previous laboratory study, one group consisting of good likenesses of target faces and the other of poor likenesses. From these composites he derived a parallel set of line transcriptions of the Photofits to provide a level of detail that approximated the original Identikit. These two sets of composites were then matched to a third group of artists' impressions. The latter were created by giving an experienced police artist each of the original Photofit pictures, along with their associated verbal descriptions, and asking her to create a portrait from them.

The three sets of materials varied in their degree of animation and realism, ranging from flat outlines represented by the line transcriptions of the conventional Photofit to the realistic, shaded portraits produced by the police artist. Their relative effectiveness as cues to recognition was assessed by asking subjects to identify the original target faces previously presented in a mug file. Overall, the Photofit pictures emerged as the best guide to likeness, followed by the line transcriptions; the portraits ranked a poor third. While all three sets of material were identified at above-chance levels, the comparative failure of the portraits may be attributed to the tendency of the artist to go beyond the information given to produce a comprehensive and lifelike picture construed by the witness as a specific individual rather than a general type. It appears that the elusive goal of the Photofit system to obtain realism without specificity was achieved.

The Artist as an Aid or Hindrance to Witness Memory?

Another area of lively debate among police personnel concerns the appropriate point at which the artist/technician should interview the witness; should it be a first priority or a last resort? Underlying this debate are concerns about the impact of the face recall interview itself on the memory of the witness and whether the demands of the task will impair subsequent testimony.

The impact of face recall on subsequent person identification has been the subject of a number of studies, the outcomes of which have been far from consistent. Mauldin and Laughery (1981) contrasted the effect of verbal recall of a face and production of an Identikit picture on subsequent ability to recognize the person presented in a mug file. Compared to control subjects who carried out neither task, Identikit construction facilitated recognition of the target, whereas verbally describing the face produced no clear effect. These findings should be contrasted with those of Davies, Ellis, and Shepherd (1978a), who found no effect of Photofit reconstruction on subsequent identification, and with those of Hall (1977), who reported a significant impairment of recognition following production of an artist's impression of the target.

Subsequent studies have failed to clarify the issue. Thompson and Laughery (1981) replicated the original facilitation effect for the Identikit, and Wogalter, Laughery, and Thompson (1987) reported similar effects when the Field Identification System was employed. However, these positive findings contrast with the significant impairments to recognition reported by Comish (1987) regarding Identikit construction and by Schooler (1987) regarding description production.

Davies (1981, 1986b) suggested that the solution to this conflict may lie in the quality of the resulting composites or descriptions, rather than in the production process itself. Jenkins and Davies (1985) have shown that observation of a misleading composite can impair subsequent recognition of a target face. If the subjects themselves generate the errors during production of their own composites, this seems likely to impair recognition. In the Hall study (1977), the artists were inexperienced and were instructed to demand exhaustive recall of detail by the witness. In the Schooler study (1987), a week elapsed between the observation and the request for a description, while in the Comish study (1987), maximum error occurred when the witness's own efforts at composite production were used to incorporate misleading detail. Conversely, facilitation has been observed with very short time delays between initial observation and recall, often no more than 30 min and never more than

2 days. Under these conditions, opportunities for trace information to be impaired or otherwise suffer deterioration have been minimized. As Laughery and his colleagues have noted, the face recall task may provide the opportunity for additional rehearsal of the target image and thus facilitate subsequent recognition (see Read, 1979).

If this interpretation is correct, then one might expect accuracy in composite production to be correlated with subsequent recognition preferences. This effect has been observed on some occasions (Wogalter, 1987) but not on others (Wogalter et al., 1987). Moreover, an inverse relationship between recall and recognition could be the result of the differing encoding demands of the two retrieval tasks, rather than the carry-over of erroneous information from one task to the other (Wells & Hryciw, 1984). Aside from the particular interpretation, current findings underline the need for training and caution among those responsible for interviewing witnesses. Unlike a verbal description, production of a face demands recall of all major features that will maximize reconstructive error among witnesses whose memory for the face has begun to fade.

Sketches and composites. There are many police officers who argue that the artist's impression is preferable to the composite method because of the superior quality of likeness achieved, despite the disparity in operational costs (Homa, 1983). Support for such a view comes from a laboratory comparison of sketches produced by trained artists and results obtained by technicians using the original Identikit. Volunteers who talked casually with a stranger for 7 to 8 min achieved with the artist likenesses of the stranger that were rated higher than those who worked with the Identikit (Laughery & Fowler, 1980). The sketches also served as a better guide to locate the targets in a mugfile than did the composites (Laughery & Smith, 1978).

A subsequent detailed analysis of the production demands of the two tasks (Laughery et al., 1986) suggested that the sketch artist elicited more information from the witnesses and gave the witnesses greater time and opportunity to arrive at final versions of each facial attribute. These findings reflect a general characteristic of the sketch artist. Unlike the composite technician, the artist has an unlimited repertoire of features, compared to the fixed number available in the kits. In this respect, the apparent superiority of the sketch over the composite parallels the superiority of the cued description over the prompted description. However, in both instances this potential superiority must be qualified by practical considerations, such as the availability of an artist gifted enough to provide the necessary flexibility and a witness with sufficient verbal fluency to describe the appearance of the suspect.

Flexibility in feature representation may not be the only factor that accounts for the observed superiority of the sketch artist. There is also the ability to manipulate the relative positions of features within a face, a procedure that is largely prescribed in rigid systems such as Photofit and Identikit. Haig (1986) used a computer graphics package to manipulate the internal positions of features within a target face and reported that observers were highly sensitive to small changes in the relative position of the eyes and the mouth to nose distance. The importance of the internal geometry of the face in securing a likeness is confirmed by the studies of Laughery et al. (1986); they noted that subjects who worked on groups of features rather than individual features achieved higher levels of rated likeness in composite construction.

Computerized composite systems. An obvious solution to the problem of manipulating the internal relationship of features is to replace the rigidities of acetate and cardboard with the versatility of a computer graphics package. Gillenson and Chandrasekaren proposed in 1975 that a computer-generated imaging system could provide the versatility of the skilled artist to the novice police interviewer. Experiments were conducted by the British Home Office, which resulted in a prototype computerized Photofit system; however, further development was abandoned because of the high cost of a production system (Kitson et al., 1978).

In recent years, the availability of computer graphics at modest costs has encouraged a number of manufacturers to develop identification packages. *Comphotofit* allows the witness and operator to build a Photofit picture on the computer screen in much the same manner as the conventional Photofit system. Features stored in the computer can be stretched or reduced to improve the likeness. Skin tone adjustment ensures that boundary lines between features are eliminated, and a painting facility allows limited coloring of the synthesized face. The final composite may be photographed or printed on a high-resolution graphics printer. Similar systems have been developed to take advantage of the graphics capabilities of the Apple MacIntosh computer. *Compusketch* allows the operator to build a library of more than 100,000 individual features, and the *Mac-A-Mug Pro* claims to provide infinite flexibility in the positioning of features and to permit the operator to change the apparent age of a face (*Mac-A-Mug Pro v. Compusketch,* 1987).

As yet, little empirical research has been conducted on this new generation of composite systems. They seem to have advantages over more traditional composite methods, yet they depend on many of the same assumptions as their predecessors about how faces are stored and retrieved from memory. Research on the original prototype computer system suggested that the similarity of likenesses achieved by volunteer witnesses was no better, or even slightly poorer, than those with the conventional Photofit (Christie, Davies, Shepherd, & Ellis, 1981). It will be unfortunate if increased technological ingenuity is not accompanied by appropriate allowances for the psychological factors that underlie facial perception and recall.

PHASE TWO: SEARCH

After a description, composite, or impression has been compiled, it must be identified, usually by a systematic search of the crime archive. Police forces have long kept records of known offenders but have had great difficulty in mobilizing this resource to trace and identify suspects. Zeiner and Zima (1983) described police records as "information cemeteries" from which few suspects emerge. With the advent of computerized data bases, many have suggested applying their power and versatility to the problem of the search for and location of suspects on the basis of descriptions supplied by witnesses. As with the electronic Photofit, however, there is a need to adapt technological sophistication to witness limitations.

The size of the problem can be illustrated by reference to the Canadian experience. The Royal Canadian Mounted Police maintains archives of approximately 1,400,000 criminal mugshots, which grow by more than 100,000 per year (J. B. O'Brien, personal communication, May 24, 1984). Routine searches of such a collection without the aid of a powerful heuristic are impractical. The search problem itself consists of two problems. First, one must devise a system for economical and effective classification and categorization of facial and other characteristics. Second, one must develop an algorithm that permits semiautomatic reduction of the collection to a subset small enough to be scanned visually.

Laughery, Rhodes, and Batten (1981) and Davies (1983) have reviewed early efforts in this field. The Houston Mugfile Project led by Laughery was the most ambitious. This envisaged a database composed of physical measurements derived from mugshots of known offenders, together with type of offense and personal details. When an offense occurred, the witness was to be interviewed to obtain verbal descriptions of the perpetrator, measurements were to be derived from a composite or impression, and vehicle descriptions that would form the input for a computerized search were to be devised. The system foundered on the difficulties of relating measurements derived from witness-generated portraits to the actual suspect photographs. Witness recall was not sufficiently accurate for the search algorithm to operate with any precision, and the power of computers in the early 1970s was inadequate to support a simultaneous search on a sufficient number of attributes (Laughery & Wogalter, in press). Perhaps the SIGMA project, which was developed by IBM for the Austrian police and which shares many similarities with the Houston approach, will avoid these pitfalls (Zeiner & Zima, 1983).

With the advent of low-cost microcomputers, vastly more powerful search routines can be employed, but the problem of integrating them with the psychological processes of witness behavior remains. One such system is the Optical Identification of Characteristics of Facial Features (OIC), developed by the Wisconsin State Police based on the work of Cormack (1979). Faces are classified on the basis of seven features, and this information is stored along with conventional criminal details. If a witness volunteers accurate information on two facial attributes, then 65% of the photographs in the collection can be eliminated. Three attributes eliminates 25% more of them, and four attributes reduces the set to 1%. Such a system is clearly dependent on accurate reporting of the critical facial features by the witness, which was the problem that caused the Houston system to fail.

Lenorovitz and Laughery (1984) reported a further attempt to solve the search problem, called Computer-Assisted Photographic Search and Retrieval (CAPSAR). The prototype database consisted of 330 randomly generated Identikit composites that were classified on 18 different dimensions. On the experimental trials, witnesses were shown a composite as a target, and then an interactive search of the database was carried out. A specimen Identikit composite from the database was shown, and the witness was requested to describe how it differed from the target. These differences would then form the basis for pruning the file of all faces that were not consistent with the description. An additional face was randomly presented from the remaining set, and the pruning algorithm was repeated until the number of faces had been reduced to 50 or fewer. These were then visually searched by the witness. Trials indicated a 53% hit rate for CAPSAR, compared to only 32% for a conventional manual search.

CAPSAR operates by systematically eliminating faces from the search set. If the witness makes a series of correct decisions, then the system is highly effective. On the other hand, if the witness makes an error, the consequences are severe because the target is eliminated from the search. This problem can be avoided by an algorithm that prioritizes rather than eliminates faces. One such system is Face Retrieval and Matching Equipment (FRAME), developed at Aberdeen University in conjunction with the British Home Office. The prototype database consisted of ratings obtained on facial attributes derived from photographs of 1,000 white men. Photographs of the 1,000 faces were stored on an optical disk, allowing immediate display of relevant pictures to the witness. In research trials, witnesses were shown a photograph of a target face, which they subsequently described to the operator. The operator then converted the description into a series of ratings on relevant facial attributes that were then fed into the FRAME computer program. This searched the database and identified, in descending order, the 10 faces that most closely fit the description. If the target was not located after the first search, the description could be modified on the basis of the faces shown and a second, and possibly a third, search initiated.

A series of experimental studies described by Shepherd (1986) yielded identification rates of between 70% and 80% using the FRAME system. Compared with conventional album searches, FRAME achieved no difference in effectiveness on distinctive faces, but it was markedly superior on faces lacking distinctive features (69% versus 44%). A working operational system of FRAME known as Face Analysis, Comparison and Elimination System (FACE) is now undergoing a full field evaluation with the Lancashire Constabulary in England. All 11,000 photographs from the files of one police division have been coded on relevant attributes, using a mixture of visual evaluation and semiautomatic measuring procedures. Results from the early operation have been encouraging. Future developments may lead to an electronic composite device ("E fit") that will utilize the same scales as FACES. This should allow a composite to be produced in parallel with the search of the suspect file, which would be a major breakthrough in forensic identification (Bennett, 1986).

PHASE THREE: IDENTIFICATION

When the police detain a suspect, the third and perhaps most critical stage in the evidence-gathering sequence can begin. This is the procedure of obtaining an identification from a lineup, a critical stage because a positive identification at this time may become direct evidence in a criminal case. In addition, a positive identification can become an important element in plea bargaining, and a nonidentification can suggest that other lines of investigation should be pursued to strengthen a case, or that an entirely new line of inquiry should be explored. Thus, lineup performance by witnesses has both informational and evidentiary importance (Twining, 1983).

The identification of a perpetrator in a lineup is a cause for concern because judges and legal scholars believe that such identifications are vulnerable to error. There can be no doubt that false identifications occur in actual criminal cases; case study documentation is readily available (see Chapter 1 and Borchard, 1932; Brandon & Davies, 1973; Devlin, 1976; Frankfurter, 1927; Levine & Tapp, 1973; O'Connor, 1974; Wall, 1965; Williams, 1955).

Known errors and the suspicion that there are many more unknown errors have led to the recruitment of psychologists to help explain why such errors occur and, if possible, to improve procedural and structural aspects of lineups. Considerable evidence has been amassed from laboratory simulations, field investigations, and case studies regarding the reliability of witness performance in identifying suspects. Such evidence points not only to conditions under which identification is likely to be unreliable but also to those procedures that are likely to prove most reliable. Thus, present research has moved beyond the documentation of the extent of recognition failures to the development of theoretical frameworks to explain how the different types of error arise and to suggest procedures that may moderate errors and increase correct identifications.

Two fundamental errors may arise in an identification situation involving lineups: the witness can fail to identify the perpetrator, or the witness can pick an innocent person (possibly a suspect) from the lineup. The psychologist's tasks are to explain the mechanisms that give rise to such errors and to determine how these errors can be avoided or at least attenuated by procedural refinements.

Factors that are known to influence lineup identification are discussed below under three perspectives on identification accuracy: the social psychology perspective, the structural perspective, and the cognitive perspective. Numerous explanations of the diversity of identification failures found throughout the psychological and psycholegal literature are interpretable within one or more of these perspectives.

The Social Psychology Perspective

Clifford and Bull (1978) argued that lineup identification is basically a cognitive-social phenomenon. More recently, Malpass and Devine (1984) suggested that there is a distinction between the witness's identification or nonidentification of someone in a lineup and the accuracy of that choice. Choosing is a behavior, and accuracy is an outcome of choosing. As Malpass and Devine indicated, the choosing-accuracy distinction has not been sharply made until recently, even though it is implicit in many psychological discussions of eyewitness identification (Levine & Tapp, 1973; Woocher, 1977) and is at the core of the issue of the effects of suggestion (Devlin, 1976; Sobel & Pridgen, 1981; Wall, 1965).

If a lineup has been properly composed, then the witness is faced with a difficult choice. If the foils resemble a perpetrator and/or suspect, the witness must decide whether or not to choose. This choice will not rest solely on a memory trace, because existing values and beliefs peculiar to the witness will also be present, although they may not be articulated or articulable (Clifford & Bull, 1978). However, they may be real and compelling to the witness. If the witness believes that a correct identification will lead to the conviction of a criminal, this will contribute to the attractiveness of choosing. Conversely, a belief that a correct identification will require further participation in protracted criminal proceedings and difficult social-emotional confrontations will contribute to the unattractiveness of choosing. If the witness is preoccupied with thoughts that a false identification could lead to the conviction of an innocent person or that nonidentification could lead to the freeing of a guilty person, then different patterns of choosing can be predicted.

These witness biases relate to the fact that social situations are also informational situations. To the extent that police exhibit confidence, deliberately or unconsciously, the witness at the lineup may reasonably make one or more of the following deductions: A lineup has been arranged because the police have a suspect; the confidence of the police suggests that the suspect is actually the perpetrator; if the witness fails to make an identification or makes a wrong identification, the police will be perturbed. It is of more than passing interest that in the appendix to the Devlin Report (1976), in cases where misidentification was demonstrated, they were predominantly focused on the police suspect.

The traditional belief that identification is solely a question of comparing a memory image with a present image is now seen to be a convenient fiction that should be discarded. In reality, the lineup identification situation is much more complex. Psychologists now argue that the behavior of a witness is best conceptualized as a decision process that results from the interplay of the information in the memory, the information available in the situation, and the beliefs and values of the witness concerning the outcomes of possible behaviors and the probabilities and consequences of these outcomes.

Choosing has dimensions that transcend the pure memory, as shown by Ainsworth and King (1988). These researchers surveyed all lineups conducted within five divisions of a large Northern England police force during a 12-month period. Witnesses were asked to answer structured questionnaires concerning the experiences and feelings they had while trying to identify the perpetrators. There were 24 male and 29 female witnesses, with ages that ranged between 14 and 76 years. The offenses they had witnessed included robbery, burglary, and indecent exposure.

Of the 53 witnesses, 40% correctly identified the suspect. Of the 32 witnesses who failed to make an identification response, 53% said they felt nervous, whereas of those who chose someone, only 24% said they were nervous. Of 32 witnesses who failed to make a choice, 34% stated that they feared reprisals from the suspect, whereas only 9% of those who chose stated such fears. Although such studies are not conclusive, this study certainly suggests that choosing is a social decision-making process as well as a cognitive memory process. Thus, social decision-making research is clearly an approach that promises to be productive in explaining lineup identification choices.

There is a more immediately practical implication to be drawn from the Ainsworth and King (1988) finding that witnesses mentioned nervousness and fear of reprisals. Modification of identification procedures to avoid face-to-face contact and the chance of perpetrators' identifying the witnesses would be desirable for the criminal justice system. If this is a desirable modification, research conducted in the informational tradition could be reconceptualized in terms of social decision making and its implications. Such research involves the question of whether lineups using photospreads, videotape recordings, or live presentations produce significantly different rates of choosing and accuracy. Conventional wisdom says that live lineups are preferred. For example, Justice Traynor of the California Supreme Court stated in his review of *People v. Gould* (1960) that "identification from a still photograph is substantially less reliable than identification of an individual seen in person" (p. 160). Likewise, Wall (1965) opined that "a corporeal identification, if properly obtained, is more reliable than a photographic one" (p. 70). The factual basis for such beliefs must be examined.

Yuille and Cutshall (1984) presented subjects with either a live or a videotaped version of a staged theft and tested identification accuracy for the perpetrator presented in a live lineup, a videotaped lineup, and a photospread. They found that the mode of lineup presentation made no difference. On the basis of this experiment, they concluded that "videotaped lineups seem to offer promise as a means of providing effective identification procedures for police." Their conclusion regarding photospreads conflicts with other research findings. Egan, Pittner, and Goldstein (1977) and Turnbull and Thompson (1984) found live lineups to be better than photospreads. The former researchers reported higher hit rates with live lineups but no difference in false positives, and the latter reported that photospreads increased false positive rates. However, Wells (1984) argued that the difference in identification accuracy between live lineups and photospreads is trivial, and his conclusion is supported by Shepherd, Ellis, and Davies (1982).

If identification accuracy is only slightly affected by the mode of presentation of the lineup (photospread, videotaped, or live), then logistical considerations concerning composition and considerations of witness judgments of consequences to themselves argue for the use of methods that minimize stressful face-to-face confrontations and possible perpetrator identification of the witness. Such changes in procedure could alter the rate of choosing. However, before this putative equality of methods is adopted for identification procedures, it must be recognized that the rate of choosing when the offender is *absent* must be known in order to estimate the degree to which correct identification reflects the ability of the witness to differentiate the offender from other individuals. The power of this manipulation of perpetrator-absent lineups will be taken up in the following discussion of the cognitive perspective, but it should be noted here that as long as studies comparing photospread, videotaped, and live lineups do not employ perpetrator-absent conditions, the comparability of different modes of lineup presentation remains to be settled.

Even though different methods of conducting identification parades may or may not affect the rate of correct identifications, there can be little doubt that methods without face-to-face confrontation are less stressful. Dent and Gray (1975) compared color slide presentations with live lineups. They reported that in the live condition witnesses appeared embarrassed and self-conscious as they looked at the men lined up in front of them and that they were less willing than the photospread subjects to look at one man for a long time. When faced with the actual perpetrator, they also appeared more anxious to end the situation quickly. Dent and Gray also found that higher accuracy rates of identification with photographs than with live lineups.

The use of one-way mirrors, videotaped lineups, or even photospreads is gaining momentum. This momentum is fueled by a perspective that emphasizes the social dimensions of the identification situation. However, even if it were possible to conduct lineup identifications with no element of confrontation, certain structural and procedural problems would still remain. These problems are best investigated under the structural perspective, to which we now turn.

The Structural Perspective

The U.S. Supreme Court (Wall, 1965) suggested that the influence of improper suggestion probably accounts for more mistaken identifications and miscarriages of justice than any other single factor or all other factors combined. An identification is considered suggestive if the police suspect is indicated to the witness by any means. The potential for suggestion exists in the procedures of the lineup (social interaction patterns such as those described above) and in the structure of the lineup (composition and number of foils). There is certainly an irreducible degree of suggestiveness in the mere holding of a lineup, but careful instructions to the witness concerning the possible presence or absence of the perpetrator can obviate the witness's inherent belief that the task is to choose a member of the lineup.

Laboratory studies have investigated manipulations of instructions given to witnesses who were about to attempt an identification. Malpass and Devine (1981) staged a live event and then sought identification of the perpetrator. They gave one group of witnesses (the biased-instruction group) instructions that indicated that the offender was present in the lineup, and they provided response forms without a category of "not present." The other group of witnesses (the unbiased-instruction group) received instructions that implied that the offender might not be present in the lineup, and their response form included the option to indicate "not present." Witnesses viewed a five-person lineup through a one-way mirror. Half of each instruction group was presented with an offender-present line-up that included the perpetrator, and the other half received an offender-absent lineup. Malpass and Devine hypothesized that biased instructions would lead to more errors in offender-absent lineups, whereas unbiased instructions would lead to more caution by witnesses and fewer identification responses in offender-absent lineups. When the perpetrator was present, 100% of witnesses given biased instructions chose someone, and 25% of their choices were errors. With unbiased instruction only 83% chose someone, and 17% of their choices were errors. When the perpetrator was absent, given biased instructions 78% of the witnesses chose someone, but only 33% made a choice when given unbiased instructions.

Hall and Ostrom (1975) asked subjects to identify the person who had recruited them for an experiment in their psychology class. When the target was present, they found a high rate of choosing under both biased (80%) and unbiased (100%) instructions. When the target was absent, errors of choosing were moderate (36%) under biased instructions but low (8%) under unbiased instructions. When the target was present in the lineup, biased instructions led to 40% errors, but no errors occurred under unbiased instructions. Thus, the instructions given to witnesses may have significant effects on the rate of choosing and the accuracy of those choices.

In a conceptually similar experiment, Egan and Smith (1979) asked subjects to play the role of witnesses. They were shown a target person through a one-way mirror, and 2 or 35 days later they were asked to indicate whether or not each member of a five-person lineup was the target. Subjects were given either lax (avoid misses) or strict (avoid false alarms) instructions. With the target present, there was little difference in error rates for the two instructions (12% for lax and 8% for strict). With the target absent, there were more erroneous choices under lax (79%) than under strict instructions (37%).

Another study reported a somewhat different pattern of results (Buckhout, 1980). Following the viewing of a film of a mugging, Buckhout asked subjects to select the perpetrator from a photospread, under either a lax or a strict criterion. When the perpetrator was present under lax instructions, 76% made a choice, but only 52% made a choice under strict instructions. When the perpetrator was absent, 74% of subjects under lax instructions made a choice, whereas under strict instruction 53% made a choice. However, accuracy differed from previous studies. With the perpetrator present, there were 86% errors under lax instructions but 90% under strict instructions. With the offender absent, there were 74% and 53% errors under lax and strict instructions, respectively.

These various studies point to the strong and consistent effects of instructional bias on choosing and on errors when the perpetrator is not present. When the perpetrator is present, the effects of instructional biases are lessened. Numerous other studies support the contention that the instructions given by the person conducting the lineup are important, but the strongest case is made by the studies discussed above that included a perpetrator-absent condition.

However, certain studies that used perpetrator-absent lineups have not confirmed the importance of instructions. Fleet, Brigham, and Bothwell (1987) staged a live event and asked witnesses to identify the perpetrator in target-present and target-absent lineups, under three types of instructional bias: positive ("We believe that the person who stole the videocamera is in one of the pictures"), neutral ("The person who stole the camera may or may not be in one of the pictures"), and negative ("We doubt that the person who stole the videocamera appears in any of the pictures"). They did not find the interaction between bias and error rate that Malpass and Devine (1981) reported. Instead, they found that error rates for the target-absent lineup were similar for the unbiased (54%) and positively biased instruction groups (46%). With target-present lineups, there was no significant difference between positively biased instructions (25%) and unbiased instructions (17%). At least one other study found no effect of differential instructions. Hilgendorf and Irving (1978) failed to find any difference in hit rates under encouraging, discouraging, and neutral instructions.

The effect of instructional bias is complex and appears to depend on situational variables, such as target presence (Malpass & Devine, 1981, 1984), such personality variables as self-monitoring (Hosch, Leippe, Marchioni, & Cooper, 1984) and neuroticism (Zanni & Offermann, 1978). Clearly, the effects of differential instruction on eyewitness memory seem to be more subtle and complex than previously assumed. Instructional bias has produced increases in the rate of choosing and decreases in the rate of lineup rejections (Hosch et al., 1984), but it must be conceded that instructions are not always successful in increasing detection of the perpetrators and in decreasing the rate of erroneous identifications.

In addition to the mental set that may be created by the instructions given to the witnesses, a greater source of potential suggestion may be the composition of the lineup. Lineups in which identification of the suspect is certain or highly likely to occur are generally considered unfair or suggestive. Malpass and Devine (1983) stated that lineups should be of sufficient size that the probability of a chance identification of an innocent suspect is low and that the potential for error is distributed across a number of persons. The size of a lineup affects the level of risk to which an innocent suspect is exposed by chance alone. The larger the lineup, the less the risk. Of course, this risk must be balanced against the practical considerations of constructing a large lineup. Not only must the number of foils be considered, but discriminability from the suspect must also be considered. This principle is concerned with the level of risk to which an innocent suspect is exposed in relation to the other members of the lineup (Malpass & Devine, 1983) and is referred to as bias in a lineup.

Fairness in size and bias are both based on similarities of the members of the lineup to each other and to the suspect. Unfairness in size results from a situation where one or more foils are not plausible choices for the witness. In this situation the lineup is functionally smaller than the number of people in the lineup. While the problem of lineup size focuses on the possibility that one or more foils will be identified with a probability less than expected by chance, the problem of lineup bias focuses only on whether the identification of the suspect departs from chance expectation. If the suspect has an identification probability greater than expectation, the lineup is biased against the suspect. If the suspect has an identification probability less than expectation, the lineup is biased in favor of the suspect.

It may be argued that the above considerations are desirable but impractical. Although this may be true to some extent, the principles have implications for actual practice. Consider the situation where the witness is white, the perpetrator is black, and the person who constructs the lineup could be either black or white. Because the witness had indicated a black perpetrator, the foils must be black, and the problem is to choose foils that do not violate the bias principle outlined above. Research on cross-racial identification (e.g., Lindsay & Wells, 1983) and other-race visual processing (e.g., Ellis, Deregowaski, & Shepherd, 1975) suggests that a black police officer should compose the lineup. As Brigham and Ready (1985) indicated, it is probable that a black officer would compose a better lineup when the perpetrator is black because a black person is better able to "see" relevant similarities and differences between the suspect and the potential foils. A lineup so composed should have less bias than might be the case were it constructed by a white.

Malpass and Devine (1983) examined the relationship between the similarities among the foils and the suspect and a number of measures of the two types of lineup fairness. Similarity was manipulated by using foils that varied from the target to different degrees in terms of the color, style, and length of hair; general body build; height; and eye color. Subjects read a description of a breaking and entering offense that included two descriptions of the suspect: one at the midpoint of the summary of the case and one at the end. They found that fairness as measured by seven different indices decreased as the dissimilarity between the suspect and the foils increased.

Psychologists who work in this area of evidence elicitation should be concerned to experimentally investigate unfairness in lineup composition (Wells, Leippe, & Ostrom, 1979). These researchers estimate the degree of bias against or in favor of the suspect by computing the reciprocal transformation of the proportion of mock witnesses who identify a suspect. Mock witnesses did not see the perpetrator at the scene of a crime; they only read a description given by a witness who was present. They are then asked to select the perpetrator from a photospread, a videotape, or a picture of a lineup on the basis of this verbal description of the perpetrator. This index of bias is the number of mock witnesses (N) divided by the number who identified the suspect (D). That is, if the number of mock witnesses who chose the suspect is 50% of all mock witnesses, then the probability (i.e., D/N) is .50 and the functional size (i.e., N/D) is 2.0.

Legal practitioners tend to grasp functional size concepts better than probability concepts. Accordingly, a lineup is biased against the suspect if the index is smaller than the number of individuals in the lineup and is biased in favor of the suspect if the index is larger. As an example, suppose there is a lineup of five foils plus the suspect, and there are 60 mock witnesses. If 40 of these mock witnesses choose the suspect, then the index is $60/40 = 1.5$. However, if only 10 of the mock witnesses choose the suspect, then the index is $60/10 = 6$. Given the simplicity of this test and its powerful evidential implications, it should be mandatory for all police forces to maintain a visual record of all lineups. This simple prescription has been resisted in the United Kingdom on the understandable but refutable grounds of expense and the infringement of the personal privacy of the innocent foils who chose to help the police form a lineup.

Several other measures of lineup size and bias have been suggested (e.g., Malpass, 1981), but as Malpass and Devine (1984) recognized, methods that require either training in statistics and measurement or technical consultation may be better suited to research than to the gathering of evidence in actual cases. (However, this degree of available expertise demonstrates the depth of the psychologist's potential contribution to the gathering and evaluation of evidence.) Simpler methods of assessing bias are available, which make explicit the assumptions upon which decisions would be made. Malpass and Devine (1983, 1984) argued that indicators of fairness in a lineup can be devised by constructing intervals around the proportion of identifications expected by chance (expressed as a proportion of choice expectations based on the nominal size). Therefore, any member of a lineup can be considered a poor alternative if the observed proportion of identifications falls below the acceptable interval. Thus, an acceptable foil could be defined by a cutoff proportion, such as .75 of chance expectation. Any foil that falls below this cutoff would be rejected as a foil.

Thus far, bias considerations have focused on characteristics of foils and lineup size as these relate to fairness. These conclusions can also be focused on the suspect. A lineup would be biased against the suspect if the suspect is identified above a criterion proportion by mock witnesses and biased in favor of the suspect if the suspect is identified less than a certain criterion.

Although fairness in the informational sense discussed above is not a concept much discussed in legal circles, it is beyond doubt that psychological research can make an important contribution to the analysis of problems in eyewitness identification (Malpass & Devine, 1984), although its direct application to the criminal justice system is limited. Courts, police stations, and legal offices are frequently located in populous locations where mock witnesses are readily available. Thus, the use of such panels may be a practical method of monitoring the validity of eyewitness identification. The use of mock witnesses should be encouraged, because we need to evaluate the fairness of a lineup independent of the judgments made by real witnesses. Fair lineups protect innocent suspects from misidentification by witnesses who do not possess adequate information about the appearance of the offender but who feel that they must attempt an identification. If a lineup is fair, then witnesses who have only general information about the appearance of the offender should not make identifications with a probability greater than chance, whereas witnesses who have firsthand information about the offender's unique appearance should be able to select at above chance levels. This rationale and the mock witness technique have been used to evaluate the fairness of lineups in actual criminal cases (Biederman, 1980; Doob & Kirschenbaum, 1973; Wells et al., 1979).

So far we have examined the fairness of a lineup after it has been constructed, as well as how police officers should instruct witnesses. However, a prior problem concerns how officers should go about constructing a lineup. Obviously, they begin with the suspect. However, suspects are usually selected only from the descriptions given by witnesses. The important question concerns the extent to which verbal descriptions accord with later visual identification, that is, how well witnesses verbalize a visual image and how well the police officer translates the verbal description into a visual image. The slippage inherent in this process is highlighted by studies that correlate witness descriptions with their later identifications.

Early researchers demonstrated that witness descriptions of criminals were generally of poor quality (e.g., Munsterberg, 1908; Stern, 1903-1906). The U.S. Supreme Court emphasized that "the accuracy of a prior description" was one of the criteria to be used in judging identification accuracy, but Wells and Murray (1983) indicated that emphasizing the need for congruence between the suspect's appearance and the witness's description may introduce a problem into the construction of a lineup when the perpetrator has not been apprehended. To the extent that there is a low correlation between prior description and later identification of a criminal, the possibility exists that witness descriptions can mislead the lineup constructor, who must begin with the suspect who has been apprehended on the basis of the witness's description. If the suspect is not the perpetrator, then the foils will not be appropriate for the perpetrator but only for the (wrong) suspect.

Laboratory studies on facial recognition (e.g., Malpass, Lavigueur, & Weldon, 1973; Sporer, in press; Wells, 1985) and studies employing staged ncidents (Pigott & Brigham, 1985; Pigott, Brigham, & Bothwell, 1985) generally produce either zero or only slightly positive correlations between description accuracy or the number and type of descriptions provided and identification accuracy. In fact, Sporer (1986) observed in a staged incident study that subjects who made an identification attempt recalled fewer physical descriptors of the target than subjects who refused to make a lineup choice.

A more encouraging study (Wells, 1985) used 88 different target faces and found a significant point-biserial correlation between description accuracy and identification accuracy. However, he pointed out that this relationship was not due to good describers making accurate identifications but to the fact that faces that are better described are better identified. That is, the descriptor-identification relationship was mediated by target factors rather than subject factors. This result tells the criminal justice system that unique faces may be better described and better identified. However, the weight of this evidence suggests that lineup construction bias and unfairness may start long before the selection of foils; it may start at the point of obtaining descriptions from the witness or victim. This lack of positive correlation between descriptions and identification has important implications for understanding what the witness is actually doing at the time of identification and suggests methods for overcoming inaccurate identification. To understand the problem, we must go to our third perspective in identification evidence.

The Cognitive Perspective

Clifford and Bull (1978) made the point that no matter how fastidiously the police go about constructing a lineup, the fundamental consideration is the basis for the witness's decision to choose one of the lineup participants. This point of choice is the critical focus of psychological theory and experiment and concerns our knowledge of the nature of memory. Recognition and identification in eyewitness situations are always the result of an approximate match between the initial memory laid down at the time of witnessing the original event and the subsequent perception of an individual in a lineup. The match will never be perfect, because of logical and practical factors. Thus, identifying is a decision-making process, and what an eyewitness decides is the degree of resemblance that is an acceptable basis for an identification. But in a lineup situation identification is even more complex than this, because the degree-of-resemblance decision is predicated on a relative judgment involving all of the other lineup members. This second facet of the decision-making process would not be present in show-up situation where the police confront the witness with only the suspect.

A study by Lindsay and Wells (1980) makes these resemblance-processing and relative-judgment points clearer. Eyewitnesses to a staged event viewed lineups that did or did not contain the perpetrator. In perpetrator-absent lineups, the foils did or did not closely resemble the (innocent) suspect who had been chosen beforehand for his resemblance to the actual perpetrator. At the lineup stage, when there was a superficial resemblance between the foils and the innocent suspect, the innocent suspect was identified as the perpetrator by 31% of the witnesses who made a choice. However, when dissimilarity existed between the foils and the innocent suspect, the innocent suspect received 70% of the choices. In other words, the innocent suspect was relatively more similar to the perpetrator in the latter condition, and this served to increase the likelihood of obtaining incriminating evidence against him. This experiment clearly demonstrates that in a lineup situation witnesses' identification choices involve two processes. First, the witness must compare each and every current lineup member with the memory of the perpetrator seen at the scene of the crime. Second, the choice involves relative judgments of how close that resemblance is for each lineup member, relative to all other lineup members, taking the lineup as a whole. The first process is what we have referred to as resemblance processing; the second process is what we have referred to as the relative judgment process.

Now, clearly, the identification problem stems from the lack of a perfect memory for the perpetrator's appearance. However, if some objective index of memory strength existed, then perhaps it would be possible to make a judgment of how lax or strict the witness must have been in making a resemblance-based identification. That is, if memory for the perpetrator was perfect, then comparison with a person currently being viewed in a lineup would be easy. To the extent that memory was not perfect, a means of measuring the degradation of that memory would afford a metric for judging veracity. Unfortunately, no such objective index exists to allow evidence gatherers and evaluators make these judgments. A number of such indices have been tried, but without much success.

We have already seen that the quality of initial description, when a witness's memory is reasonably fresh, does not predict eventual identification accuracy. The U.S. Supreme Court has always argued strongly that confidence or level of certainty should be given weight, whereas in the United Kingdom Devlin (1976) suggested that the witness's demeanor (mainly confidence) should be given consideration. The idea of a positive relationship between confidence and accuracy is intuitively appealing, and certainly jurors are more likely to believe a witness who is certain (Lindsay, Wells, & Rumpel, 1981). However, the literature fails to substantiate this view (Deffenbacher, 1980; Leippe, 1980; Wells & Murray, 1984). A meta-analysis (Bothwell, Brigham, & Deffenbacher, 1985) across 33 samples found a mean correlation between confidence and accuracy of only +0.28, with the 95% confidence interval ranging from −0.09 to +0.64. However, several recent field studies have reported significant correlations (Brigham, Maass, Snyder, & Spaulding, 1982; Fleet, Brigham, & Bothwell, 1987; Hosch & Platz, 1984; Krafka Penrod, 1985; Piggott et al., 1985), but once again, the correlations are low.

A reasonable conclusion is that we do not know whether confident identifications made by witnesses at a lineup should be given more weight than identifications by less confident witnesses. Certainly, confidence is not an index of memory strength in the field of eyewitness identification.

Another question concerns the relationship between the amount of time that elapsed from witnessing a crime to providing an identification and the strength of the memory trace. Could elapsed time be an index of memory strength and thus an indicator of whether the witness used a lax or strict criterion of resemblance in making an identification choice? Again, the evidence is not consistent. It is certainly the case that laboratory studies of memory for faces have generally found little or no decline in memory over intervals of many weeks (for reviews see Ellis, 1984; Shepherd, 1981). Egan et al. (1977) presented two targets for later identification and found identifications from photospreads to be high and not to decline over a period of 8 weeks. However, false identifications increased quite substantially, from which it can be inferred that memory had degraded. Shepherd and Ellis (1973) showed subjects photographs of faces and tested them either immediately, after 6 says, or after 35 days. Memory became progressively poorer as time passed, but only for faces of average attractiveness. Memory for faces of high and low attractiveness exhibited little or no decline over time. Using normal faces, Laughery, Fessler, Lenorovitz, and Yoblick (1974) and Goldstein and Chance (1971) also failed to demonstrate a significant drop in identification accuracy with the passage of time.

In light of this conflicting evidence, Shepherd et al. (1982) conducted a series of experiments to elucidate the effect of delay on facial memory over periods of 1 week to 11 months. In one study, a man burst into a lecture and demanded that the owner of a car speak out. Following intervals of 1 week, 1 month, 3 months, and 11 months, the subjects were required to identify this target from a videotaped array of nine men. No significant decline in accuracy was found over intervals of 1 week to 3 months. Memory declined over 11 months, but false alarm rates did not differ among any of the delay intervals. This finding on false alarms differs from that by Egan et al. (1977). Perhaps the fact that the latter study employed two perpetrators but used only one in a lineup could account for this effect, since recognition accuracy decreases as the number of perpetrators increases (Clifford & Hollin, 1981). The general conclusion from these studies is that the amount of delay cannot be used as an objective index of the strength of the memory trace that a witness has for a perpetrator and thus cannot be employed to judge the extent to which resemblance processing has occurred.

Rather than searching for possible situations or factors that could be used to infer the degree of presence of relative-judgment resemblance processing, a more beneficial approach would be to assume such processing always occurs, because of the nature of memory, and to seek procedural changes in the identification situation on that basis (Clifford & Bull, 1978; Wells, 1984). It is important to reiterate the psychological assumptions underlying the proposed changes, in order for them to be clear. No two representations of the same person will ever be identical. To the extent that no two representations are ever identical, we are in the realm of resemblance, and judgments about how closely one thing resembles another are a matter of degree and are subject to influence. In a lineup situation, one source of influence is the foils (see Lindsay & Wells, 1980, 1985). If it is accepted that we are dealing with relative rather than absolute matching of memory and perceptual images when eyewitnesses are identifying in a lineup situation, and that the lineup composition and procedure can increase the probability of witnesses choosing someone, irrespective of the true match between the memory image of the perpetrator and the currently perceived lineup member; changes in lineup procedures may be required.

Following this line of reasoning, psychologists have recommended the use of blank lineups, both by researchers and by police in the field (e.g., Clifford & Bull, 1978; Dunning, Ellsworth, & Ross, 1985; Lindsay & Wells, 1985). In both cases, the rationale is that to the extent that the witness is choosing on the basis of approximate similarity (resemblance) rather than absolute similarity (identicality), errors will be made on the blank (perpetrator-absent) lineup, and this will indicate the unreliable witnesses.

The use of blank lineups as a research tool is aimed at providing police with a method for deciding whether their lineups contain the real perpetrators or not. This is felt to be important because at the time of conducting a lineup, the police can never truly know whether *their suspect* is the *perpetrator*. Thus, they can never know whether, in essence, they have a perpetrator present or a perpetrator-absent (blank) lineup. After obtaining a judgment from a witness who has viewed a lineup, the police and prosecution must decide whether the evidence can be relied upon. If the witness positively identified the suspect, it must be decided whether the identification was correct (i.e., the suspect was the perpetrator) or incorrect (i.e., the suspect was an unfortunate innocent in a blank lineup). Conversely, if the witness fails to identify the suspect, the police must decide whether the witness's memory was not up to the task (but the lineup contained the perpetrator) or whether the suspect was truly innocent (and the lineup was blank). Pardons and miscarriages of justice following wrongful lineup identifications demonstrate that these are very real issues for the police. It is here that research on blank lineups may be of help.

Unlike the police in the field, experimental psychologists in the research situation do know whether they are conducting perpetrator-present or perpetrator-absent lineups because they arrange the total event. To the extent that the behavior of witnesses in the two types of lineup differs, then knowledge of these patterns of difference can be used to help to judge whether real-life police lineups are blank or valid, that is, whether the suspect is actually the perpetrator. That is the theory; practice has not yet caught up. To date, nothing has been found in witnesses's patterns of choices that allows discrimination of a valid from a blank lineup. Thus, this is a contribution that psychology may be able to make in the future.

More practically, however, it has been suggested that blank lineups can be used as screening devices. Thus, it has been suggested that police set up two lineups, the first one not containing the suspect. Any witness who identifies from the first (blank) lineup is immediately excused as a reliable witness. But there are practical difficulties here. To use two lineups requires recruiting more than the normal number of foils. Rejecting witnesses because of blank lineup errors is a serious matter for police forces, especially if they only have one witness. In addition, diffusion into the general population of the information that two lineups are usually used and that the first is blank would render the system useless. Thus, what is required is a lineup procedure that, on the one hand, reduces the tendency to employ relative-judgment strategies without, on the other hand, eliminating witnesses, increasing police man-hours devoted to constructing lineups, and allowing witnesses to predict the placement of suspects in a lineup. Lindsay and Wells (1985) suggest that the sequential lineup procedure best achieves this end.

In a sequential lineup, witnesses see lineup members one at a time and, while knowing that there are other members of the lineup still to be seen, must make a yes or no decision concerning the person currently being viewed. This procedure greatly reduces the relative-judgment process that occurs when witnesses survey all lineup members simultaneously. It also serves to emphasize to the witness the need to identify solely in terms of the absolute resemblance of the current person to his or her existing memory trace of the actual perpetrator.

That these two benefits accrue to the sequential lineup is indicated by the fact that the chief function of such a lineup is to reduce false positives while leaving unchanged the rate of true identifications. In this, sequential lineups may prove to be a major contribution to the criminal justice system. Like other procedural refinements, such as instructions (e.g., Malpass & Devine, 1981), manipulated similarity of foils (e.g., Lindsay & Wells, 1980), and the use of blank lineups (Wells, 1984), sequential lineups seem to operate by reducing the witness's reliance on relative-judgment resemblance processing. The sequential lineup suggestion is a good example of the psychologist-criminal justice interface, where psychological knowledge makes known the human factors that operate in specific situations and the criminal justice system sets the boundaries within which practical changes can be effected to accommodate these psychological factors in ways that better ensure justice.

Voice Identification

Voice identification is an area that has been much less investigated than visual identification. Eliciting descriptions and searching databases cannot be appropriately applied to voice identification because no research of any quality exists on the description of the voices of perpetrators, and there are no voice banks for known perpetrators. Only the third phase of eliciting testimony has been investigated: voice identification situations. This dearth of research and strategic investigation of voice identification is unfortunate, because it is often forgotten that in three landmark cases in the United States (see Bull & Clifford, 1984; Clifford, 1983) voice identification was critical. Furthermore, for obscene phone calls, bomb hoaxes, ransom demands, hooded rapes or muggings, and crimes committed in darkness, the perpetrator's voice may be the only tangible piece of evidence available to facilitate police investigation.

Although three major reviews on voice identification exist (Clifford, 1980, 1983; Bull & Clifford, 1984), space permits only a summary of the major findings. There is a marked similarity of findings in voice and visual identification studies, which suggests that conclusions regarding the visual mode will also prove to be correct for voice, although it is likely that the absolute level of performance for voice identification will be lower than for visual identification (e.g., Yarmey, 1986). For example, voice recognition of familiar voices is very good but is much poorer for unfamiliar voices. As with visual identification, the unexamined extrapolation from familiar to unfamiliar stimuli is crucial to the status of voice identification as direct evidence in courts of law. This simple generalization from familiar to unfamiliar stimuli is no less dangerous in voice than in visual identification cases, as the sparse research clearly demonstrates.

The duration of a speech sample makes little difference to later identification accuracy for adults, provided that at least one sentence is heard; it appears that children's recall can benefit from longer exposure (Clifford, Bull, & Rathborn, 1980). As with visual identification, the effects of delay are equivocal, but there is a suggestion that length of time between hearing a perpetrator's voice and eventual identification is less important. The confidence-accuracy relationship, which is ambiguous in face identification, is also unclear in voice investigations. Several researchers (e.g., Rathborn, Bull, & Clifford, 1981) have reported positive correlations between confidence and objective accuracy in voice identification under optimal testing conditions. In terms of individual differences, very young and very old earwitnesses are less accurate than middle-aged witnesses. A same-sex effect has been demonstrated in voice identification, wherein women are better at recognizing female voices and men are better at recognizing male voices. Concerning the effect of race, one must conclude from the exploratory work of Goldstein, Knight, Bailis, and Conover (1981) that there is no clear evidence of cross-racial problems in speaker identification. Voice disguise has been shown to be a powerful factor in preventing correct voice identification (e.g., Saslove & Yarmey, 1980).

In reviewing the existing voice identification research, two major conclusions emerge, paralleling those of facial recognition research. First, there is an apparent lack of a trainability component in voice recognition. As far as encoding processes are concerned (e.g., Bull & Clifford, 1984), trainability does not seem very promising. Second, extremely low levels of accuracy are obtained for voice identification in studies that achieved, or approximated, ecologically valid conditions. Saslove and Yarmey

(1980) examined voice identification when subjects were either informed or not informed that a subsequent voice-memory test would be administered. The performance of the uninformed group was only 62% accurate under very favorable conditions of listening.

In a staged-event experiment, where subjects did not expect a criminal event and did not anticipate a voice identification test, Clifford and Denot (1982) found that earwitness performance was 49% correct after 1 week and only 8% correct after 3 weeks. Clifford and Fleming (1981) studied voice and visual identification in shopkeepers and bank clerks in situations that simulated counterfeiting and fraud. Voice identification was attempted either immediately, 1 hr, 4 hr, or 24 hr after the perpetrator-witness interaction. Performance declined rapidly over time, falling from 50% to 33% to 17% to chance level at the four testing lags, respectively. Thus, a delay effect in voice identification may be present when the witnesses are unaware that a criminal incident is happening.

Even this brief survey reveals that voice identification is under researched. It is unfortunate that voice and face identification conditions have not been in tandem, as in the Clifford and Fleming study (1981). If more studies had done so, we would be able to provide practical suggestions to the criminal justice system in matters of voice identification. Psychological researchers should remedy this situation. However, it is true that corporeal identifications far outweigh voice identifications in number and importance.

In summarizing the psychologist's contribution to investigating and gathering evidence, the examples chosen throughout the text have illustrated that certain suggestions and practices are well advanced, some are already in the field-trial stage, and others are only gleams in a theoretical psychologist's eye. In all cases, however, we have tried to demonstrate that psychologists are progressively addressing problems raised by the criminal justice system and that the psychologist's preferred solutions have usually been informed and constrained by consideration of practical possibilities within the existing criminal justice framework.

ACKNOWLEDGMENTS

The authors are indebted to Detective Sergeant Peter Bennett (Metropolitan Police) and Inspector Robert Ashcroft (Warwick Constabulary) for valuable discussions of identification methods and procedures.

REFERENCES

Ainsworth, P. B., & King, E. (1988). Witness perceptions of identification parades. In P. Morris, M. Gruneberg, & J. Sykes (Eds.), *Practical aspects of memory: Current research and issues* (Vol. 1, pp. 66–70). New York: John Wiley.
Allison, H. (1973). *Personal identification.* Boston: Holbrook Press.
Bennett, P. (1986). Face recall: A police perspective. *Human Learning, 5,* 197–202.
Biederman, I. (1980). *A non-obvious factor in assessing the fairness of a lineup.* Unpublished manuscript, State University of New York at Buffalo.
Borchard, E. M. (1932). *Convicting the innocent: Errors of criminal justice.* New Haven: Yale University Press.
Bothwell, R. K., Brigham, J. C., & Deffenbacher, K. (1985). *Optimality revisited, a meta-analysis of the confidence-accuracy relationship in eyewitness identification.* Unpublished manuscript, Florida State University, Tallahassee.
Brandon, R., & Davies, C. (1973). *Wrongful imprisonment.* London: Allen & Unwin.
Brigham, J. C., Maass, A., Snyder, L. D., & Spaulding, K. (1982). Accuracy of eyewitness identification in a field setting. *Journal of Personality and Social Psychology, 42,* 673–681.
Brigham, J. C., & Ready, D. J. (1985). Own-race bias in lineup construction. *Law and Human Behavior, 9,* 415–424.
Buckhout, R. (1980). Nearly 2000 witnesses can be wrong. *Bulletin of the Psychonomic Society, 16,* 307–310.
Bull, R., & Clifford, B. R. (1984). Earwitness voice recognition accuracy. In G. L. Wells & E. F. Loftus (Eds.), *Eyewitness testimony: Psychological perspectives* (pp. 92–123). New York: Cambridge University Press.

Christie, D., Davies, G., Shepherd, J., & Ellis, H. (1981). Evaluating a new computer-based system for face recall. *Law and Human Behavior, 5,* 209–218.

Christie, D., & Ellis, H. (1981). Photofit reconstructions versus verbal descriptions of faces. *Journal of Applied Psychology, 66,* 358–363.

Clifford, B. R. (1980). Voice identification by human listeners: On earwitness reliability. *Law and Human Behavior, 4,* 373–394.

Clifford, B. R. (1983). Memory for voices: The feasibility and quality of earwitness evidence. In S. Lloyd-Bostock & B. R. Clifford (Eds.), *Evaluating witness evidence: Recent psychology research and new perspectives* (pp. 189–218) Chichester: John Wiley.

Clifford, B. R., & Bull, R. (1978). *The psychology of person identification.* London: Routledge & Kegan Paul.

Clifford, B. R., Bull, R., & Rathborn, H. (1980). *Voice identification,* Report (Res. 741/1/1) London: Home Office.

Clifford, B. R., & Denot, H. (1982). *Visual and verbal testimony and identification under conditions of stress.* Unpublished manuscript, North East London Polytechnic.

Clifford, B. R., & Fleming, W. (1981). *Face and voice identification in a field setting.* Unpublished manuscript, North East London Polytechnic.

Clifford, B. R., & Hollin, C. (1981). Effects of the type of incident and the number of perpetrators on eyewitness memory. *Journal of Applied Psychology, 66,* 364–370.

Comish, S. (1987). Recognition of facial stimuli following an intervening task involving the Identi-Kit. *Journal of Applied Psychology, 72,* 488–491.

Cormack, S. J. (1979). *The police artist's reference.* Pewaukee, WI: Wakusha County Technical Institute.

Darnbrough, M. (1977). *The use of facial reconstruction methods by the police.* Paper presented at the Annual Conference of the British Psychological Society, Exeter, Devon.

Davies, G. (1981). Face recall systems. In G. Davies, H. Ellis, & J. Shepherd (Eds.), *Perceiving and remembering faces* (pp. 227–250). London: Academic Press.

Davies, G. (1983). Forensic face recall. In S. Lloyd-Bostock & B. Clifford (Eds.), *Evaluating witness evidence: Recent psychological research and new perspectives* (pp. 103–124). Chichester: John Wiley.

Davies, G. (1986a). Capturing likeness in eyewitness composites: The police artist and his rivals. *Medicine, Science and the Law, 26,* 283–290.

Davies, G. (1986b). The recall and reconstruction of faces: Implications for theory and practice. In H. Ellis, M. Jeeves, F. Newcombe, & A. Young (Eds.), *Aspects of face processing* (pp. 388–397). Dordrecht, The Netherlands: Martinus Nijhoff.
Davies, G., Ellis, H., Flin, R., Milne, A., Shepherd, J., & Shepherd, J. (1982). *Face retrieval techniques.* (Contracts PR/80, 13/53/1, and PR/81, 13/53/1.) London: Home Office.
Davies, G., Ellis, H., Shepherd, J. (1978a). Face identification: The influence of delay upon accuracy of Photofit construction. *Journal of Police Science and Administration, 6,* 35–42.
Davies, G., Ellis, H., & Shepherd, J. (1978b). Face recognition accuracy as a function of mode of representation. *Journal of Applied Psychology, 63,* 180–187.
Davies, G., Milne, A., & Shepherd, J. (1983). Searching for operator skills in face composite reproduction. *Journal of Police Science and Administration, 11,* 405–409.
Davies, G., Shepherd, J., Shepherd, J., Flin, R., & Ellis, H. (1986). Training skills in police Photofit operators. *Policing, 2,* 35–46.
Deffenbacher, K. A. (1980). Eyewitness accuracy and confidence: Can we infer anything about their relationship? *Law and Human Behavior, 4,* 243–260.
Deffenbacher, K., & Horney, J. (1981). Psycho-legal aspects of face identification. In G. Davies, H. Ellis, & J. Shepherd (Eds.), *Perceiving and remembering faces* (pp. 221–226). London: Academic Press.
Dent, H., & Gray, F. (1975). Identification on parade. *New Behavior, 1,* 366–369.
Devlin, P. (1976). *Report to the Secretary of State for the Home Department of the Departmental Committee on Evidence of Identification in Criminal Cases,* London: Her Majesty's Stationary Office.
Domingo, F. (1984). *Survey to study the feasibility of conducting a national composite artist conference.* Unpublished report, City of New York Police Department.
Doob, A., & Kirschenbaum, H. (1973). Bias in police line-ups—partial remembering. *Journal of Police Science and Administration, 1,* 287–293.
Dunning, D., Ellsworth, P. C., & Ross, L. (1985). *Why blank lineups are essential: Accuracy, confidence, and memory rehearsal.* Unpublished manuscript.
Egan, D., Pittner, M., & Goldstein, A. G. (1977). Eyewitness identification: Photographs vs live models. *Law and Human Behavior, 1,* 199–206.

Egan, D. M., & Smith, K. H. (1979, October). *Improving eyewitness identification: An experimental analysis*. Paper presented at the Meeting of the American Psychology-Law Society Convention. Baltimore, MD.

Ellis, H. (1984). Practical aspects of face memory. In G. L. Wells & E. F. Loftus (Eds.), *Eyewitness testimony: Psychological perspectives* (pp. 12–37). Cambridge: Cambridge University Press.

Ellis, H. (1986). Face recall: A psychological perspective. *Human Learning, 5,* 189–196.

Ellis, H., Deregowaski, J. B., & Shepherd, J. (1975). Descriptions of white and black faces by white and black subjects. *International Journal of Psychology, 10,* 119–123.

Ellis, H., Shepherd, J., & Davies, G. (1980). The deterioration of verbal descriptions of faces over different time delays. *Journal of Police Science and Administration, 8,* 101–106.

Fleet, M. L., Brigham, J. C., & Bothwell, R. K. (1987). The confidence-accuracy relationship: The effects of confidence assessment and choosing. *Journal of Applied Social Psychology, 17,* 171–187.

Flin, R., Markham, R., & Davies, G. (in press). Making faces: Developmental trends in the construction and recognition of Photofit face composites. *Journal of Applied Developmental Psychology.*

Flin, R., & Shepherd, J. (1986). Tall stories: Eyewitness ability to estimate height and weight characteristics. *Human Learning, 5,* 29–38.

Frankfurter, F. (1927). *The case of Sacco and Vanzetti.* New York: Little, Brown.

Gillenson, M., & Chandrasekaren, B. (1975). A heuristic strategy for developing human facial images on a CRT. *Pattern Recognition, 7,* 187–196.

Goldstein, A. G., & Chance, J. E. (1971). Visual recognition memory for complex configurations. *Perception and Psychophysics, 9,* 237–241.

Goldstein, A., Knight, P., Bailis, K., & Conover, J. (1981). Recognition memory for accented and unaccented voices. *Bulletin of the Psychonomic Society, 17,* 217–220.

Griffiths, A. (1908). *Mysteries of police and crime* (Vol. 1). London: Cassell.

Haig, N. (1986). Investigating face recognition with an image processing computer. In H. Ellis, M. Jeeves, F. Newcombe, & A. Young Eds.), *Aspects of face processing* (pp. 410–425). Dordrecht, The Netherlands: Martinus Nijhoff.

Hall, D. (1977, October). *Obtaining eyewitness identifications in criminal investigations: Two experiments and some comments on the Zeitgeist in forensic psychology.* Paper presented at the American Psychology-Law Conference, Snowmass, Colorado.

Hall, D. F., & Ostrom, T. M. (1975, August). *Accuracy of eyewitness identification after biasing and unbiasing instructions.* Paper presented at the meeting of the American Psychological Association, Chicago.

Hilgendorf, E. L., & Irving, B. L. (1978). False positive identification. *Medical Science and the Law, 18,* 255–262.

Homa, G. (1983). *The law enforcement composite sketch artist.* West Berlin, NJ: privately printed.

Hosch, H. M., Leippe, M. R., Marchioni, P. M., & Cooper, S. D. (1984). Victimization, self-monitoring, and eyewitness identification. *Journal of Applied Psychology, 69,* 280–288.

Hosch, H. M., & Platz, S. (1984). Self-monitoring and eyewitness accuracy. *Personality and Social Psychology Bulletin, 10,* 289–292.

Jenkins, F., & Davies, G. (1985). Contamination of facial memory through exposure to misleading composite pictures. *Journal of Applied Psychology, 70,* 164–176.

Kitson, A., Darnbrough, M., & Shields, E. (1978). Let's face it. *Police Research Bulletin, 30,* 7–13.

Krafka, C., & Penrod, S. (1985). Reinstatement of context in a field experiment on eyewitness identification. *Journal of Personality and Social Psychology, 49,* 58–69.

Kuehn, L. (1974). Looking down a gun barrel: Person perception and violent crime. *Perceptual and Motor Skills, 39,* 1159–1164.

Laughery, K., Duval, C., & Wogalter, M. (1986). Dynamics of face recall. In H. Ellis, M. Jeeves, F. Newcombe, & A. Young (Eds.), *Aspects of face processing* (pp. 373–387). Dordrecht, The Netherlands: Martinus Nijhoff.

Laughery, K., Fessler, P. K., Lenorovitz, D. R., & Yoblick, D. A. (1974). Time delay and similarity effects in facial recognition. *Journal of Applied Psychology, 59,* 490–496.

Laughery, K., & Fowler, R. (1980). Sketch artist and Identikit procedures for recalling faces. *Journal of Applied Psychology, 65,* 307–316.

Laughery, K., Rhodes, B., & Batten, G. (1981). Computer-guided recognition and retrieval of facial images. In G. Davies, H. Ellis, & J. Shepherd (Eds.), *Perceiving and remembering faces* (pp. 251–270). London: Academic Press.

Laughery, K., & Smith, V. (1978). Subject identification following exposure to sketches and Identikit composites. *Proceedings of the Human Factor Society, 22nd Annual Meeting, Detroit,* 631-635.

Laughery, K., Smith, V., & Yount, M. (1980). Visual support devices: Evaluation of a new technique for constructing facial images. *Proceedings of the Human Factors Society, 24th Annual Meeting, New York,* 1-4.

Laughery, K., & Wogalter, M. (in press). Forensic applications of facial memory research. In A. Young & H. Ellis (Eds.), *Handbook of face processing,* Amsterdam: North Holland.

Leippe, M. R. (1980). Effects of integrative memorial and cognitive processes on the correspondence of eyewitness accuracy and confidence. *Law and Human Behavior, 4,* 261-274.

Lenorovitz, D., & Laughery, K. (1984). A witness-computer interaction system for searching mug-files. In G. Wells & E. Loftus (Eds.), *Eyewitness testimony: Psychological perspectives* (pp. 38-63). Cambridge: Cambridge University Press.

Levine, F. J., & Tapp, J. L. (1973). The psychology of criminal identification: The gap from Wade to Kirby. *University of Pennsylvania Law Review, 5,* 1079-1131.

Lindsay, R. C. L., & Wells, G. L. (1980). What price justice? Exploring the relationship of lineup fairness to identification accuracy. *Law and Human Behavior, 4,* 303-314.

Lindsay, R. C. L., & Wells, G. L. (1983). What do we really know about cross-race eyewitness identification? In S. Lloyd-Bostock & B. R. Clifford (Eds.), *Evaluating witness evidence; Recent psychological research and new perspectives.* (pp. 219-234). Chichester: John Wiley.

Lindsay, R. C. L., & Wells, G. L. (1985). Improving eyewitness identifications from lineups: Simultaneous versus sequential lineup presentation. *Journal of Applied Psychology, 70,* 556-564.

Lindsay, R. C. L., Wells, G. L., & Rumpel, C. (1981). Can people detect eyewitness identification accuracy within and across situations? *Journal of Applied Psychology, 66,* 79-89.

Mac-A-Mug Pro v. Compusketch. (1987, February-March). *The Blues,* pp. 18-21.

Macleod, M., & Shepherd, J. (1986). Sex differences in eyewitness reports of criminal assaults. *Medicine, Science and the Law, 26,* 311-318.

Malpass, R. S. (1981). Effective size and defendent bias in eyewitness identification lineups. *Law and Human Behavior, 5,* 299-309.

Malpass, R. S., & Devine, P. G. (1981). Eyewitness identification: Lineup instruction and the absence of the offender. *Journal of Applied Psychology, 66*, 482–489.

Malpass, R. S., & Devine, P. G. (1983). Measuring the fairness of eyewitness identification lineups. In S. Lloyd-Bostock & B. R. Clifford (Eds.), *Evaluating witness evidence; Recent psychological research and new perspectives* (pp. 81–102). Chichester: John Wiley.

Malpass, R. S., & Devine, P. G. (1984). Research on suggestion in lineups and photospreads. In G. L. Wells & E. F. Loftus (Eds.), *Eyewitness testimony: Psychological perspectives* (pp. 64–91). London: Cambridge University Press.

Malpass, R. S., Lavigueur, H., & Weldon, D. E. (1973). Verbal and visual training in face recognition. *Perception and Psychophysics, 14*, 285–292.

Mauldin, M., & Laughery, K. (1981). Composite production effects upon subsequent facial recognition. *Journal of Applied Psychology, 66*, 351–357.

Munsterberg, H. (1908). *On the witness stand: Essays on psychology and crime.* New York: Clark Boardman.

O'Connor, J. (1974). "That's the man": A sobering study of eyewitness identification and the polygraph. *St. John's Law Review, 1*, 27–29.

People v. Gould, 54 Cal. 2d 621 (1960). 7 *Cal. Reporter* 273, 278, 354 P. 2d 865, 870.

Pigott, M. A., & Brigham, J. C. (1985). Relationship between accuracy of prior description and facial recognition. *Journal of Applied Psychology, 70*, 547–555.

Pigott, M. A., Brigham, J. C., & Bothwell, R. K. (1985). *A field study on the relationship between description accuracy and identification accuracy.* Unpublished manuscript. Florida State University, Tallahassee.

Rathborn, H., Bull, R., & Clifford, B. R. (1981). Voice recognition over the telephone. *Journal of Police Science and Administration, 9*, 280–284.

Read, J. (1979). Rehearsal and recognition of human faces. *American Journal of Psychology, 92*, 71–85.

Saslove, H., & Yarmey, D. A. (1980). Long term auditory memory: Speaker identification. *Journal of Applied Psychology, 65*, 111–116.

Schooler, J. (1987). *Verbalizing non-verbal memories: Some things are better left unsaid.* Unpublished doctoral dissertation, University of Washington, Seattle.

Shepherd, J. W. (1981). Social factors in face recognition. In G. M. Davies, H. D. Ellis, & J. W. Shepherd (Eds.), *Perceiving and remembering faces* (pp. 55–80). London: Academic Press.

Shepherd, J. W. (1986). An interactive computer system for retrieving faces. In H. Ellis, M. Jeeves, F. Newcombe, & A. Young (Eds.), *Aspects of face processing* (pp. 398–409). Dordrecht, The Netherlands: Martinus Nijhoff.

Shepherd, J. W., & Ellis, H. D. (1973). The effect of attractiveness on recognition memory for faces. *American Journal of Psychology, 86*, 627–633.

Shepherd, J. W., Ellis, H. D., & Davies, G. M. (1982). *Identification evidence: A psychological evaluation*. Aberdeen: Aberdeen University Press.

Sobel, N. R., & Pridgen, D. (1981). *Eyewitness identification: Legal and practical problems*. New York: Clark Boardman.

Sporer, S. L. (1986). *Person description and person identification: A critical review of some fresh evidence*. Paper presented at the Biennial Meeting of the American Psychology-Law Society, Tucson, Arizona.

Sporer, S. L. (in press). Verbal and visual processes in person identification. In H. Wegener, F. Losel, & J. Haisch (Eds.), *Criminal behaviour and the justice system: Psychological perspectives*. New York/Heidelberg: Springer.

Stern, L. W. (1903–1906). *Beiträge zur Psychologie der Aussage*. 2 Volumes. Leipzig: Barth.

Thompson, B., & Laughery, K. (1981). *Facial memory: Effects of recall efforts on subsequent recognition*. Paper presented at the Annual Meeting of the Psychonomics Society, Phoenix, Arizona.

Turnbull, D. G., & Thompson, D. M. (1984, May). *Eyewitness testimony: Photographic vs live lineups*. Paper presented at the Experimental Psychology Conference, Deakin University, Geelong, Australia.

Tversky, B., & Baratz, D. (1985). Memory for faces: Are caricatures better than photographs? *Memory and Cognition, 13*, 45–49.

Twining, W. (1983). Identification and misidentification in legal processes: Redefining the problem. In S. Lloyd-Bostock & B. R. Clifford (Eds.), *Evaluating witness evidence: Recent psychological research and new perspectives* (pp. 255–284). Chichester: John Wiley.

Wall, P. M. (1965). *Eyewitness identification in criminal cases*. Springfield, IL: Charles C. Thomas.

Wells, G. L. (1984). The psychology of lineup identification. *Journal of Applied Social Psychology, 14,* 89-103.
Wells, G. L. (1985). Verbal descriptions of faces from memory: Are they diagnostic of identification accuracy? *Journal of Applied Social Psychology, 70,* 619-626.
Wells, G. L., & Hryciw, B. (1984). Memory for faces: Encoding and retrieval operations. *Memory and Cognition, 12,* 338-344.
Wells, G. L., Leippe, M. R., & Ostrom, T. M. (1979). Guidelines for empirically assessing the fairness of a lineup. *Law and Human Behavior, 3,* 285-293.
Wells, G. L., & Murray, D. M. (1983). What can psychology say about the Neil vs. Bigger's criteria for judging eyewitness identification accuracy? *Journal of Applied Social Psychology, 68,* 347-362.
Wells, G. L., & Murray, D. M. (1984). Eyewitness confidence. In G. L. Wells and E. F. Loftus (Eds.), *Eyewitness testimony: Psychological perspectives* (pp. 155-170). Cambridge: Cambridge University Press.
Williams, G. (1955). *The proof of guilt: A study of the English criminal trial.* London: Stevens.
Wogalter, M. (1987). *Face memory: Effects of verbal description and visual rehearsal.* Unpublished manuscript, University of Richmond, Virginia.
Wogalter, M., Laughery, K., & Thompson, B. (1987). *Eyewitness identification: Composite construction on subsequent recognition performance.* Unpublished manuscript, University of Richmond, Virginia.
Woocher, F. D. (1977). Did your eyes deceive you? Expert psychological testimony on the unreliability of eyewitness testimony. *Stanford Law Review, 29* 969-1030.
Yarmey, D. A. (1986). Verbal, visual and voice identification of a rape suspect under poor illumination. *Journal of Applied Psychology, 71,* 363-370.
Yuille, J. C., & Cutshall, J. L. (1984). *Live vs video media in eyewitness events and line-ups.* Unpublished manuscript, University of British Colombia, Vancouver.
Yuille, J., & Cutshall, J. (1986). A case study of eyewitness memory. *Journal of Applied Psychology, 71,* 291-301.
Zanni, G. R., & Offermann, J. T. (1978). Eyewitness testimony: An exploration of question wording upon recall as a function of neuroticism. *Perceptual and Motor Skills, 46,* 163-166.
Zeiner, W., & Zima, H. (1983). *The "Sigma" project: A new approach to personal description data.* Auswig: IBM.

Field Studies of Eyewitness Memory of Actual Crimes

3

Judith Cutshall and John C. Yuille

The recent centennial of the publication of Ebbinghaus's (1885) classic text, *On Memory*, provided an occasion for researchers of human memory to examine the successes and failures in their 100-year effort to determine the nature and functions of memory. On balance, this self-examination reveals a disappointing state of affairs. One major failure is the inability of researchers to generate knowledge that is applicable to real-life situations. In his introduction to the proceedings of the first Practical Aspects of Memory Conference, Neisser (1978) lamented the lack of research on practical issues related to memory. In addition, he questioned the ecological validity of much of the laboratory-based memory research.

Neisser is not alone in his lament. Psychologists with a variety of interests have expressed concerns about the narrowness of most memory research and have questioned the generalizability of laboratory findings to real-world situations (e.g., Newell, 1974; Tulving & Madigan, 1970). Although doubts have been raised about the ecological validity of much of the memory research of the past century, there have been some notable exceptions. At the 1978 conference an encouraging array of real-world memory research, including everyday memory, memory aids, and individual differences, was presented (see Gruneberg, Morris, & Sykes, 1978). Nine years later, at the Second International Conference on Practical Aspects of Memory the offerings of real-world research had increased substantially. The published proceedings expanded to encompass two volumes (see Gruneberg, Morris, & Sykes, 1988), and the research included such diverse topics as autobiographical memory, prospective memory, memory for broadcasts, and memory and aging. At both conferences one type of research that is particularly exciting was presented as an exemplar of ecologically valid memory research: the study of eyewitness memory.

In this chapter we focus on eyewitness memory research and its applicability to real-life situations. Before discussing our research findings, we briefly consider the current status of eyewitness research, its ecological validity, and the implications of generalizing research findings to actual witness situations.

Eyewitness research, although mostly laboratory-based, typically involves the assessment of memory for complex events, such as films of crimes, films of accidents, or live staged events. Unlike much of the memory research of the past century, which was based on the use of single words, nonsense syllables, and similar impoverished materials, eyewitness studies seem to have more ecological validity because of the complexity of the events employed. Given the apparent value of eyewitness research, there has been rapid growth in this area of research. During the past 15 years so much attention has been devoted to eyewitness memory that the editor of *Law and Human Behavior* was prompted to complain that forensic researchers have concentrated on eyewitness memory to the exclusion of other interesting forensic and legal problems (Saks, 1986).

Although excessive attention may have been paid to eyewitness research, from the perspective of memory researchers enthusiasm for the study of eyewitnesses is understandable. Eyewitness research provides an opportunity to study basic issues concerning the nature of memory and to simultaneously obtain information that can be of value to police, lawyers, and the courts. Thus, eyewitness research appears to have successfully applied scientific methodology to achieve generalizable results.

Because of the presumed ecological validity of eyewitness research, some of the most active researchers in the field have advocated extensive application of the results of experimental eyewitness research to the criminal justice context. For example, Buckhout (1974) pioneered the presentation of behavioral science evidence in courts to demonstrate the weaknesses and problems associated with eyewitness testimony. More recently, Loftus (1979, 1986) has become the leading advocate of the application of experimental findings to real-world witnesses (see also Lloyd-Bostock & Clifford, 1983; Wells & Loftus, 1984; Yarmey, 1979). This application is of considerable importance, since the laboratory work suggests that witnesses make a variety of errors in their accounts. They forget information quite rapidly, and they are susceptible to suggestion. On the basis of some experimental literature, it is tempting to suggest that eyewitness memory should be given little credence because it is too prone to error and distortion.

During the past 4 or 5 years, however, the supporters of the application of eyewitness research to real-world witnesses have begun to meet stiff criticism. In an issue of *Law and Human Behavior* totally devoted to the debate concerning this application, Buckhout (1986) and Loftus (1986) used a combination of experimental findings and examples drawn from selected criminal cases in which they had served as consultants to show the usefulness of findings from experimental research to problems of eyewitnesses in actual cases. Critics such as McCloskey, Egeth, and McKenna (1986) and Konecni and Ebbesen (1986) pointed to a variety of problems concerning the applications of the experimental results; they raised the basic issue of the ecological validity of the laboratory research. The very theme that has been used to promote the usefulness of eyewitness research has become the principal focus of criticisms.

The typical eyewitness study employs a group of student volunteers who are exposed to an event. The subjects may or may not be expecting the event, but research ethics require that they not be personally affected by it. In order to achieve the face validity of the studies as eyewitness experiences, staged crimes or accidents are the typical events presented to subjects. The events may be recorded and presented via slides, videotape, or film, or they may involve actors in a live sequence. After viewing the staged crime or accident, the subjects are asked to respond to a series of questions. The questions may be open-ended and general ("Tell me what you saw.") or specific ("What was the thief wearing?"), or they may include multiple-choice options ("Was the woman wearing trousers, a skirt, or shorts?"). Specific and multiple-choice formats are preferred because they are easily scored and yield readily quantifiable data. In addition to answering questions about the event, the subjects may be asked to examine a lineup or photospread that may or may not include the perpetrator.

The preceding description of typical eyewitness research raises a number of questions relevant to the generalizability of this research to real-life contexts. For example, how comparable is a filmed or staged event to an actual criminal event? Many of the cues available in real-life situations may not be present in a staged event and are even less likely to occur in a filmed event. The level of arousal associated with an actual crime is usually lacking or at least mitigated in the experimental context.

Another question concerns the comparability of the typical laboratory eyewitness to a witness of an actual crime. Witnesses to actual crimes are likely to be affected by the crime they observe; usually the witnesses are also victims (Cutshall, 1985). In addition, witnesses to crimes often become involved in the criminal justice system by being interviewed by police, witnessing a lineup, or testifying in court. Because the criminal justice process involves very serious proceedings and issues, witnesses are generally aware of the potential consequences of their actions. The information they may provide may produce dramatic effects on them, as well as on the accused and others. Laboratory witnesses, on the other hand, are relatively unaffected by the events to which they are exposed. The information they provide to the experimenter typically has trivial consequences for the witnesses and those involved in the experiment.

These questions relating to the contextual differences between the laboratory and the real world are at the heart of the debate concerning the generalizability of experimental eyewitness research. Our understanding of the relationship between the behavior of witnesses to actual crimes and the behavior of laboratory witnesses, is limited, because systematic information has been available concerning only laboratory witnesses in contrived situations; information about real witnesses has been anecdotal. However, recent field research has begun to address this issue. Brigham, Maas, Snyder, and Spaulding (1982) and Krafka and Penrod (1985) tested the recognition memory of store clerks who had previously interacted with a confederate who pretended to be a customer, and Peters (1988) examined the recognition memory of adults who received inoculations.

Field studies provide valuable data because they move beyond the university setting and explore memory processes in naturalistic field settings with a nonstudent population. These studies are limited, however, in regard to the type of event that was witnessed; the events employed lacked the drama, arousal, and consequences generally associated with criminal events. In addition, these studies focused solely on recognition memory rather than witnesses's verbal recall, and the latter is central in many criminal cases. Therefore, these field experiments are insufficient for assessing the relationship between laboratory witnesses and real-world witnesses to actual crimes. In order to address this issue, we need data from actual witnesses who have observed real crimes. During the past 5 years our research team has begun to collect this type of data. The remainder of this chapter focuses on a summary of the results of our research to date.

STUDYING WITNESSES TO ACTUAL CRIMES

Since several problems present major barriers to doing this kind of research, it is understandable that researchers have avoided working with witnesses to actual crimes. At the outset it is necessary to obtain the cooperation of the witnesses. Often the event they have witnessed has caused them loss, pain, injury, or other difficulties, and they may be less than eager to recall the details for research purposes. In addition, the witnesses must be located through law enforcement agencies, requiring the cooperation of these agencies. Even if one secures the cooperation of police and witnesses at least two major difficulties remain. The statements obtained from witnesses are usually idiosyncratic in form and not easily amenable to analysis. Some means of reliably analyzing the content of witness accounts must be devised. In addition, in real-world crimes we don't know what actually happened during the event; the criteria normally available in laboratory situations are inapplicable for these situations. The criminal event must somehow be reliably reconstructed.

A variety of circumstances enabled us to find tentative solutions to these problems. The Royal Canadian Mounted Police (RCMP) had an interest in researching actual witness behavior, and their cooperation was the initial step in making such research possible (see Yuille, 1986). We were able to establish a working relationship with two RCMP detachments in the greater Vancouver area (the RCMP function as municipal police in a variety of Canadian cities; see Yuille, 1984). The RCMP allowed us to examine their files of closed cases, which served as the basis for our initial research. We have subsequently formed a working relationship with the Vancouver City Police and have expanded the number and type of criminal cases we have examined.

The first step in our procedure involved conducting a survey of thousands of police files in order to determine the characteristics of witnesses to different types of crimes (Yuille, 1986). Then we searched for special cases that would allow an investigation of the eyewitness abilities of individuals who had witnessed a crime. We looked for cases in which there had been multiple witnesses and in which there was sufficient forensic evidence to reconstruct what had actually happened. The crimes we selected were not representative of typical crimes, because typical crimes involve only one witness (the victim) and the details of the event typically remain unknown (Cutshall, 1985). We chose these specific criminal events because they were amenable to research.

After selecting a case we transcribed the accounts that witnesses had provided to the police at the time of the incident. We then contacted the witnesses and arranged to interview them about the event. We obtained two accounts of the incident from each witness: one recorded by the police at the time of the event and one obtained by our research staff after a delay that varied from 4 months to 3 years after the event. The research interview followed a format similar to the police interview. We initially asked witnesses to describe the incident in their own words, and then we asked specific questions to clarify the information given and to provide more facts about critical aspects of the event.

Each eyewitness account was subjected to an evaluation procedure that we developed for this purpose. This procedure began with a transformation of each witness's interview transcript from a narrative format into a list of action details and a list of descriptive details of both people and objects. The two aspects of each statement, the free account and the responses to specific questions, were initially analyzed separately (e.g., Cady, 1924; Lipton, 1977; Yuille & McEwan, 1985). However, because no systematic differences were found between the free accounts and the answers to questions, this distinction was collapsed. Repetitions of details that occurred in the free recall portion of the statement and the responses to questions were thus eliminated from the analysis. Unresolved contradictions, however, were included. For example, if a witness described an automobile as a Pontiac at one point during the interview and as an Oldsmobile at another point in the same interview, both descriptions would be entered into the analysis unless the witness made it clear in subsequent questioning that one response was correct and the other incorrect. The reliability of the transformation procedure was ascertained by comparing transcripts transformed by three independent raters. The variance among raters was less than 5%.

After transforming witnesses's interviews into both action and descriptive details, each component was tallied separately in terms of the number of details reported. The details were scored by assigning 1 point for each specific, unique bit of information. Scoring the descriptive details involved partitioning the details in relation to noun and adjective phrases. For example, the statement "He was 5 ft, 11 in, and wore a blue sweater" contains three descriptive details. Action details, on the other hand, are revealed primarily in verb and adverb phrases. For example, the statement "He jumped on the guy and stuck a knife in his stomach" contains three details. Nonspecific information, such as "She was short," was assigned ½ point. The total number of action and descriptive details were tallied separately for both the police and research interviews.

Two other features of the accuracy criteria should be noted. First, the procedure we employed was conservative with respect to the degree of confidence expressed by the witness. Thus, a statement "I'm sure he wore a blue shirt" was given equal weight to a statement "He might have worn a blue shirt, I'm not sure." In addition, credit was not given to the witness's account when it deviated from objective reality, even when the witness's impression had been correct. For example, one witness reported that "the thief looked like he was in his early twenties." The thief did, in fact, appear younger than his actual age of 35, but this was scored as an error for that witness.

The next stage in our analysis involved an evaluation of the details given by each witness. Each detail was classified as either correct, incorrect, or unclassifiable. This determination was made on the basis of a reconstruction of the event. As noted above our choice of criminal cases was guided primarily by the availability of forensic evidence that would allow a reconstruction of the witnessed event. We began by assembling all of the pertinent forensic materials: police and laboratory reports of weapons recovered at the scene, locations of blood stains, photographs of the crime scene, detailed descriptions of the perpetrator (deceased in three cases) and his clothing, and autopsy and medical reports. We also obtained reports given by ambulance attendants and public safety personnel at the scene of the incident and verbatim statements given by each witness of the event. Using these materials, we reconstructed the event.

Reconstruction of the descriptive details was relatively straightforward. Except for the bank robberies reported below, police reports and photographs of the scene provided concrete descriptions of the perpetrator and the victim, their clothing, the weapons used, and nearby automobiles or pertinent objects. Determination of the sequence of action details and their veracity was more difficult and required an interpretative technique more similar to that of the historian (Stern, 1939) than the experimentalist. Since none of the actions had been preserved on film (as had some of the objects at the scene) and because of the fleeting nature of an action sequence, verification of the action details was more difficult than that of concrete, relatively long-lasting objects. However, by combining the forensic evidence and the reports of all witnesses, police, and support personnel, and by employing the constraints of logic, we were able to reconstruct the events reported below. Using these sources, outlines of the criminal event were reconstructed independently by three raters, and a research sequence was abstracted that reflected agreement among the three raters. The resulting outline represented an interpretation of the event rather than an objective reconstruction of the event, since the latter was not possible. However, it should be noted that the reconstruction relied primarily on forensic evidence and a logical analysis.

Consensus among various witnesses played a role in the reconstructions, but only when witnesses's reports were given independently and from different viewing angles and when they were consistent with a logical analysis of other information. Information given by witnesses, even with agreement from other witnesses, was not considered sufficient for inclusion in our reconstruction unless it could be corroborated by other evidence or by witnesses with different viewing perspectives. Following these guidelines, we were able to ascertain the accuracy of the majority of details given by witnesses concerning the event in question. Across the various events reported in this chapter, the number of unclassifiable details ranged from 4% to 6% of reported details pertinent to the criminal event.

The following sections report the results of our investigations of four separate cases involving three shooting deaths and one set of bank robberies. We review and contrast the findings from each of the four cases and draw some general conclusions about the memories of witnesses for serious crimes.

Gun Store Robbery and Shooting

This case constitutes the first published scientific investigation of adult eyewitness memory for an actual crime (Yuille & Cutshall, 1986). The event occurred on a spring afternoon when a robber entered a gun store. He tied up the store owner, took some money and a box of handguns, and left the store. The robber ran to his car, which was parked at the curb in front of the store. He stood by the driver's door and placed the box of guns on the hood of the car. Meanwhile, the store owner freed himself, grabbed a loaded revolver, and ran into the street in front of the store. The robber and store owner faced each other at a distance of 2 m. The robber fired two shots at the store owner and wounded him. The store owner then fired all six shots from his revolver, killing the robber. The 21 witnesses to this event were interviewed by the RCMP immediately after the incident. Of the 19 witnesses whom we contacted, 13 agreed to a research interview, which we conducted 4 to 5 months after the incident. We analyzed the police and research interviews of those 13 witnesses.

Both accounts provided by each witness were analyzed. The total number of both action and descriptive details was determined, and those that could be classified according to the forensic information were then labeled as either correct or false. The witnesses comprised two groups: a central group of individuals ($n = 7$) who were close to the event, and a peripheral group ($n = 6$) who observed less of the event. The central group provided the police with an average of 71.9 details, and they provided an average of 103.7 details in their research interview. The comparable figures for the peripheral group were 24.3 details in the police interview and 55.2 details in the research interview. Although the two groups differed in the amount of information they provided, they did not differ in their accuracy. Table 3.1 provides the average witness accuracy for each interview. The most striking result was the uniformly high rate of accuracy which did not decrease over the months that intervened between the first and second interviews. This evidence suggests that there are circumstances in which eyewitness memory can be detailed, accurate, and persistent.

Table 3.1. Percent Accuracy of Recall for the Gun Store Incident

Type of detail	Police interview	Research interview
Action	81.9	81.9
People description	75.6	72.7
Object description	88.5	85.5
Total details	82.1	80.7

Adapted from Yuille & Cutshall (1986)

In addition, we analyzed the consistency between the interviews provided to the researchers and those provided to the police. The primary difference between the two statements was the increased elaboration obtained in the research interviews. Across the 13 witnesses, 60% of the information given at the time of the research interview had not been reported to the police. The average accuracy rate of 81% for this new information compares favorably to the 84% accuracy rate at the time of the police interview. These data show that witnesses were not simply repeating to researchers what they had earlier told the police, and it suggests that their memories at the time of the research interview were not due solely to retellings of the event. This supposition was further supported by witnesses's responses to a question concerning the color of a blanket that covered the dead perpetrator, a detail not reported earlier and unlikely to be included in retellings of the event. Of the 6 witnesses who remembered seeing the blanket, 5 accurately reported its color.

Although the eyewitnesses made relatively few errors, we performed a qualitative analysis to determine the nature of these errors. Figure 3.1 shows the distribution of the errors, several features of which are relevant to our current comparisons among crimes. The most frequent type of error is labeled multiple action; two-thirds of the errors of this type were committed by three witnesses. Two male teenagers, who viewed the event from a sharp angle, mistakenly reported that the store owner and robber had struggled. The other inaccurate witness was a woman

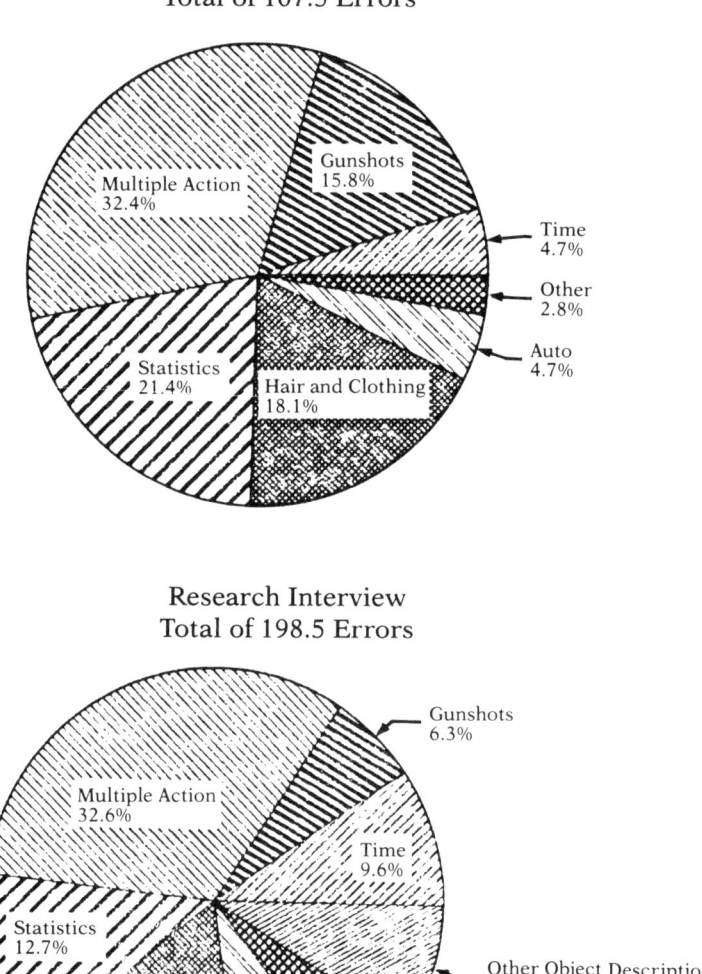

Figure 3.1. Distribution of errors in the police and research interviews. From Yuille & Cutshall (1986).

who passed by the scene driving a car. Her late arrival led her to misperceive some aspects of the event. In short, most of the action errors were not memory errors per se but reflected initial misperceptions of the event itself (for details see Yuille & Cutshall, 1986).

Another interesting feature of the pattern of errors was that the witnesses were poor at providing height, weight, and age estimates (labeled "Statistics" in Figure 3.1). Fully 50% of these estimates in both the police and research interviews were incorrect, and they constituted 52% of the person-description errors in the police interview and 37% of the errors in the research interview. Once again, these may not be errors of memory but rather may reflect the difficulties inherent in providing such estimates. Memory may serve to enhance the errors in such estimates, but errors of estimation should not be viewed as a weakness of memory per se. The final point to be noted from the analysis of the errors is that color information associated with hair and clothing was often incorrect. This feature is further discussed later in this chapter.

During our research interviews we tried to mislead the witnesses about the color of the robber's car and the existence of a broken headlight by employing Loftus's (1974) procedure. For example, we asked witnesses if they had seen either *the* or *a* broken headlight on the robber's car. In contrast to laboratory studies reporting that such suggestions are effective in misleading witnesses (e.g., Loftus, 1975; Loftus & Zanni, 1975), the wording of the questions had no effect. Ten of the witnesses reported no broken headlight or noted they hadn't noticed this detail. One witness had not noticed the automobile, and of the remaining 2 witnesses, 1 acquiesced to the misleading information and 1 acquiesced to the control question. Our attempt to mislead these witnesses may have been less successful than laboratory research because of the elapsed time since the event; therefore, we are unable to draw firm conclusions concerning the susceptibility of real witnesses to suggestive wording. However, most witnesses firmly replied that they had not seen a particular detail even when we suggested that they had, which leads us to suspect that actual witnesses may not be as readily misled as laboratory witnesses who view slide or film sequences. More research is needed in field settings to address this question.

We also asked the witnesses to rate their degree of stress during and after the event. The 5 witnesses who reported the highest degree of stress were significantly more accurate in their reports than the witnesses who indicated less stress. Because degree of stress was confounded with proximity to the event, no firm conclusions can be drawn about the effect of stress on memory. However, there was no evidence in this study that stress had a negative effect on eyewitness recall.

In summary, data from this study suggest that witnesses can be highly accurate in their verbal reports of criminal events. Particularly striking is the fact that accuracy of recall can be maintained over a period of 4 to 6 months. It is also instructive to note that the lowest accuracy levels were found in regard to (1) descriptions of people, particularly in relation to height, weight, and age estimations, and (2) assignment of color. Data concerning suggestibility and the effects of stress are more ambiguous, but the data suggest that stress does not necessarily impair performance and that suggestibility may be less prominent in vividly remembered real-world situations. This single study does not supply sufficient data from which to draw firm conclusions about the relationship between laboratory witnesses and actual witnesses to real crimes. The critical question for the generalizability of the present results concerns the uniqueness of this particular set of witnesses and this type of event. To address this question, we now examine our analyses of similar criminal events witnessed by different individuals.

A Restaurant Shooting

This incident began when a robber entered a bank, placed a gun in front of a teller, and demanded money. The teller alerted her supervisor and handed money to the robber. The robber left the bank and was followed by the branch manager, who alerted a pedestrian to follow the robber while the manager flagged a passing police car. The pedestrian followed the robber down an alley and into the rear entrance of a fast-food restaurant. A struggle between the robber and the pedestrian began in the kitchen of the restaurant. Upon seeing the robber's gun, the pedestrian backed away and took cover. A police officer entered the kitchen, and the robber pointed his gun at the officer, who fired a single shot that killed the robber.

Eight witnesses to the struggle and shooting in the restaurant were interviewed by the Vancouver City Police. We were able to contact four of these witnesses, all of whom agreed to be interviewed. These interviews were conducted 2 years after the incident. The interviews and statement analysis procedures were the same as those employed in the previously reported incident.

The police interviews of the eight restaurant witnesses had been very cursory, because the police basically knew what had occurred (a police officer had been present during much of the event), and they had asked for few details from the witnesses. As a result of the cursory interviews in this incident, the police obtained an average of only 7.2 classifiable details from the witnesses. This is approximately one-fourth of the information that the witnesses had provided the police in the incident described earlier in this chapter. Since the police were not interested in descriptions of the thief, most of the obtained details concerned actions (81.2% of the total). The descriptive and action information that the witnesses provided to the police was 100% accurate.

Table 3.2 summarizes the information provided by the four restaurant employees who completed a research interview. They were the central witnesses to the event.

Table 3.2. Amount and Percent Accuracy of Recall for the Restaurant Shooting Incident

Type of detail	Police interview		Research interview	
	Amount	(%) Accuracy	Amount	(%) Accuracy
Action	9.6	100	43.3	97.1
People description	0.0	—	25.5	79.1
Object description	2.0	100	8.1	100
Total details	11.6	100	76.9	92.3

More than seven times as much information was obtained in the research interview, reflecting that our interviews with each witness lasted from 60 to 90 min, and we encouraged them to recall as much information as they could. The figures in Table 3.2 reveal a pattern similar to that reported for the gun shop incident. Overall accuracy was 92.3%, with person descriptions accounting for most of the errors. One-third of these errors concerned estimates of the robber's age, height, and weight. The remaining errors concerned the description of the color and nature of the robber's clothing. Half of these errors occurred in the account of the only male witness, and the rest were distributed among the three female witnesses.

The results of this study are consistent with those reported in the gun shop incident. The accuracy of the witnesses's accounts at the time of the event was very high, although the number of details obtained by the police was extremely limited. There was no decrease in the accuracy of recall over the delay of 24 months between the event and the research interview. Again, it appears that a striking event of this sort leads to virtually no loss in the amount or accuracy of recall over a long retention interval. The types of errors that witnesses made were the same in both studies and concerned descriptions of people. Estimates of age, height, and weight and memory for colors of clothing and hair seem to be particularly prone to error.

The Breadline Shooting

This event took place on a fall afternoon in 1984. A man was standing in a food line, holding his daughter in his arms. Another man who was standing in front of him turned around and pushed him. The two men began to exchange insults, and when they reached the top of the stairs outside of the building, the assailant stabbed the man with the child twice in the stomach. At first the man was unaware of his wound. When he noticed the blood on his stomach, he handed his child to his wife and went after the assailant, who threatened him with his knife. At this point he noticed a police car and stopped it (this event took place within a block of the central police headquarters). He pointed out the assailant to the police officer, who used his radio to report a stabbing. The officer then approached the assailant and asked him to drop his knife. A brief struggle ensued, and the officer was stabbed in the chest, below the armpit. These events occurred on the sidewalk and in the street. An off-duty police officer noticed the incident, got out of his car, and drew his gun. The wounded officer and the assailant now separated, and the wounded officer also drew his gun. Both officers demanded several times that the assailant drop his knife. The assailant demanded that the officers drop their guns. They lowered their weapons, again requesting that he discard his knife. He then moved toward the wounded officer, who backed up, stumbled at the curb, and backed into the street. He continued to pursue this officer, and the wounded officer fired six shots and fell onto his back. Although wounded, the assailant continued toward the wounded officer and began to attack him. The officer kicked the assailant in self-defense and at this point the off-duty officer shot and killed the assailant.

Eighteen witnesses to this event were interviewed by the Vancouver City Police. Because the incident took place in the skid row area of Vancouver, most of the witnesses were itinerant, and we were unable to contact them more than 1 year after the event. However, of the 11 we were able to locate, 6 agreed to a research interview. The research interviews were conducted between 13 and 18 months after the event, and both interviews were subjected to the same form of analysis employed for the other two incidents.

Table 3.3 provides a summary of the information provided by the 6 witnesses. The police obtained an average of 37.7 facts from each witness, of which 76.1% (28.7 facts) could be classified by the forensic evidence. The police were content with simple interviews in this case since they required only that the witnesses confirm the forensic evidence and the information provided by the police officers involved in the incident.

The research interviews were more extensive than the police interviews and produced an average of 65.2 facts from each witness, an increase of 72.3% relative to the police interviews. This increase was accounted for almost entirely by the descriptive

Table 3.3. **Amount and Percent Accuracy of Recall for the Breadline Incident**

Type of detail	Police interview		Research interview	
	Amount	(%) Accuracy	Amount	(%) Accuracy
Action	16.8	88.3	19.2	91.6
Description	11.8	97.0	22.6	78.7
Total	28.7	92.1	41.8	84.6

facts, which virtually doubled in the research interview. This reflects the lack of need for the police to obtain a description of the assailant. Descriptions of the assailant also accounted for the increased error rate in the research interview. As in the previous two incidents, almost all of these errors were in estimates of age, height, and weight and in the description of the nature and color of clothing.

This third incident is consistent with the pattern of results observed in the previous two studies. Eyewitness memory for a striking incident was highly accurate immediately after the event and accuracy declined only slightly across a delay of 13 to 18 months. Even with a long retention interval, the details provided by eyewitnesses were more extensive than those initially obtained by the police in this case.

Bank Robberies

The previous three studies had a common focus on eyewitness recall for a violent event. The pattern of results across the three studies suggests that witness memory for such events may remain accurate and detailed over long periods of time. An obvious question concerns the pattern of memories of witnesses to a criminal event that is not overtly violent. This study provided a preliminary look at eyewitness memories of a nonviolent event consisting of a series of robberies of financial institutions by two individuals. One of these men, whom we call Jake, robbed 16 institutions in the same municipality, and the other, identified here as Frank, robbed 4 institutions in the same area. We were able to interview 13 of the 39 witnesses to Jake's robberies and 4 of the 13 witnesses to Frank's robberies.

Neither robber used a weapon, although both implied that they possessed one. Jake robbed individual tellers by passing them a note, whereas Frank informed everyone in the bank that he was robbing it. Neither wore a disguise. In each case the witnesses were interviewed by the RCMP immediately after the event. Approximately one-fourth of the witnesses were aware of each robbery as it was occurring, and the other witnesses became aware of the robbery only as the robber was leaving the bank or after it was completed.

Table 3.4 provides a summary of the recall pattern for both interviews for the 17 witnesses, and it indicates that the number of details provided during the police interviews was small.

This is not because the police were disinterested in obtaining information. Unlike the previous incidents in which the perpetrator was killed, the police interviewed these witnesses to obtain information to assist in finding the bank robber. In part, the small amount of recall reflects the fact that both central and peripheral witnesses are grouped together in these averages. The pattern changes somewhat when these two groups are separated. In the police interview, the 4 central witnesses provided an average of 23.8 details about the robberies, which is more than twice as much information as the average of 11.2 details provided by the 13 peripheral witnesses.

The information given by witnesses in police interviews was highly accurate, with the majority of errors occurring in the

Table 3.4. Amount and Percent Accuracy of Recall for the Bank Robberies

Type of detail	Police interview		Research interview	
	Amount	(%) Accuracy	Amount	(%) Accuracy
Action	6.0	98.9	9.4	82.8
Description	8.3	84.1	11.7	79.7
Total	14.3	90.2	21.1	82.0

descriptions of the robbers. As in the previous cases, the errors occurred in estimates of age, height, and weight and in the descriptions of the color and style of clothing.

The accuracy of recall remained high during the later research interview. These interviews occurred, on the average, 2 years after the event. The increased error rate associated with action details was due to errors about the temporal aspects of the events. In the research interview, many witnesses provided erroneous information about the day, date, and time of the event.

The most striking difference between the present results and those of the three previous incidents is the smaller increase in the amount of recall in the research interview. The increase from the police to the research interview was less than 50%. More importantly, the amount of recall was less than half that of the breadline incident and approximately half of that associated with the other two shootings. Even when the amounts recalled by the central and peripheral witnesses are calculated separately, this effect remains. The central witnesses recalled an average of 30.0 details during the research interview, and the peripheral witnesses recalled an average of 18.4 details.

The studies previously outlined focused on the amount and accuracy of eyewitness recall. This investigation of a series of bank robberies afforded an opportunity to explore recognition memory. At the end of the research interview, each witness was shown a photospread containing eight pictures. The robber's picture and a number of similar-looking foils were provided by the RCMP. During the research interview, 10 of the witnesses viewed a photospread that included a photograph of the actual robber, and 6 witnesses were shown a photospread that contained eight foils and no photograph of the robber. One witness was not shown a photospread. In each case, the witness was asked to identify the robber's photograph if they thought it was present or to reject the photospread if they thought the robber's photograph was not included.

Four of the 10 witnesses who were shown a photospread that included the robber correctly identified the photograph of the robber, 1 rejected the photospread, and 5 incorrectly identified one of the foils. All 6 of the witnesses who were shown the blank photospread incorrectly identified one of the foils. Overall, 50% of the witnesses made incorrect identifications. Furthermore, the 4 central witnesses incorrectly chose foils, 3 from the photospread containing the robber's photograph and 1 from the blank photospread. These results indicate a high rate of false identification among witnesses to real crimes. The level of false identification was higher than has been reported in laboratory studies of eyewitness memory, especially when the photograph of the robber was present (e.g., Shepherd, Ellis, & Davies, 1982; Wells & Lindsay, 1985).

The amount of information that witnesses retain about a crime appears to depend on the nature of the crime. The violent events were well remembered; the nonviolent robberies were not. It is not clear that violence per se is the basis for this difference, but it may have played a role. In the cases of robberies, the central witnesses recalled more than the peripheral witnesses. However, all of the witnesses to the bank robberies recalled less about this type of event, particularly during the later interview.

The bank robberies provided a first opportunity to examine recognition memory in the context of an actual crime. The present results support findings from experimental research that suggest that witnesses tend to select someone from a photospread whether or not the perpetrator's photograph is included. In particular, the present results, involving a retention interval of 2 years, are consistent with Shepherd's finding of a strong detrimental effect of long retention intervals on facial recognition memory (Shepherd, 1983). Although these findings strongly suggest the possibility of a high false positive rate when witnesses view photospreads, additional data are needed in order to draw firm conclusions about recognition memory for perpetrators of actual crimes.

GENERAL DISCUSSION

A century of research has demonstrated the selective and complex nature of human memory. Perhaps the one generalization that can be drawn about memory concerns its variety. It is possible to demonstrate rapid forgetting (e.g., with a standard verbal learning task) or long-term retention (e.g., flashbulb memories) or rapid acquisition (e.g., the use of mnemonics) or slow acquisition (e.g., learning of nonsense syllables). What we remember depends upon our relevant knowledge, our mood, our intention, the nature of the event, the consequences of the event, whether we recall the event immediately, and our use of retrieval aids, to name only a few of the large number of factors that affect human memory (c.f. Gruneberg et al., 1988). Because of the large number of factors that influence human memory, it is risky to make generalizations from one context to another about the characteristics of memories.

Our concern about the generalizability of laboratory-based eyewitness research to actual witness situations led us to implement the previously described research program. The four studies presented in this chapter represent the initial development of an empirical basis for understanding eyewitness memory for real-life events. This is only a beginning, however. At present we know little about eyewitness memory of real crimes, and overgeneralizing our findings would be a mistake. With this caution in mind, we believe our results suggest that in constrast to traditional laboratory findings, witnesses can have detailed and accurate memories about some aspects of striking events and that these memories may show little loss over long retention intervals. However, our results also provide support for the typical laboratory findings that witnesses demonstrate considerable error in identifying and describing perpetrators. Our results also suggest that certain types of events (e.g., a shooting incident) are better remembered than other events (e.g., a nonviolent robbery). Our explanations for these differences are speculative, but the data suggest that we look more closely at the characteristics of striking events (c.f. Conway & Bekerian, 1988).

There is a long list of similar questions that require empirical examination. For example, when a witness's recall is fairly detailed, how forensically useful is it? What accounts for the types of errors made by witnesses, such as poor color memory and inaccurate descriptions and recognition of perpetrators? Can

Can the occurrence or impact of these errors be minimized? Which aspects of laboratory eyewitness memory (e.g., recognition memory) generalize to real eyewitnesses?

The tentative nature of the results reported in this chapter reflects the problems of field research, which is less precise than laboratory research. Actual witnesses have different vantage points, different interpretations of the event, different reasons for cooperating, and different ways of telling their versions of the event. In addition, field research is costly in terms of time and money, and it requires cooperation of the police, governments, and the public. It depends on unfortunate circumstances occurring in ways that are amenable to analysis. Despite the difficulties inherent in field research, we believe that the present studies demonstrate that such research can be done and that useful data can be obtained. Furthermore, the impact and nature of many crimes cannot be re-created in the laboratory. Therefore, it is likely that memory for violent, threatening events can be studied only as these events occur in real life; complete simulation is ethically and practically impossible. It is our contention that anyone interested in fully understanding the nature of human memory for such striking events must also study actual crimes.

As noted earlier, some of the conclusions presented in this chapter are at variance with those found in the laboratory-based literature. For example, Clifford and Lloyd-Bostock (1983) noted that researchers have generally been "concerned with showing the witness's fallibility and his inability to recall accurately physical actions, person descriptions or verbalizations" (p. 286). The results of our field research indicate that witnesses may have difficulty with some aspects of person descriptions but not with physical actions. The level of accuracy of real witnesses for striking events may be higher than laboratory studies have generally suggested. It should be noted, however, that some laboratory studies have also reported high levels of accuracy (e.g., Geiselman, Fisher, MacKinnon, & Holland, 1985; Wigmore, 1909).

Another example of the variant findings of our study concerns the claim that the Ebbinghaus forgetting curve applies to eyewitness memory; that is, the assertion that memory declines dramatically over time (e.g., Penrod, Loftus, & Winkler, 1982). Our data demonstrate that this is simply not true for some events. For three of the four events we investigated, memory remained detailed and accurate over months and years. In addition, we tested the effectiveness of misleading questions concerning witnesses's descriptions of objects in one of the incidences, but our attempt to distort the memory of real witnesses was unsuccessful.

There are also some similarities between our findings and those of the laboratory. One similarity concerns the problems witnesses have with color memory (e.g., Munsterberg, 1908; Stern, 1910; Whipple, 1910). Also, as noted earlier, the high rate of errors by our witnesses who were asked to make identifications of the bank robbers is consistent with the laboratory literature (e.g., Shepherd, 1983).

Comparison between our field research and laboratory research thus reveals a mixed picture in terms of the similarities and differences between laboratory witnesses and actual witnesses to real-world crimes. It remains unclear precisely which laboratory findings are generalizable to specific criminal situations. It is clear, however, that we need to look more closely at this problem and to generate data that can provide an empirical basis for generalizing our findings to the forensic context.

At this point in time our field data suggest that psychologists have, at times, erred in generalizing from laboratory-based studies of human memory to memory in forensic contexts. The desire to generalize research to forensic settings is understandable. Police, lawyers, and judges must deal with problems of human memory on a daily basis. When psychologists have claimed to possess relevant knowledge and theory, forensic professionals have been eager to listen. The laboratory work has face validity; showing a group of students a film of a robbery seemed to simulate the event of a witness watching an actual robbery. Our data suggest that these events may not be completely analogous for forensic purposes.

We suggest that the application of experimental findings to real crime contexts contains some errors because such applications have failed to appreciate the special aspects of forensic contexts that may affect human memory. Similarly, we caution against hasty generalization from our findings. Our database is quite small at this time, and generalizations to the forensic arena should be tempered by an awareness of the potential impact of research in this area. Not only may long-standing principles of law be modified on the basis of research results, but defendants, victims, and their families may also be greatly affected by inferences drawn from eyewitness research (Konecni & Ebbesen, 1979). With so much at stake, as eyewitness researchers it is incumbent upon us to look closely at the validity of our methodologies and the relevance and applications of our research findings.

The research reported in this chapter represents an initial effort to generate forensically relevant information, but more representative data are needed. As we noted, our cases do not represent the average criminal event. Most crimes involve only one or two witnesses, most often only the victim. Research focusing on actual victims of crimes is therefore needed. In addition, to enhance the forensic relevance of field research, more emphasis should be placed on exploring individual differences among witnesses to crimes. Group averages are of little use within the forensic context. It's interesting that 5 of the 13 witnesses in the gun shop incident scored above 90% in their overall accuracy. It would be of interest to explore what distinguishes this group of witnesses from the others. Recent research by Bothwell, Brigham, and Pigott (1987) has explored personality variables that may affect eyewitnessing abilities. These authors suggest that arousal may have a facilitating effect on stable personalities and a debilitating effect on neurotic personalities (as measured by the Eysenck Personality Inventory). The generalizability of this research has not yet been ascertained, but it suggests some intriguing possibilities.

We end this chapter with a call for systematic field research to examine real eyewitness memory. The questions about real eyewitnesses are as interesting as they ever were, and the time has come for us to apply our methodologies to answer these questions directly.

ACKNOWLEDGEMENTS

The research reported in this chapter was supported by grants to John C. Yuille from the Social Sciences and Humanities Research Council of Canada. The authors wish to thank Doreen Kum and Mark Turner for their assistance in the collection of the data and to express special thanks to the Royal Canadian Mounted Police and to the Vancouver City Police for making this research possible.

REFERENCES

Bothwell, R. K., Brigham, J. C., & Pigott, M. A. (1987). An exploratory study of personality differences in eyewitness memory. *Journal of Social Behavior and Personality, 2,* 335–343.

Brigham, J. C., Maas, A., Snyder, L. D., & Spaulding, K. (1982). Accuracy of eyewitness identifications in a field study. *Journal of Personality and Social Psychology, 42,* 673–681.

Buckhout, R. (1974). Eyewitness testimony. *Scientific American, 231,* 23–31.

Buckhout, R. (1986). Personal values and expert testimony. *Law and Human Behavior, 10,* 127–144.

Cady, H. M. (1924). On the psychology of testimony. *American Journal of Psychology, 35,* 110–112.

Clifford, B. R., & Lloyd-Bostock, S. M. A. (1983). Witness evidence: Conclusion and prospect. In S. M. A. Lloyd-Bostock & B. R. Clifford (Eds.). *Evaluating witness evidence* (pp. 285–290). New York: Wiley.

Conway, M. A., & Bekerian, D. A. (1988). Characteristics of vivid memories. In M. M. Gruneberg, P. E. Morris, & R. N. Sykes (1988). *Practical aspects of memory: Current research and issues* (Vol. 1, pp. 519–524). New York: Wiley.

Cutshall, J. (1985). Eyewitness characteristics and memory: An in situ analysis. Unpublished master's thesis, University of British Columbia, Vancouver.

Ebbinghaus, H. E. (1964). *Memory: A contribution to experimental psychology.* New York: Dover. (Original work published in German in 1885)

Geiselman, R. E., Fisher, R. P., MacKinnon, D. P., & Holland, H. L. (1985). Eyewitness memory enhancement in the police interview: Cognitive retrieval mnemonics versus hypnosis. *Journal of Applied Psychology, 70,* 401–412.

Gruneberg, M. M., Morris, P. E., & Sykes, R. N. (Eds.). (1978). *Practical aspects of memory*. New York: Academic Press.
Gruneberg, M. M., Morris, P. E., & Sykes, R. N. (Eds.). (1988). *Practical aspects of memory: Current research and issues* (Vols. 1 & 2). New York: Wiley.
Konecni, V. J., & Ebbesen, E. B. (1979). External validity of research in legal psychology. *Law and Human Behavior, 3*, 39-70.
Konecni, V. J., & Ebbesen, E. B. (1986). Courtroom testimony by psychologists on eyewitness identification issues: Critical notes and reflections. *Law and Human Behavior, 10*, 117-126.
Krafka, C., & Penrod, S. D. (1985). Reinstatement of context in a field experiment on eyewitness identification. *Journal of Personality and Social Psychology, 49*, 58-69.
Lipton, J. P. (1977). On the psychology of eyewitness testimony. *Journal of Applied Psychology, 62*, 90-93.
Lloyd-Bostock, S. M. A., & Clifford, B. R. (Eds.). (1983). *Evaluating witness evidence*. New York: Wiley.
Loftus, E. F. (1974, December). Reconstructing memory: The incredible eyewitness. *Psychology Today*, pp. 116-119.
Loftus, E. F. (1975). Leading questions and the eyewitness report. *Cognitive Psychology, 7*, 560-572.
Loftus, E. F. (1979). *Eyewitness testimony*. Cambridge: Harvard University Press.
Loftus, E. F. (1986). Ten years in the life of an expert witness. *Law and Human Behavior, 10*, 241-263.
Loftus, E. F., & Zanni, G. (1975). Eyewitness testimony: The influence of the wording of a question. *Bulletin of the Psychonomic Society, 5*, 86-88.
McCloskey, M., Egeth, H., & McKenna, J. (1986). The experimental psychologist in court: The ethics of expert testimony. *Law and Human Behavior, 10*, 1-13.
Munsterberg, H. (1908). *On the witness stand: Essays on psychology and crime*. New York: Clark, Boardman.
Neisser, U. (1978). Memory: What are the important questions? In M. M. Gruneberg, P. E. Morris, & R. N. Sykes (Eds.), *Practical aspects of memory* (pp. 3-24). New York: Academic Press.
Newell, A. (1974). You can't play 20 questions with nature and win. In W. G. Chase (Ed.), *Visual information processing* (pp. 283-285). New York: Academic Press.
Penrod, S., Loftus, E. F., & Winkler, J. (1982). In N. L. Kerr & R. M. Bray (Eds.), *The psychology of the courtroom* (pp. 119-168). New York: Academic Press.

Peters, D. P. (1988). Eyewitness memory and arousal in a natural setting. In M. M. Gruneberg, P. E. Morris, & R. N. Sykes (Eds.), *Practical aspects of memory: Current research and issues* (Vol. 1, pp. 89–94). New York: Wiley.
Saks, M. J. (1986). The law does not live by eyewitness testimony alone. *Law and Human Behavior, 10*, 279–280.
Shepherd, J. W. (1983). Identification after long delays. In S. M. A. Lloyd-Bostock & B. R. Clifford (Eds.), *Evaluating witness evidence* (pp. 173–187). New York: Wiley.
Shepherd, J. W., Ellis, H. D., & Davies, G. M. (1982). *Identification evidence: A psychological evaluation.* Aberdeen: Aberdeen University Press.
Stern, L. W. (1910). Abstracts of lectures in the psychology of testimony and on the study of individuality. *American Journal of Psychology, 21*, 270–282.
Stern, L. W. (1939). The psychology of testimony. *Journal of Abnormal and Social Psychology, 34*, 3–20.
Tulving, E., & Madigan, S. A. (1970). Memory and verbal learning. *Annual Review of Psychology, 21*, 437–484.
Wells, G. L., & Lindsay, R. C. L. (1985). Methodological notes on the confidence-accuracy relation in eyewitness identifications. *Journal of Applied Psychology, 70*, 413–419.
Wells, G. L., & Loftus, E. F. (Eds.). (1984). *Eyewitness testimony: Psychological perspectives.* Cambridge: Cambridge University Press.
Whipple, G. M. (1910). Recent literature on the psychology of testimony. *Psychological Bulletin, 7*, 365–368.
Wigmore, J. H. (1909). The psychology of testimony. *Illinois Law Review, 3*, 399–434.
Yarmey, A. D. (1979). *The psychology of eyewitness testimony.* New York: Free Press.
Yuille, J. C. (1984). Research and teaching with police: A Canadian example. *International Review of Applied Psychology, 33*, 5–23.
Yuille, J. C. (1986). Meaningful research in the police context. In J. C. Yuille (Ed.), *Police training and selection* (pp. 225–243). Dordrecht, The Netherlands: Martinus Nijoff.
Yuille, J. C., & Cutshall, J. L. (1986). A case study of eyewitness memory of a crime. *Journal of Applied Psychology, 71*, 291–301.
Yuille, J. C., & McEwan, N. H. (1985). The use of hypnosis as an aid to eyewitness memory. *Journal of Applied Psychology, 70*, 389–400.

Legal Issues in Eyewitness Evidence

4

James M. Doyle

The legal system relies heavily on eyewitness testimony, and nowhere more so than in the law enforcement context. Despite this reliance, the courts have always regarded eyewitness versions with some wariness. Long before systematic psychological study of eyewitness performance was attempted, anecdotal evidence of misidentifications found its way into legal memoirs. At least since the late 19th century, experimental results challenging eyewitness capacity have drawn the attention of legal commentators (Levine & Tapp, 1973).

To its credit, the legal system's response to increased psychological knowledge about the eyewitness process has not been complacent. Various courts and rule-making bodies, persuaded that eyewitnesses are vulnerable to error, have at various times designed and instituted special procedures to guard against mistakes. Unfortunately, the system of filters that has resulted from these procedures does not fit perfectly with either the growing fund of psychological knowledge or with the exigencies of day-to-day law enforcement activities.

Perhaps no perfect system is possible. The psychologists' information is inherently statistical and probabilistic; the legal system's task is clinical and diagnostic. Even when a psychologist can present an opinion describing how an eyewitness might perform in 75% of similar cases, the legal system must decide how to use that information in determining whether this case is one of the 75% or one of the 25%. The translation can never be simple and mechanical.

The current, imperfect state of the legal system's treatment of the psychologically complex problem of eyewitness evidence compels the attention of everyone interested in investigation and trials. Failing to grasp its peculiarities will enhance the likelihood that one of two potential major problems will become a reality.

The first of these problems is that an incorrect identification will slip through the legal system and result in the conviction of an innocent person. The conviction of an innocent citizen, bad enough in itself, also has important collateral consequences. The actual perpetrator is likely to escape justice, and the discovery of an erroneous conviction can undermine public faith in the law enforcement community in general. A television segment describing the mistaken incarceration of a blameless neighbor is not a spectacle to be welcomed.

The second problem may occur even more frequently. If the operation of the legal system, with all of its complexities and idiosyncrasies, is not understood, accurate identification evidence can be excluded because the investigating officials failed to anticipate the legal system's requirements for admissibility. This is not the type of mistake anyone enjoys having to explain to a crime victim. Even if eyewitness testimony is eventually admitted, failure to appreciate how it will be handled in a courtroom setting can result in an accurate identification being made to look so implausible that the expected conviction will be jeopardized.

Nothing can provide complete protection against these dangers, but a survey of the legal system's attempts at structuring the use of eyewitness evidence can be a productive first step. The following sections attempt to provide such a survey. They discuss reform efforts in three broad historical contexts. The first of these is the context of the traditional common-law jury trial, the second is the era of prophylactic procedures mandated by the Warren Court in the 1960s, and the final segment is the contemporary debate over the advisability of expert testimony concerning eyewitness psychology.

THE EYEWITNESS IN THE TRADITIONAL TRIAL

There were jury trials before there were psychologists. What is more, because there were jury trials before there were fingerprint examiners and forensic laboratories, early trials relied even more heavily on eyewitness accounts than do today's. Many commentators now argue that the jury trial as routinely practiced provides inadequate safeguards against eyewitness error and juror overconfidence in eyewitness testimony.

These arguments can best be understood by looking briefly at the way in which juries decide cases. Practically speaking, they tend to use two sorts of information: specific data generated by the evidence, and general principles derived from their commonsense experience, which help them to weigh and interpret the specific data and to arrive at a conclusion. For example, if specific testimony is introduced showing that there is blood on a club, the system relies on the jurors' everyday experience to supply the general principle that if there is blood on the club, someone was hit with it. In eyewitness trials the specific data are often easy to generate—for example, the witness is confident, or the witness was under stress. Many contemporary psychologists worry that at the level of general interpretive principles, the jurors are very likely to apply commonsense principles, such as confidence means accuracy or stress enhances alertness and accuracy. However, psychological research has called these principles into question. Many psychologists and lawyers now wonder whether the eyewitness trial presents an unusual case in which the faith in the jurors' everyday experience, on which the trial system relies, is misplaced.

These questions are important, but they must be kept in perspective. It would be a mistake to allow their alarming implications to obscure the fact that the traditional jury trial does provide some devices for controlling eyewitness testimony and juror credulity. A look at those devices will suggest the dimensions of the problem.

The Eyewitness and the Voir Dire

At least in theory, jury selection in traditional trials presents an opportunity to mute the most aggravated instances of jurors' overconfidence in eyewitnesses (National Jury Project, 1983). If the lawyers conducting the jury selection process are successful in efforts to identify and challenge jurors who possess extreme misconceptions about eyewitness reliability, then perhaps no further remedial steps are necessary. Unfortunately, this safeguard functions only in theory.

Lawyers conducting jury selection always have more than one goal (Amsterdam, Segal, & Miller, 1983). Aside from identifying jurors with disadvantageous misconceptions about eyewitness accuracy, they will be trying to preview for the jurors their theories of the case, to win the trust of the jurors, and to dampen the impact of the opposing side's strongest points. It will almost never be possible to give absolute priority to uncovering jurors who mistakenly believe, for example, that there is a strong correlation between an eyewitness's confidence and an eyewitness's accuracy (Loftus & Doyle, 1987).

Even if it were possible to concentrate exclusively on eyewitness psychology, the mechanics of the voir dire make it nearly impossible to do that effectively. When a lawyer succeeds in identifying a juror with an advantageous picture of eyewitness performance, the process will reveal to the opposing lawyer that the same picture of eyewitness performance is disadvantageous for the other side. There will be exceptions, of course, but the most likely outcome of such an eyewitness-centered voir dire is an impasse, rather than a correction of the jury's collective misconceptions of the eyewitness process (Doyle, 1984).

Cross-examination of the Eyewitness

It is an article of faith among lawyers that cross-examination represents "[T]he greatest legal engine ever invented for the discovery of the truth" (Wigmore, 1974, Sec. 1367). A wealth of judicial opinions assert that whatever problems may exist with eyewitness testimony, cross-examination is their solution (*Smith v. United States*, 1978; *United States v. Amaral*, 1973).

It is certainly true that a lawyer can accomplish a great deal in cross-examining an eyewitness. In fact, when it comes to generating specific data about the crime or incident that the witness observed, there is virtually no limit to what an aggressive lawyer can achieve. If the lighting was poor, the encounter brief, the description sketchy, and the assailant a stranger, all of these things can be put before the jury using cross-examination in its most traditional form.

For the critics of eyewitness testimony, however, two peculiarities of the eyewitness case diminish confidence in the efficacy of cross-examination. First, in cross-examining an eyewitness, a lawyer risks eliciting specific facts that a psychologist would consider signals for caution in evaluating an eyewitness' testimony (e.g., the incident provoked a high level of stress), but jurors may actually believe such factors should have the reverse effect.

Second, the traditional ammunition of the cross-examiner consists of facts known by the witness but withheld during the direct examination. Cross-examination of a dissembling witness is expected to elicit this suppressed information and to provoke a demeanor consistent with dissembling, including gestures, pauses, and hesitations that will convince the jurors that the witness's testimony must be weighed with caution. Unfortunately, psychological research seems to suggest that it is a feature of eyewitness testimony that eyewitnesses, no matter how mistaken, are by the time of their testimony utterly and sincerely convinced that their identification is correct (Woocher, 1977). That the witness's confidence could well be the product of information introduced after the event is something known to psychologists but not to the jurors. As a result, a lawyer who aggressively cross-examines a mistaken eyewitness simply digs a deeper hole for the client by emphasizing to the jurors the witness's sincerity and conviction (Woocher, 1977).

In the eyes of critics, the specific data that cross-examination is well suited to elicit provides only the raw material of correct decision making. A correct decision, they would say, cannot be made without a framework of information that will help the jurors to use the raw material accurately. In the traditional trial, the principal vehicles for integrating legal and evidentiary principles with specific facts have been the closing arguments and the judge's instructions to the jury.

Instructions and Argument

In American jury trials, jury instructions are agreed upon before the closing arguments begin, and trial lawyers are taught to integrate (into their own accounts of the evidence) the principles that the judge will announce to the jurors. In the United Kingdom, the trial judge's instructions are likely to deal more closely with the facts of the specific case being tried, but typically, the lawyers will have an early notion of the general principles that the judge will provide. Taken together, the arguments of counsel and the instructions by the judge possess powerful potential for correcting whatever frailties the combination of eyewitness error and juror overconfidence may create. There are considerations, however, at the level of policy and at the level of mechanics that tend to brake the full use of the corrective power of instructions and arguments.

It may be clearest to begin with the text of a standard instruction. The instruction that follows is the most basic form. Having been approved by the U.S. Court of Appeals for the Seventh Circuit, it is an instruction that a trial judge (at least in that circuit) can use without fear of criticism or reversal:

> The reliability of eyewitness identification has been raised as an issue in this case and deserves your attention. Identification testimony is an expression of belief or impression by the witness. Its value depends upon the opportunity the witness had to observe the offender at the time of the offense and later to make a reliable identification, and upon the influences and circumstances under which the witness made the identification.
>
> You must consider the credibility of each identification witness in the same way as any other witness. Consider whether he is truthful, and consider whether he had the capacity and

opportunity to make a reliable observation on the matter covered in his testimony. (*United States v. Hodges*, 1975, p. 656)

It should be obvious that cautious form instructions of the foregoing variety will do very little to quiet the anxieties of commentators who are worried about juror overreliance on eyewitnesses. The instruction does no more than point out that identification evidence must be weighed like any other evidence. It makes no effort to address the possibility that the jurors will begin by weighing it too heavily.

The U.S. Court of Appeals for the District of Columbia Circuit attempted to improve on the standard version of jury instructions in its influential opinion in *United States v. Telfaire* (1972). Despite the fact that the court was apparently sensitive to the dangers of misidentification and obviously believed that it was doing something useful in proposing a new model instruction, the *Telfaire* instruction does no more than draw the jurors' attention to potential areas of danger, without explicitly stating that they are dangerous or why they are dangerous. For example, in one crucial paragraph, it is suggested that jurors be advised that "[y]ou may take into account both the strength of the identification and the circumstances under which the identification was made" (pp. 558–559). If strength of the identification is interpreted to mean the witness's confidence in the identification, the instruction actually contradicts the results of several experiments that seem to show that there is no correlation between confidence and accuracy. The phrase "circumstances under which the identification was made" is not controversial; on the other hand, it is not helpful. It conveys nothing to the jurors of the variety, subtlety, or power of various kinds of postevent information that an identification procedure might introduce.

The somewhat bland nature of the *Telfaire* instruction becomes easier to understand, however, when one considers the problems encountered when an instruction takes the next step and actually attempts to import psychological studies into the deliberative process. For example, in *People v. Wright* (1980) the California Supreme Court addressed cross-racial identification by stating that "[s]tudies show that when the witness and the person he is identifying are of different races, and particularly when the witness is white and the offender is black, the identification tends to be less reliable than if both persons are of the same race" (p. 729). There is certainly a growing body of literature that agrees with the court's assertion, but it is not quite true to say that the extent and the contours of the cross-racial identification problem are entirely beyond debate (Johnson, 1984). Most legal commentators would agree that as long as a proposition of this sort is debatable, it should be the subject of an adversary debate between the parties, not an unchallenged (and practically unchallengeable) pronouncement by the judge.

In short, attempts to use instructions to improve jurors' ability to weigh eyewitness evidence produce a dilemma. On one hand, the existence of the jurors' strongly held preexisting misconceptions seems to require strong, explicit, categorical corrective language. On the other, the judge's categorical announcement of the answers to debated questions seems to threaten the fundamental basis of the jury trial.

Once the instructions are cast in a somewhat temporizing mode, the contents of counsel's arguments become predictable. One lawyer is likely to argue that obviously eyewitnesses are reliable, the opposing lawyer that obviously they are not. The jurors will decide these cases, of course, but little in the decision-making process is likely to assuage the worries of critics of eyewitness testimony. The critics would argue that a jury decision in a traditional trial depends on the preconceptions that the jurors brought to court and not on anything that happened in the courtroom. For the critics at least, the jurors' preconceptions are erroneous, and their decisions suspect.

THE PREVENTIVE APPROACH TO EYEWITNESS ERROR

Some psychological research indicates that no matter how many protective devices the trial process provides against eyewitness error, they are simply provided too late. Many psychologists believe that the nature of the eyewitness process causes eyewitnesses to integrate into their own accounts of crime or incident postevent information provided during the investigative process. This feature of the eyewitness is particularly dangerous since the eyewitness is very likely to be unconscious of the fact that the information was not part of the initial memory (Loftus & Doyle, 1987, pp. 75–86). Between witnessing the crime and providing testimony, the uncertain, frightened, and hesitant eyewitness may be transformed into a confident, convinced, and compelling narrator. The witness is no more accurate than on the night of the crime but has been made immune to cross-examination by the investigative process.

During the 1960s the U.S. Supreme Court appeared to acknowledge this problem by instituting a framework of preventive rules intended to reach out from the courthouse into day-to-day law enforcement identification practices. An understanding of these rules and their psychological underpinnings is crucial to investigators. It is true that eyewitnesses can be unconsciously influenced by a suggestive lineup; it is also true that in designing that lineup, investigators may unconsciously build in suggestive elements. When that occurs, an incorrect identification may result in either an erroneous conviction, or a subsequent court finding of suggestivity may result in the suppression of a correct identification and an erroneous acquittal. Knowing and conforming to the procedural requirements for the admissibility of identification testimony is indispensable to the successful conclusion of an eyewitness case.

The U.S. Supreme Court has chosen two separate constitutional guarantees as the vehicles for its efforts to improve pretrial identification procedures: the Sixth Amendment right to counsel and the Fifth and Fourteenth Amendments guarantee of due process of law.

The Right to Counsel

Since its opinion in *United States v. Wade* in 1967, the Supreme Court has applied a three-part test to determine whether a suspect has a right to counsel in an identification procedure, and the Court mandated that identification testimony gathered in violation of this right must be suppressed. At the time of its announcement, the *Wade* rule evoked a strong protest from the law enforcement community. Although a large number of investigatory identification procedures meet the first test in *Wade* (i.e., they will be "critical stages" of a prosecution), at 20 years' distance it is somewhat easier to see that the elements of the test confine the test's direct effects to a rather narrow range of cases.

A criminal suspect does not have a right to counsel until the commencement of formal judicial proceedings (*Moore v. Illinois*, 1977). The Court has provided no "bright-line" test for when the commencement of formal proceedings occurs; however, it has provided a number of examples. It is clear that either the indictment of the defendant or arraignment after the arrest on a warrant suffice to trigger the right to counsel (*Brewer v. Williams*, 1977).

It is equally clear, however, that many of the most frequently used identification procedures are entirely beyond the reach of the right to counsel. A showup at the scene, soon after a crime, will almost never require that counsel be provided. Similarly, routine viewings of photoarrays will ordinarily occur before proceedings have commenced.

The photoarray technique is beyond the reach of the right to counsel case for another reason. The Court has held that the protections afforded by the right to counsel are not necessary unless there is an actual, physical confrontation between the defendant and the witness. The postarraignment line-up requires that counsel be present; a viewing by the same witness of a photograph of the same lineup does not (*United States v. Ash*, 1977).

Even if the range of impact of the right to counsel on identification cases is limited, the strength of the remedy that will be applied when a violation occurs can be substantial. An identification obtained in contravention of the right to counsel is *per se* inadmissible (*United States v. Wade*, 1967). In order to use identifications that were obtained after a Sixth Amendment violation, the prosecutor must prove by clear and convincing evidence that the subsequent identifications were not tainted by the earlier, illegal one.

The litigation context, however, drastically dilutes the effect of the *Wade* rule. Perhaps partly as a result of *Wade*, a typical investigation now progresses from a showup (no right to counsel) through a photographic identification (no right to counsel). Only after that point, at which time most psychologists would believe its purpose is largely ceremonial, is there a postarraignment lineup where the right to counsel applies (Dunning, Ellsworth, & Ross, 1980). Even where a violation may have occurred at the lineup stage, the earlier identifications will ordinarily be admissible and ample to convict. Moreover, the lower courts, in interpreting *Wade*, have not been willing to require that counsel actually do anything at the lineup. The use of a stand-in counsel, unacquainted with the defendant and uninformed about the facts of the case, often has been held to be sufficient (*United States v. Jones*, 1973).

The effect of the *Wade* rule is largely indirect. It has encouraged a regularized, professional approach to the conduct of pretrial identification proceedings by investigative authorities (Loftus & Doyle, 1987, pp. 241–242). Although its force will now be felt in relatively few cases, it can be significant. When it is important for authorities to conduct a postarraignment, live lineup, it must be conducted properly if it is to provide admissible evidence.

Due Process of Law

If identification procedures are "so unnecessarily suggestive as to give rise to a very substantial likelihood of irreparable misidentification" (*Manson v. Braithwaite*, 1977), the due process clause forbids the use of the evidence that they generate. The due process protection is independent of the right to counsel; rather, it supplements and overlaps it. A lineup at which counsel was present can nevertheless be subject to a suppression order if its makeup singled out the defendant. In contrast to the right to counsel, the due process clause reaches a comprehensive range of identification procedures. It covers showups, lineups, photoarrays, and courtroom identifications, regardless of when they occur. As a result, a defense lawyer in a criminal case can almost always find some reason to file a motion to suppress identification testimony. As a practical matter, however, suppression rarely occurs.

In evaluating due process attacks on identification procedures, courts do not react reflexively to any single element. Instead, they weigh the totality of the circumstances to determine whether, even assuming that suggestive elements existed, the identification obtained was reliable. Some courts have used a two-step approach to due process claims by considering whether an identification is reliable only after it has been shown that the procedures were unnecessarily suggestive (*United States v. Phillips*, 1981). Other courts collapse the two issues into one, weighing the evidence of suggestiveness against the reliability of the evidence in all cases (*Green v. Loggins*, 1980). Under either procedure, however, courts are frequently called upon to decide whether the evidence meets the amorphous test of reliability. To aid the lower courts in that task, the U.S. Supreme Court provided a set of guidelines that illustrate the somewhat ambivalent relationship between the legal system and the findings of contemporary psychology.

In *Manson v. Braithwaite* (1977) the U.S. Supreme Court directed the attention of courts to a list of psychological factors relevant to the determination of the reliability of the identification. These included the opportunity to view the offender, the degree of attention during the crime, the accuracy of the description of the offender, the time between the crime and the identification, and the witness's certainty that the identification was correct. With the exception of the last element (there is little, if any, experimental verification of a correlation between confidence and reliability), most psychologists would find the *Manson v. Braithwaite* list to be unobjectionable as far as it goes. Many, however, would find its catalogue of factors to be radically oversimplified. For example, many psychologists would consider advertance to the witness's degree of attention useful only if the court's definition of degree of attention included the concept of weapon focus, the tendency of a witness to focus on a dangerous or threatening object rather than on a face. Others would point out that the phrase "opportunity to view" is useful only when it is understood to encompass a range of fairly subtle factors (e.g., stress), not merely the duration of the crime.

Nothing in the Supreme Court's tests for the reliability of identifications forbids lower courts to integrate their standards for reliability with the more elaborate understanding of the eyewitnessing process supported by psychologists (see Chapters 1, 2, and 3). A review of the reported opinions, however, shows very little movement in this direction. In fact, the lower courts sometimes seem to strain to apply the most forgiving versions of reliability in order to allow the identification to be presented to the jury. Identifications of criminals who were masked at the time of the offense (*Simons v. State*, 1980) or by victims who were temporarily blinded by liquids (*People v. Lutz*, 1982) have been admitted into evidence and upheld on appeal.

The context of criminal litigation also limits the impact of the due process test on trials. The proper remedy for a suggestive identification procedure is the suppression of the identification it produced and all subsequent identifications that were the products of the improper procedure and not products of the witness's view of the criminal at the time of the crime. For example, consider a sequence consisting of an inadmissible showup, a fair photoarray, and a fair lineup. If the defense succeeds in suppressing all of the identification procedures, the defense will win. If any one of the identifications is admitted into evidence, however, it will be in the interests of the defense to seek the admission of the improper showup in order to argue to the jury that it was the suggestive nature of the showup that created the witness's subsequent identifications (Loftus & Doyle, 1987). In part because of the structure of the constitutional protections afforded, and in part because of the reluctance of the lower courts to apply them, the loss of an eyewitness identification prosecution in pretrial litigation is increasingly rare; it is fair to say that the vast majority of eyewitness cases now go to the jury.

It would not, however, be fair to say that the much-maligned Warren Court's foray into the world of eyewitness investigation was entirely without impact. It had an important threefold effect on the ways in which the law enforcement community handles its cases. It prompted research into the reliability of traditional procedures, the institution of new procedures, the education of investigators in more reliable approaches, all of which resulted in more intelligent handling of the large but invisible number of eyewitness cases that are disposed of in the screening process (Gross, 1987). The legendary lineups of six nuns and a suspect and showups where the police ostentatiously point at the suspect are rarely encountered now. The most egregiously dangerous end of the spectrum of identification practices has been drastically pruned by increased police professionalism and court scrutiny.

When all is said and done, however, the elimination of the most flagrantly suggestive identification procedures still leaves a broad range of identifications to be evaluated by the jurors. Persistent doubts about the jurors' ability to perform that task with traditional tools have led to calls for direct participation by psychologists as expert witnesses in the trial process (Loftus, 1986).

THE PSYCHOLOGIST AS EXPERT WITNESS

A spirited debate is raging over the efficacy, desirability, and propriety of expert psychological testimony concerning the psychology of eyewitness identification. There are psychologists on both sides of the debate, legal scholars on both sides of the debate, and courts on both sides of the debate. The controversy is fascinating because it reveals the variety of opinions held by psychologists concerning the legal system and a similar diversity of confidence among lawyers about psychological research. Most interestingly, it reveals the uneasy and imperfect relations between the two professions as they focus on a shared problem. The outcome of the debate may have important consequences for investigators.

The impetus for expert psychological testimony is generated by two matters already discussed: the arguable inadequacy of traditional jury trial methods of dealing with eyewitness reliability and the tendency of pretrial remedies to place squarely on the jury trial the responsibility for weighing growing numbers of eyewitness cases. Opposition to expert testimony sometimes focuses on the unreliability of psychology in general, but only rarely. More typically, attacks on expert testimony dwell on either or both of two themes. The first of these themes is that psychological testimony will so dazzle the jurors with its aura of expertise that the jurors will surrender their free will, the psychologist will run away with the case, and eyewitness testimony, which is indispensable in many cases, will be lost in a sea of useless skepticism. The second theme holds that the traditional devices of adversary attack can convey the idea behind expert testimony without necessitating the attendant dangers and expenses of a battle of the experts in every eyewitness case. It is worth spending some time scrutinizing these challenges to expert testimony.

It simplifies matters if the law of evidence is looked on as providing a series of screens insofar as scientific evidence is concerned. The first of these screens is designed to eliminate what might be called bad science—information ostensibly based on scientific techniques that is simply wrong. Different courts design this screen in different ways; some accept the testimony of any qualified expert (McCormick, 1972), some require a showing that the scientific information offered has been "generally accepted" by the relevant scientific community (*Frye v. United States*, 1923), and some require that it aid the trier of fact.

Whatever test is applied, expert psychological testimony about perception, memory, and recall will pass through this screen without much difficulty. Although there is debate within the psychological community about various aspects of eyewitness psychology, the general acceptance standard requires only that the general explanatory theory of the work (here, the general scientific approach of experimental psychology) be accepted (*Ibn-Tamas v. United States*, 1979). The debate within the scientific community does not challenge the basic methods or the results of the experiments; it questions the inferences and conclusions drawn from them (McCloskey & Egeth, 1983b). To put it another way, there is little doubt that the research to which critics of eyewitness performance refer is valid, but its significance is hotly contested. Arguments over the significance of valid scientific information, however, present essentially legal, not scientific problems. They are problems that must be resolved by considering whether the jurors will misuse concededly valid information.

Some courts believe that an expert witness stands in "a posture of mystic infallibility in the eye of a jury of laymen" (*United States v. Addison*, 1974, p. 744). This belief survives despite the fact that, as one authority notes, "the clear weight of the available hard data calls into question the assumption . . . that scientific testimony overwhelms the typical lay juror" (Imwinkelreid, 1983, p. 570). It is a belief that has frequently contributed to the exclusion of expert testimony about eyewitness psychology—ironically, an area in which the belief is least tenable.

Despite the absence of hard data, there is something intuitively appealing about the idea that jurors tend to defer to experts. Assuming for the sake of argument that some jurors will defer to some experts, it is difficult to believe that all jurors will defer to different experts to the same degree. Jurors realize that their knowledge of neurology is limited, and a testifying neurologist can expect to receive some deference. The same is not true of psychologists testifying about a process that is part of each juror's everyday life. As one commentator put it, "[M]ost jurors probably consider themselves better amateur psychologists than amateur physicians, chemists, or metallurgists. They are likely to be less swayed by testimony about perception and memory than by testimony about cervical discs" (Convis, 1983, p. 584).

An expert witness in the area of eyewitness psychology is particularly vulnerable to adversary attack (Loftus & Doyle, 1987, pp. 313–318). The attackers will generally have the jurors' preconceptions on their side. The judge will remind the jurors that it is their role, not the expert's, to decide the case. Finally, the expert psychologist is likely to be seen by the jurors as participating in a contest with the eyewitness. In that contest the eyewitness enjoys several significant advantages.

The most obvious of these advantages is that the jurors are likely to find the eyewitness—a layperson like themselves, caught in a trial by circumstance—easier to identify with than the expert who possesses advanced degrees and is compensated for testifying. A second advantage held by the eyewitness is that the eyewitness and the psychologist are offering two different kinds of information. The psychologist's information is statistical and deals with general probabilities; the eyewitness's information is clinical and deals with the specific incident of central concern in this trial. Research seems to show that in making decisions, people have a tendency to discount the importance of statistical and base rate information in favor of the facts of the specific situation (Edwards & VonWinterfeldt, 1986). Finally, it is reasonable to expect the jurors to be impressed with the fact that the eyewitness was present during the event, whereas the expert is merely relying on experiments that attempt to duplicate crime conditions, sometimes unrealistically.

Although there may be cases in which expert testimony presents dangers, in light of the control devices available there does not seem to be any justification for adhering to an across-the-board embargo of expert testimony about eyewitness psychology based on the presumed aura of expertise. As a growing number of courts now recognize, the issue must be examined on a case-by-case basis.

The second theme of opponents of expert testimony is that the psychologist's information can be conveyed by other means. It draws a similar answer: Sometimes it can, and sometimes it cannot. As noted in earlier discussion, the traditional adversary methods of the trial are problematic solutions to the rather novel discontinuity between psychological knowledge about the eyewitness process and the lay jury's preconceptions. In weighing the question of substitute means of communicating psychological knowledge, as in evaluating the distorting effect of the expert's prestige, there seems to be no escape from a case-by-case analysis. A growing number of appellate courts now seem to agree that trial courts must scrutinize each individual offer of expert testimony in light of the facts of the case on trial.

The initial reception given to offers of expert testimony on the psychology of eyewitness identification in the courts was decidedly hostile. The opinions rehearsed the two themes set out in the preceding sections, accepted their validity, and frequently added the observation that to require expert testimony on this subject would swamp the court system in myriad battles of the experts (*State v. Chapple*, 1983, dissenting opinion of J. Hayes). Although few of the opinions actually forbade the introduction of expert testimony, they did state that the trial judge was not compelled to permit its introduction. A tone of wariness about the costs and benefits of expert testimony pervaded judicial writings on the subject.

In 1983 the Arizona Supreme Court became the first state supreme court to hold that it was an abuse of the trial judge's discretion to exclude relevant expert psychological testimony (*State v. Chapple*, 1983). Subsequently, several federal courts of appeal advanced similar views. Although judicial opinion is by no means uniform on the point, it is fair to say that there is a discernible trend toward admitting relevant expert testimony, unless it carries substantial disadvantages (*People v. MacDonald*, 1984; *United States v. Downing*, 1985).

Courts that have favored admissibility have pointed to the special need for expert testimony in cases that raise the possibility of psychological phenomena, such as the forgetting curve, unconscious transference, and postevent information, with which jurors are likely to be unfamiliar. The existence of other evidence corroborating the eyewitness's account has also been a factor in determining whether the refusal to admit expert testimony requires reversal.

Courts have shown an enhanced willingness to admit expert testimony when the expert's observations are general and do not purport to comment on the accuracy of the particular witness testifying in the case on trial. In general, the analytical framework provided by the U.S. Court of Appeals for the Third Circuit in *United States v. Downing* (1985) can stand as a summary version of the way in which most courts now approach the issue of admissibility:

> First, the evidence must survive preliminary scrutiny in the course of an in limine proceeding conducted by the district judge. This threshold inquiry . . . is essentially a balancing test, centering on two factors: (1) the reliability of the scientific principles upon which the expert testimony rests, hence the

potential of the testimony to aid the jury in reaching an accurate resolution of a disputed issue; and (2) the likelihood that the testimony may in some way mislead or overwhelm the jury. Second, admission depends upon the "fit," i.e., upon a specific proffer showing that scientific research has established the particular features of the eyewitness testimony involved may have impaired the accuracy of those identifications.

Even the most avid partisans of expert testimony cannot claim that it is a panacea for the problems implicit in the eyewitness's encounters with the legal system. The more vociferously one argues that it is safe to admit expert testimony, the more one is forced to consider whether part of that safety lies in the fact that no one is paying much attention to the testimony anyway. There is no question that case-by-case analysis not only uncovers cases where expert testimony is sufficiently helpful to justify the time, effort, and money it consumes, but it also uncovers cases where it is not justified.

The legal debate over the admissibility of expert psychological testimony is accompanied by a similar but distinct debate within the psychological community, which concerns the professional propriety of testimony concerning eyewitness performance. All psychologists agree that there is more research to be done in the field; some feel that the existence of gaps does not excuse psychologists from sharing with the legal system as much as is understood (Loftus, 1986). Other psychologists believe that the incomplete state of psychological knowledge argues against participation.

It is important to understand that the doubts concerning the propriety of expert testimony are founded as much upon the psychologists' perceptions of the legal system as upon doubts concerning the validity of particular experiments. Psychologists on both sides of the expert testimony debate enjoy generally good relations with each other and benefit from a lively dialogue concerning the significance of ongoing research (Loftus, 1986; McCloskey & Egeth, 1983b). All are agreed that the area is an important one and that research should continue. The dispute is over whether it can be constructively continued within the intensely adversarial atmosphere of the trial courts. Psychologists who are wary of allowing psychologists to assume the role of expert witness express two levels of concern. The first of these focuses on the potentially distorting impact of partisan expert testimony on individual cases; the second focuses on the damage that partisan psychological testimony in a relatively controversial area might inflict on the prestige of the profession.

Opponents of expert testimony seem to envision something like the following situation. A psychologist is tempted by a vigorous lawyer to overstate psychological findings concerning eyewitness error. That lawyer portrays the psychologist as a magician. The jury assents to that portrayal and accepts the erroneous psychology, at least until the opposing lawyer argues that psychologists are not magicians at all but rather charlatans. Perhaps the opposing lawyer will call an expert witness of his own to prove that the first psychologist is a knave or a fool. (For opponents, one potential solution—an expert called by the court rather than the parties—is no solution at all. It simply results in one witness being abused by two lawyers rather than two eyewitnesses being abused by one lawyer each.) The ultimate result, the opponents hold, will be a jury awash in pointless skepticism concerning eyewitness performance and unwarranted cynicism about the ethics of psychological researchers.

Such situations are certainly worth avoiding, but it is difficult to believe that they will arise with great frequency. It seems unduly pessimistic, for example, to expect that psychologists will routinely be prepared to risk the professional ignominy that overstated testimony (in an area where contradiction is readily at hand) will inevitably bring. It also seems to underestimate the resources of the adversary process and to overestimate the credulity of jurors to suppose that whenever psychologists testify erroneously, their testimony will be swallowed without question in the courtroom.

Moreover, the damage to the prestige of the profession that is anticipated as a result of a battle of psychological experts may be a phantom. Medical doctors, economists, metallurgists, and engineers all regularly find themselves involved in forensic battles, and none of their professions has been crippled as a result. The only battles of experts that have produced observable skepticism about particular fields concern those fields (such as clinical psychology and forensic psychiatry) that require relatively subjective, diagnostic tasks not embodied in testimony concerning the eyewitness. Indeed, it seems at least arguable that the honest expression of conflicting views among psychologists will portray a profession prepared to learn and grow and enhance the prestige of the profession, whether it occurs in the courtroom or in the pages of professional journals (Levine, 1974).

Even the strong belief that testimony can be safely provided, however, does not answer the question of whether it should be provided. There is no doubt that expert testimony, in terms of money and time alone, is extremely costly. That cost may be justified, but only if the increase in dollars and hours results in a corresponding decrease in the likelihood of error and the cost of the error when it occurs (Posner, 1978). Unfortunately, that crucial question can only be answered by rigorous, case-by-case analysis. There will be cases in which the traditional tools of the trial process succeed in modulating the impact of eyewitness testimony and confining the possibility of error at an acceptable level. There will be other cases in which the traditional tools do not suffice. There will be still other cases in which a potential for error that might be acceptable in another context (e.g., a simple assault prosecution) becomes intolerable because of the cost of the error should it occur (e.g., in a capital case). As appealing as a categorical, across-the-board answer to the expert witness controversy may be, it cannot be the correct answer for every case. The case-by-case process of arriving at that answer argues strongly for efforts at mutual education by the legal and psychological professions.

CONCLUSION

When one steps back and views the legal system's response to the psychological study of eyewitness performance, the impression is one of an immense, ungainly, jury-rigged mechanism, constructed from a number of unrelated protective devices, that nevertheless may work pretty well some of the time and well enough most of the time. However, in evaluating the legal mechanisms provided for curing the problems in eyewitness testimony, it is impossible to escape the conclusion that the best solution is to prevent the problems at the outset (see Chapter 2 for a detailed description of identification procedures).

The opportunities and responsibility for achieving that goal fall on the investigative community, which typically encounters the eyewitness long before the legal system becomes involved. Although previously it seemed important to focus on slipshod law enforcement practices as the most prevalent cause of misidentifications, now it seems obvious that a focus on investigative professionalism presents the best hope for a cure.

REFERENCES

Amsterdam, A., Segal, B., & Miller, M. (1983). *Trial manual 3 for the defense of criminal cases.* Philadelphia: ALI-ABA.

Brewer v. Williams, 430 U.S. 387 (1977).

Convis, F. (1983). Testifying about testimony: Psychological evidence on perceptual and memory factors affecting the credibility of witnesses. *Duquesne Law Review, 21,* 579–594.

Doyle, J. M. (1984). Applying lawyers' expertise to scientific experts: Some thoughts about trial court analysis of the prejudicial effects of admitting and excluding scientific evidence. *William and Mary Law Review, 25,* 619–658.

Dunning, E., Ellsworth, R., & Ross, R. (1980). Effect of choosing an incorrect photograph on later identification by an eyewitness. *Journal of Applied Psychology, 65,* 16–29.

Edwards, J., & VonWinterfeldt, E. (1986). Cognitive illusions and their implications for law. *Southern California Law Review, 59,* 225–271.

Frye v. United States, 293 F.2d 1013 (D.C. Cir. 1923).

Green v. Loggins, 614 F.2d 219 (9th Cir. 1980).

Gross, S. R. (1987). Loss of innocence: Eyewitness identification and proof of guilt. *Journal of Legal Studies, 26,* 395–452.

Ibn-Tamas v. United States, 407 A.2d 626 (D.C. 1979).

Imwinkelried, E. (1983). The standard for admitting scientific evidence: A critique from the perspective of juror psychology. *Villanova Law Review, 28,* 554–587.

Johnson, S., (1984). Cross-Racial Identification In Criminal Cases, Cornell Law Review, 69, 934–989.

Levine, B., & Tapp, J. L. (1973). The psychology of criminal identification: The gap from Wade to Kirby. *University of Pennsylvania Law Review*, 121, 1079–2009.
Levine, M. (1974). Scientific method and the adversary model: Some preliminary thoughts. *American Psychologist*, 29, 661–677.
Loftus, E. F. (1986). Ten years in the life of an expert witness. *Law and Human Behavior*, 10, 241–263.
Loftus, E. F., & Doyle, J. M. (1987). *Eyewitness testimony: Civil and criminal.* New York: Kluwer Law Book Publishers.
Manson v. Braithwaite, 432 U.S. 98 (1977).
McCloskey, M., & Egeth, H. (1983a). Eyewitness identification: What can a psychologist tell a jury? *American Psychologist*, 38, 573–575.
McCloskey, M., & Egeth, H. (1983b). A time to speak, or a time to keep silence? *American Psychologist*, 38, 573–575.
McCormick, E. (1972). *McCormick On Evidence.* Minneapolis: West Publishing.
Moore v. Illinois, 434 U.S. 220 (1977).
National Jury Project, (1983). *Jurywork.*
Posner, R., (1973). An economic approach to legal procedure and administration. *Journal of Legal Studies*, 2, 399–421.
People v. Lutz, 431 N.E.2d 753 (Ill. 1982).
People v. MacDonald, 37 Cal.3d 351 (1984).
People v. Wright, 729 P.2d 280 (Cal. 1980).
Simons v. State, 389 So.2d 262 (Fla. Dist. App. 1980).
Smith v. United States, 389 A.2d 1356 (D.C. 1978).
State v. Chapple, 660 P.2d 1208 (Ariz. 1983).
United States v. Addison, 498 F.2d 741 (D.C. Cir. 1974).
United States v. Amaral, 488 F.2d 1148 (9th Cir. 1973).
United States v. Ash, 413 U.S. 300 (1977).
United States v. Downing, 753 F.2d 616 (3d Cir. 1985).
United States v. Hodges, 515 F.2d 650 (7th Cir. 1975).
United States v. Jones, 477 F.2d 1213 (D.C. Cir. 1973).
United States v. Phillips, 640 F.2d 87 (7th Cir.), *cert. denied*, 991 (1981).
United States v. Telfaire, 469 F.2d 552 (D.C. Cir. 1972).
United States v. Wade, 388 U.S. 218 (1967).
Wigmore, J. H. (1974). *Evidence.* Boston: Little, Brown.
Woocher, J. (1977). Did your eyes deceive you? Expert psychological testimony on the unreliability of eyewitness identification. *Stanford Law Review*, 29, 969–1021.

Interviewing and Assessing Witnesses, Victims, and Suspects

II

Investigative Hypnosis 5

Martin Reiser

In 1976 in Chowchilla, California, 26 children and the driver of their school bus were kidnapped at gunpoint by three masked men. They were taken to a quarry and buried 6 ft underground. Hours later, they were able to dig themselves out and were rescued. Despite questioning many of the victims, the Federal Bureau of Investigation could not elicit specific descriptions of the suspects or other pertinent information. Ed Ray, the bus driver, agreed to a hypnosis interview and was able to recall all but one digit of the license plate on the suspect's white van. This led to the apprehension of three males who were subsequently convicted of the crime (Hatton, 1978; *People v. Woods et al.*, 1977).

A 15-year-old girl hitchhiking alone in northern California was picked up by a man driving a van. He tied her up, sexually abused and raped her, and then chopped off both of her forearms with an ax. He then stuffed her into a highway drainage tunnel. After he had gone, the victim crawled out, stopped a passing vehicle, and was taken to a hospital. Highly traumatized, she was able to recall only limited details of the suspect and the events. Later, during a hypnosis interview, the victim recalled the suspect's name, his occupation, and other items of conversation.

She described the vehicle and was able to assist the police artist in constructing a composite drawing. This information, which was subsequently corroborated by physical evidence and other witnesses, led to the identification and conviction of the criminal (*People v. Singleton*, 1980; Vollmer, 1979).

The sole available witness to a homicide was admittedly intoxicated on alcohol and other drugs during the crime event. When questioned by detectives, she could recall very little, stating, "I was bombed out of my skull." At a dead end, the detectives wondered if hypnosis might help her to recall the events. During a hypnosis interview, she remembered details of a drug transaction between her deceased boyfriend and a suspect. These details included conversation, clothing, and a physical description. A composite drawing made from her descriptions led to the identification of several suspects and the validation of her recall under hypnosis (Reiser, 1974). This case was important because it lent support to the hypothesis that recall is enhanced when the original learning state is recreated (Swanson & Kinsbourne, 1979). It also helped confirm Hilgard's (1977) concept of the hidden observer; which proposes that the observing portion of the ego remains aware of what is happening in the real world regardless of the level of regression experienced by the hypnotized subject and that that information is processed at conscious and subconscious levels simultaneously.

The use of hypnosis interviews to assist in overcoming problems of witnesses' memories in these cases provides striking examples of the effectiveness of investigative hypnosis for developing useful information in criminal cases. Since there is substantial debate about the validity and utility of information obtained during hypnosis interviews, the procedures and guidelines for such applications will be presented next, in order to provide descriptions of the specific techniques and the constraints on how they are used in actual practice. This is followed by a brief history and background of hypnosis and extensive discussions of the controversies surrounding the phenomena associated with hypnosis, the investigative utility of hypnosis interviews, and some of the legal and political issues related to its uses in the context of criminal investigation.

THE INVESTIGATIVE HYPNOSIS PROCESS

The investigative hypnosis process can be divided into seven phases (Reiser, 1980). The first phase involves preliminary activity that must be accomplished before the hypnosis session proper. This includes reviewing basic crime information with the case investigators in order to learn about the time frame, the setting, and other key parameters of the situation. It is useful to briefly outline the areas of information desired by the investigators, such as vehicle, weapon, location, conversations, and descriptions of suspects. It is also desirable to review the overall context of the decision to do a hypnosis session and to determine if any special consultation is necessary because of brain injury, hearing impairment, drugs or medications, or psychiatric problems. Logistical arrangements can be established, including time, location, and whether the setting may affectively impact the subject.

The hypnosis session proper usually consists of six stages, beginning with the preinduction phase. Audiotaping and/or videotaping equipment should be running and in plain view when the subject enters the office. Lapel microphones are attached; the date, time, place, and subject's name are announced; introductions are made; taping procedures are explained; and the subject's reactions are discussed. The identity and role of each person present during the hypnosis session should be explained. They may include a police artist, a case investigator, or a researcher. Except in special situations such as a small child needing support or security, family members or friends should be excluded from the session because of possible inhibiting and negative emotional effects on the subject. Comfort needs should be addressed, including the level of light in the room, the temperature, removing contact lenses, and bathroom use.

Building rapport with the witness is important before proceeding with the hypnosis. There should also be a discussion of common misinformation and misconceptions about hypnosis and a brief explanation of the reasons for forgetting and of the possibilities of recall. Verifying the subject's motivation for the hypnosis interview is helpful, as is giving a preview of what will be done during the interview in order to allay anxiety and demystify the process. The subject should have an opportunity to raise any questions before beginning the induction. Observations of the witness during the preinduction phase will assist the hypnotist in choosing hypnosis and recall techniques appropriate to the subject. Typical techniques used during the induction phase include eye fixation, the Spiegel eye roll, deep breathing, muscle relaxation, and repetition of instructions to relax.

The next stage is the deepening phase, in which the subject is assisted in reaching an optimal level of comfort and functioning. Typical deepening techniques include counting from ten to zero; imagining going down several floors by elevator, escalator, or stairway; and ideomotor responses such as arm levitation, opening and closing the eyes, and the use of imagery that may include scenes of a beach, the country, or mountains.

In beginning the stage of information elicitation, the crime scene and time parameters are established for recall. Permissive instructions for self-paced recall are used, with the subject being told to recall as much or as little as is safe and feasible. Techniques commonly used to elicit information include the induced dream, the television technique, ideomotor finger signals, and time regression. Utilizing a police artist to construct a composite drawing of a suspect during this stage can be very effective. Identikits provide less flexibility, but they may be more readily available for the composite work. A phase of permissive posthypnotic suggestions can be used to increase the possibility of later recall or to prepare for any follow-up hypnosis sessions.

The dehypnotization phase includes instructions for feeling calm, relaxed, and normal in every way. It can be useful to indicate to the subject that over time it may become easier to deal with the crime experience in a more constructive way. A general instruction for feeling normal in every way will help remove any temporary suggestions for lightness, heaviness, or ideomotor responses that were given during hypnosis. The subject can either be aided out of hypnosis by counting or by instruction to come out at "your own rate, fully awake and alert, feeling clearheaded, refreshed, relaxed, and perfectly normal in every way. This will have been a most interesting experience for you."

Guidelines

The following guidelines have been utilized at the Los Angeles Police Department to help ensure that hypnosis interviews are conducted in a professional and ethical manner:

1. The hypnosis project director screens all requests for investigative hypnosis to determine appropriateness.
2. The hypnosis session is conducted by a qualified hypno-investigator or health professional.
3. Informed consent is obtained from the subject or guardian.
4. The entire hypnosis session is recorded on audiotape or videotape.
5. The person conducting the hypnosis session shall not be otherwise involved in the conduct of the investigation in which the subject was a victim or witness.
6. Hypnosis interviews will be conducted with volunteer witnesses but not with suspects or defendants.
7. The welfare of the hypnosis subject is primary and takes precedence over any other considerations. (Los Angeles Police department Hypnosis Guidelines. Undated.)

Some federal agencies have developed similar guidelines for utilization of investigative hypnosis (Ault, 1980; Hibler, 1984).

BRIEF HISTORY

During the 1950s sporadic efforts were made to train police in hypnosis techniques for investigative purposes and to have them utilize this tool in-house (Arons, 1967). Apparently, those attempts were premature, and the application of hypnosis to the law enforcement domain remained infrequent and restricted to the province of a few interested mental health consultants and lay hypnotists (Dorcus, 1960).

In 1972 I began using hypnosis interviewing in selected major crime cases at the Los Angeles Police Department (Reiser, 1974). This was initiated by a request from detectives who were at a dead end in a homicide case but were convinced that the key witness had perceived important details not recalled during routine interviews. Success in this and several subsequent cases led to an interest among other detectives and a significant increase in requests for hypnosis interviews (Reiser, 1976).

Two years of hypnosis experience with witnesses, 11 years of clinical hypnosis background, prior success in training paraprofessionals to do therapy (Sperber & Reiser, 1971), and a jammed work schedule led me to propose that experienced detectives be trained in hypnosis-interviewing techniques (Reiser, 1980). A 1-year research demonstration project was designed with the assistance of an outside panel of professional consultants. Initial administrative skepticism was eventually overcome, allowing the feasibility study to proceed. Begun in June 1975, the project handled approximately 70 major crime cases during the 1-year period. The program was considered a success, and the investigative hypnosis model was subsequently incorporated into other existing investigative procedures of the Department (Ross, 1977).

In 1976 requests from a variety of other criminal justice professionals led to the presentation of investigative hypnosis training outside of the Los Angeles Police Department (Reiser & Nielsen, 1980). Since that time, it is estimated that approximately 1,500 criminal justice and mental health professionals representing local, state, and federal agencies have been trained (Gilbert, 1980).

MYTHS, MISINFORMATION, AND MISUNDERSTANDINGS

The fiction of mind control by hypnosis is one of the most pervasive myths about hypnosis (Orne, 1972). Du Maurier's novel *Trilby* (1895) graphically established the popular image of the sinister hypnotist using powerful mental magic to exert control over the limp, compliant subject (Schneck, 1978). However, the ability to be hypnotized is present in most individuals to some degree. The hypnotist is essentially a guide or teacher who instructs the subject in how to tap into this latent ability. In some instances the instruction may come primarily from books or tapes. Since all hypnosis is basically self-hypnosis, the subject is taught how to manage his or her own trance capability. This applies to the learning of either self- or hetero-hypnosis (Spiegel & Spiegel, 1978).

Another widely held myth about hypnosis is that it has truth-detecting or truth-compelling capability. In fact, neither hypnosis nor any known drugs can compel or guarantee truthfulness (Gottschalk, 1961; Spiegel, 1980). The hypnotic subject retains volitional control in hypnosis. Therefore, the same considerations affecting truthfulness and accuracy of perceptions are operative in the hypnotized and nonhypnotized subject (Hibbard & Worring, 1981).

The myth of the dangerousness of hypnosis still abounds, though, among health professionals as well as the public. Occasional instances of misuse of the hypnosis situation, usually in the psychotherapeutic or entertainment areas, have been reported (Weitzenhoffer, 1979; West & Deckert, 1965).

However, there is no substantive evidence that hypnosis per se is dangerous. Janet (1925) said, "Even in bad hands, suggestion and hypnotism do not seem to have been able to do much harm" (p. 346). Cheek and Le Cron (1968) stated that more harm results from ignorance of hypnosis than is possible when it is used intelligently. Conn (1972) examined this question in detail and emphatically concluded that the danger attributed to hypnosis is mythical.

Misinformation about hypnosis may be based on ignorance or on emotional, guild, or propaganda motives. In the investigative hypnosis realm, such misinformation focuses on the problems supposedly inherent in police use of this technique. One widely held point of view is that despite training, police officers cannot safely and professionally use investigative hypnosis techniques (Perry & Laurence, 1983). The objections raised include the fear that police will coerce confessions from defendants, that they will wittingly or unwittingly suggest information to the subject, and that they are not therapists and cannot deal with the traumatized witness adequately (Diamond, 1980; Orne, 1979; Udolf, 1983).

Because police do not use hypnosis with suspects or defendants, it is unlikely that confessions will be coerced by this means. As Conn (1982) pointed out, the coercive power of hypnosis is chimerical. In most cases where investigative hypnosis is requested, there are no suspects in mind and the police are searching for leads because little investigative information is available. It is impossible to suggest to a witness what is not known by the investigator. The notion that police are unqualified to use hypnosis interviewing because the subject often has been traumatized and police are not mental health professionals seems difficult to defend. It is the stated job of the police to assist the victims of crime in the community, including those who have been brutalized (Gottfredson, Reiser, & Tsegaye-Spates, 1987). With specific training in investigative hypnosis, officers merely have another tool to use in working with witnesses and victims. Spiegel (1980) stated that in the area of police investigation, it is the psychologist or psychiatrist who is the layperson.

The failure to differentiate between the phenomena of investigative hypnosis and those relevant to therapeutic hypnosis has resulted in unnecessary confusion and argument about their problems, dangers, and outcomes (Reiser, 1984). Both of these specialties utilize hypnosis techniques; however, hypnotherapy and investigative hypnosis are distinct areas of application. Hypnotherapy does not usually concentrate on factual recall but on impression and affect (Kroger, 1977). The hypnotherapist is more interested in dreams, fantasies, and unconscious material. In therapy, the task orientation and demand characteristics are aimed at identifying and resolving conflict.

In contrast to therapeutic uses of hypnosis, investigative hypnosis focuses on the recall of details of a recent, actual crime event, one that is often traumatic in nature. The information-eliciting instructions are designed to maximize the possibility of accurate recall by witnesses. Though the same tool is used in therapy and investigation, different training and expertise are required of practitioners for these distinctly different applications.

Milton Erickson strongly supported the training of police officers in investigative hypnosis techniques. He recognized the clear distinction between hypnotherapy and police investigation

(Reiser, 1982). Several misunderstandings exist about investigative hypnosis that appear to be based on outdated information, confusion among basic constructs, or inappropriate extrapolation of laboratory data to field situations.

In the field of criminal investigation, it is my experience that competent detectives trained in investigative hypnosis interviewing are usually the most qualified to work with victims and witnesses in major crime cases when posttraumatic amnesia is a barrier to investigation (Reiser, 1980). In exceptional cases involving some child victims or witnesses having psychiatric problems or severe physical injuries, it may be desirable to use a trained mental health professional to do the hypnosis interview. During my 15 years of experience with investigative hypnosis at the Los Angeles Police Department, virtually all of the witnesses who participated subsequently reported the experience as positive and often as having unexpected benefits (Los Angeles Police Department, 1982).

Perhaps the major construct misunderstood about the use of hypnosis is suggestibility. The belief that hypersuggestibility automatically occurs during hypnosis was popularized initially by Charcot (1877) and later reiterated by Hull (1933). Currently, there is a scientific consensus that suggestibility plays a relatively small role in hypnotic processes (Bowers, 1977; Chertok, 1981; Frankel, 1976; Hilgard, 1965, 1981; Sheehan & Perry, 1976). Almost a century ago, Bernheim (1890/1980) stated that hypnosis and suggestibility were independent of each other. More recently, Erickson, Rossi, and Rossi (1976) reaffirmed the fact that hypersuggestibility does not necessarily occur in trance states: "This is a major misconception that has frustrated and discouraged many workers in the past and has impeded the development of hypnosis as science. Trance is a special state that intensifies the therapeutic relationships and focuses the patient's attention on inner realities. Trance does not insure the acceptance of suggestions" (p. 312).

Kroger (1977) also cited the universal nature of suggestion and belief systems in everyday life. He pointed out that people are suggestible in varying degrees, with or without hypnosis. Common examples are the power of suggestion in advertising and the placebo effect in doctor-patient relationships. These effects rely on trust and belief in the powerful authority (Conn, 1959). Other everyday examples of nonhypnotic suggestion are religious conversions, faith healing, confidence games, and love relationships. Additionally, studies of voodoo, attitudes, beliefs and values, communications, and general systems theory all indicate that suggestibility is ubiquitous in normal waking life (Barber, 1961; Rokeach, 1968; Von Bertalanffy, 1968; Watzlawick, 1978).

Hypnotic suggestibility is often confused with two other variables having distinct properties. One is hypnotic ability, an innate capacity of the individual to utilize hypnosis; the other is hypnotic susceptibility, which is related to the subject's motivation and trust in the hypnotist in the particular situation (Barber, 1980; Hilgard, 1977).

Overall, it seems that suggestibility is a universal phenomenon that is neither unique to hypnosis nor equated with it. Trust in an authority figure and belief in the information communicated appear to be the key factors giving rise to suggestibility, with or without hypnosis.

CONTROVERSIAL ISSUES IN INVESTIGATIVE HYPNOSIS

Memory Theory

Recent research on memory has focused on processes of acquisition, encoding, storage, and retrieval of information. The conditions under which information can be deeply or permanently stored in its originally acquired form are being examined (Lachman, Lachman, & Butterfield, 1979; McGaugh, 1980; Spear, 1978; Tulving, 1972). Long-term memory, amnesia, and hypermnesia are of central interest in the area of investigative hypnosis. To date, the data suggest that episodic material involving imagery seems to be processed more deeply and permanently (Craik & Lockhart, 1972; Paivio, 1969). Empirical observations and research on flashbulb memories (Benderly, 1981; Brown & Kulik, 1977), eidetic images (Crawford, Wallace, & Slater, 1986;

Kihlstrom, 1981), flashbacks (Fischer, 1977), memorable events (Neisser, 1982; Rubin, 1982), and recall with traumatized witnesses (Dorcus, 1960; Reiser, 1980) suggest that hypermnesia is primarily a problem of retrieval strategies.

Recently, attention has been given to the fact that memory involves subconscious as well as conscious processes. Kihlstrom (1987) has stated, "One thing is now clear: Consciousness is not to be identified with any particular perceptual-cognitive function such as discriminative response to stimulation, perception, memory, or the higher mental processes involved in judgment or problem-solving. All of these functions can take place outside of phenomenal awareness" (p. 237). Dual recording of information at both levels simultaneously (Hilgard, 1977) makes the issue of accessing subconscious memory very important (Cheek, 1975; Raikov, 1982). Since a witness may not know consciously what has been registered in memory (Key, 1973), retrieval strategies such as hypnosis become an important research tool (Reiser, 1980). Evans (1988) stated, "The easy reversibility of the amnesia suggests that the experienced events may be stored with minimal organization in a temporary memory buffer, in which the retrieval case itself is the primary organizational strategy that is to be used when it is appropriate to retrieve the material" (p. 186).

Critics of investigative hypnosis (Laurence & Perry, 1988; Loftus, 1979; Orne, 1979) have stated that law enforcement practitioners hold a mistaken theory of memory, the taperecorder model proposed by Penfield (1952). However, there is a long history of such theories in the literature. Nilsson (1979) discusses the two critical factors leading to current memory research that appeared in the 1950s. One was the view of information based on cybernetics and communications theory (Miller, Galanter, & Pribram, 1960), which made inevitable the notion of a memory system able to hold information from one occasion to another. The other factor having considerable impact on memory research was computer terminology (Broadbent, 1958). The concept of memory was translated into computer language, which led to the development of human information-processing theory. This led to an enormous amount of research and the formulation of numerous models and minitheories. The metaphor of the human being as information processor yielded the distinctions between short-term and long-term memory. It permitted the conceptualization of memory in new terms such as coding, storage, and retrieval (Tulving, 1979).

Cheek and LeCron (1968), working in the clinical hypnosis area, wrote, "Everything that has ever happened to us is stored in memory in complete detail, and hypnosis can bring out forgotten memories even back to infancy" (p. 90). However, the reconstruction model of memory is asserted by critics as the operative theory with proven validity. Craik and Jacoby (1979) discuss memory as state setting versus a trace system and agree that the memory-as-background theory can provide a basis for feelings of familiarity but does not allow a description of memory for specific episodes. They suggest that the cognitive system can work in a variety of modes, ranging from comprehension, in which past learning serves as background, to remembering, in which new inputs (retrieval cues) act as the background and the attention focus is on the restoration of some encoded aspect of past experience. "The event will be well retrieved to the extent that the retrieval cue can be elaborated in turn to reconstruct the specific target encoding and not other, similar encodings" (p. 163).

In fact, there is no single proven model of memory. Neisser (1978) and Tulving (1979) point out that despite 100 years of laboratory-based research on memory, we still do not have agreement among the majority of reachers and theorists concerning the concepts that are important or necessary. The effect of investigative hypnosis techniques on recall of meaningful, traumatic events has received relatively scant attention from researchers. Ecologically valid laboratory studies and crime-related field research are sorely needed to better answer some of the unanswered memory questions.

Hypermnesia

Whether or not hypnosis can improve recall of information stored in memory has been debated for years among laboratory researchers (Augustynek, 1977; Barber & Calverly, 1966; Cooper & London, 1973; De Piano & Salzberg, 1981; Dhanens & Lundy, 1975; Nogrady, McConkey, & Perry, 1985; Putnam, 1979; Sears, 1954; Zelig & Beidleman, 1981). The controversy spilled over into the investigative hypnosis arena, with experts taking positions for hypnosis (Dorcus, 1960; Geiselman, Fisher, & MacKinnon, 1985; Kroger & Douce, 1979; Raginsky, 1969; Ready, 1986; Reiser, 1974; Sanders, Gansler, & Riesman, 1987; Stager, 1974; Yuille & Kim, 1987) and against (Diamond, 1980; Frankel, 1988; Orne, 1979; Sloane, 1981; Udolf, 1983).

Normal forgetting appears to be linked to cognitive associational processes over time (Postman & Underwood, 1973). Amnesias following distressing situations are seen most vividly in posttraumatic stress disorders resulting from war, crime events, or physical injuries (Menninger, Mayman, & Pruyser, 1963).

Amnesias have also been studied in laboratory investigations of memory (Kihlstrom & Evans, 1979). In retrograde amnesia cases, an individual in a fugue state forgets his or her basic identity and associated memories. Hypnosis techniques have been used successfully to lift the amnesia and recover the split-off memories (Brunn, 1968; Dorcus, 1960; Stross & Shevrin, 1968). Fischer (1977) examined altered states of consciousness and identified an area of amnesia between state of intoxication and one of sobriety. He postulated that the recovery of memory from any specific state or level involves the particular spatiotemporal neuronal-synaptic firing pattern that prevailed during the initial experience, and that this must be reinstated. In the same way, Fischer believes that amnesia may follow a violent crime. Dorcus reported that the likelihood of accurate witness recall was positively related to the level of emotional involvement of the subject during the event.

Recently, studies of victimology have broadened the categories of traumatic events that may lead to posttraumatic stress effects (Task Force Report on Victims of Crime and Violence, 1984). Victims of crime and some witnesses are often severely traumatized, leading to the use of the defenses of denial, dissociation, and repression (Spiegel, 1986). The need to ward off the unpleasant memories results in the conscious forgetting of crime details important to the investigation. However, the fended-off feelings and information remain at a subconscious level, dissociated but often in unaltered form. The task of the investigator is to assist the subject to retrieve this information while protecting the safety needs of the individual. In these cases, investigative hypnosis interviewing is the method of choice.

There have been several recent reviews of the literature on hypnotic hypermnesia. Relinger (1984) described three types of studies: recall of nonmeaningful material, recall of meaningful material, and laboratory simulations of forensic situations. He concluded that the literature clearly shows that hypnosis does enhance the recall of meaningful material when recall is measured in a free narrative format. Orne, Whitehouse, Dinges, and Orne (1988) acknowledged that contextually meaningful material tends to enhance hypnotically aided memory. Geiselman and Machlovitz (1987) reviewed 35 experiments in 27 articles on hypnotic recall published between 1930 and 1985. Twenty-two of the 35 experiments reported significantly more correct information with hypnosis, 10 reported no effect with hypnosis, and 3 reported significantly less information with hypnosis. Another recent independent review of the hypnosis literature similarly concluded that only recall of meaningful material yielded positive outcomes, and almost uniformly so (Erdelyi, Dinges, Orne, Whitehouse, & Orne, 1985).

Eyewitness Testimony

Those who oppose the testimony of previously hypnotized witnesses claim that a variety of memory distortions, increased confidence, and loss of critical judgment make such evidence inadmissible (Diamond, 1980; Orne, Dinges, & Orne, 1984; Perry & Laurence, 1983). One of the complications in the debate is that ordinary eyewitness testimony in itself is often unreliable (see Chapters 1, 2, and 3) since ordinary memory retrieval is also problematical (Baddeley, 1976; Bahrick, 1979; Ellison & Buckhout, 1981; Neisser, 1978; Nilsson, 1979). Typical problems of ordinary eyewitness recall and testimony involve the quality of the original perceptions, witness responses to leading questions, degree of witness trauma, confidence as related to accuracy, and appropriateness of recall cuing techniques (Bregman & McAllister, 1982; Deffenbacher, 1980; Loftus, 1979; Parker, 1980).

Memory distortions attributed to hypnotized witnesses include confabulation, loss of critical judgment, and hardening of memory (Diamond, 1980; Orne, 1979). Confabulation, the filling in of gaps in memory with invented material, is possible with or without hypnosis. However, the idea that confabulation is inevitable in hypnosis (Diamond, 1980; Orne, 1979) does not appear to be supported by the available data (Relinger, 1984). The confabulation concept was extrapolated from hypnotherapy, age regression, and false information experiments (Orne, 1951; Putnam, 1979; Udolf, 1983) and applied uncritically to the area of investigative hypnosis (Reiser, 1985).

The scientific literature on confabulation is extremely limited. Griffin (1980) compared recall of hypnotized and waking subjects at intervals of 2 to 30 days and found that hypnotized witnesses did not confabulate more than nonhypnotized witnesses. Rainer (1983) found no specific distortion for hypnotized subjects. Overall, data showed that the acceptance of misleading information was the same for hypnotized or nonhypnotized subjects, and for high or low susceptibility subjects. Sheehan (1988) reviewed the research literature having reliable and consistent findings and concluded there is no general, pervasive distortion effect for hypnosis. "Evidence on the whole has been against, rather than in support of, the hypothesis that hypnosis generally creates inherent distortion in memory reports" (p. 99).

Only recently have studies specifically examined this issue in the investigative hypnosis realm. These data show that there is little difference in the number of inaccurate responses between hypnotized and nonhypnotized subjects if misleading manipulations are not used (Ready, 1986; Timm, 1981, 1983).

Unlike the laboratory, witnesses to actual crimes are positively motivated toward recall of a meaningful recent life event having emotional and psychological impact. Independent corroboration of information recalled by witnesses and recent controlled studies having ecological validity do not support the confabulation thesis for investigative hypnosis (Geiselman et al., 1985; Reiser, 1982; Yuille & McEwan, 1985). The confabulation and misperception questions have been focused more directly in the area of eyewitness identifications. The frequency of misidentification of suspects by nonhypnotized witnesses indicates that the problem is actually a generic one involving cognitive functions such as perception, attitudes, and beliefs (Buckhout, 1974; Loftus, 1979; Yarmey, 1979), rather than the hypnosis itself.

The misconceptions of loss of critical judgment, hardening of memory, and other notions about memory distortion that have been applied to investigative hypnosis are also derived from psychotherapy, age regression, and induced distortion situations. Relinger's (1984) review of the hypnosis literature does not reveal any general research support for the concept of loss of critical judgment in hypnosis. Orne's (1972) research showed that subjects retain their values, morality, and decision-making abilities while under hypnosis. Hilgard's (1977) neodissociation research reveals the operation of an observing, reality-connected part of the ego independent of the subject's hypnotic depth. Field experience in actual crime cases confirms that with investigative hypnosis, the subject retains the same critical judgment and decision-making abilities as before (Hibbard & Worring, 1981; Reiser, 1986).

It has been stated that hypnosis causes hardening of the memory and decreased accuracy of recall (Diamond, 1980; Orne, 1979). Recent research shows that in investigative hypnosis, subjects tend to recall more information about a meaningful crime event than do nonhypnotized subjects and that their recall is more accurate (Geiselman et al., 1985; Ready, 1986; Yuille & Kim, 1987). The results of numerous investigative hypnosis cases conducted by the author indicate that the hypnotized witnesses were usually able to differentiate what they remembered before, during, and after the hypnosis interview. They did not develop hardening of perceptions or become absolutely certain of their recall (Reiser, 1985). Individuals tended to utilize their preexisting level of cognitive abilities during and after the hypnosis experience. In general, the mere passage of time seemed to have a greater effect than hypnosis on uncertainty or certainty, just as with nonhypnotized subjects (Edmonston, 1981).

Yarmey (1979) pointed out that hypnotic memory performance is not different in kind from other memory states; it is susceptible to similar kinds of problems in recall. However, evidence is accumulating that recall during hypnosis interviewing is somewhat better than in the waking state (Stager & Lundy, 1985), particularly for traumatic, emotionally arousing events (Benderly, 1981; Fischer, 1977; Goldstein & Siprelle, 1970; Reiser, 1984). Bowers and Hilgard (1988) point out that "considerable care is needed to avoid attributing to hypnosis problems that really belong to the domain of memory per se. Only when the separate complexities of memory and hypnosis are appreciated are we apt to understand how they interact to engender specific mnemonic distortions and/or benefits" (p. 17).

A commonly misunderstood issue is the difference between witness truthfulness and the accuracy of witness testimony. Witnesses are sworn to tell the truth. However, honest perceptions can be distorted. In a legal context, absolute accuracy is not a requirement, only testimony having probative value. No testimony, whether from a hypnotized or a nonhypnotized witness, must be proven to be absolutely accurate in order to be admissible (Spector & Foster, 1977, 1979).

RESEARCH ON THE UTILITY OF INVESTIGATIVE HYPNOSIS

One of the primary difficulties with laboratory research in investigative hypnosis is that of limited ecological validity (Neisser, 1982). Further complicating the situation are research designs based on coercive questioning or the imparting of false information, or questionable sample size (Loftus, 1979; Putnam, 1979; Wagstaff, 1982). Few studies have adequately addressed such important questions as the meaningfulness and level of emotional arousal of the event, the utilization of retrieval for relevant information cues, the use of real police interviewers, and the testing of the claims of hardening of memory and the imposibility of cross-examination of witnesses after hypnosis interviewing.

Recently, several studies have attempted to address these issues by utilizing designs closer to real world conditions. Timm (1981) simulated an assassination and tested the 45 subjects for recall 2 months later under hypnosis or one of two nonhypnosis conditions. The results showed more accurate recall for the two experimental groups using hypnosis or regression. There was no increase in inaccurate information found with hypnosis interviewing.

Geiselman et al. (1985) compared the effects of hypnosis interviewing with cognitive and standard police interviews, using 89 subjects in a more ecologically valid controlled setting. Emotionally arousing police training films of violent crime scenes were shown to subjects, and experienced law enforcement personnel conducted all of the interviews 48 hr later. Both hypnosis and cognitive procedures elicited significantly more correct information than did standard police interviewing. The number of incorrect items was not different across the three interview conditions.

Yuille and McEwan (1985) showed a videotape of a simulated bank robbery to 72 subjects who were interviewed 1 week later in one of three states: hypnotized, relaxed, or waking. Interviewers utilized imagery or guided memory instructions. Misleading questions were included in the design, along with a photograph identification task and questions about the "live" context of the viewing room. Overall recall accuracy for the video and live events was high. Analysis of responses to the misleading questions showed that the hypnotized subjects were found not to be more susceptible to suggestion. Confidence of subjects on the photograph identification task correlated positively with the amount of information recalled and with the accuracy of choice. In this research, hypnosis did not aid memory; the accuracy of the hypnotized subjects was not statistically different from the other groups.

Yuille and McEwan (1985) suggested the possibility that hypnosis interviewing helps in situations involving emotionally disturbing events that cannot be ethically replicated in the laboratory. Although these findings did not support the use of hypnosis as a memory aid, they did not find any negative effects. Hypnosis subjects were not more susceptible to leading information, nor more likely to select a photograph from the photospread, or more prone to provide longer or more detailed responses than subjects in the other groups. This study did not reinforce the negative image in the existing literature on eyewitness memory. Recall accuracy averaged between 69% and 78% for the videotaped event and between 73% and 80% for the live event, which are better performances than reported previously.

Following the work of Geiselman et al. (1985) and Yuille and McEwan (1985), Ready (1986) examined the effects of hypnosis and guided memory on eyewitness recall and suggestibility. One hundred subjects were placed in an emotionally charged situation involving the expectation of being publicly evaluated on an impromptu speech that would be videotaped. They then watched a 6 min videotape of a student giving a speech and being harshly criticized by a person acting as a professor. Two days later, subjects' memories were tested by use of questionnaires and photograph lineups containing both leading and nonleading items. Subjects in the hypnosis conditions were not less accurate on suggestive questions or lineups. Also, they did not differ from controls on either leading or nonleading questions or in confidence about the accuracy of their responses. Hypnotized subjects were able to correctly identify the targets of photograph lineups at higher rates than controls, and confidence in lineup choices was not affected by hypnosis. Guided memory did not assist recall but did interact with hypnosis to improve recognition on one lineup. Motivational instructions did not influence subject behavior, but greater hypnotic susceptibility did aid accuracy of recall across all conditions.

The results of Ready's (1986) study contradicted prior research that found hypnotized subjects to be significantly less accurate than controls on recognition and recall tasks containing misleading information. Also, a hypnotically linked increase in subjects' confidence was not found. Smith (1983) had criticized early studies in this area because in each case the incorrect answer to leading questions was simply yes or no. She indicated that the results of these studies may only indicate that hypnotized subjects are more acquiescent than controls, rather than more accepting of misinformation, but Ready found that hypnosis subjects were not more acquiescent than controls.

The results of the Ready (1986) study also failed to support Orne's (1979) contention that the memory of hypnotized witnesses would be more easily distorted by suggestion than non-hypnotized witnesses. Ready found that hypnotized or not, most individuals' memory is distorted by indirect suggestion. Redston and Knox (1983) found that hypnotized subjects do not typically become very confident in the material they produce in hypnosis. Only one of eight previous studies had reported an increase in subject confidence due to hypnosis (Sheehan, Griggs, & McCann, 1984), and Ready's study found no evidence for Orne's (1979) assertion that hypnosis will increase witness confidence. Crawford and Allen (1983) found evidence for increased memory accuracy for pictorial material in hypnosis and Erdelyi (1988) stated that a hypermnesic effect with pictures is reliable and very powerful.

Studies that examined the effect of hypnosis on photograph lineup responses lack consistency in their findings. Sanders and Simmon (1983) found that hypnosis subjects did comparatively poorly on both regular and suggestive lineups. In three other studies of lineups, hypnosis subjects were equally accurate or more accurate than controls (Ready, 1986; Wagstaff, 1982; Yuille & McEwan, 1985).

Overall, the Ready (1986) study did not support any of Orne's (1979) contentions about the negative side effects of hypnosis. His study also failed to support Wagstaff's (1982) suppositions that the use of motivational instructions can explain most of the effect of hypnosis on recall, or that the relaxation resulting from hypnosis may improve memory. Ready found that subjects who were very relaxed at recall were less accurate than those who experienced a moderate degree of arousal. Hypnosis, not relaxation, appeared to account for the memory enhancement found in his study.

Another interesting finding reported by Ready (1986) was that subjects who were high in hypnotic susceptibility had an advantage on the recall tasks, regardless of the condition tested. The highest correlations between susceptibility to hypnosis and task performance were scattered among the nonhypnosis conditions. This calls into question the practice of separating subjects into treatments using a hypnotic susceptibility rating. Ready also found a curvilinear relationship between arousal at the time of recall and arousal during the original events. Subjects who were moderately anxious at time of recall had consistently higher accuracy scores than subjects in the high- and low-anxiety groups. This suggests that it is important to induce an optimal amount of arousal in the witness in order to maximize accurate recognition and recall.

Shields and Knox (1986) studied the concept of depth of processing of information, as formulated by Craik and Lockhart (1972), and its effect on hypermnesia. In the first of their two studies, 40 subjects rated high in hypnotic susceptibility were divided into a hypnosis group and a relaxed/motivated group. Twenty subjects rated low in hypnotic susceptibility were used as a simulating group. Instructional cues were used to cause shallow or deep processing of a list of words. As predicted, hypnotic hypermnesia was found for words processed at a deep level. The superior performance of the hypnotized group as compared to the simulating group indicated that the gain was not simply a result of complying with the demand characteristics of the experiment. Rather, the improvement in memory appeared to be related to the instructions for hypermnesia within the hypnosis framework. Contrary to Orne's (1979) argument that hypnotically aided recall will result in confabulation, it was found that hypnotized subjects did not exhibit more confabulation than controls. It was concluded that a criterion shift theory cannot explain the results.

A second study by Shields and Knox (1986) examined recall and recognition errors. New samples of 30 subjects high in hypnotic susceptibility and 10 subjects low in hypnotic susceptibility were used. As in the first study, subjects reliably recalled more deeply processed words than shallowly processed words.

Hypnotized subjects recognized more deeply processed words than the controls and failed to recognize more shallowly processed words. These results support the view that depth of processing is crucial to eliciting hypnotic hypermnesia. Together, the two studies provide evidence that hypnotic suggestions can modestly improve recall and recognition of verbal material that has been processed at a deep level.

Sanders et al. (1987) attempted to maximize ecological validity by studying the effects of hypnosis on eyewitness testimony and cross-examination. Fifty-five volunteers from the community witnessed a simulated crime and were then interviewed by professional police investigators to obtain evidence. Witnesses were randomly assigned to one of three groups: hypnosis-neutral, hypnosis-vivid (using instructional cues of vivid and accurate recall), and control. All witnesses were examined approximately 2 weeks later and cross-examined by a pair of practicing criminal attorneys. Their testimony was videotaped and then evaluated by two volunteer community residents serving as jurors.

The attorneys and jurors rated the confidence level of all 55 witnesses. The results did not support the excessive confidence hypothesis. Hypnosis alone or in combination with other variables had no significant effect on perceived confidence, credibility, or amenability of the witness to cross-examination. Trance depth was not correlated with extreme confidence or unusual reactions to cross-examination. The data in this study did not support the assumptions of hypersuggestibility and excessive confidence on the part of hypnotized witnesses. Rather, it was found that the commonly accepted practice of lawyers briefing the witness before testifying had much more impact on the certainty displayed by witnesses.

Sanders et al. (1987) found no evidence of confabulation and hypersuggestibility with hypnotic testimony. Hypnotized witnesses were more complete and internally consistent than controls without an accompanying increase in erroneous details. These results are consistent with many studies reviewed by Geiselman and Machlovitz (1987). They also support the contention by Reiser (1980) that when hypnosis is properly employed, it can increase the completeness of eyewitness testimony without an increase in erroneous information.

Consistent with 100 years of research on eyewitness testimony, the Sanders et al. (1987) study found that, in general, witness reports will likely contain some distortion of the perceived incident. However, hypnosis did not alter this unreliability. The authors concluded that jurors who hear testimony do not change the weight they give to evidence because of the use of hypnosis. These findings confirm that hypnosis can be a valuable investigative aid, and when properly used, it does not require any special actions by the courts in terms of admissibility or special instructions to the jury.

Geiselman and Machlovitz (1987) provide the most recent review of published experiments from 1930 to 1987, which addresses the issue of hypnotically aided recall. They examined 30 articles that reported a total of 38 experiments. Generally, the experiments had low ecological validity for evaluating the forensic use of hypnosis. Twenty-one of these studies reported more correct information with hypnosis, 13 reported no hypnosis effect, and 4 reported significantly less correct information with hypnosis. Overall, the reviewers found that the three factors of type of interview, sample size, and retention interval could significantly predict the success or failure of hypnosis-aided recall in eliciting additional correct information. Hypnosis recall was more successful when forensic conditions were approximated on several dimensions: an interactive interview with a skilled interviewer, longer-delayed tests of recall, and use of realistic materials that have arousal effects. In this regard, Geiselman et al. (1985) found that experienced police detectives produced 35% more correct facts with hypnosis than with standard police interviews.

Field Research and Experience

Very little field research has been reported in the area of investigative hypnosis. Only two controlled studies investigating the use of hypnosis interviews with witnesses during the investigation of actual cases have been published (Sloane, 1981; Yuille

& Kim, 1987). Sloane examined the comparative effectiveness of hypnosis and goal-directed recall strategies for memory refreshment in criminal cases. Forty-four witnesses/victims were randomly assigned to one of four treatment conditions after standard interrogations were completed. Ten experienced hypno-investigators were randomly assigned to do interviews utilizing hypnosis, nonhypnosis, visual recall instructions, or nonvisual recall instructions. Both waking and hypnotized subjects produced approximately 9% new information. The combined waking state conditions produced 95% accuracy on confirmed data, which did not differ from the mean accuracy scores of 97% derived from the hypnosis conditions. Overall, the study showed that hypnotized witnesses did not produce more new information of greater accuracy than waking subjects. It also found that hypnosis subjects showed no differences from waking subjects in confabulation. Several problems combined to limit the generalizability of the findings. The sample size was small, which contributed to excessive within-group variance; the semantic differential measure used to assess arousal was inappropriate; the time interval available for corroboration of information was too short; multivariate analyses would have been desirable; and the interviews were conducted by personnel with varying expertise.

Yuille and Kim (1987) retrospectively studied cases from police files in which hypnosis had been used to aid memory. From a total of 41 cases, 7 were selected for detailed analysis because the cases were solved and the complete files were available. From the 7 cases, a total of nine subjects was studied. Each had provided a standard police interview prior to giving a hypnosis-aided interview, which was conducted by a police hypnotist. The average elapsed time between the crimes and the prehypnosis interviews was 3.5 days, while the hypnosis interviews occurred at an average of 13.5 days after the prehypnosis interviews. Two of the subjects had provided two standard police interviews prior to the hypnosis interview, and 1 subject had a posthypnosis standard interview in addition to the prehypnosis and hypnosis interviews. All interviews were recorded. Comparisons were made with the evidence in each case and across interviews using a statement analysis technique.

Compared to the standard interviews, the hypnosis interviews averaged 177% increase in total information, almost triple the amount previously provided, and every subject showed an increase. On average, witnesses provided 204.1% more descriptive details when hypnotized and an increase in action details that averaged 80.6%. The 2 subjects having two prehypnosis interviews did not provide significantly more information merely by being reinterviewed, but they provided significantly more information during the hypnosis interviews. Of the descriptive facts in the prehypnosis interviews that could be compared to forensic evidence, an average of 84.4% were accurate. During hypnosis interviews, verifiable facts averaged 82%. Thus, there was no apparent sacrifice in the accuracy of information due to hypnosis. Of the facts that were compared between the standard and hypnosis interviews, there was a high degree of consistency. Yuille and Kim concluded that the results supported the value of hypnosis as an aid to memory in criminal investigations. This study reinforces the findings of field workers that the hypnosis procedure assists in the retrieval of information.

Other field research with actual crime witnesses consists of survey data and case reports. Ross (1977) reported a pilot study conducted at the Los Angeles Police Department where 67 hypnosis sessions were conducted during a 1-year period. The cases involved homicide, robbery, burglary, sex crimes, bombing, grand theft, attempted homicide, and vandalism. Survey questionnaires completed by the investigating detectives indicated that new investigative leads were obtained during hypnosis interviews in 77.6% of the cases. Additionally, it was determined that 16.5% of the cases were solved during the year of the study as a direct result of the information gained in the hypnosis interviews. Reiser (1982) reported the results of the investigative hypnosis project begun at the Los Angeles Police Department in 1975. Survey data provided by case detectives showed that in 600 major crimes, new information was elicited during hypnosis interviews in 75% of the cases. Approximately half of this new information permitted a validation test, which showed approximately 90% corroboration.

Stratton (1977) reported the results of a pilot program in investigative hypnosis at the Los Angeles County Sheriff's Department and found that in over 50 hypnosis interviews conducted since the implementation of the program, 90% of the sessions resulted in information helpful to the investigations. Schaefer and Rubio (1978) conducted investigative hypnosis interviews for a variety of California police departments and attorneys. Of the 13 cases where hypnosis was actually utilized, 10 were judged to have been materially helped by the hypnosis-elicited information. Ault (1980) reported on the Federal Bureau of Investigation team approach to investigative hypnosis, in which health professionals were used to induce hypnosis and trained agents did the interviewing. Of more than 50 hypnosis cases, it was found that additional useful information was obtained in 60% of them.

Numerous case reports have been published documenting the usefulness of hypnosis interviews by both law enforcement and defense attorneys (Arons, 1967; Block, 1976; Ferrara & Wade, 1982; Kroger & Douce, 1979; Reiser, 1974; Sannito & Mueller, 1980). Kleinhauz, Horowitz, and Tobin (1977) evaluated the use of hypnosis as a memory enhancement tool in Israeli police investigations beginning in 1973. In all, hypnosis was used with 40 subjects. It was found that the amount of information increased with the meaningfulness of the material to be recalled and the level of anxiety involved. Several bombing cases were solved with the aid of hypnosis interviewing, and the researchers concluded that hypnosis is a useful and effective tool in criminal investigations.

In addition to crime situations, investigative hypnosis has been used to enhance the recall of surviving witnesses in plane and car accidents. Raginsky (1969) described a case where hypnosis interviewing of an airline pilot who survived a plane crash overcame his amnesia for the event, allowing the cause of the accident to be determined. Similarly, a hypnosis interview with the victim of a helicopter crash was used 4 years after the incident in a civil suit involving personal injury. New details about the accident were obtained and later used in court (*Wyller v. Fairchild-Hiller Corporation*, 1974).

Hiland and Dzieszkowski (1984) reported a study evaluating the efficacy of hypnosis interviews of 10 witnesses to six recent naval aircraft accidents. All of the witnesses were interviewed after routine reporting was completed. Prior to hypnosis, they were asked to give a narrative account of the accident. All were able to remember some important information during the hypnosis interview. Sixty percent of the information was rated by aeromedical evaluators within the upper third on the scale of importance. In 70% of the interviews, the information gained was considered highly compatible with known or suspected factors of the accidents. It was also found that the hypnosis interviews did not result in the development of improbable or irrelevant information about the circumstances of the accidents. This study led to the conclusion that hypnosis techniques can be very beneficial in the memory enhancement of some witnesses to aircraft accidents. As with aircraft accidents, hypnosis interviews of survivors of car crashes have aided in determining the reasons for the accidents, where the witness has posttraumatic amnesia for the event (*Kline v. Ford Motor Co., Inc.*, 1975).

Comments on Research

All critiques of the vast amount of laboratory research in the areas of hypnotic hypermnesia, memory, and eyewitness testimony agree that there is a dire need to increase the ecological validity of future studies by better replicating real-world conditions (Neisser, 1978; Relinger, 1984; Shepherd, Ellis, & Davies, 1982). Problems requiring special attention in researching the effectiveness of investigative hypnosis include the uniqueness and meaningfulness of the stimulus material, levels of emotional arousal and anxiety at the time of information acquisition and retrieval, and the need to use experienced interviewers who employ a free-recall format prior to focused questioning. Because experienced investigative interviewers do not use misleading or false information, introducing such procedures into the design is inappropriate for a test of the investigative hypnosis procedure. Studies having greater ecological validity (Geiselman et al., 1985; Ready, 1986; Sanders et al., 1987; Timm, 1981; Yuille & Kim, 1987; Yuille & McEwan, 1985) are more likely to yield results comparable to those found with witnesses in real crime cases.

LEGAL AND POLITICAL ISSUES

An example of inequity involving investigative hypnosis is contained in the California Supreme Court's decision in *People v. Shirley* (1982), which permitted previously hypnotized defendants to testify in court, but not witnesses or victims of crime (Watson, 1985). The U. S. Supreme Court in *Rock v. Arkansas* (1987) affirmed the right of a defendant to introduce hypnotically aided recall in court. The Court cited cross-examination, expert testimony, and cautionary instructions as means of assessing accuracy of testimony. In recent years, the interest in victims' rights has been growing (Bard & Sangrey, 1979), which is exemplified in the final report of the President's Commission on Crime and Violence. It includes recommendations designed to provide a variety of aid to crime victims (President's Commission Report on Victims of Violent Crime, 1983). Additionally, the American Psychological Association Task Force on Victims of Crime and Violence reviewed research and practices regarding victims and recommended changes for psychologists and others in the criminal justice system (Task Force Report on Victims of Crime and Violence, 1983).

In California, the swing of the pendulum toward victims' needs led to the passage of Proposition 8, the so-called "Victims' Bill of Rights." One part of this law reaffirms the right to have a jury hear all of the evidence in criminal cases and to decide its weight, rather than allowing important information to be excluded on technicalities and by expert opinion. This application of the law remains to be tested in regard to investigative hypnosis. Three recent reviews summarize the legal issues from differing vantage points (Brown, 1985; Henderson, 1985; Sies & Wester, 1985). The legal status of investigative hypnosis is discussed in Chapter 10 in this volume.

Unfortunately, disagreements over investigative hypnosis are not limited to factual, scientific questions (Reiser, 1984). The guild interests of mental health professionals, distrust of police, and personal attacks on those advocating police use of hypnosis have been prominent in much of the recent writing and organizational activity of some mental health professionals (Laurence

& Perry, 1988; Orne et al., 1984; Perry & Laurence, 1983). Three organizations have passed resolutions decrying police use of hypnosis interviewing (American Medical Association, 1985; International Society of Hypnosis Resolution, 1979; Society for Clinical and Experimental Hypnosis, 1979). In two instances they declared it unethical to train or consult with police who practice this technique. The major organization of practitioners of investigative hypnosis responded with its own resolution, which pointed out the antipolice and emotional, rather than scientific, basis for the assertions of its opponents (International Society for Investigative and Forensic Hypnosis Resolution, 1980).

Thirty years ago, a leading hypnosis expert pointed out that the prejudice against police departments using hypnosis for crime detection was irrational and that over time people would become less unreasonable (Estabrooks, 1957). More recently, Kroger (1977) pointed out that hypnosis cannot be claimed by any medical specialty or school of psychotherapy. Weitzenhoffer (1979) addressed one of the central problems underlying a significant proportion of the current controversy by stating, "Speaking of only hypnotism research done during the last 45 years, I find much of it, and the associated writings, to have been of low scientific caliber. There has been far more pseudoscience than science in it" (p. 353).

Spiegel (1980) cogently suggested that it would be more desirable for police and psychologists to join in sharing knowledge, rather than in condemning and excluding other professionals.

CONCLUSIONS

More applied research is necessary to further identify the significant parameters operative in investigative hypnosis (Reiser, 1980). Ideally, this research should be based in the real world of police work and should study victims/witnesses who are involved in criminal cases, as was the case in the Yuille and Kim (1987) study. Future laboratory studies need to achieve greater validity by use of nonstudent populations, police interviewers, realistic "live" crime events, and close replication of law enforcement investigative procedures. In addition to yielding important new information about the effects of hypnosis interviews, research in the natural "setting" of forensic investigations will likely provide meaningful data on the important questions of how memory is acquired, stored, and retrieved.

The results of existing research and the state of the art of investigative hypnosis permit the practitioner-researcher to make four pragmatic inferences: (1) hypnosis does not invariably result in hypersuggestibility; (2) investigative hypnosis is a legitimate specialty located within the domain of police science rather than in the therapy domain; (3) the hypnotized witness is not transformed into a different person by hypnosis and retains critical cognitive abilities to judge and discriminate among events; (4) memory is not automatically tainted by hypnosis and confabulation is not an invariable consequence in recalling information about recent, meaningful crime events (Nelson, 1987).

In sum, the personal experience of the author over a 15-year period of using investigative hypnosis at the Los Angeles Police Department in serious crime cases has been essentially positive. Although not a panacea and as subject to abuse or misuse as any tool, the investigative hypnosis process works in a meaningful number of dead-end cases to assist the criminal justice process.

REFERENCES

American Medical Association. (1985). *Scientific status of refreshing recollection by the use of hypnosis.* Council on Scientific Affairs. Chicago.

Arons, H. (1967). *Hypnosis in criminal investigation.* Springfield, IL: Charles C. Thomas.

Augustynek, A. (1977). Recalling in state of awareness and under hypnosis. *Przeglad Psychlogiczny, 20,* 193–705.

Ault, R. L., Jr. (1980, January). Hypnosis—the FBI's team approach. *FBI Law Enforcement Bulletin,* pp. 5–8.

Baddeley, A. D. (1976). *The psychology of memory.* New York: Basic Books.

Bahrick, H. P. (1979). Broader methods and narrower theories for memory research: Comments on the papers by Eysenck and Cermak. In L. A. Cermak & F. I. M. Craik (Eds.), *Levels of processing in human memory* (pp. 151–156). Hillsdale, NJ: Erlbaum.

Barber, J. (1980). Hypnosis and the unhypnotizable. *The American Journal of Clinical Hypnosis, 23*(1), 4-9.
Barber, T. X. (1961). Death by suggestions. *Psychomatic Medicine, 23,* 153-156.
Barber, T. X., & Calverly, D. S. (1966). Effects on recall of hypnotic induction, motivational suggestions and suggested regression: A methodological and experimental analysis. *Journal of Abnormal Psychology, 71,* 169-180.
Bard, M., & Sangrey, D. (1979). *The crime victim's book.* New York: Basic.
Benderly, H. P. (1981, June). Flashbulb memory. *Psychology Today,* pp. 71-74.
Bernheim, A. M. (1980). *New studies in hypnotism.* New York: International Universities Press. (Original work published 1890.)
Block, E. B. (1976). *Hypnosis: A new tool in crime detection.* New York: McKay.
Bowers, K. S. (1977). *Hypnosis for the seriously curious.* New York: Aronson.
Bowers, K. S., & Hilgard, E. R. (1988). Some complexities in understanding memory. In H. M. Pettinati (Ed.), *Hypnosis and memory* (pp. 3-181). New York: Guilford Press.
Bregman, N. J., & McAllister, H. A. (1982). Eyewitness testimony: The role of commitment in increasing reliability. *Social Psychology Quarterly, 45,* 181-184.
Broadbent, D. E. (1958). *Perception and communication.* London: Pergamon Press.
Brown, R. J. (1985). Hypnosis in Canadian criminal law. *American Journal of Clinical Hypnosis, 27*(13), 153-158.
Brown, R., & Kulik, J. (1977). Flashbulb memories. *Cognition, 5,* 73-79.
Brunn, A. D. (1968). Retrograde amnesia in a murder suspect. *American Journal of Clinical Hypnosis, 12,* 209-213.
Buckhout, R. (1974). Eyewitness testimony. *Scientific American, 231,* 23-31.
Charcot, J. M. (1877). *Lectures on the diseases of the nervous system.* London: New Syndenham Society.
Cheek, D. B. (1975). Maladjustment patterns apparently related to imprinting at birth. *American Journal of Clinical Hypnosis, 18,* 75-82.
Cheek, D. B., & Le Cron, L. M. (1968). *Clinical hypnotherapy.* New York: Grune & Stratton.
Chertok, L. (1981). *Sense and nonsense in psychotherapy: The challenge of hypnosis.* New York: Pergamon Press.

Conn, J. H. (1959). Cultural and clinical aspects of hypnosis, placebos, and suggestibility. *International Journal of Clinical and Experimental Hypnosis, 7,* 179–186.

Conn, J. H. (1972). Is hypnosis really dangerous? *International Journal of Clinical and Experimental Hypnosis, 20,* 61–79.

Conn, J. H. (1982). The myth of coercion under hypnosis. In J. K. Zeig (Ed.), *Ericksonian approaches to hypnosis and psychotherapy* (pp. 357–367). New York: Brunner/Mazel.

Cooper, L. M., & London, P. (1973). Reactivation of memory by hypnosis and suggestion. *International Journal of Clinical and Experimental Hypnosis, 21,* 312–323.

Craik, F. I. M., & Jacoby, L. L. (1979). Elaboration and distinctiveness in episodic memory. In L. G. Nilsson (Ed.), *Perspectives on memory research* (pp. 145–166). Hillsdale, NJ: Erlbaum.

Craik, F. I. M., & Lockhart, R. S. (1972). Levels of processing: A framework for memory research. *Journal of Verbal Learning and Verbal Behavior, 4* 671–684.

Crawford, H. J., & Allen, S. N. (1983). Enhanced visual memory during hypnosis as mediated by hypnotic responsiveness and cognitive strategies. *Journal of Expermental Psychology: General, 112,* 662–685.

Crawford, H. J., Wallace, B., & Slater, H. (1986). Eidetic-like imagery in hypnosis: Here but there. *American Journal of Psychology, 99,* 527–546.

Deffenbacher, K. A. (1980). Eyewitness accuracy and confidence: Can we infer anything about their relationship? *Law and Human Behavior, 4,* 243–260.

De Piano, F. A., & Salzberg, H. C. (1981). Hypnosis as an aid to recall of meaningful information presented under three types of arousal. *International Journal of Clinical and Experimental Hypnosis, 29,* 383–400.

Dhanens, T. P., & Lundy, R. M. (1975). Hypnosis and waking suggestions and recall. *International Journal of Clinical and Experimental Hypnosis, 23,* 181–216.

Diamond, B. L. (1980). Inherent problems in the use of pretrial hypnosis on a prospective witness. *California Law Review, 68,* 313–349.

Dorcus, R. M. (1960). Recall under hypnosis of amnestic events. *International Journal of Clinical and Experimental Hypnosis, 7,* 57–61.

Du Maurier, G. (1895). *Trilby.* New York: Harper.

Edmonston, W. E. (1981). *Hypnosis and relaxation.* New York: Wiley-Interscience.

Ellison, K. W., & Buckhout, R. (1981). *Psychology and criminal justice.* New York: Harper & Row.
Erdelyi, M. H. (1988). Hypermnesia: The effect of hypnosis, fantasy, and concentration. In H. M. Pettinati (Ed.), *Hypnosis and memory* (pp. 64–94). New York: Guilford Press.
Erdelyi, M. H., Dinges, D. F., Orne, M. T., Whitehouse, W. G., & Orne, E. C. (1985, October). *The stimulus and the test in hypnotic hypermnesia.* Paper presented at Institute of Pennsylvania Hospital, Philadelphia.
Erickson, M. H., Rossi, E. L., & Rossi, S. I. (1976). *Hypnotic realities.* New York: Irvington Press.
Estabrooks, G. H. (1957). *Hypnotism.* New York: E. P. Dutton.
Evans, F. J. (1988). Posthypnotic amnesia: Dissociation of content and context. In H. M. Pettinati (Ed.), *Hypnosis and memory* (pp. 157–192). New York: Guilford Press.
Ferrara, S. J., & Wade, N. L. (1982). Hypnotic testimony: To be or not to be? *Journal of the Society of Medical Hypnoanalysts, 3,* 112–117.
Fischer, R. (1977). On flashback and hypnotic recall. *International Journal of Clinical and Experimental Hypnosis, 25,* 217–233.
Frankel, F. (1976). *Hypnosis: Trance as a coping mechanism.* New York: Plenum Medical Books.
Frankel, F. H. (1988). The clinical use of hypnosis in aiding recall. In H. M. Pettinati (Ed.), *Hypnosis and memory* (pp. 247–264). New York: Guilford Press.
Geiselman, R. E., Fisher, R. P., Mac Kinnon, D. P., & Holland, H. L. (1985). Eyewitness memory enhancement in the police interview: Cognitive retrieval mnemonics versus hypnosis. *Journal of Applied Psychology, 70,* 401–412.
Geiselman, R. E., & Machlovitz, H. R. (1987). Hypnosis memory recall: Implications for forensic use. *American Journal of Forensic Psychology, 5*(1), 37–47.
Gilbert, J. N. (1980). *Criminal investigation.* Columbus, OH: Merrill.
Goldstein, M. S., & Siprelle, C. N. (1970). Hypnotically induced amnesia versus ablation of memory. *International Journal of Clinical and Experimental Hypnosis, 18,* 211–216.
Gottfredson, G. D., Reiser, M., & Tsegaye-Spates, C. R. (1987). Psychological help for victims of crime. *Professional Psychology: Research and Practice, 18,* 316–325.
Gottschalk, L. A. (1961). The use of drugs in interrogation. In A. Biderman & H. Zimmer (Eds.), *Manipulation of human behavior* (pp. 96–144). New York: John Wiley.

Griffin, G. R. (1980). Hypnosis: Toward a logical approach in using hypnosis in law enforcement. *Journal of Police Science and Administration, 8,* 385-389.

Hatton, K. L. (1978, February 13). Hypnosis takes hold as a legitimate police tool. *The Cleveland Plain Dealer.*

Henderson, M. D. (1985). The admissibility of hypnotically enhanced testimony. *Journal of Legal Medicine, 6,* 293-331.

Hibbard, W. S., & Worring, M. A. (1981). *Forensic hypnosis: The practical application of hypnosis in criminal investigations.* Springfield, IL: Charles C. Thomas.

Hibler, N. S. (1984). Forensic hypnosis: To hypnotize or not to hypnotize, that is the question. *American Journal of Clinical Hypnosis, 27,* 52-57.

Hiland, D. N., & Dzieszkowski, P. A. (1984, December). Hypnosis in the investigation of aviation accidents. *Aviation, Space and Environmental Medicine,* 1136-1142.

Hilgard, E. R. (1965). *The experience of hypnosis.* New York: Harcourt, Brace, & World.

Hilgard, E. R. (1977). *Divided consciousness: Multiple controls in human thought and action.* New York: Wiley-Interscience.

Hilgard, E. R. (1981). Hypnotic susceptibility scales under attack: An examination of Weitzenhoffer's criticisms. *The International Journal of Clinical and Experimental Hypnosis, 29*(1), 24-41.

Hull, C. L. (1933). *Hypnosis and suggestibility.* New York: Appleton-Century-Crofts.

International Society of Hypnosis Resolution. (1979). *The International Journal of Clinical & Experimental Hypnosis, 27,* 453.

International Society for Investigative and Forensic Hypnosis Resolution (1980). *Newsletter, 2,* 31.

Janet, P. (1925). *Psychological healing.* London: Allen and Unwin.

Key, W. B. (1973). *Subliminal seduction.* New York: Prentice-Hall.

Kihlstrom, J. F. (1981). Puzzles of imagery. *Journal of Mental Imagery, 5,* 43.

Kihlstrom, J. F. (1987). The cognitive unconscious. *Science, 237,* 1445-1452.

Kihlstrom, J. F., and Evans, F. J. (1979). *Functional disorders of memory.* Hillsdale, NJ: Erlbaum.

Kleinhauz, M., Horowitz, I., & Tobin, Y. (1977). The use of hypnosis in police investigation: A preliminary communication. *Journal of Forensic Science Society, 17,* 77-80.

Kline v. Ford Motor Co., Inc., 523 F.2d 1067. (1975).

Kroger, W. S. (1977). *Clinical and experimental hypnosis* (2nd ed.). Philadelphia: Lippincott.

Kroger, W. S., & Douce, R. G. (1979). Hypnosis in criminal investigation. *International Journal of Clinical and Experimental Hypnosis, 27*, 358–374.

Lachman, R., Lachman, J. L., & Butterfield, E. L. (1979). *Cognitive psychology and information processing.* Hillsdale, NJ: Erlbaum.

Laurence, J. R., & Perry, C. (1988). *Hypnosis: Will and memory.* New York: Guilford Press.

Loftus, E. F. (1979). *Eyewitness testimony.* Cambridge, MA: Harvard University Press.

Los Angeles Police Department. (1982) Hypnosis Survey Los Angeles Police Department.

McGaugh, J. L. (1980, December). Adrenaline: A secret agent in memory. *Psychology Today*, p. 132.

Menninger, K., Mayman, M., & Pruyser, P. (1963). *The vital balance.* New York: Viking Press.

Miller, G. A., Galanter, E., & Pribram, K. H. (1960). *Plans and the structure of behavior.* New York: Holt, Rinehart & Winston.

Neisser, U. (1978). Memory: What are the important questions? In M. M. Gruneberg, P. E. Morris, & R. N. Sykes (Eds.), *Practical aspects of memory* (pp. 3–24). London: Academic Press.

Neisser, U. (1982). *Memory observed.* New York: Freeman.

Nelson, S. A. (1987). Investigative hypnosis in criminal cases. *Convictions, 1*(4), 1–2.

Nilsson, L. G. (Ed.). (1979). *Perspectives on memory research.* Hillsdale, NJ: Erlbaum.

Nogrady, H., McConkey, K. M., & Perry, C. (1985). Enhancing visual memory: Trying hypnosis, trying imagination, and trying again. *Journal of Abnormal Psychology, 94*, 195–204.

Orne, M. T. (1951). The mechanisms of hypnotic age regression. *Journal of Abnormal and Social Psychology, 46*, 213–225.

Orne, M. T. (1972). Can a hypnotized subject be compelled to carry out otherwise unacceptable behavior? *International Journal of Clinical and Experimental Hypnosis, 20*, 109–117.

Orne, M. T. (1979). The use and misuse of hypnosis in court. *International Journal of Clinical and Experimental Hypnosis, 27*(4), 311–339.

Orne, M. T., Dinges, D. F., & Orne, E. C. (1984, December). The forensic use of hypnosis. *Research in Brief* (National Institute of Justice), pp. 1–6.

Orne, M. T., Whitehouse, W. G., Dinges, D. F., & Orne, E. C. (1988). Reconstructing memory through hypnosis: Forensic and clinical implications. In H. M. Pettinati (Ed.), *Hypnosis and memory* (pp. 21-63). New York: Guilford Press.
Paivio, A. (1969). Mental imagery in associative learning and memory. *Psychological Review, 76*, 241-263.
Parker, L. C., Jr. (1980). *Legal psychology: Eyewitness testimony and jury behavior.* Springfield, IL: Charles C. Thomas.
Penfield, W. (1952). Memory mechanisms. *Archives of Neurology and Psychiatry, 67*, 178-198.
People v. Shirley, 31 Cal. 3rd 18, CA (1982).
People v. Singleton, 112 Cal. App. 3rd 418 (November 1980).
People v. Woods et al., no. 63187 ABNC (Alameda Co., CA, December 15, 1977).
Perry, C., & Laurence, J. R. (1983). The enhancement of memory by hypnosis in the legal investigative situation. *Canadian Psychology, 24*, 155-167.
Postman, I., & Underwood, B. J. (1973). Critical issues in interference theory. *Memory and Cognition, 1*, 19-40.
President's Commission Report on Victims of Violent Crime. (1983). Washington, DC: U.S. Department of Justice.
Putnam, W. H. (1979). Hypnosis and distortions in eyewitness testimony. *International Journal of Clinical and Experimental Hypnosis, 27*, 437-448.
Raginsky, B. B. (1969). Hypnotic recall of an aircraft crash. *International Journal of Clinical and Experimental Hypnosis, 27*, 1-19.
Raikov, V. L. (1982). Hypnotic age regression to the neonatal period: Comparisons with role playing. *International Journal of Clinical and Experimental Hypnosis, 30*, 108-115.
Rainer, D. (1983). *Eyewitness testimony: Does hypnosis enhance accuracy, distortion and confidence?* Unpublished doctoral dissertation, University of Wyoming, Cheyenne.
Ready, D. J. (1986). *The effects of hypnosis and guided memory on eyewitness recall and suggestibility.* Unpublished doctoral dissertation Florida State University, Tallahassee.
Redston, M. T., & Knox, J. (1983, October). *Is the recognition of faces enhanced by hypnosis?* Paper presented at the Annual Meeting of the Society of Clinical and Experimental Hypnosis, Boston.
Reiser, M. (1974). Hypnosis as an aid in a homicide investigation. *The American Journal of Clinical Hypnosis, 17*, 84-87.

Reiser, M. (1976). Hypnosis as a tool in criminal investigation. *Police Chief, 46,* 39–40.
Reiser, M. (1980). *Handbook of investigative hypnosis.* Los Angeles: LEHI Publishing.
Reiser, M. (1982). Erickson and law enforcement: Investigative hypnosis. In J. K. Zeig (Ed.), *Ericksonian approaches to hypnosis and psychotherapy* (pp. 349–356). New York: Brunner/Mazel.
Reiser, M. (1984). Police use of investigative hypnosis: Scientism, ethics and power games. *American Journal of Forensic Psychology, 2,* 115–143.
Reiser, M. (1985). Some current issues in investigative hypnosis. *International Journal of Investigative and Forensic Hypnosis, 8,* 41–56.
Reiser, M. (1986). Admission of hypnosis-induced recollections into evidence. *American Journal of Forensic Psychology, 4,* 19–26.
Reiser, M., & Nielsen, M. M. (1980). Investigative hypnosis: A developing specialty. *American Journal of Clinical Hypnosis, 23,* 75–84.
Relinger, H. (1984). Hypnotic hypermnesia: A critical review. *American Journal of Clinical Hypnosis, 26,* 212–225.
Rock v. Arkansas, 97 L. Ed. 2d 237 (1987).
Rokeach, M. (1968). *Beliefs, attitudes and values.* San Francisco: Jossey-Bass.
Ross, K. (1977). *Evaluation study of the Los Angeles Police Department hypnosis project.* Baccalaureate project, University of Redlands, California.
Rubin, D. C. (1982). Very long term memory for prose and verse. In U. Neisser (Ed.), *Memory observed—Remembering in natural contexts* (pp. 289–310). San Francisco: Freeman.
Sanders, G. S., Gansler, D. A., & Riesman, S. (1987). *The effect of hypnosis in eyewitness testimony and reactions to cross-examination.* State University of New York, Albany.
Sanders, G. S., & Simmon, W. L. (1983). Use of hypnosis to enhance eyewitness testimony: Does it work? *Journal of Applied Psychology, 68,* 70–77. Unpublished manuscript.
Sannito, T., & Mueller, P. (1980). The use of hypnosis in a double manslaughter defense. *Trial Diplomacy, 3,* 30–35.
Schaefer, D. W., & Rubio, R. (1978). Hypnosis to aid the recall of witnesses. *International Journal of Clinical and Experimental Hypnosis, 26,* 81–91.
Schneck, J. M. (1978). Henry James, George Du Maurier and mesmerism. *International Journal of Clinical and Experimental Hypnosis, 26,* 76–80.

Sears, A. B. (1954). A comparison of hypnotic and waking recall. *Journal of Clinical and Experimental Hypnosis, 2,* 81–91.

Sheehan, P. W. (1988). Confidence, memory and hypnosis. In H. M. Pettinati (Ed.), *Hypnosis and memory* (pp. 95–127). New York: Guilford Press.

Sheehan, P. W., Griggs, L., & McCann, T. (1984). Memory distortion following exposure to fake information in hypnosis. *Journal of Abnormal Psychology, 93,* 259–265.

Sheehan, P. W., & Perry, C. W. (1976). *Methodologies of hypnosis: A critical appraisal of contemporary paradigms of hypnosis.* Hillsdale, NJ: Erlbaum.

Shepherd, J. W., Ellis, H. D., & Davies, G. M. (1982). *Identification evidence: A psychological evaluation.* Aberdeen: Aberdeen University Press.

Shields, I. W., & Knox, V. J. (1986). Levels of processing as a determinant of hypnotic hypermnesia. *Journal of Abnormal Psychology, 95,* 358–364.

Sies, D. E., & Wester, W. C. (1985). Judicial approaches to the question of admissibility of hypnotically refreshed testimony: A history and analysis. *De Paul Law Review, 35,* 97–124.

Sloane, M. C. (1981). *A comparison of hypnosis vs. waking state and visual vs. non-visual recall instructions for witness/victim memory retrieval in actual crime cases.* Unpublished doctoral dissertation, Florida State University, Tallahassee.

Smith, M. C. (1983). Hypnotic memory enhancement of witnesses: Does it work? *Psychological Bulletin, 94,* 387–409.

Society for Clinical and Experimental Hypnosis Resolution. (1979). *International Journal of Clinical and Experimental Hypnosis, 27,* 452.

Spear, N. (1978). *The processing of memories: Forgetting and retention.* Hillsdale, NJ: Erlbaum.

Spector, R. G., & Foster, T. E. (1977). Admissibility of hypnotic statements: Is the law of evidence susceptible? *Ohio State University Law Journal, 38,* 567.

Spector, R. G., & Foster, T. E. (1979). The utility of hypno-induced statements on the trial process: Reflections on People v. Smrekar. *Loyola Chicago Law Journal, 10,* 691–707.

Sperber, Z., & Reiser, M. (1971). Utilizing non-professional aides in the treatment of psychotic children at an out-patient clinic. *Psychotherapy, 3,* 224–230.

Spiegel, D. (1986). Dissociating damage. *American Journal of Clinical Hypnosis, 29*, 123–131.
Spiegel, H. (1980). Hypnosis and evidence: Help or hindrance? *Annals of the New York Academy of Sciences, 347*, 73–85.
Spiegel, H., & Spiegel, D. (1978). *Trance and treatment.* New York: Basic Books.
Stager, G. (1974). The effect of hypnosis on the learning and recall of visually presented material. *Dissertation Abstracts International, 35*(6), 3075B.
Stager, G., & Lundy, R. M. (1985). Hypnosis and the learning and recall of visually presented material. *International Journal of Clinical and Experimental Hypnosis, 33*, 27–39.
Stratton, J. G. (1977). The use of hypnosis in law enforcement criminal investigations. A pilot program. *Journal of Police Science and Administration, 5*, 399–406.
Swanson, J. M., & Kinsbourne, M. (1979). State-dependent learning and retrieval: Methodological cautions and theoretical considerations. In J. F. Kihlstrom & F. J. Evans (Eds.), *Functional disorders of memory* (pp. 275–299). Hillsdale, NJ: Erlbaum.
Stross, L., and Shevrin, H. (1968). Thought organization in hypnosis and the waking state. *Journal of Nervous and Mental Disease, 147*(3), 272–288.
Task Force Report on Victims of Crime and Violence (1984). Washington, DC: American Psychological Association.
Timm, H. W. (1981). The effect of forensic hypnosis techniques on eyewitness recall and recognition. *Journal of Police Science and Administration, 9*, 188–194.
Timm, H. W. (1983). The factors theoretically affecting the impact of forensic hypnosis techniques on eyewitness recall. *Journal of Police Science and Administration, 11*, 442–450.
Tulving, E. (1972). Episodic and semantic memory. In E. Tulving & W. Donaldson (Eds.), *Organization of memory* (pp. 381–403). New York: Academic Press.
Tulving, E. (1979). Memory research: What kind of progress? In L. G. Nilsson (Ed.), *Perspectives on memory research* (pp. 19–34). Hillsdale, NJ: Erlbaum.
Udolf, R. (1983). *Forensic hypnosis.* Lexington, MA: Lexington Books.
Vollmer, T. (1979, March 24). Seaman guilty in multilation, rape of girl. *Los Angeles Times.*
Von Bertalanffy, L. (1968). *General systems theory.* New York: Braziller.

Wagstaff, G. F. (1982). Hypnosis and recognition of a face. *Perceptual and Motor Skills, 55,* 816–818.
Watson, Donald E. (1985, March 13). How the California Supreme Court mesmerized the law. Unpublished manuscript.
Watzlawick, P. (1978). *The language of change.* New York: Basic Books.
Weitzenhoffer, A. M. (1979). Hypnotism and altered states of consciousness. In A. A. Sugarman & R. E. Tartar (Eds.), *Expanding dimensions of consciousness.* New York: Springer Publishing Co.
West, L. J., & Deckert, G. H. (1965). Dangers of hypnosis. *Journal of the American Medical Association, 192,* 9–12.
Wyller, v. Fairchild-Hiller Corporation, 503 F.2d 506 (Ninth Cir., 1974).
Yarmey, D. A. (1979). *Eyewitness testimony.* New York: Free Press.
Yuille, J. C., & Kim, C. K. (1987). A field study of the forensic use of hypnosis. *Canadian Journal of Behavioural Science, 19,* 418–429.
Yuille, J. C., & McEwan, N. H. (1985). Use of hypnosis as an aid to eyewitness memory. *Journal of Applied Psychology, 70,* 389–400.
Zelig, M., & Beidleman, W. B. (1981). The investigative use of hypnosis: A word of caution. *International Journal of Clinical and Experimental Hypnosis, 29,* 401–412.

The Cognitive Interview Technique for Victims and Witnesses of Crime

R. Edward Geiselman and Ronald P. Fisher

In a recent study, sheriff's deputies and detectives across the state of New York were asked, "What is the central and most important feature of criminal investigations?" (Sanders, 1986). The majority of the respondents answered, "Eyewitnesses." Nevertheless, few reported that they had had any training in interviewing witnesses. Interrogation methods for interviewing suspects are taught at most police academies, but they have little application to willing witnesses who are experiencing difficulties in reconstructing what they have seen. Although hundreds of studies have examined the recall performance of witnesses (Loftus, 1979; Yarmey, 1979), only recently has research been conducted on interview techniques for maximizing the completeness of witnesses' reports.

Our research has focused on developing interview techniques that can be used to enhance the quality and quantity of information obtained from victims and witnesses of crime. We have labeled these methods *the cognitive interview*. The cognitive interview has been successful in several experiments, and a number of investigators have reported success in using the techniques in the field. Volunteer off-duty detectives from police departments in Los Angeles and Inglewood, California; and Metro-Dade County, Florida; and other law enforcement agencies have provided valuable assistance in this work. We have taken great care to include in the cognitive interview format only those recall enhancement techniques that have received considerable attention by psychologists and that have been demonstrated to be reliable and effective. Thus, the cognitive interview should meet the requirements of *Frye v. United States* (1923).

THE COGNITIVE INTERVIEW

The cognitive interview consists of four general memory enhancement techniques, plus several specific methods for increasing a witnesses' recall of events. Although some investigators already use one or more of the cognitive methods in some form, our experiments have shown improved recall when experienced law enforcement professionals conducted the complete cognitive interview as compared to a standard witness interview. These memory guidance techniques can easily be incorporated into the standard police interview.

In the standard interview, the victim or witness first is asked to give a narrative report of what happened. The narrative report is followed by specific questions that serve to enhance the completeness of the report. The same general format is followed in the cognitive interview, but this procedure is augmented with the following instructions given to the witness prior to eliciting the narrative report.

Reconstruct the Circumstances: "Try to reconstruct in your mind the context that surrounded the incident. Think about what the surrounding environment looked like at the scene of the crime, such as rooms, the lighting, the weather, any smells, any nearby people or objects. Also think about how you were feeling at the time, and think about your reaction to the incident. Mentally, put yourself back there at the time this incident happened."

Be Complete: "Some people hold back information because they are not quite sure that the information is important. Please do not edit anything out of your report, even things you think may not be important."

Recall in Different Orders: "It is natural to go through the incident from beginning to end. However, you also should try to go through the events in reverse order. Alternatively, try starting with the thing that impressed you the most in the incident and then go from there, going both forward and backward in time."

Change Perspectives: "Try to recall the incident from different perspectives that you may have had, or adopt the perspectives of others who were present during the incident. For example, try to place yourself in the role of a prominent character in the incident, and think about what he or she must have seen."

How the human memory system operates is still very much in debate. Some believe that memory can operate much like a tape-recording that can be played back using tools such as hypnosis (Reiser, 1980). Others believe that memory is a malleable and incomplete abstraction of what happened (Loftus, 1979). In either case, most researchers agree that the more closely the context at the time of the interview resembles the situation as it actually was received, the more complete memory recall is likely to be. Mentally reinstating the context that surrounded a to-be-remembered event has been shown to be a powerful memory aid in numerous laboratory experiments (Smith, 1979). This technique certainly is easier to carry out than returning physically to the scene of a crime, and it may be preferable because the scene of a crime may have changed, thus creating a negative cuing effect (Loftus, Manber, & Keating, 1983).

Asking the victim or witness to be complete has two positive effects. First, we have found that many people do not have a good idea of the investigative value of any particular item of information and thus hold back information. Second, the act of being complete sometimes leads people to remember an important detail simply by thinking about seemingly unimportant details. Such associations are likely to be formed in memory because the important details were experienced contiguously with the unimportant details.

While events typically would be recalled in the order that they occurred, recalling the events in reverse order induces victims or witnesses to examine the memory record without the influence of their general knowledge of the type of crime in question (Geiselman & Callot, 1988). When events are recalled in forward order, some people reconstruct in their minds what they think must have happened based on their knowledge of similar crime scenarios (crime schemata). Geiselman and Callot found that this reconstruction can lead to incomplete or even inaccurate reports. In contrast, recall in reverse order is less schematic and often leads to recall of actions that are incidental to the crime scenario. Because these actions are more unique than actions consistent with a given crime scenario, they often are critical for linking one crime to others.

Mentally changing perspectives while recalling an event also appears to enhance the completeness of reports. In many cases, victims or witnesses experienced the incident from a variety of perspectives, but there is a tendency for people to report what they remember from a unitary, static perspective. Also, by recalling the reaction of others who were present, new details concerning the suspect's actions are recalled.

Specific Mnemonics

In addition to the four general methods, the cognitive interview utilizes a series of specific techniques that can be used, following the narrative phase of an interview, to elicit specific items of information. Instructions to use these techniques are given to the witness when the interviewer feels that they are needed. These specific techniques include the following:

Physical Appearance: "Think about whether the suspect reminded you of anyone you know. If you were reminded of someone, try to think of why. Was anything unusual about the physical appearance or clothing?" (For example, in one case this technique elicited from a witness that the suspect reminded him of Groucho Marx because of the way he walked. The peculiar walk was not reported earlier in the interview.)

Names: "If you think that a name was spoken but you cannot remember what it was, try to think of the first letter of the name by going through the alphabet. Afterward, try to think of the number of syllables."

Numbers: "Was the number high or low? How many digits were in the number? Were there any letters in the sequence?"

Speech Characteristics: "Think of whether the voice reminded you of someone else's voice. If you were reminded of someone, try to think why. Was there anything unusual about the voice?"

Conversation: "Think about your reactions to what was said, and the reactions of others. Were there any unusual words or phrases used?"

The cognitive interview has been found to be effective for enhancing eyewitness memory in seven studies described in this chapter. The amount of correct information was increased significantly when compared to standard interview procedures, even for the most critical items from the crime scenarios. Furthermore, the amount of incorrect information generated did not change.

Experiment 1

To enhance the validity of our evaluation of the cognitive interview, we conducted experiments in which the stimulus materials were emotionally arousing films of simulated violent crimes used for police trainees; the eyewitness interviews were interactive, as in real police interviews; and the interviews were conducted by experienced law enforcement personnel. The first major study (Geiselman, Fisher, MacKinnon, & Holland, 1985) compared the cognitive interview to two interview procedures that have been used by investigators, the hypnosis interview and the standard police interview. Eighty-nine students at the University of California at Los Angeles (UCLA) were interviewed to generate a total of more than 120 hr of recorded interviews.

Each taperecorded interview was transcribed. The information contained in the transcriptions was categorized into three exhaustive lists concerning the persons, objects, and events described for each film. The person category included physical appearance, clothing, mannerisms, and speech characteristics of each person described. The objects category included guns, knives, cars, and carried articles. The events category included movements of the persons, number of shots, interperson contacts, conversation, and general sequencing of events. This catalogue of information was used to score the transcribed report given by each subject for (1) the number of correct items of information recalled, (2) the number of incorrect items of information generated (e.g., the wrong hair color of a suspect), and (3) the number of confabulated items of information generated (e.g., a description of a suspect's face when the face was not shown in the film).

The results are presented in Table 6.1. Both the cognitive interview and the hypnosis interview elicited 35% more correct information from the witnesses than did the standard police interview. This observed memory enhancement for the cognitive and hypnosis interviews was not accompanied by an increase in incorrect or confabulated information. Neither the amount of time spent questioning the subject nor heightened subject or interviewer motivation could explain the results. We concluded

Table 6.1. Mean Number of Facts Recalled with the Three Types of Interview

Performance measure	Type of interview		
	Cognitive	Hypnosis	Standard
Number correct	41.2	38.0	29.4
Number incorrect	7.3	5.9	6.1
Number confabulated	0.7	1.0	0.4

that the memory enhancement effects were produced by the guided memory components of the cognitive and hypnosis interviews.

Although the cognitive and hypnosis procedures were equally effective, the cognitive interview can be easily learned and applied by interviewers after relatively little training. In addition to the savings in training time, the results showed that much less time was required to instruct a witness in the general cognitive mnemonics than to perform a hypnotic induction. Perhaps most important, the cognitive interview circumvents the present legal problems that surround forensic hypnosis (see Chapter 10). Thus, the cognitive interview is a viable memory enhancement technique that is effective, efficient, and legally acceptable. It remains to be determined whether or not hypnosis is more effective in cases where the victim or witness has experienced severe trauma (Reiser, 1980).

Experiment 2

Our second study (Geiselman, Fisher, MacKinnon, & Holland, 1986) was conducted to assess the effectiveness of the cognitive interview with a nonstudent population. This research was important because the memory retrieval techniques had been previously developed and evaluated only with student samples.

An argument can be made that the cognitive interview might be less effective with nonstudents because nonstudents are less practiced at using memory search strategies, and all of the research on the retrieval mnemonics in the cognitive interview has been carried out with college students. A competing argument could be made that the cognitive interview might be more effective with nonstudents either because (1) students are poorer observers due to their "preoccupation with competing thoughts" (McCarty, 1960), and thus much information is not stored for later retrieval in any case, or (2) students are more likely to know about and use retrieval mnemonics without being instructed to do so, and thus subjects in the standard interview carry out their own version of the cognitive interview.

Fifty-one paid volunteers, with a mean age of 32 years, served as subjects. The methodology was the same as in the first experiment, except that hypnosis was not studied. The results are shown in Table 6.2 and provide another demonstration of the memory enhancement qualities of the cognitive interview. As in the previous experiment, the cognitive interview elicited significantly more correct information than the standard police interview, without increasing incorrect or confabulated information. Thus, the cognitive interview was effective with a subject population that was more representative of those who are more likely to be victims or witnesses of crime.

Experiment 3

The third test of the cognitive interview was to determine whether the memory enhancement techniques affect witness responses to leading questions (Geiselman, Fisher, Cohen, Surtes, & Holland, 1986), as has been claimed for hypnosis (Putnam, 1979). We had found in our research that law enforcement professionals appear to ask very few leading questions, but in this study we intentionally asked leading questions. We staged an event in which two men entered a classroom and stole a slide projector. One of the men carried a *blue* backpack. When the students were questioned 48 hr later, some were asked near the beginning of the interview, "Was the guy with the *green* backpack nervous?" Near the end of the interview, they were asked, "What color was the backpack?"

Table 6.2. Recall Performance as a Function of Type of Interview and Level of Education

	College		No college	
Performance measure	Cognitive	Standard	Cognitive	Standard
Number correct	42.2	35.3	40.5	35.9
Number incorrect	8.1	8.2	9.9	8.9
Number confabulated	1.6	3.3	1.8	1.3

There are two possible ways in which the cognitive interview might influence the recollection of details for which misleading information has been presented. On the one hand, the interview might produce a strong bond between the interviewer and the witness, as is suspected with the hypnosis interview, and the witness may be more easily misled by the interviewer. On the other hand, the cognitive interview may *reduce* a subject's susceptibility to misleading questions. If a misleading question serves to create a second memory that coexists with the original one (Bekerian & Bowers, 1983), rather than replacing the original one (Greene, Flynn, & Loftus, 1982; Loftus, 1979), then reinstatement of the original context with the cognitive interview should lead the subject to retrieve the original (correct) memory at the time the misleading questions are asked.

The subjects were 42 undergraduate students recruited from UCLA. During the first meeting with the subjects, a staged incident was carried out by three research assistants from the Theater Arts Department at UCLA. A woman played the role of an experimenter from the Psychology Department, and two men played the roles of intruders. The experimenter greeted the students upon arrival and informed them that they would be expected to memorize a long list of words. The words were presented one at a time on a screen at the front of the room. After approximately 20 slides had been presented, the men entered the room and turned on the lights. One intruder pushed a cart that held a taperecorder and a typewriter. The other intruder carried a blue backpack with a yellow cord hanging out of it. They stated that they were there to pick up the projector because it was scheduled to be used by a professor. A verbal exchange ensued between the intruders and the experimenter, during which several bits of key information were presented. Despite objections by the experimenter, the intruders put the projector on their cart and left. The entire incident lasted between 45 sec and 1 min.

Each subject returned 48 hr after observing the incident and was randomly assigned to one of two interview conditions, cognitive or standard. Both groups were asked to recall as much information as they could about the incident. The group that received the cognitive interview was first instructed in the use of the four memory retrieval mnemonics to aid their recall.

At the beginning of the specific-questions phase of the interviews, which immediately followed the narrative phase, time was provided for the subjects to write their answers to three questions in the response booklets. For each subject, one of these questions contained misleading (incorrect) information, another contained leading (correct) information, and the remaining (control) questions contained no supplemental information.

At the end of each of the interviews, time was provided for the subjects to answer three questions designed to assess the impact of the leading and misleading questions. Immediately prior to asking these assessment questions, the experimenter in the cognitive interview condition briefly reviewed the four general mnemonics for the subjects. Subjects in the standard interview condition waited for a comparable period of time (1 min).

The results are presented in Table 6.3. The students who were questioned using the cognitive interview were somewhat less likely to report the color of the backpack as green than were students who were questioned using standard interview procedures. Thus, the cognitive interview did not render the subjects

Table 6.3. Proportion of Subjects Giving Each Type of Answer to the Target Question in Experiment 3

Type of question	Type of answer			
	Correct	Misleading alternative	Other alternative	"Don't know"
Leading				
Cognitive	.55	.09	.05	.31
Standard	.65	.05	.10	.20
Control				
Cognitive	.55	.05	.18	.22
Standard	.50	.05	.25	.20
Misleading				
Cognitive	.15	.49	.05	.31
Standard	.05	.60	.10	.25

more susceptible to leading questions but actually helped to reduce the effects of leading questions on accurate memory recall. This outcome is logical if we assume that the cognitive interview guides the witness back to the original (correct) memory for what happened.

Experiment 4

A fourth experiment examined the effectiveness of the cognitive interview with child witnesses, aged 7 to 12 years old (Geiselman & Padilla, in press). The legal and social service fields need better techniques for improving children's reports of experienced and witnessed events. In recent years an increasing number of children have been asked to testify concerning criminal events. Many court cases have been dismissed because of inadequate testimony and charges of faulty interviewing. Therefore, it is crucial to develop interview techniques that are nonsuggestive and that are not likely to be construed as suggestive in the courtroom. Based on the results of Experiment 3, the cognitive interview would appear to be a promising alternative.

The literature on child development suggests that the cognitive interview would be useful with child witnesses. With respect to reinstatement of context, Pressley and Levin (1980) observed that imagery instructions enhanced the recall performance of children. With respect to amount of information spontaneously recalled, in some studies children recalled less than adults (King & Yuille, 1987; Marin, Holmes, Guth, & Kovac, 1979). However, Goodman, Aman, and Hirschman (1987) reported only minor effects of age on recall. With respect to the order of items recalled, the ability to recall in correct serial order has been shown to develop gradually with age (Brown, 1975; Piaget, 1969). The ability to take the perspectives of others also has been shown to develop gradually with age (Flavell, 1986). Thus, assistance with these procedures is likely to enhance the completeness of children's reports. Many studies have examined the memory performance of children versus that of adults, but little research has been conducted on interview methods for maximizing the completeness of a child's report from a memory perspective.

The subjects were 15 children from 7 to 12 years of age. Before agreeing to participate in the study, all parents and children were informed that they would be viewing a film depicting a violent crime and that they would be interviewed about the contents of the film 3 days later. The film, which was also used in Experiment 1, presents a street perspective of a liquor store holdup that is rich in quantifiable information, including person descriptions, mannerisms, weapons, and sequences of events.

After a 3-day delay, the subjects were interviewed by a graduate research assistant about what they had seen in the film. Seven children were randomly assigned to be interviewed using a standard interview format, and 8 children were randomly assigned to be interviewed using the cognitive interview. All interviews were taperecorded for later analysis.

The subjects who received the standard interview were first asked to describe in their own words what they remembered about the film (open-ended report). Then, and only then, they were asked specific questions about the film (Loftus, 1979). These questions were based on the narrative account given by the witness, who then was asked to elaborate on any persons, objects, and events previously mentioned. As in an actual police interview, the interviewer continued until it appeared that the child had exhausted the memory for the event. This form of interactive questioning was selected to preserve the ecological validity of the results. This is especially important because the type of questioning chosen to elicit information is known to affect the resulting evaluation of children's memory (Goetze, 1981; Goodman & Reed, 1986).

The general structure of the cognitive interview was the same as that for the standard interview, except that memory guidance techniques were used in conjunction with the questions. Before the subjects gave their narrative accounts of the event, the interviewer asked the subjects to try to reconstruct mentally the circumstances that surrounded the event, such as the nature of the weather, the lighting, and nearby people or objects, and to think about how they were feeling and their reactions during the event. The interviewer also asked the subjects to be complete and not to hold back any information, even if they thought that the information was not important. They were told, "Think about how you were feeling while you were watching the movie, and think about what the whole area in the movie looked like. Think about where things were, what the weather was like. Also, I want you to tell me everything that you can remember. Sometimes people will not say some things because they think they are not important, but I want you to tell me everything."

Following the narrative report by the subject, the interviewer asked the subject to recall the events in reverse order, starting at the end and pretending that the film was being shown in reverse, "as if the movie had been shown backwards." Also, the subjects were asked to imagine that they were some other person that was present at the scene and to recall the events from the perspective of that person: "Pretend you are the bad guy and tell me what happened." When appropriate, a series of specific memory-jogging techniques were used to elicit specific kinds of information. For names, the subjects were told, "Go through the alphabet and see if you can find the first letter of the name" (Gruneberg & Monks, 1976). For further descriptions of suspects, they were asked, "Did the suspect(s) remind you of anyone you know, and if so, why?"

Each taperecorded interview was transcribed by research assistants trained by the authors. They were blind to the research hypotheses. The transcriptions of the tapes then were given to another member of the research team who categorized the information for each film into three exhaustive lists concerning persons, objects, and events. The persons category included physical appearance, clothing, mannerisms, and speech characteristics. The objects category included guns, knives, cars, and carried articles. The events category included movements, number of shots, interpersonal contacts, conversation, and general sequencing. These exhaustive lists were compiled and matched against the information contained in the film to determine the accuracy of each subject's report.

This catalogue of information then was used to score each subject's transcribed report for the number of correct bits of information, the number of mistakes (inaccurate reporting of information that appeared in the film), and the number of confabulated items of information (reporting of information that did not appear in the film in any form). This scoring was carried out by members of the research team, who checked one another's work and resolved discrepancies by majority vote.

In addition to the memory variables, the length of the interviews was also obtained. This measure was used as a covariate to assess recall effects corrected for questioning time. Since the film used here was the same as that used by Geiselman et al. (1985) with college students, the present data were compared with the adult data. This comparison is tenuous, however, because the adults were interviewed by experienced law enforcement professionals, and the two samples of subjects were not matched on demographic variables.

Table 6.4 presents the three recall measures as a function of type of interview. The comparison data for the adults were taken from Geiselman et al. (1985). With respect to the children, the cognitive interview produced 21% more correct items of information than the standard interview. The number of mistakes and confabulations did not differ as a function of type of interview.

This analysis was carried out without considering the relative importance of the information that was generated. Thus, it was possible that the extra details produced with cognitive

Table 6.4. Performance Measures as a Function of Type of Interview and Age Group

Type of interview	Performance measure		
	Correct	Mistakes	Confabulation
Cognitive			
Adults	57.3	8.0	0.6
Children	37.1	5.0	6.4
Standard			
Adults	29.9	8.1	0.7
Children	30.7	6.4	6.3

Note. The adult data are taken from Geiselman et al. (1985).

interviewing were unimportant or trivial. Therefore, the 20 most important facts from the film were chosen for selective scoring. A list of the 20 most important facts was generated independently by each of the five members of the research group, and the lists were merged at a joint meeting of the group in the manner described in Geiselman et al. (1985). As before, adult comparison data were taken from Geiselman et al. (1985). Although the increase in recall of critical facts with the cognitive interview was not as great for the children as it was for the adults, the small observed increase was reliable. Thus, the results of this analysis mimic those of the full analysis (see Geiselman & Padilla, in press, for details of these analysis). This outcome is important because any one of these critical details could lead to a successful case resolution.

To determine if the difference in total amount of correct recall for the two interview methods could be attributed to the length of the interviews, an analysis of covariance was carried out. There was no significant difference in the average lengths of the two types of interviews, and the difference between them in the total amount of correct recall remained significant.

While these results confirmed that the cognitive interview with children is an improvement over the standard interview, the cognitive interview was considerably more effective when law enforcement professionals interviewed adults (see Table 6.4). This difference cannot be attributed to inferior encoding or retention by the children, because they did not differ from the adults in the amount of correct recall when standard interviews were administered (see Table 6.4). This was true even though the interviews of the children required nearly 15 min less than those of the adults. Thus, these children may have been less successful than adults either in understanding some of the cognitive techniques or in executing them effectively.

Finally, while the children produced somewhat fewer mistakes than the adults, they generated approximately 10 times the number of confabulations. This comparison between the recall of children and that of adults is guarded, however, as noted above, because no attempt was made to equate the two populations on clinical or demographic characteristics.

Experiment 5

The purpose of this part of the research program (MacKinnon, O'Reilly, & Geiselman, 1988; Mende, MacKinnon, & Geiselman, 1986) was to extend the scope of cognitive interviewing to the important problem of witness memory for license plates. While most law enforcement professionals would likely agree that recall of a license plate can be a critical factor in case solution (e.g., for bank robberies), memory for license plates has received little attention in the eyewitness research literature. In fact, a computer search of the psychological and police science literature discovered no study that directly addressed memory for license plates.

The research described here was designed to develop and test techniques to enhance the completeness and accuracy of eyewitness reports for license plate information. Among the techniques studied were an innovative questioning routine that included mental reinstatement of contextual information and a license plate simulation device to aid the witness in visualizing characters on the plate. The plate simulation device was constructed of colored paper and vinyl alphanumeric characters such that the characters could be inserted and interchanged in the plate shell upon the subjects' command. The purpose of the device was to reinstate the visual context of a license plate and to provide an opportunity for the witness to generate character configurations for inspection.

The questioning routine began with the visualization instructions, "Visualize the car in your mind. Did the car remind you of anyone else's car? Now visualize the back end of the car. Focus in on the truck . . . the tail lights . . . now the bumper. Were there any stickers on the bumper? Now center in on the license plate." The witness then was asked, "Did the letters or numbers remind you of any words or things? Did the characters have lines, curves, or anything special about them? Did the characters appear to be close together?" and so on.

More than 300 subjects were shown slides that depicted what was described simply as a "suspicious event." The set of 10 slides depicted a man who carried a television set, placed it in his car in a hurried manner, and drove the car down the street. Two sets of slides were used, with a different car and license plate in each set. Immediately after the last slide, the witness was asked to give a written description of the events presented in the slides. After this unstructured narrative recall, the witness received one of four types of interview to recall the license plate. The interviews were created from the combination of two factors: (1) cognitive questioning or no cognitive questioning, and (2) license plate simulator or no plate simulator. The control subjects (no cognitive questioning and no license plate simulator) were asked a series of questions, generated from a poll of several detectives in the Los Angeles, California, area regarding their interview techniques for license plates, such as "Was there a frame on the plate? Was it a personalized plate?"

Both the cognitive interview and the license plate simulation device resulted in significant increases in correct plate information generated by the subjects. While the standard interview of the control subjects produced 1% more correct characters than incorrect characters, the subjects who either received cognitive interviews or worked with the plate simulation device produced 10% more correct characters than incorrect characters. Furthermore, the combination of cognitive interview and license plate simulator produced an interactive improvement. These subjects performed best of all, showing a 33% increase that represented an average production of two additional correct characters. These increases were not achieved by spending more time with the witnesses because performance was unrelated to questioning time, and there is no evidence that simply motivating the subjects to try harder enhances the retrieval of memories (Weiner, 1966). Thus, the cognitive questioning and the plate simulator were both useful for enhancing witness recall of plate information. These data represent another instance where mental reinstatement of context is a powerful technique for enhancing witness memory retrieval.

While the techniques studied here rarely led to the recall of an entire plate (average recall was 3.9 of the 7 characters presented), the two-character increase dramatically reduced the number of possibilities for investigation and computer search.

For example, if the characters given by a witness were recalled in their correct order (only 10% of the errors observed were transposition errors), then recalling four characters instead of two on a California license plate would reduce the number of possibilities from 676,000 plates to 260 plates. These results are encouraging.

REFINING THE COGNITIVE INTERVIEW

Our initial refinements of the cognitive interview were based on carefully analyzing interviews conducted in the laboratory. There were characteristic differences between effective and ineffective interviewers. One typical difference was that effective interviewers asked more open-ended questions and allowed the witness to dominate the interview, whereas ineffective interviewers asked more direct, short-answer questions and played a more central role in the interview. We therefore modeled good interviewers by building in the attributes of good interviewers and deleting the faults characteristic of poor interviewers.

To increase the validity of our observations, we also examined police interviews conducted in the field (Fisher, Geiselman, & Raymond, 1987). Although the interviews varied considerably, three problem techniques appeared universally. First, interviewers often interrupted the eyewitness in the middle of a narrative description. On the average, interviewers interrupted within 7.5 sec after the respondent began his response. Second, interviewers used an excessive number of short-answer questions. The average interview contained 3 open-ended questions and 26 short-answer questions. Short-answer questions are often less valuable than open-ended questions, especially when used extensively, since they elicit less elaborated responses. Third, in many of the field interviews the sequence of questions seemed unplanned and generally unrelated to the mental activities of the witness. Furthermore, it appeared that this haphazard question order frequently created a barrier that obstructed memory. Several other errors were also noted, often reflecting poor wording or presentation style.

After analyzing the laboratory and field interviews, we revised the original cognitive interview (Fisher, Geiselman, Raymond, Jurkevich, & Warhaftig, 1987). The revised cognitive interview includes four basic principles: event-interview similarity, focused retrieval, extensive retrieval, and witness-compatible questioning. The following is a brief description of the core principles.

Event-Interview Similarity

This principle is identical to the "reconstruct the circumstances" principle of the original cognitive interview. Memory of an event, such as a crime, is enhanced when the psychological environment at the interview is similar to the environment at the original crime. The interviewer, therefore, should try to reinstate in the witness's mind the external (e.g., weather), emotional (e.g., feelings of fear), and cognitive (e.g., relevant thoughts) features that were experienced at the time that the crime occurred. The witness need not be placed physically back in the same environment; mentally recreating the environment is sufficient.

Focused Retrieval

Memory retrieval, like other mental acts, requires concentrated effort. One of the interviewer's roles, then, is to assist the witness to focus concentration. Any disruptions of the retrieval process, such as noise disturbances or interruptions of the witness's report, will impair performance. Frequently, witnesses will not attempt to search memory in a concentrated manner because of the additional mental effort involved. In these instances, the effective interviewer must encourage the witness to make the extra effort.

Extensive Retrieval

In general, the more attempts the witness makes to retrieve a particular episode, the more information will be recalled. Witnesses should therefore be encouraged to conduct as many retrieval attempts as possible. Many witnesses will terminate their retrieval after the first unsuccessful effort. This is a particular problem for older witnesses. It is important, therefore, for the interviewer to encourage witnesses to continue trying to retrieve, even if they claim not to know a particular detail.

Witness-Compatible Questioning

Successful retrieval of an event will depend, in part, on how compatible the questions are to the form in which that witness has learned the information. It is important, therefore, for the interviewer to tailor the interview to the witness. A uniform style of questioning, asked of all witnesses alike, will not effectively tap the memories of each witness. It is more effective for interviewers to be flexible and to alter their interviewing style to meet the needs of each witness than for them to use a rigid, uniform style of questioning and to force witnesses to adjust their memory to the interviewers' questioning. Try to place yourself in the witness's frame of mind and then ask questions that are relevant to that perspective.

Experiment 6

Two experiments were conducted to examine the revised cognitive interview. In this first experiment (Fisher, Geiselman, Raymond, Jurkevich, & Warhafting, 1987), subjects were shown the videotape of either the bank or the liquor store robbery used in the previous experiments (Geiselman et al., 1985; Geiselman, Fisher, MacKinnon, & Holland, 1986). Two days later, the witnesses were interviewed about the film by research assistants trained to use the original or revised cognitive interview. The interviews were taperecorded and scored for accuracy against the original film. As seen in Table 6.5, the revised cognitive interview elicited approximately 45% more information than the original technique, which had been shown earlier to be 30% to 35% more effective than a standard witness interview (Geiselman et al., 1985; Geiselman, Fisher, MacKinnon, & Holland, 1986). Furthermore, the advantage of the revised technique did not

Table 6.5. Recall in Revised and Original Cognitive Interviews

	Type of cognitive interview	
	Revised	Original
Number correct	57.5	39.6
Error rate	.17	.19

come at the expense of additional errors. The error rates were approximately 18% in both groups. When compared to similar observation conditions in the earlier studies, the revised cognitive interview elicited almost twice as many correct statements (96%) as the standard police interview.

Experiment 7

Having demonstrated reliably in the laboratory that the cognitive interview can elicit more information than the standard witness interview, we entered the most important phase of the research program: testing the cognitive interview in the field (Fisher, Geiselman, & Amador, 1988). Does the cognitive interview elicit more information when detectives conduct interviews with actual victims and witnesses of crime?

We again enlisted the assistance of the Metro-Dade Police Department to conduct the field research. Initially, 16 experienced detectives from the Robbery Division were selected for the study, all of whom taperecorded their next several interviews. In all, 79 interviews were recorded, primarily with victims of commercial robberies or purse-snatchings. Based on these preliminary interviews and on the recommendations of the detectives' commanding officer, two equivalent groups were formed. One group was trained in the cognitive interview. The second group served as a control.

The effectiveness of the cognitive interview can be examined in two ways: by comparing the number of facts elicited before and after training for each of the 7 detectives who completed the entire training program, and by comparing the number of facts elicited by the trained versus the untrained detectives. The cognitive interview was found effective in both the before-and-after comparison and in the trained-untrained groups comparison. As a group, the 7 trained detectives elicited 47% more information after than before training (39.6 facts vs. 26.8 facts). Of these 7, 6 elicited more information (65% to 173% more) after than before training. Only one detective did not do appreciably better after training than before. An analysis of the posttraining interviews showed that he was the only one of the 7 detectives who did not follow the recommended procedures. Across the two groups, the trained detectives collected 63% more information than the untrained detectives (39.6 facts vs. 24.2 facts). Prior to training, the two groups were equivalent.

As with the laboratory studies, we were concerned not only with the amount of information elicited by the cognitive interview but also with its accuracy. To what degree might the additional information elicited by the cognitive interview simply reflect lower accuracy? To estimate accuracy, therefore, we examined corroboration rates, the degree to which elicited statements were corroborated by other reliable sources of information (e.g., other victims or witnesses to the crime). Of 24 interviews where corroborating information was available (16 by pretraining and 8 by posttraining interviews), there were 325 corroboratable statements. Overall, the confirmation rates were extremely high and were not different for the pretraining (93.0%) and posttraining (94.5%) interviews. The similar corroboration rates for the cognitive interview and the standard witness interview duplicates the laboratory findings on accuracy rates and again suggests that the added information elicited by the cognitive interview does not come at the expense of additional incorrect information.

CONCLUSIONS

Historically, little training has been available to investigators on interviewing witnesses and victims, but our critiques of both laboratory and field interviews indicate that current standard interviewing techniques can be improved considerably through training. The results of each of the studies reported here confirm that cognitive interviewing reliably enhances the completeness of a witness's recollection, without increasing the number of incorrect or confabulated bits of information generated. Based on the examination of several interviews, a revision of the original cognitive interview was made, which was found to further enhance the quality of witness reports. The procedures are easy to learn and can be readily adopted in routine police interviews. In fact, the cognitive interview is currently in use as standard training at several police departments and at other law enforcement agencies.

The effectiveness of the cognitive interview generalizes to a variety of populations. In previous work, the cognitive interview was found to be successful both with college-educated witnesses and with those who had not attended college. The present research shows that the cognitive interview is effective with both adults and children.

Most important, the cognitive interview was found to be successful in the field, in comparison to both standard detective interviews and uniformed officer reports. As noted by Malpass and Devine (1980), "No matter how well executed or elegant our studies are, they will be of questionable relevance at best without a knowledge of the differences between eyewitnessing in real situations compared with research situations" (p. 344). In our field study, the "research situation" was the "real situation," and the cognitive interview increased eyewitness recollection.

ACKNOWLEDGEMENTS

This research was supported by two grants from the National Institute of Justice (USDJ-83-IJ-CX-0025 and USDJ-85-IJ-CX-0053).

REFERENCES

Bekerian, D. A., & Bowers, J. M. (1983). Eyewitness testimony: Were we misled? *Journal of Experimental Psychology: Learning, Memory, and Cognition, 9,* 139–145.

Brown, A. (1975). The development of memory: Knowing, knowing about knowing, and knowing how to know. In H. W. Reese (Ed.), *Advances in Child and Behavior*, Vol. 10, pp. 156–166). New York: Academic Press.

Fisher, R. P., Geiselman, R. E., & Amador, M. (1988). Field testing of the cognitive interview. Manuscript submitted for publication.

Fisher, R. P., Geiselman, R. E., & Raymond, D. S. (1987). Critical analysis of police interview techniques. *Journal of Police Science and Administration, 15*, 177–185.

Fisher, R. P., Geiselman, R. E., Raymond, D. S., Jurkevich, L. M., & Warhaftig, M. L. (1987). Enhancing enhanced eyewitness memory: Refining the cognitive interview. *Journal of Police Science and Administration, 15*, 291–197.

Flavell, J. H. (1986). The development of children's knowledge about the appearance-reality distinction. *American Psychologist, 41*, 418–425.

Frye v. United States 293 F. 1013 (1923).

Geiselman, R. E., & Callot, R. (1988). Reverse versus forward recall of script-based texts. *Journal of Applied Cognitive Psychology*.

Geiselman, R. E., Fisher, R. P., Cohen, G., Surtes, L., & Holland, H. L. (1986). Eyewitness responses to leading and misleading questions under the cognitive interview. *Journal of Police Science and Administration, 14*(1), 31–39.

Geiselman, R. E., Fisher, R. P., MacKinnon, D. P., & Holland, H. L. (1985). Eyewitness memory enhancement in the police interview: Cognitive retrieval mnemonics versus hypnosis. *Journal of Applied Psychology, 70*, 401–412.

Geiselman, R. E., Fisher, R. P., MacKinnon, D. P., & Holland, H. L. (1986). Enhancement of eyewitness memory with the cognitive interview. *American Journal of Psychology, 99*, 385–401.

Geiselman, R. E. & Padilla, J. (in press). Interviewing child witnesses with the cognitive interview. *Journal of Police Science and Administration*.

Goetze, H. J. (1981). The effect of age and method of interview on the accuracy and completeness of eyewitness accounts. *Dissertation Abstracts International, 42*, order # 8113913.

Goodman, G. S., Aman, C., & Hirschman, J. (1987). Child sexual and physical abuse: Children's testimony. In S. J. Ceci, D. F., Ross, & M. P. Toglia (Eds.), *Children's eyewitness memory* (pp. 1–23). New York: Springer-Verlag.

Goodman, G. S., & Reed, R. S. (1986). Age differences in eyewitness testimony. *Law and Human Behavior, 10*, 317–332.

Greene, E., Flynn, M., & Loftus, E. F. (1982). Inducing resistance to misleading information. *Journal of Verbal Learning and Verbal Behavior, 21*, 207–219.

Gruneberg, M. M., & Monks, J. (1976). The first letter search strategy. *IRCS Medical Science: Psychology and Psychiatry, 4*, 307.

King, M. A., & Yuille, J. C. (1987). Suggestibility and the child witness. In S. J. Ceci, D. F. Ross, & M. P. Toglia (Eds.), *Children's eyewitness memory* (pp. 24–35). New York: Springer-Verlag.

Loftus, E. F. (1979). *Eyewitness testimony.* Cambridge, MA: Harvard University Press.

Loftus, E. F., Manber, M., & Keating, J. F. (1983). Recollection of naturalistic events: Context enhancement versus negative cueing. *Human Learning, 2*, 83–92.

MacKinnon, D. P., O'Reilly, K. E., & Geiselman, R. E. (1988). Memory for license plates. *Journal of Applied Cognitive Psychology.*

Malpass, R. S., & Devine, P. G. (1980). Realism and eyewitness identification research. *Law and Human Behavior, 4*, 347–358.

Marin, C., Holmes, D., Guth, M., & Kovac, P. (1979). The potential of children as eyewitnesses. *Law and Human Behavior, 3*, 295–305.

McCarty, M. (1960). *Psychology and the law.* Englewood Cliffs, NJ: Prentice-Hall.

Mende, L., MacKinnon, D. P., & Geiselman, R. E. (1986). Memory for license plates as a function of exposure time. *Journal of Police Science and Administration, 15*(1), 68–71.

Piaget, J. (1969). *The child's conception of time.* London:

Pressley, M., & Levin, J. (1980). The development of mental imagery retrieval. *Child Development, 51*, 558–560.

Putman, W. H. (1979). Hypnosis and distortions in eyewitness memory. *International Journal of Clinical and Experimental Hypothesis, 27*, 437–448.

Reiser, M. (1980). *Handbook of investigative hypnosis.* Los Angeles: LEHI.

Sanders, G. S. (1986). On increasing the usefulness of eyewitness research. *Law and Human Behavior, 10*, 333–336.

Smith, S. (1979). Remembering in and out of context. *Journal of Experimental Psychology: Human Learning and Memory, 5*, 460–471.

Weiner, B. (1966). The effects of motivation on the availability and retrieval of memory traces. *Psychological Bulletin, 65*, 24–37.

Yarmey, A. D. (1979). *The psychology of eyewitness testimony.* New York: Free Press.

Criteria-Based Statement Analysis

7

Max Steller and Guenter Koehnken

In Germany, the assessment of the credibility of statements by child witnesses in cases of sexual abuse is made by psychologists who are appointed as expert witnesses by trial courts. The psychological assessment is based on three elements:

1. Analysis of the individual characteristics of the child witness
2. Analysis of the possible motives for the witness to make a false accusation
3. Analysis of the content of the statement itself

The methods to assess the individual characteristics and motives of the witness are identical to those used for other psychodiagnostic problems. They include biographical interviews, behavioral assessments, and psychometric or other tests. The analysis of the individual characteristics of the witness and possible motives for making a false accusation enable the psychologist to make an overall assessment of the person. This includes the general intellectual and emotional attributes of the witness.

Older approaches to witness psychology in Germany dealt with "general trustworthiness" as a kind of personality construct and inferred from the personality diagnosis the credibility of the witness in a particular case. In contrast to this outdated point of view, statement analysis aims to assess the veracity of the specific testimony of a witness. It is a trivial fact that a generally honest person may have motives to deceive in a particular case and that a person who is generally dishonest may be truthful concerning a certain issue. Therefore, assessing the general trustworthiness of a person does not contribute to solving a case. It is not the general credibility of the person but the credibility of the statement in the specific instance that is of interest for judicial decisions.

The analysis of a statement is conducted according to criteria applied to the content, the so-called reality criteria. The analysis of the quality of a statement by use of reality criteria is made against a background of the individual's personality and cognitive and verbal competencies. Therefore, some type of analysis of the individual is included in assessing the veracity of the statement, although it does not make use of the construct of "general trustworthiness" for assessing the credibility of statements about specific issues. Evaluation of the quality of a statement by means of reality criteria requires some knowledge of the intellectual and verbal abilities of the witness. In this meaning, individual assessment is part of statement analysis. Certain reality criteria can be evaluated properly only by taking the cognitive abilities of a person into account. The material that follows is confined to a description of statement analysis by means of content (reality) criteria, a procedure that is called *criteria-based statement analysis*.

SYSTEM OF CONTENT CRITERIA

The basic assumption of criteria-based statement analysis is that statements based on observations of actual (self-experienced) events differ in quality from statements that are not based on direct experience but are products of fantasy or invention. The reality criteria or content criteria reflect specific features that differentiate truthful from invented testimonies.

In the 1930s reality criteria were first described in German psychological and juristic literature. In 1954 the German

Criteria-Based Statement Analysis 219

Supreme Court held a hearing and ruled (Undeutsch, 1982, pp. 37–38) that expert witnesses must be appointed to assess the truthfulness of statements, if the testimonies of children or juveniles are the only or main evidence. As the number of practical cases has increased enormously, German psychologists have conducted many thousands of interviews with children and adolescents and have gathered considerable experience in the juridical field (Arntzen, 1982).

Statement analysis has only recently been described in English by Undeutsch (1982,1984), who is considered the pioneer of the present practice of statement analysis in the courts of West Germany. After Undeutsch's (1967) first extensive description of reality criteria, Arntzen (1970, 1983) and Szewczyk (1973; cf. also Dettenborn, Froehlich, & Szewczyk, 1984) published similar compendia in German. In 1963 in Sweden, Trankell described a technique of analyzing witness statements by reality criteria (Trankell, 1972).

Although all authors use the term *reality criteria*, Trankell's (1972) technique for the assessment of witness reports cannot be directly compared with those of Undeutsch, Arntzen, and Szewczyk. While Trankell described a holistic-intuitive approach, Undeutsch, Arntzen, and Szewczyk presented detailed lists of different criteria. Undeutsch (1967, 1982, 1984) and Szewczyk (1973) simply presented several criteria by naming them and giving examples, whereas Arntzen (1970) provided the first classification of criteria, as presented in Table 7.1. Sporer (1983) presented a critical discussion of these concepts with particular reference to Arntzen's (1970) criteria.

The organization of criteria by Arntzen (1970) is unsystematic and unconvincing (Koehnken, 1982). For example, *incontinence* defines a criterion that is fulfilled if the sequence of events is reported by a witness in an unorganized, disarranged manner but can still be put together into a chronological and meaningful event by the evaluator. Therefore, it is a content criterion rather than something that can be assessed by observation of the witness's behavior accompanying the testimony, as proposed by Arntzen.

On the basis of Arntzen's (1970) classification of criteria, it can be shown that until now all authors have improperly used

Table 7.1. Criteria for the Credibility of Testimony by Arntzen (1970)

1. Criteria from the development of testimony over time
   a. Constancy over several reports
   b. Type of supplementations
2. Criteria from the content of testimony
   a. Amount and specificity of details
      Reproduction of conversations
      Description of inner events
      Description of typical but not understood phenomena
      Interconnectedness with temporary external circumstances
      Negative complications in the course of action
      Complicated response chains
      "Onion structure" of contents
      Unusual (minor) details
   b. Offense specific details
3. Criteria from the expressive format of testimony
   a. Differentiation of emotions
   b. Incontinence (conclusiveness despite lack of organization)
   c. Naturalness and spontaneity (lack of control)
4. Criteria from the context of testimony
   a. Inferred underlying motivations

Note. From Sporer, S. L. (1983). *Content Criteria of Credibility: The German Approach to Children's Eyewitness Testimony.* Used by permission.

the term *reality criteria* to refer to quite different subject matters. Under the heading *reality criteria*, topics were listed that must be applied in a general fashion when assessing the credibility of statements. On the other hand, the term *reality criteria* was also used to refer to features of the content of a statement that may or may not be fulfilled in specific instances. For example, the motivation of a witness to make a false accusation is not a reality criterion. However, motivation must be analyzed during the credibility assessment of a witness's allegations. The same is true for observable behavior that accompanies the testimony.

The term *reality criteria* should be reserved exclusively for criteria that refer to the contents of a statement. *Content criteria* can be used synonymously with *reality criteria*, as they can both be assessed by analyzing the content of a written transcript of the witness's statement. This procedure is known as *criteria-based statement analysis*. Reality criteria can be judged as present or not present, or rated in terms of the strength or extent to which they are fulfilled in a certain statement.

Table 7.2 presents a revised system of content criteria used in statement analysis. It consists of five major categories containing 19 individual criteria. This system constitutes an integration of the criteria listed by Undeutsch (1967), Arntzen (1970, 1983) Szewczyk (1973), and Dettenborn et al. (1984). As a result of the criticism that these researchers' approaches suffered

Table 7.2. Content Criteria for Statement Analysis

General Characteristics
    1. Logical structure
    2. Unstructured production
    3. Quantity of details

Specific Contents
    4. Contextual embedding
    5. Descriptions of interactions
    6. Reproduction of conversation
    7. Unexpected complications during the incident

Peculiarities of Content
    8. Unusual details
    9. Superfluous details
    10. Accurately reported details misunderstood
    11. Related external associations
    12. Accounts of subjective mental state
    13. Attribution of perpetrator's mental state

Motivation-Related Contents
    14. Spontaneous corrections
    15. Admitting lack of memory
    16. Raising doubts about one's own testimony
    17. Self-deprecation
    18. Pardoning the perpetrator

Offense-Specific Elements
    19. Details characteristic of the offense

from a substantial lack of systematic organization and precise definitions and distinctions, this newly organized system of reality criteria was developed.

General Characteristics

The first major category includes general characteristics of the statement. These reality criteria are related to the complete testimony, the statement taken as a whole. They can be looked upon as the first step of a statement analysis and can be assessed without reference to the details of the content of the statement.

Criterion 1: Logical Structure

Testimonies, especially extensive ones, must be examined for their logical consistency and/or contextual homogeneity (contextual coherence). Trankell (1972, p. 129) stated that the homogeneity criterion is fulfilled when different, independent details in a statement all describe the same course of events. Undeutsch (1967, p. 138) described this as an inner coherence and consistency. Arntzen (1983) interpreted a homogeneous testimony as being one in "which the contextual details can be combined as a whole, without any discrepancies or inconsistencies; also that these details can be brought together in an integrated organic coherency in which the contents of the testimony are also consistent" (p. 51).

It should be taken into consideration that neither the accounts of unusual details (criterion 8) nor the appearance of unexpected complications in the events (criterion 7) necessarily interfere with the logical consistency.

Criterion 2: Unstructured Production

One aspect of the validity of a statement can be assessed in terms of the manner in which the essential aspects of the case are reported. This criterion is meaningful only when dealing with statements in which a witness has given a free account of the event without interference from too much structure induced by direct questioning by the interviewer.

Arntzen (1983) used the label *incontinence* to characterize a "testimony without control," a statement that has an "incoherent, disconnected (desultory), unorganized manner of representation" (p. 80). The factual elements of the case are scattered throughout the statement or completely disarrayed in their descriptions. They are accompanied by temporary digressions, and the sequence of events is not reported in chronological order. However, fragments of the statement must be capable of being joined together into a unified whole that indicates the logical consistency of the content of the testimony. Fabricated testimonies and fantasies are usually characterized by a continuous, structured, generally chronological manner of presentation, with clear attempts by the witness to demonstrate causal connections. An expressive style showing lack of constraint and producing an unstructured presentation is considered a sign of the validity of the statement. However, if the statement shows inconsistencies that cannot be resolved within the context of the entire statement, it violates logical structure (criterion 1), which is an indication of the lack of credibility of the statement.

Criterion 3: Quantity of Details

According to Arntzen (1983), a considerable number of details in a statement is an indication of its credibility because "it is impossible for the majority of witnesses to embellish a false testimony with numerous details" (p. 27). Abundant detail in a statement is present when, for instance, the exact place is described, persons are described in detail from different aspects, or the succession of events is described step by step. However, repetitions of the same details should not be counted again; only distinct facts or details should be considered.

Specific Contents

The second major category of content criteria concerns the specific contents of the statement. In this second step of the analysis of the statement, specific parts of the testimony are assessed in terms of the presence or strength of certain types of descriptions.

Criterion 4: Contextual Embedding

Undeutsch (1967) mentioned that "real incidents have a temporal and spatial basis" (p. 139), and Dettenborn et al. (1984, p. 313) emphasized the anchoring of the contents of a statement into the whole of a situation. According to Arntzen (1983), "diverse intertwinings of the essential facts of the event under investigation with those of the external, changeable circumstances" (p. 35) also support the credibility of the testimony. Such space-time interrelations can be, for example, "everyday occurrences, habits, the family, acquaintances, residential relationships" (p. 35). When a deceiving person describes events of peripheral interest, such a close fusion of major events with irrelevant details or mutual influences is not expected in the statement.

All credible statements cannot be expected to fulfill this criterion because an account of a brief event or one that took place without being connected to the prevailing circumstances can be recounted only in the way in which it actually happened. However, if contextual embeddings are reported, this can be considered an indicator of the credibility of a statement.

Criterion 5: Descriptions of Interactions

Arntzen (1983) reported that descriptions of interactions can appear in truthful statements. He stated, "Here it concerns a chain of mutual actions and reactions of both the witness and of that person to whom the testimony refers, above all, those deeds and discussions that are mutually dependent and are reported fluently" (p. 34). We do not agree with Arntzen's restriction that the descriptions must be fluently reported. To fulfill this criterion, it is sufficient if the child describes interactions, even if in a clumsy or awkward manner. If conversation is reproduced verbatim by the child, it is scored under criterion 6 and also under criterion 5 if it describes an interaction. Dettenborn et al.

(1984, p. 314) observed that accounts of interactions containing misperceptions and misunderstandings constitute a stronger instance of this criterion. Descriptions of any kind of interaction are considered signs of the credibility of a statement.

Criterion 6: Reproduction of Conversation

Arntzen (1983, p. 32) stated that a clue to the veracity of a statement occurs when accounts of conversation are provided. In contrast to criterion 5, with this type of interaction we are dealing only with dialogue. The different speakers should be recognizable in the reproduced dialogues. This requirement is especially fulfilled when the witness includes in the perpetrator's speech vocabulary that is atypical for the age of the witness, or reasoning used by the accused is included, or conversations that reveal the different attitudes of the perpetrator and the victim/witness are presented.

On the whole, this criterion is not satisfied by a report about the content of a dialogue; it is satisfied only when there is a virtual replication of the utterances of at least one person. The report should create the impression that the witness reexperienced the verbal context of the situation when providing the statement. With regard to verbal interactions, this criterion differs from criterion 5 by being a stronger indication of credibility. If the witness reports a verbal interaction with the perpetrator, criterion 5 is fulfilled. However, the witness must provide a virtual replication of the actual wording of at least some part of the verbal interaction in order to fulfill criterion 6 (as with criterion 5, it does not have to be done fluently). Szewczyk (in Dettenborn et al., 1984, p. 314) added that hints by the perpetrator that are reproduced but not understood by the child are especially strong instances of this criterion.

Criterion 7: Unexpected Complications During the Incident

The appearance of accounts of unexpected complications during the incident (Arntzen, 1983, p. 33; Dettenborn et al., 1984,

p. 313; Undeutsch, 1967, p. 153), supports the credibility of a statement. The range of these complications can extend from an unforseen interruption or difficulty to the spontaneous stopping of the event before its logical completion.

Peculiarities of Content

Criteria relating to peculiarities of the content of a statement comprise another category of reality criteria. They include features of a statement that enhance its concreteness and vividness. For this category, one deals with individual instances in a statement that increase the quality of its content and that can be found in different parts of the statement.

Criterion 8: Unusual Details

In this aspect of the content analysis, emphasis is placed on the degree of concreteness and the vividness of the testimony. A statement can become concrete and vivid through accounts of unusual or unique details, such as the appearance of odd details that are not obviously unrealistic.

This criterion can also be found in Trankell's (1972, p. 129) "Uniqueness Criterion"; it was enlarged upon by Undeutsch (1967, p. 138), Arntzen (1983, p. 39), and Dettenborn et al. (1984, p. 313). Since unusual details have a low probability of occurrence, they would not be expected to appear in invented accusations.

Criterion 9: Superfluous Details

Details that are not essential for the accusation but that are described by the witness in connection with the allegations can be considered signs of the validity of a statement. Lying persons probably would not think about inventing irrelevant, superfluous details that do not contribute to the affirmation of the alleged act.

Criterion 10: Accurately Reported Details Misunderstood

This criterion is fulfilled if the child reports actions or provides details that are misunderstood by the child but are understood by the interviewer. This criterion was also mentioned by Arntzen (1983, p. 31) and Szewczyk (1973, p. 57), echoing Undeutsch (1967, p. 141) who spoke of details that lie "beyond the horizon of the comprehension of the witness." This criterion occurs in a statement when the child witness incorrectly interprets a correctly described observation.

Criterion 11: Related External Associations

An additional peculiarity of the content of a statement is the occurrence of related external associations. A related external association is present when the witness reports conversations that refer to other events such that each of the conveyed accounts contains "an overlapping interlocking of at least two relationships" (Arntzen, 1983, p. 38). For example, in the report of an incestuous relationship, a related external association would be present if the witness (the daughter) described a conversation with the perpetrator (the father) in which they discussed the sexual experiences of the daughter with other partners. The association is external to the allegation but related to its content. Arntzen (1983, p. 38) reported that he has never found such interlockings in false statements.

Criterion 12: Accounts of Subjective Mental State

The account of the child's own mental state during the event is also of qualitative importance. This criterion includes descriptions of feelings, such as fear or disgust, as well as reports of cognitions, such as thinking about how to escape while the event was in progress. This criterion can be found in Arntzen (1983, p. 29) and Dettenborn et al. (1984, p. 314). Arntzen also pointed out the value of accounts concerning the development of emotions and their changes during the course of the event.

Criterion 13: Attribution of Perpetrator's Mental State

Undeutsch (1967, p. 143) pointed out that the states of mind and motives that are attributed by the child to the alleged perpetrator are signs of the credibility of a statement. Dettenborn et al. (1984, p. 314) also listed descriptions of affective reactions and of physiological states of the perpetrator as reality criteria.

Motivation-Related Contents

The fourth group of criteria includes contents that refer to the motivation of the child to make a statement or an allegation. At this point, the expert considers details of the statement that define the relationship between the witness and the testimony given by the witness. This information provides an opportunity to draw conclusions about the possible motivation of the child to make a false accusation. They are content criteria because they can be inferred solely from the content of the statement (for example, from a typed transcript) without considering other information regarding the motivation of the witness for false accusations.

In the preceding second and third major categories, the cognitive characteristics were emphasized. They dealt with the question of whether or not a witness would be able to fabricate contents with qualities such as those described by the criteria. In the fourth major category of criteria, the motivational aspects are emphasized. The criteria in this category are used to assess the probability that a witness giving false testimony would mention details of the sort described by these criteria.

Criterion 14: Spontaneous Corrections

Spontaneously correcting oneself during the interview or providing newer or clearer recollections are regarded as characteristics that favor the credibility of a statement, or at least argue against a completely fictitious account or one that was influenced by a third person. Undeutsch (1967, p. 152) attached much importance to spontaneous corrections or improvements of one's own statement. Because persons who deliberately give false testimony feel compelled to convey a good impression and not put themselves in question through improvements or corrections of their statements, this criterion would not be expected to occur in fabricated accusations. Dettenborn et al. (1984, p. 313) emphasized, however, that this criterion cannot be considered fulfilled when a correction or an improvement is not spontaneous but instead occurs through questioning, suggestions, or other direct influences by the interviewer.

Criterion 15: Admitting Lack of Memory

When admitting lack of memory, a witness is in a psychological situation similar to that which occurs when he or she spontaneously corrects a former statement. It is assumed that persons deliberately giving false testimony would rather answer questions completely than admit a lack of memory of certain details. Therefore, the occurrence of admitted lack of memory in a statement is considered a sign of its credibility.

Criterion 16: Raising Doubts About One's Own Testimony

According to Undeutsch (1967), the raising of "objections to the correctness of one's own testimony" (p. 153) is also a clue to the credibility of the statement. It can be assumed that a person who is attempting to appear credible when giving a false statement will not be inclined to raise any doubts about the credibility of the allegation.

Criterion 17: Self-Deprecation

The mention of personally unfavorable, self-incriminating details in a statement also speaks for the veracity of the testimony. According to Undeutsch (1967, p. 153) and Dettenborn et al. (1984, p. 314), self-accusation of a witness "due to a self-critical attitude concerning the witness's own behavior with the perpetrator" favors the credibility of a witness. Such confessions of improper or wrong behavior would not be expected in deceitful testimony that is aimed at falsely incriminating the accused.

Criterion 18: Pardoning the Perpetrator

If a statement tends to favor the accused (e.g., explanations or exonerations of the behavior are given) or if the witness does not make use of obvious possibilities for further incriminations, Undeutsch (1967, p. 153) considers this to be an indication of the veracity of a statement.

Offense-Specific Elements

Elements of the testimony that do not relate to the general vividness of the statement but do relate to the crime in a typical way must be assessed specifically. This extraordinary status is based on the fact that reality criteria of this category do not occur often in credible testimonies. On the other hand, the expert must have specific knowledge and experience concerning typical ways in which sexual crimes are perpetrated in order to deal with this category of reality criteria.

Criterion 19: Details Characteristic of the Offense

Undeutsch (1967) added the description of "specific deviations from common notions about sexual behavior" (p. 137) as an example of concreteness and vividness. Such accounts embody special qualities characteristic of the offense. Similar to Undeutsch, we place value on offense-specific elements in the statement that contradict everyday knowledge, such as descriptions that contradict the commonly held belief that sexual assaults of children are usually committed by strange, unknown persons who employ violence.

In cases of incest, for example, some might question the veracity of the victim because the descriptions include lack of resistance by the victim and a long and continuing incestuous relationship, beginning with relatively harmless sexual behavior that progressively develops along with a change in the attitude of the victim toward the perpetrator. As shown by empirical research, these elements can be considered offense-specific for incestuous sexual relationships; at the same time, they are contradictory to beliefs commonly held by nonprofessionals. This criterion is based on empirical criminological findings about the typical courses and characteristics of specific sexual crimes. Agreement between the testimony and the known characteristics of offenses is taken as an indication of the veracity of the statement.

CRITERIA-BASED STATEMENT ANALYSIS IN JUDICIAL PROCESSES

The content criteria described above can be judged simply as present or absent, or they can be rated in terms of the strength and extent to which they are fulfilled in the statement. An overall judgment of the degree to which content criteria are present in a statement leads to an assessment of the quality of the statement. This provides an evaluation of the degree of veracity of the statement, in other words, a probabilistic assessment of whether or not the witness actually experienced the alleged event.

At present there are no formalized decision rules for combining content criteria or for determining cutoff scores to differentiate between truthful and deceptive statements on the basis of the amount or strength of the content criteria that are present. In German practice there is a rule of thumb that "at least three reality criteria must be given . . . in order to classify a testimony as credible" (Arntzen, 1970, p. 46), but this rule of thumb is misleading. It should be pointed out that the various reality criteria have different values for assessing the veracity of a statement (Koehnken, 1982). For example, accurately reported but misunderstood details and reports of offense-specific elements are apparently of more significance than relatively simple descriptions of interactions or contextual embeddings.

In the following section, the scientific problems of criteria-based statement analysis as a psychodiagnostic method will be outlined, including the problem of determining the appropriate weights for different reality criteria as predictors of the veracity of statements. At present, the practical use of statement analysis represents a semistandardized approach, the result of which is based on clinical-intuitive judgments rather than formalized decision rules.

The content quality of a statement is dependent not only on whether or not a witness described a self-experienced or invented event but also on the cognitive abilities of the reporting person and the nature of the reported event. As the intellectual abilities of a witness increase and the complexity of an event decreases, the application of statement analysis by content criteria becomes more and more difficult, or even meaningless. A positive outcome of an analysis of the quality of a statement is less convincing if the cognitive and verbal abilities of a witness are highly developed. On the other hand, a negative outcome of statement analysis that is due to lack of complexity of the reported event has little meaning for the evaluation of the credibility of the report by the witness. Therefore, as was pointed out earlier, assessing the credibility of statements by child witnesses in cases of alleged sexual abuse also implies personality analysis by means of psychometric and other diagnostic methods.

In addition to the nature of the event and the cognitive abilities of the witness, the amount of reality criteria in a given statement also depends on the length of the statement. The length of a statement is partially determined by the interview technique used by the investigator, but the techniques of interviewing child witnesses are beyond the scope of this chapter (see Steller, Raskin, Esplin, & Boychuk, 1989, for a discussion of interview techniques). It should be sufficient to point out that statement analysis requires extensive narratives and that leading or suggestive questions during the interview can produce a statement that cannot be properly analyzed by the content criteria.

In Germany, statement analysis is a specialty practiced by psychologists who are appointed as expert witnesses by trial courts.

This restriction is due to procedural rules established by the courts and has no relation to the logic of the technique. Knowledge of criteria-based statement analysis and its underlying assumptions and implications for interview techniques is especially important and useful in the earliest stages of the investigation. Therefore, police investigators, social workers, and case workers should be trained in the assessment and investigative techniques of criteria-based statement analysis.

We should also consider whether criteria-based statement analysis can be used only on testimony provided by witnesses, or if it can also be used to assess the veracity of statements by accused persons. Although Undeutsch (1967) made no distinction between statements of a witness and an accused, Arntzen (1970, p. 8) pointed out that statement analysis refers only to the statements of witnesses. The range of application of statement analysis is not determined simply by the opinions of experts, but by the scientific assumptions on which it is founded.

As stated previously, the basic assumption of criteria-based statement analysis is that true and fictitious reports differ in quality. Conclusions as to whether or not a person has experienced an alleged event are drawn from the presence or absence of content criteria in the statement. In principle, the use of criteria-based statement analysis is independent of whether the reporting person is an accused or a witness. However, in forensic applications, statement analysis is generally restricted to the assessment of witness reports because in most cases accused persons do not describe an event or experience of long duration and complexity; they simply deny the events that are described by the witness. The lack of material necessary to conduct a criteria-based statement analysis is the typical situation when dealing with the statement by the accused. It is more appropriate to use a properly conducted polygraph examination of the accused (for applications in sexual abuse cases, see Raskin & Steller, 1989; for technical and scientific issues, see Chapter 8 in this book).

Since the results of statement analysis by content criteria depend on the cognitive abilities of witnesses as well as the nature of the reported event, criteria-based statement analysis should be restricted to the assessment of children's statements in cases where they state that they were personally involved in the events, especially cases of sexual abuse. In such cases, other kinds of evidence are usually lacking, and the usefulness of criteria-based statement analysis as an assessment method for investigative and judicial purposes is obvious.

SCIENTIFIC BASIS OF CRITERIA-BASED STATEMENT ANALYSIS

The crucial question concerning criteria-based statement analysis is whether it is sufficiently valid to discriminate truthful from fictitious statements. The validity of statement analysis refers to the validity of individual content criteria as well as the validity of the overall decision about truth or deception that is based on these criteria. Since the validity of the above-described integrative system of content criteria is related to the validity of the methods by which they were developed, the methods and results of empirical validation studies of the original approaches are discussed in the following section, in order to evaluate the present empirical basis of statement analysis.

The major methodological strategy to assess the validity of statement analysis has been the field study. The basic material for evaluation consists of witness statements that have been analyzed and classified as truthful or fictitious by psychological experts. If this classification is later confirmed either by confession of the perpetrator or by any other type of evidence, it has been regarded as correct and an indication of the validity of the method (Arntzen, 1983). Therefore, the basic external criteria for the truthfulness of a witness statement are the confession of the perpetrator and, to a lesser extent, additional evidence that confirms the statement.

Undeutsch (1982, 1984), however, pointed out that it is extremely difficult to determine a single objective, independent, and reliable criterion in a field setting. He stated that "it is virtually impossible in most criminal cases to get to the 'basic reality,' to establish some sort of 'ground truth'" (1984, p. 64). Thus, Undeutsch suggested that all of the separate pieces of evidence should be combined into a "specific and non-interchangeable configuration of facts" (1984, p. 64). If the conclusions and inferences drawn by the expert on the basis of statement analysis fit into this configuration, it may be regarded as a confirmation of the diagnostic method.

Experimental procedures that would allow absolute control over the credibility of statements were explicitly rejected by Undeutsch (1982, 1984), Arntzen (1983), and Trankell (1972). Undeutsch (1982) stated that "experiments conducted in the laboratory lack ecological validity and realism" (p. 48). Similarly, Arntzen (1983) stated that experimental simulations could never produce the significant personal and emotional involvement that is particularly relevant in cases of sexual abuse. According to Arntzen, the artificial interview situation in an experiment would have little or no resemblance to a real criminal investigation, and experiments are of no value for the validation of statement analysis.

Arntzen (1982, 1983) reported that he and his co-workers have analyzed approximately 24,000 eyewitness statements in actual court cases. Ninety-two percent of the psychological investigations were made in cases of sexual offenses with children or female juveniles. The majority of these investigations (64%) were conducted by order of the prosecution, and the remaining 36% by order of the courts. According to Arntzen (1983), the courts concurred with the conclusions of the psychological experts concerning the credibility of the eyewitnesses in more than 90% of the cases. Approximately about 60 to 70% were found to be truthful. In 866 of these cases, the perpetrators had confessed to the crime in question after the statement of the witness was diagnosed as truthful by the psychological expert. In "several hundred further cases" (Arntzen, 1983, p. 12), external evidence was available that confirmed at least part of the witness statements and thereby validated the results of the statement analysis. Based on this case material, Arntzen concluded that few areas of applied psychology have been subject to such extensive and rigorous control as that applied to the method of statement analysis.

Undeutsch (1982, 1984) has conducted about 1,500 statement analyses, the majority of them in cases of sexual offenses with children or female juveniles. Ninety percent of the statements were diagnosed as truthful, and in 95% of these cases the accused was convicted by the court. "Not one of those convicted defendants has ever been shown to have been innocent by the later discovery of conflicting evidence" (Undeutsch, 1982, p. 50). Undeutsch gave no indication concerning the proportion of cases where confessions supported the results of the statement analyses, since he ascribed only limited value to confessions as a criterion for the validity of the diagnosis. However, Undeutsch is very optimistic about the results that are achieved with the method of statement analysis. He stated that

> although this method has been applied in many thousands of cases in Germany and Sweden during the last three decades, there is not a single case reported in the literature or otherwise documented, in which the analysis of the statement led to the clear finding that the statement had to be considered as the truthful account of a personally experienced real event, and which, later in the criminal proceeding or afterwards turned out to be in conflict with other relevant evidence. (1982, p. 49)

This is taken by Undeutsch (1984) as a "strong indication of the accuracy of the approach" (p. 64).

Littmann and Szewczyk (1983) and Szewczyk and Littmann (1982) have reanalyzed the material of 173 statement analyses obtained in cases of sexual offenses between 1965 and 1976. The witnesses were between 5 and 18 years of age, and 90% were female. Of the 173 statements, 42% were judged as certainly truthful according to the results of statement analyses; 35% were diagnosed either as clearly deceptive, or there was at least considerable doubt regarding their credibility. The remaining 23% were rated as partially truthful. For the final analysis, only material from the first two groups (certainly truthful and clearly deceptive or doubtful statements) was selected. The authors then compared the frequency of occurrence of individual content criteria in those statements that were finally judged as truthful or deceptive. It should be noted that the design of this validation study is flawed since the final classification of the statements as truthful or deceptive was not independent of the presence of the content criteria. Therefore, the results of this study indicate only relationships between the occurrence of any given criterion of credibility and the classification of statements as truthful or deceptive by the psychological expert. Keeping this limitation in mind, some interesting inferences may be drawn from the results of this study.

One point of interest is the fact that some of the criteria considered indicative of truthful statements also were found with considerable frequency in statements that were later classified as deceptive. Some of the other criteria did not significantly discriminate between truthful and deceptive statements. Obviously, no single criterion is sufficient to discriminate reliably between truthful and deceptive accounts. Furthermore, differential weights are assigned to the various criteria, and a final decision is derived from the configuration of content characteristics rather than from a simple additive combination of criteria. This contrasts with Arntzen (1983, p. 22), who indicated that a statement may be judged as truthful if at least three reality criteria are fulfilled.

Another problem with statement analysis evident in the report by Littmann and Szewczyk (1983) is the low frequency of occurrence of some criteria. For example, supplementations were observed in only 8.7% of all cases, spontaneous corrections occurred in only 20.7% of the statements, and the quantity of details was relevant in only 35.8%. Only the criteria of consistency over time with repeated questioning, resistance to suggestions, and admission of lack of memory were scored in more than 50% of the cases. Using only these criteria may result in a considerable restriction of data such that the amount of usable data may be insufficient to allow a final decision about truth and deception. Furthermore, the investigator may have only limited potential to stimulate the production of diagnostically relevant verbal material by the witness.

The approach of validating criteria-based statement analysis exclusively in field studies, using confessions of defendants as the external criterion for the truthfulness of the witness statements, has been criticized by Koehnken (1982) and Koehnken and Wegener (1985). The general problems that arise from the lack of randomization and control of variables are well known, and there is no need to repeat them here (see Cook & Campbell, 1976). There are, however, some particular problems associated with the use of confessions as external criteria. Since criteria-based statement analysis is not used to predict confessions of defendants but only the truth of witness statements, confessions are only an indicator of the ultimate criterion. It must be established that the confessions occur only when the statement is true and not because of any other factor. This is obviously not always the case. For example, Gudjonsson and MacKeith (1982) have discussed the dangers of false confessions, and they listed several possible reasons for a defendant to make a false confession, even in very serious cases.

There may be good reasons for a defendant to confess to a crime even when not guilty. For example, if there is no chance of avoiding a guilty verdict, it may be a beneficial strategy to confess to a crime not committed, since this is usually considered as repentance by the court and results in a reduction of the penalty. This is even more likely in the frequent plea-bargain arrangements in the United States. Even more important, the expert diagnosis about the truth of a central witness's statement may influence the defendant to confess or not confess to a crime.

Statement analyses by psychological experts are usually obtained if no other incriminating or exonerating evidence is available. If, under such conditions, an incriminating statement is judged as truthful, the chances for the defendant to obtain an acquittal decrease dramatically. According to Undeutsch (1982, 1984) and Arntzen (1982), about 90% to 95% of the defendants in their cases were convicted. On the other hand, there is no reason for the defendant to confess to a crime if the expert witness has judged the major witnesses' statement to be deceptive. As a result, the probability of a confession may be influenced by the diagnosis itself, and the attempt to validate this diagnosis by the confession is clearly circular.

Another problem arises from the selectivity of the material. In Germany, it is not the investigator but the prosecutor and/or the courts who decide whether or not a statement analysis must be conducted. This has led to an extremely selective database that is almost completely confined to statements by female children or adolescents in cases of sexual offenses. According to Arntzen (1982), 92% of the analyzed statements are of this type. Consequently, the empirical basis of statement analysis must be limited to these types of cases. Up to now, there has been no research evidence that statement analysis may be generalized to different crimes or to adult witnesses.

Only one experimental approach to evaluate the validity of certain selected content criteria has been reported in the literature (Koehnken & Wegener, 1982). In this study the statements of a group of female adolescents 16 and 17 years of age were analyzed with regard to three content criteria. Half of the subjects were shown a film about 10 min in length, and the remaining half received a verbal description of the contents of this film. Prior to viewing the film or listening to the description, all subjects had been instructed that their task would be to give a statement about the event to one of five randomly assigned interviewers. Half of the subjects in each group gave the first report immediately after this procedure and again 3 weeks later. The other half made their statement after a time delay of 3 weeks. Finally, the statement was divided into a free narrative that always constituted the first part of the interview, followed by a structured interview. This manipulation resulted in a factorial design $2 \times 2 \times 2$ (original observation vs. instructed statement, immediate vs. delayed recollection, free narrative vs. structured interview), with form of report as a within-subject factor.

The interviews were taperecorded and later transcribed verbatim. The transcriptions were randomly assigned to five trained coders who were blind with respect to the purpose of the experiment and the actual experimental conditions of the subjects. First, the statements were segmented into small action units that were subjected to further analysis (e.g., "The man entered the car"; "The boy rang the doorbell"). The major dependent variables were the amount of details and the constancy of these details in two consecutive statements.

Following Arntzen (1983) and Undeutsch (1967, 1982), it was hypothesized that statements about a personally observed event, as compared to a verbally described event would be characterized by a greater number of details and a higher proportion of consistently mentioned details in the two statements. A detail was defined as each action (usually described by a verb) and each further description of this action (usually described by an adverb). Repetitions of the same action were not used. After extensive training, the mean agreement of the coders in three randomly selected interview transcriptions was quite high ($r = .95$).

The results for the number of details supported the initial hypothesis. There were, however, some exceptions to the general superiority of the film group. Subjects in the film group produced significantly more details than did the subjects in the fantasy group in immediate and delayed free narratives and in the immediate structured interview. However, the difference between the delayed structured interviews, although in the expected direction, did not reach significance. Therefore, a free narrative seems to be a more diagnostically sensitive method to assess the credibility of a statement than a structured interview. A similar conclusion may be drawn if the effects of the first interview are treated as a pretreatment factor. In this analysis, the pretreatment produced a higher number of details in the free narratives of the film group, but not of the fantasy group. No significant differences emerged in the structured interviews. As a result, the discrepancy in the number of details between the film and the fantasy group was highest in a repeated free narrative.

In a further analysis, only those subjects who gave two statements, one immediately after the experimental manipulation and the other after a time delay of 3 weeks, were considered. This comparison showed that subjects in the film group initially produced more details than subjects in the fantasy group. This difference was more pronounced in the free narrative than in the structured interview. However, while the number of details remained fairly constant in the second statement by the fantasy group, it decreased in the film group. As a result, this variable did not reliably discriminate between the two groups in the second structured interview. Again, the free narrative proved to be a more sensitive method than the structured interview.

Contrary to expectations, the proportion of concordantly produced details in two consecutive statements did not differ significantly between the film and the fantasy group. The reason for this failure is not clear, since the assessment of concordance in this study differed somewhat from the descriptions of Arntzen (1983) or Undeutsch (1967). Although Arntzen emphasized that concordance is important for central but not for peripheral details, that distinction was not considered in this study. Furthermore, neither of the above-mentioned authors discussed the problem of a possible confounding such that the more details produced by the witness, the higher the absolute number of concordant details. To control for this dependency, the proportion of concordantly produced details relative to the total number was computed. It is, therefore, unlikely that the subjectively experienced importance of concordance is simply the result of a confounding with the higher absolute number of details in truthful statements. Interestingly, Littmann and Szewczyk (1983) also concluded from their material that the impact of the concordance variable may be overestimated in practice.

The present empirical basis of criteria-based statement analysis is unsatisfactory. The predominantly used methodological approach of field studies is not only incompletely documented but also it lacks the basic requirements of randomization and sufficient control over variables. Its material is highly selective, and the external criterion used as an indicator for the validity of the method may have been influenced by the diagnoses.

The first field study of the validity of our system of content criteria was recently reported by Boychuk, Esplin, and Raskin (1989). They analyzed statements obtained from 40 child witnesses in sexual abuse cases. Twenty of the statements had been confirmed as truthful by confessions of the accused (18) in the absence of plea-bargain arrangements and/or strong corroborating physical evidence of sexual abuse (16). The other 20 statements had been judged to be of highly doubtful validity on the basis of a lack of any corroborating physical evidence, persistent denials by the accused and truthful polygraph test outcomes on the 13 for whom tests were available, and judgments by a psychologist that there was a low probability of abuse.

Criteria-based statement analysis was performed by blind evaluation of the typed transcripts of the interviews to assess the occurrence of each of the 19 content criteria listed in Table 7.1. A score of 2 was assigned if a criterion was strongly fulfilled, a score of 1 was assigned if it was simply present, and a score of zero was assigned if it was absent. The scores were then totalled for each statement, and the mean total score was 23.7 for the confirmed truthful group and only 3.6 for the highly doubtful group. There was no overlap in the distributions for the two groups.

The findings of this recent field validity study provide the strongest available evidence in support of the basic hypothesis of statement analysis and the system of content criteria described in this chapter. However, a broader empirical base and additional analyses are needed to establish the validity of this approach and the specific diagnostic utilities of each of the 19 content criteria.

In addition, more information about the reliability of the individual reality criteria and the final diagnosis is badly needed. Leaving aside these shortcomings, the validity of the method may still be limited to the analysis of the statements of young children or adolescents in cases of alleged sexual offenses.

CONCLUDING REMARKS

In the preceding section it was pointed out that criteria-based statement analysis still lacks sufficient systematic scientific research to demonstrate its validity for assessing the veracity of children's or juveniles' testimonies in cases of sexual abuse. In spite of that, it should be taken into consideration that statement analysis has a long tradition in German-speaking countries, and the method reflects a great deal of expert knowledge based on extensive practical experience. Statement analysis has some empirical basis, although this consists mainly of unsystematically gathered case experiences. In addition, some content criteria have a high degree of face validity and plausibility, and at least the criterion of quantity of details has been shown in a controlled experimental environment to discriminate reliably between truthful and deceptive statements. The recent field study by Boychuk, Esplin, and Raskin (1989) provides the first assessment of criteria-based statement analysis, and the results are very encouraging in terms of its validity.

Considering all of the available evidence, a total endorsement of criteria-based statement analysis would be unwise and premature. However, it should be applied with caution until more research results are available. The first and most basic step would be to assess the interrater reliability for each content criterion and for the overall decision about truth and deception. Next, empirical studies must be conducted to investigate the discriminating power of each criterion. This would allow a determination of the differential weights to be applied to each criterion within a multivariate approach. We would strongly recommend the use of experimental methods to examine criteria-based statement analysis in a highly controlled environment combined with investigations of the generalizability of these methods by field studies of real cases.

The practical and scientific advantages of the above-described integrative system of content criteria should be pointed out. Our categorization is based on a logical structure that can be easily examined. Furthermore, it integrates the existing different approaches of statement analysis, and each of the individual criteria listed in the literature is included in our descriptive system.

Our system can be directly used in practice. The assessment of testimonies can be conducted by employing the sequence of categories in the system. First, the expert considers the statement as a whole. Then, attention is directed to the details of the statement, which become progressively more specific. The system not only structures the method of analyzing the statement but also simultaneously provides a structure for reporting the conclusions based on the analysis of the statement. Standardizing the assessment procedure by structuring individual steps is an important means of reducing subjectivity and increasing reliability in the analysis of statements (for a detailed exposition and expansion of this approach, see Steller, Raskin, Esplin, & Boychuk, 1989).

Our integrative system is also of heuristic relevance for future research. The criteria listed can be supplemented by those discovered in future research. Clear descriptions and distinctions among content criteria, which had been previously lacking, permit systematic empirical research as described above. Considering the possible traumatic effects of falsely classifying child victims of sexual abuse as deceptive witnesses, as well as the life-destroying effects of falsely classifying innocent adults as sexual offenders, we should make every effort to improve our knowledge about assessing the credibility of children's statements in cases of sexual abuse. Criteria-based statement analysis is a promising psychological technique for that purpose.

REFERENCES

Arntzen, F. (1970). *Psychologie der Zeugenaussage. Einfuehrung in die forensische Aussagepsychologie.* Goettingen: Hogrefe.

Arntzen, F. (1982). Die Situation der forensischen Aussagepsychologie in der Bundesrepublik Deutschland. In A. Trankell (Ed.), *Reconstructing the past* (pp. 107–120). Stockholm: Norstedt & Soners.

Arntzen, F. (1983). *Psychologie der Zeugenaussage. Systematik der Glaubwuerdigkeitsmerkmale.* Muenchen: C. H. Beck.

Boychuk, T., Esplin, P. W., & Raskin, D. C. (1989). *Children's statements of sexual abuse: Validity of criteria-based content analysis.* Manuscript submitted for publication.

Cook, T. D., & Campbell, D. T. (1976). The design and conduct of quasi-experiments and true experiments in field settings. In M. D. Dunnette (Ed.), *Handbook of industrial and organizational psychology* (pp. 223–326). Chicago: Rand McNally.

Dettenborn, H., Froehlich, H., & Szewczyk, H. (1984). *Forensische Psychologie.* Berlin: Deutscher Verlag der Wissenschaften.

Gudjonsson, G. H., & MacKeith, J. A. C. (1982). False confessions: Psychological effects of interrogation. A discussion paper. In A. Trankell (Ed.), *Reconstructing the past* (pp. 253–269). Stockholm: Norstedt & Soners.

Koehnken, G. (1982). *Sprechverhalten und Glaubwuerdigkeit: Eine experimentelle Studie zur extralinguistischen und textstilistischen Aussageanalyse.* Unpublished doctoral dissertation, University of Kiel.

Koehnken, G., & Wegener, H. (1982). Zur Glaubwuerdigkeit von Zeugenaussagen. Experimentelle Ueberpruefung ausgewaehlter Glaubwuerdigkeitskriterien. *Zeitschrift fuer Experimentelle und Angewandte Psychologie, 29,* 92–111.

Koehnken, G., & Wegener, H. (1985). Zum Stellenwert des Experiments in der Forensischen Aussagepsychologie. *Zeitschrift fuer Experimentelle und Angewandte Psychologie, 32,* 104–119.

Littmann, E., & Szewczyk, H. (1983). Zu einigen Kriterien und Ergebnissen forensisch-psychologischer Glaubwuerdigkeitsbegutachtung von sexuell missbrauchten Kindern und Jugendlichen. *Forensia, 4,* 55–72.

Raskin, D. C., & Steller, M. (1989). Assessing credibility of allegations of child sexual abuse: Polygraph examinations and statement analysis. In H. Wegener, F. Loesel, & J. Haisch (Eds.), *Criminal behavior and the justice system: Psychological perspectives.* (pp. 290–302). Heidelberg: Springer-Verlag.

Sporer, S. L. (1983, August). *Content criteria of credibility: The German approach to children's eyewitness testimony.* Paper presented at the American Psychological Association, Los Angeles.

Steller, M., Raskin, D. C., Esplin, P. W., & Boychuk, T. (1989). *Child sexual abuse: Forensic interviews and assessments.* Unpublished manuscript. New York: Springer-Verlag.

Szewczyk, H. (1973). Kriterien der Beurteilung kindlicher Zeugenaussagen. *Probleme und Ergebnisse der Psychologie, 46,* 47–66.

Szewczyk, H., & Littmann, E. (1982). Untersuchungen zur Glaubwuerdigkeitsbeurteilung kindlicher Zeugen. In A. Trankell (Ed.), *Reconstructing the past* (pp. 73–103). Stockholm: Norstedt & Soners.

Trankell, A. (1972). *Reliability of evidence.* Stockholm: Beckmans.

Undeutsch, U. (1967). Beurteilung der Glaubhaftigkeit von Aussagen. In U. Undeutsch (Ed.), *Handbuch der Psychologie Bd.11: Forensische Psychologie* (pp. 26–181). Goettingen: Hogrefe.

Undeutsch, U. (1982). Statement reality analysis. In A. Trankell (Ed.), *Reconstructing the past* (pp. 27–56). Stockholm: Norstedt & Soners.

Undeutsch, U. (1984). Courtroom evaluation of eyewitness testimony. *International Review of Applied Psychology, 33,* 51–67.

Polygraph Techniques for the Detection of Deception

8

David C. Raskin

Physiological methods for the assessment of credibility had their beginnings in Italy around the end of the 19th century (Lombroso, 1895). Interest in such techniques soon spread to Germany, the United States, and the Soviet Union, and some of the most notable figures in the history of psychological science have conducted research on the detection of deception (for historical reviews, see Barland, 1988; Barland & Raskin, 1973; Trovillo, 1939). In spite of its European origins, physiological detection of deception is not used at all by Europeans, and it is now applied predominantly in the United States, Canada, Japan, Turkey, South Korea, and Israel (Barland, 1988). However, the validity and utility of polygraph techniques are extensively debated (Gale, 1988; Raskin, 1986).

This chapter describes methods of physiological detection of deception (polygraph tests) that are currently used, scientific data concerning their reliablity and validity, recent developments in examination techniques and methods for evaluating the outcome of polygraph tests, and some of the technical and practical problems surrounding their applications. Legal issues affecting their admissibility as evidence are discussed in detail in Chapter 10.

Polygraph techniques may be divided into two major categories: deception tests, which are designed to directly test if a person is deceiving, and information tests, which attempt to determine if a person possesses specific information that would imply knowledge or involvement in a criminal incident. Each of these two types of tests utilizes physiological responses to questions to make inferences concerning a person's involvement or knowledge of a crime. However, they are based on somewhat different psychological and psychophysiological assumptions, and they use different procedures for the conduct and interpretation of the test outcomes. The major techniques in both categories are described below.

DECEPTION TESTS

Deception tests are the most commonly used and generally applicable techniques for the investigation of criminal cases. They are designed to make assessments of credibility by asking the subject direct questions concerning involvement in or knowledge of the crime or incident. All questions are formulated so that the subject can answer with a simple yes or no, and they are reviewed with the subject during the pretest interview. The relevant questions typically embody a major aspect of the incident, and other questions are included for various purposes that depend on the type of deception test employed.

Deception tests must deal only with actions or events about which the subject has direct knowledge or experience and a clear memory (Raskin, 1986). The relevant questions should not attempt to directly assess a subject's state of mind during the incident or the subject's interpretation of the meaning of such acts or events. However, motives, intentions, or legal conclusions may sometimes be inferred from the content and the meaning of the questions that the examiner and subject discuss during the pretest interview.

For example, the subject in a rape case might be asked, "Did you use physical force or threats to get Lucretia to have sex with you on September 11?" The subject's veracity in denying a rape can be directly inferred from the test outcome on the issue of physical force or threat. It is also necessary for the examiner to discuss and define the meaning of *physical force* and *threat* in terms of the allegations and descriptions provided by the witness/victim. However, the subject should never be asked, "Did you rape Lucretia on September 11?" This question is unsuitable because it requires the subject to draw a legal conclusion.

In most cases, the relevant questions can be worded in simple, concrete terms that allow an unambiguous interpretation of their meaning. Any relevant question that is ambiguous or that requires the subject to draw conclusions or make interpretations can cause problems in drawing inferences about truth or deception, regardless of the actual guilt or innocence of the person tested.

Most tests for deception employ 3 or 4 relevant questions in a test sequence of 10 to 12 questions that includes other types of questions. The nature and purposes of the other questions vary according to the type of technique and the purposes of the examination, and the methods for evaluating test outcomes vary for different techniques. The major deception tests are described in the following sections.

Relevant-Irrelevant Test

The first widely used test for deception, the relevant-irrelevant technique, was developed from the research of Marston (1917) for use in law enforcement applications (Keeler, 1933; Larson, 1932). Although it was the dominant polygraph technique for about 2 decades, it is now used infrequently in criminal investigation (Raskin, 1986).

Test Structure and Administration

The typical relevant-irrelevant test employs a series of 10 to 15 questions comprised of relevant questions (e.g., "Did you shoot

Fred?") and irrelevant (neutral) questions (e.g., "Are you sitting down?"). The questions are presented to the subject while continuous recordings are made with the polygraph. The recordings usually include respiratory activity, obtained from a tube attached around the thorax and/or abdomen, changes in relative blood pressure, obtained from a partially inflated cuff placed around the upper arm, and electrodermal activity (galvanic skin response), obtained from electrodes placed on the palmar surface of two fingers. The latter is a measure of the activity of the sweat glands in the palms of the hands, which is a very sensitive index of emotional arousal. Peripheral vascular activity is also measured on some instruments. It provides an index of vasoconstriction in the blood vessels of the skin, and it is obtained by means of a photoplethysmograph attached to the palmar surface of a finger.

Interpretation of the Results

Relative strengths of physiological reactions to the various questions are used to determine whether or not the subject was truthful or deceptive in answering the relevant questions. Since most individuals display some autonomic reactivity to almost any type of question, neutral questions serve to establish a base line of reactivity against which to compare the strength of the reactions produced by the relevant questions.

The basic rationale of the relevant-irrelevant test is that a person who is deceptive in answering the relevant questions will be concerned about being discovered, which will cause involuntary autonomic reactions to occur with greatest strength in response to questions that are answered deceptively. Thus, guilty individuals are expected to show their strongest reactions to relevant questions, whereas truthful subjects are expected to show no difference in their reactions to relevant and neutral questions. Therefore, the polygraph examiner looks for heightened reactivity to the relevant questions, and the presence of such a pattern of reactions leads to the conclusion that the subject was practicing deception on the relevant issues. If no difference in reactions to relevant and neutral questions is observed, the examiner concludes that the subject was truthful in answering the relevant questions.

The assumptions and interpretations of the relevant-irrelevant test are simplistic and psychophysiologically naïve (Podlesny & Raskin, 1977), and interpretations of truth and deception based on the results of such tests present profound problems (Raskin, 1986). It is generally agreed among psychophysiologists that there is no "specific lie response" or pattern of reactions that is peculiar to deception (Raskin, 1979). That is to say, an inspection of the physiological responses of an individual to a particular question cannot provide the sole basis for concluding that the subject's answer was deceptive or nondeceptive. Although some progress has been made in identifying patterns of reactions that may be helpful in this regard (Honts, Kircher, & Raskin, 1988; Kircher & Raskin, 1982), considerably more research is needed before that approach can be applied successfully in criminal investigation.

A variety of factors may cause subjects to react with greater strength to questions about crimes of which they are suspected than to the innocuous neutral questions. Serious accusations, the emotional impact of the questions (e.g., if they mention the death of a spouse or friend), the nervousness of the individual, the thought processes and images evoked by the content of the questions, or anger and disgust concerning the accusation (e.g., sexual abuse of one's own child) may cause autonomic reactions to relevant questions even when they are answered truthfully. Neither polygraph examiners nor psychophysiologists are able to distinguish with any reasonable accuracy such reactions from those that occur as a result of deception.

Validity of the Relevant-Irrelevant Test

There are no standardized and systematic methods for interpreting the outcome of a relevant-irrelevant test, and it would be expected to produce a high rate of false positive errors (diagnosing an innocent person as deceptive). Although the relevant-irrelevant test has been widely used for more than several decades, the first scientific laboratory study of its accuracy was conducted very recently (Horowitz, 1988). In this study, quantitative evaluations of polygraph charts yielded 100% correct outcomes on guilty subjects, but only 20% of the innocent subjects were correctly classified (see Table 8.5). Thus, the relevant-irrelevant test was extremely effective in detecting guilty subjects, but it was extremely poor in identifying innocent subjects. Furthermore, the relevant-irrelevant test does not protect against hyperreactive or hyporeactive subjects who do not show differential reactions to relevant and neutral questions. Such persons might be erroneously diagnosed as truthful even when they are deceptive (false negative errors).

Although many studies claim to support the accuracy of the relevant-irrelevant test in field applications (Barland & Raskin, 1973), none meets reasonable scientific standards for internal or external validity (Office of Technology Assessment [OTA], 1983). Because of its many inherent problems, the relevant-irrelevant test is seldom used in federal law enforcement investigations. In Utah, it is illegal to administer a relevant-irrelevant test without prior approval from the Utah Department of Public Safety, and such permission has never been granted.

Control Question Test

Control question tests were developed to overcome some of the problems of the relevant-irrelevant test. The concept of the control question was first described by Summers (1939), who referred to them as "emotional standards" designed to "evoke within the individual rather intense psychogalvanic reactions due to surprise, anger, shame or anxiety over situations which he would ordinarily prefer to conceal" (p. 341).

Reid (1947) further refined the concept and application of control questions. He modified procedures then in common use, adding what he termed the "comparative response question" and reviewing the questions in advance with the subject. Reid named it the comparative response question:

> because the magnitude of the response to that question is to be compared with responses to questions pertaining to the actual

crime, and it may therefore serve to include or exclude definitely the subject as a suspect in the crime under investigation. If the examiner is fortunate enough to have in his possession certain information concerning a situation or offense involving the subject (but of less importance than the actual crime being investigated) which the examiner knows or feels reasonably sure the subject will lie about, a question based on such information and actually lied to will serve very well to indicate the subject's responsiveness when lying. Such a question thereby affords a basis for evaluating the nature of the response to the questions pertinent to the offense under investigation. (p. 544)

Reid's approach to the formulation and uses of control questions was modified by Backster and the U.S. Army (Barland & Raskin, 1973). However, this traditional control question test has been more broadly conceived within the framework of current concepts in psychology and psychophysiology (see Raskin, 1979, 1982, 1986).

Control questions are designed to give an innocent suspect an opportunity to become more concerned about questions other than the relevant questions, thereby causing the innocent suspect to react more strongly to the control than to the relevant questions. If the subject does react with greater strength to the control questions, the result is interpreted as truthful. On the other hand, stronger reactions to the relevant questions are interpreted as indicating that the subject was deceptive to the relevant questions. The problem of no "specific lie response" is circumvented by the procedure of drawing inferences about truth or deception by comparing the relative strength of this particular subject's reactions to relevant and control questions.

Although the concept of the control question is simple and its effectiveness is an empirical question, some psychologists have argued that it cannot possibly work because it is based on a scientifically faulty premise (Furedy & Heslegrave, in press; Lykken, 1979). They have argued that the control question is not a control in the scientific sense because a true control would provide "a reasonable estimate of what the subject's response to the relevant question ought to be if he is answering truthfully [to the relevant question]" (Lykken, 1979, p. 49). This argument betrays a lack of understanding of the nature and function of the control question. The control question actually serves to determine whether the subject is more concerned or less concerned about the relevant question, and it comes closer to providing an estimate of what the reaction to the relevant question would be if the subject answered it *deceptively* (Raskin & Kircher, in press).

Introducing the Control Question

Control questions deal with acts that are similar to the issue of the investigation. However, they are more general in nature, deliberately vague, and cover long periods of time in the life history of the subject. Virtually every criminal suspect has difficulty in unequivocally answering them with a simple, truthful no. An example of a control question in an examination regarding a theft is "Prior to 1987, did you ever take something that did not belong to you?" The test usually includes two or three control questions that are reviewed with the subject after the relevant questions have been discussed and reviewed, and they are presented in a manner designed to encourage the subject to answer them with a denial.

A typical introduction of the control questions by the examiner during the pretest interview is as follows:

> Since this is a matter of a theft, I need to ask you some general questions about yourself in order to assess your basic character with regard to honesty and trustworthiness. I need to make sure that you have never done anything of a similar nature in the past and that you are not the type of person who would do something like stealing that ring and then would lie about it. Therefore, I need to ask you some questions for that purpose. So, if I ask you, "Before the age of 23, did you ever lie to get out of trouble or to cause a problem for someone else?" you could answer that no, couldn't you?

Most subjects initially answer no to the control questions. If the subject answers yes, the examiner asks for an explanation. The typical response is a minor admission, such as lying about taking some change from a parent at an early age. The examiner then responds by saying, "Well, that was when you were a child and didn't know better. You never did anything like that when you were older and knew better, did you?" Most subjects then answer in the negative, and the question is used in its original form or reworded to "Other than what you told me, before age 23 did you ever . . . "

The manner of introducing and explaining the control questions is designed to pose a dilemma for the subject. It leads the subject to believe that admissions will cause the examiner to form the opinion that the subject is dishonest and is therefore guilty. This discourages admissions and maximizes the likelihood that the negative answer is untruthful. However, the manner of introducing and explaining the control questions also causes the subject to believe that deceptive answers to them will result in strong physiological reactions during the test and will lead the examiner to conclude that the subject was deceptive with respect to the relevant issues concerning the theft. In fact, the converse is true.

Stronger reactions to control questions will be interpreted as indicating that the subject's denials to the relevant questions were truthful. If the subject shows stronger reactions to control questions, this will be interpreted as indicating that the subject was more concerned about failing the test because of deception in answering the control questions or lack of confidence that the answers to them were absolutely truthful. However, if the subject shows stronger reactions to the relevant questions in spite of these procedures, the results will be interpreted as indicative of deception to the relevant questions.

Pretest Interview

The control question polygraph examination begins with a detailed pretest interview that usually requires at least 1 hr. Prior to meeting the subject, the examiner has become familiar with the case facts by reading incident reports and/or meeting with the relevant investigators or attorneys. At the outset of the pretest interview, the subject is informed of the purpose and issues of the examination, is advised concerning his or her relevant legal rights, and consents to undergo the examination. It is strongly recommended that the examiner taperecord the entire examination, including the advisement of rights, and the subject should be informed at the outset that such a recording will be made. A complete recording provides a record for later review, as well as protection for the subject and the examiner if any questions are subsequently raised about the manner in which the examination was conducted and its specific contents. The recording is very useful for an independent evaluation of the examination and for training polygraph examiners.

The pretest interview includes a brief medical and psychiatric history to uncover any serious physical or mental problems that might affect the validity of the test. The examiner then discusses the allegations or issues of the test and encourages the subject to describe and relate any events or knowledge that may be important for the examiner to know. This provides an opportunity to discuss the incident from the subject's point of view and to clarify any ambiguities or misunderstandings that might interfere with a valid test. It also assists in establishing an atmosphere of professional objectivity and trust.

The examiner then places the polygraph transducers on the subject and briefly explains the polygraph test and why people show strong involuntary physiological reactions when they are deceptive and not when they are truthful. A demonstration (stimulation) test is then performed to convince the subject that the polygraph is effective at detecting deception and verifying truthfulness. This usually takes the form of a number test in which the subject is asked to choose a number between 3 and 6, to disclose the number to the examiner, and to deny having chosen any of the numbers 1 through 7 while recordings are made with the polygraph.

After completing the number test, the subject is informed that a clear reaction occurred in response to the lie on the chosen number and that little change was observed in response to the other numbers. The subject is also told that the examiner now knows the characteristics of the subject's physiological reactions during deception and truthfulness and that there should be no problem on the test as long as the subject is completely truthful to every question. The subject is also told that any deception to any question on the test will produce even larger reactions than the reaction on the number test because such deception is more serious. Number tests have been shown to increase the accuracy of the polygraph test (Bradley & Janisse, 1981), and they are strongly recommended. Unfortunately, some polygraph practitioners fail to recognize their value and do not use them.

The specific wording of each question is then reviewed with the subject so that no ambiguities are present in the relevant questions, and the control questions are introduced in the manner previously described. A typical control question test includes 3 or 4 relevant questions embedded in a sequence of 10 to 12 questions, as shown in Table 8.1. These questions would be used in a test concerning the theft of a ring from an office. The sequence includes three relevant questions (R1, R2, R3), three control questions (C1, C2, C3), and three neutral questions (N1, N2, N3). The first two questions (I, SR) are buffers designed to habituate the reactions that normally occur to whatever question is presented first and to the first presentation of a question

Table 8.1. Control Question Sequence

I. Do you understand that I will ask only the questions we have discussed? "Yes"
SR. Regarding the theft of that ring, do you intend to answer all of the questions truthfully? "Yes"
N1. Do you live in the United States? "Yes"
C1. During the first 20 years of your life, did you ever take something that did not belong to you? "No"
R1. Did you take that ring? "No"
N2. Is your name Rick? "Yes"
C2. Prior to 1987, did you ever do something dishonest or illegal? "No"
R2. Did you take that ring from the desk? "No"
N3. Were you born in the month of November? "Yes"
C3. Before age 21 did you ever lie to get out of trouble or to cause a problem for someone else? "No"
R3. Did you participate in any way in the theft of that ring? "No"

that embodies the relevant issue of the test. The reactions to these buffer questions should not be evaluated. Each relevant question has a control question adjacent to it.

Administration of the Test

The subject is instructed not to move around or talk during the asking of questions, except to answer each question yes or no. Just before asking the questions, the examiner reminds the subject to answer every question truthfully. The examiner also instructs the subject that if anything else comes to mind during the test, it should be mentioned right after the test, not during the test. The questions are presented at a rate of one question every 25 to 35 sec while physiological activity is recorded on the polygraph charts. The sequence is repeated at least three times. The neutral and control questions are rotated through their three locations across repetitions of the question sequence in order to prevent the subject from producing anticipatory reactions caused by expecting the questions to be presented in a fixed order. If the results are not conclusive after three repetitions, two additional repetitions made be adminstered.

After each presentation of the question sequence, the examiner should discuss any concerns that the subject may express and review the questions in order to ensure that the control questions remain salient and that the relevant questions are clear and straightforward. If the subject makes an admission on a control question or provides additional information that changes the meaning of a relevant question, appropriate adjustments should be made in the affected questions and reviewed with the subject. However, the subject should not be given any information about the physiological reactions observed to the specific questions nor any indication of how the subject is doing on the test. Any specific information about the reactions can affect the outcome and interfere with the integrity of the test.

It is critical that the polygraph examiner's demeanor and behavior be professional and objective. If the subject is suspicious of the examiner or feels that the examiner is not competent or is biased, the accuracy of the test is compromised.

Some examiners are psychologically insensitive and abusive, and they sometimes convey an impression of disbelief in the subject's version of the events or attempt to interrogate the subject prior to the completion of the test. Such behaviors on the part of the examiner are likely to increase the risk of a false positive error (an example is presented by Raskin, 1986, p. 70).

Interpretation of the Results

The outcome of a control question test is evaluated by comparing the relative strengths of physiological reactions to relevant and control questions. Although different methods may be used for these comparisons, the decision rules are basically the same. If the reactions are generally stronger to the relevant questions, the outcome is considered deceptive on the relevant questions; if the reactions are stronger to the control questions, the outcome is considered truthful on the relevant questions; if there is no consistent difference in either direction, the outcome is considered inconclusive. It is the examiner's task to determine which of these conclusions applies to the polygraph charts obtained in the examination.

Global evaluation. This is the oldest method for assessing the truthfulness of the subject. It includes an overall inspection of the polygraph charts to form a general impression concerning the relative strengths of reactions to the various questions. This subjective impression is somehow integrated with information derived from the case reports, observations of the subject's demeanor and verbal behavior, and other sources of information that may be idiosyncratic to the particular examiner.

Although the global method is still advocated by some field polygraph examiners (e.g., Reid & Inbau, 1977), scientific research has shown it to be inferior to the more systematic methods based on numerical evaluation (Raskin, Barland, & Podlesny, 1978). They reported that blind numerical interpetation of polygraph charts from confirmed criminal cases produced only 1% errors, but global evaluation yielded 12% errors on the same charts.

Numerical evaluation. Numerical evaluation was developed by Backster, and Backster's system was modified by the U.S. Army and further modified on the basis of scientific research conducted at the University of Utah (for a discussion of the basic approaches and differences in results obtained with these three systems, see Weaver, 1980, 1985). Since the scientific evidence indicates that the Backster system is inherently biased against the innocent subject and produces an unacceptable number of false positive errors (Raskin, 1986; Weaver, 1985), the Utah version of the numerical scoring system forms the basis for all further descriptions and results obtained with numerical scoring in this chapter.

Numerical evaluation is a systematic approach to the evaluation of the outcome of a polygraph examination, and it attempts to rely solely on information obtained from the polygraph charts. All other sources of information, such as verbal and nonverbal behavior and case information, are formally excluded from the decision-making process. It begins with an inspection of the polygraph charts, and comparisons are made of the relative strengths of reactions to the relevant and control questions. Beginning with the first relevant question (R1), a score is assigned for each of the physiological parameters (electrodermal activity, blood pressure, and respiration). This score can range from −3 to +3, and it represents the direction and magnitude of the observed difference in the reactions elicited by the relevant question and its nearby control question (C1). If the observed reaction is stronger to the relevant question, a negative score is assigned; a positive score is assigned when the reaction is greater to the control question. The magnitude of scores can vary from 0 (no observed difference) to 1 (a noticeable difference) to 2 (a strong difference) to 3 (a dramatic difference). Most assigned scores are 0 or 1; scores of 2 are less common, and scores of 3 are unusual.

The examiner proceeds through the polygraph charts, assigning a score for each physiological parameter for each comparison of the responses to the relevant question and the nearby control question. This is repeated for each relevant question on the chart and for each chart. The scores are then summed to provide a total score for the test, and the outcome is based on this total. If the total is −6 or lower, the outcome is deceptive; if the total is +6 or higher, the outcome is truthful (or nondeceptive); and scores between −5 and +5 indicate an inconclusive outcome. These rules apply to tests that consist of three charts or five charts.

Different decision criteria are employed if the test questions and the issues make it possible for the subject to answer one or more relevant questions truthfully and one or more relevant questions deceptively, on the same test. Under these circumstances, total scores of −3 and +3 for a particular relevant question are used to arrive at a definite decision of deception or truthfulness, respectively. For example, a suspect in a bank robbery might have played one of several different roles, such as the shooter, the accomplice who took the money from the teller, or the driver of the getaway car. Assume that the subject was the driver of the car and did not go into the bank. When asked relevant questions about each of these possibilities, the subject would be truthful in denying being the shooter or being inside the bank, but deceptive when denying being the driver. The outcome of such a test would be evaluated separately for each of the three relevant questions, using cutoff scores of −3 and +3 for the totals on each of the three relevant questions.

The reliability of numerical evaluation has been determined by having different raters interpret the same sets of polygraph charts. Correlations among the total numerical scores assigned by the original examiner and by blind raters tend to be very high. In laboratory studies that used mock crime paradigms and field polygraph methods (e.g., Dawson, 1980; Kircher & Raskin, 1983, 1988; Podlesny & Raskin, 1978; Raskin & Hare, 1978; Rovner, Raskin, & Kircher, 1979), interrater reliabilities are typically in excess of .90. Similar results have been obtained in field studies (Raskin et al., 1978; Raskin, Kircher, Honts, & Horowitz, 1988). Numerical scoring by adequately trained and experienced interpreters produces extremely high reliablity that competes favorably with any psychological test interpreted by humans.

Computer interpretations. In order to provide more powerful, objective, and totally reliable polygraph chart interpretation and decision making, computer methods have been developed at the University of Utah (Kircher & Raskin, 1981, 1988). The computer methods have been validated on data from confirmed polygraph examinations of criminal suspects (Raskin et al., 1988), and they are based on extensive analyses of features extracted from physiological recordings obtained from guilty and innocent subjects. Discriminant functions were developed to yield optimal separation of the groups based on linear combinations of the physiological data. The discriminant scores for individual subjects are entered into Bayes' Theorem to calculate the probability (ranging from 0 to 1.0) that the obtained physiological data indicate that the subject was truthful.

The results obtained with the computer model are quite encouraging (Kircher & Raskin, 1988; Raskin et al., 1988). The computer diagnoses were somewhat more accurate than blind interpretations by skilled numerical evaluators, although the field study showed that the original examiners were slightly more accurate than the computer model. Apparently, the original examiners used the case information and their interactions with the subjects to adjust their numerical scoring to be more accurate. However, in terms of interpretations based solely on the polygraph charts, the computer outperformed the human interpreters. The results of these studies indicate that computer evaluations are extremely useful and are worthy of field implementation at this time. Such efforts are underway in some federal and state law enforcement agencies, and they report them to be useful and effective.

Validity of the Control Question Test

The validity of control question polygraph tests has become a subject of intense debate among scientists (e.g., Lykken, 1979; OTA, 1983; Raskin & Podlesny, 1979). Although the majority of psychophysiologists have expressed generally positive attitudes concerning the usefulness of polygraph tests for assessment of credibility (Raskin, 1988, pp. 96-97), the American Psychological Association expressed serious concerns about their scientific basis and some of their specific applications (see Raskin, 1986,

p. 73). A detailed examination of the scientific literature is necessary to provide answers to this complex, empirical question.

In the last 20 years, there has been a great deal of research, development, and experience with various techniques that employ physiological measures for assessing credibility with regard to specific acts, events, or knowledge (Raskin, 1986). Interestingly, the first laboratory study of the control question technique was conducted less than 20 years ago (Barland & Raskin, 1972), although the technique has been in widespread use since it was introduced more than 40 years ago by Reid (1947).

The debate about the accuracy of control question tests for investigative and forensic purposes centers on two general sources of data from which the accuracy of such tests may be estimated. Data may be obtained either from laboratory simulations of criminal situations (mock crime studies) or studies of actual cases that include testing of one or more suspects in a criminal investigation. Each type of study has advantages and disadvantages, and both types are needed to provide an overall picture of test accuracy.

Laboratory studies. The most accepted type of laboratory study simulates a mock crime in which subjects are randomly assigned to guilty and innocent treatment conditions (Raskin, 1982). Guilty subjects enact a realistic crime, and innocent subjects are merely told about the nature of the crime and do not enact it. All subjects are motivated to produce a truthful outcome, usually by a substantial cash bonus for passing the test. For example, one such study used prison inmates who were offered a bonus equal to one month's wages if they could produce a truthful outcome (Raskin & Hare, 1978).

The advantages of careful laboratory simulations include total control over the issues that are investigated and the types of tests that are used, consistency in their administration and interpretation, specification of the subject populations that are studied, control over the skill and training of the examiners, and absolute verification of the accuracy of test results. Carefully designed and conducted studies that closely approximate the methods and conditions characteristic of high-quality practice by polygraph professionals and that use subjects similar to the target population, such as convicted felons or a cross-section of the general community, provide the most generalizable results. The four studies that fulfilled these criteria to the greatest extent (Kircher, Horowitz, & Raskin, 1988) produced the results shown in Table 8.2.

The laboratory polygraph examinations produced decisions that were 97% accurate on guilty subjects and 93% accurate on innocent subjects. However, it should be noted that there were more errors that indicated deception by innocent subjects (7% false positive errors) than truthfulness by guilty subjects (3% false negative errors).

Field studies. The major disadvantage of laboratory simulations is the difficulty of completely simulating the real-life situation in which a person suspected of a crime is administered a polygraph test. To estimate test accuracy under these conditions, it is necessary to use tests conducted on actual criminal suspects. However, field studies of criminal suspects also have

Table 8.2. Percent Accuracy of Control Question Polygraph Tests in Mock-Crime Experiments

Experimental group	Raskin & Hare (1978)	Podlesny & Raskin (1978)	Rovner, Raskin, & Kircher (1979)	Kircher & Raskin (1988)	Weighted combined results
Guilty subjects	(24)	(10)	(24)	(50)	(108)
Correct	88	80	88	88	87
Wrong	0	10	0	4	3
Inconclusive	12	10	12	8	10
Decisions correct	100	89	100	96	97
Innocent subjects	(24)	(10)	(24)	(50)	(108)
Correct	88	90	88	86	87
Wrong	8	0	8	6	6
Inconclusive	4	10	4	8	7
Decisions correct[a]	91	100	91	93	93

[a] Decisions correct was obtained by excluding inconclusive outcomes and calculating percent correct using only decisions, i.e., Correct/(Correct + Wrong). Number of subjects in each sample is shown in parentheses.

inherent problems. The major problem is obtaining verification of the accuracy of the test outcomes, which can be very difficult in real cases.

Two general methods have been used to develop a criterion of guilt and innocence against which to assess the accuracy of field polygraph tests (Raskin, 1987). The best and most common method utilizes confessions to verify the guilt and innocence of the examinees. Law enforcement cases that involve polygraph tests produce rates of confessions in the range of 30% to 80% (OTA, 1983), but it is not known how these cases compare to those that did not produce confessions.

The other method relies on a panel of legal experts who review the case facts in order to provide judgments concerning the guilt or innocence of individual suspects. The use of panel decisions produces greater problems than a criterion based on confessions (Raskin, 1987). Since the panel criterion for guilt and innocence is merely an educated guess, it is subject to error. Furthermore, our legal standard of guilt requires conviction "beyond a reasonable doubt," and the panel is more likely to say "not guilty" for suspects who are actually guilty than it is to say "guilty" for suspects who are actually innocent. Whenever the polygraph result differs from the judgment of the panel, it is not known which was wrong. If the panel decided that the suspect was innocent and the polygraph result indicated deception, the panel may have been correct and the polygraph test may have produced a false positive error, or the polygraph may have been correct and the panel may have made a false negative error. Therefore, we cannot place much confidence in the results of panel studies, such as those reported by Bersh (1969) and Raskin et al. (1978).

The other major problems with field studies concern the representativeness of the cases selected, the training and skill of the polygraph examiners who conducted the tests, and the adequacy of the test methods and diagnostic procedures employed. To estimate the accuracy of polygraph tests on criminal suspects, it is necessary to select cases in which the subjects were suspects, not victims or witnesses. Although it is generally recognized that polygraph tests are most likely to produce false positive errors on victims of serious crimes (Mervis, 1986; Raskin, 1986), at least one major field study (Horvath, 1977) used a large number of tests in which verified innocent victims had been tested (see Raskin, 1986).

It is important that field studies select cases according to scientifically acceptable sampling procedures, using only cases in which properly trained polygraph examiners employed standard field methods for conducting the tests and interpreting their outcomes. Several of the frequently cited studies (Horvath & Reid, 1971; Hunter & Ash, 1973; Kleinmuntz & Szucko, 1984; Slowik & Buckley, 1975; Wicklander & Hunter, 1975) failed to adhere to these principles (Raskin, 1987). As a result, they provide limited information concerning the accuracy of properly conducted and interpreted polygraph tests.

The Kleinmuntz and Szucko study (1984) stands out because it embodied all of the serious methodological errors. They used only cases in which persons suspected of theft were ordered by their employers to take tests from a commercial polygraph firm, and they did not describe how they selected cases from the files of the commercial polygraph firm. In addition, they based the results on interpretations made by students in a commercial polygraph training course who were not trained in the proper methods of test interpretation, and they required the student examiners to make definite judgments of guilt or innocence on the basis of reactions to a single relevant question. It is not surprising that their study produced low rates of accuracy. Gross violations of acceptable scientific methodology and polygraph procedures render the study totally meaningless for estimating the accuracy of standard field polygraph examinations conducted by competent examiners under appropriate conditions.

Unfortunately, there are few field studies from which we can estimate the accuracy of properly conducted control question tests. The OTA (1983) selected 10 field studies that they felt had at least some degree of scientific merit. The studies included all of the field studies mentioned above and 2 others (Davidson, 1979; Raskin et al., 1978), and the overall accuracy of the polygraph decisions was 90% on criterion-guilty suspects and 80% on criterion-innocent suspects. In spite of the inclusion of many studies with serious methodological problems, accuracy in field cases was higher than is claimed by some of the most vocal critics (Lykken, 1987).

Given the range of training and the quality of performance of field polygraph examiners, it is reasonable to assume that the results obtained by some agencies and examiners are more accurate than the average of 85% reported by the OTA (1983), and some are probably lower. In order to estimate the higher levels of polygraph accuracy that may be achieved by criminal investigative agencies, a major field study was recently completed using data from polygraph examinations conducted in criminal investigations by the U.S. Secret Service (Raskin et al., 1988). The U.S. Secret Service was selected for the study because their polygraph program is noted for its high quality and effectiveness (Raskin, 1986). The Secret Service selects polygraph examiners from their Special Agents, all of whom possess at least a baccalaureate degree; many have advanced degrees in psychology or related disciplines. The effectiveness of their polygraph program is demonstrated by the high rate of case resolution produced by confessions following polygraph examinations (OTA, 1983).

The study sampled cases from criminal investigations that included polygraph examinations conducted during the 3-year period beginning in 1983. Polygraph examinations were selected if they fulfilled two criteria. The first criterion was a confession that inculpated or exculpated a suspect who had been administered a polygraph test. The second criterion required corroboration of the confession by physical evidence, such as seizure of the counterfeit money described in a confession or a fingerprint of the suspect found on a forged check. Using these criteria, subjects were classified as confirmed truthful and confirmed deceptive on one or more relevant questions in the test.

The outcomes were classified according to the interpretations by the original examiners and also by blind evaluations performed by other Secret Service examiners. Numerical evaluations were performed at the level of individual questions, and the results are shown in Table 8.3. The original examiners were highly accurate on confirmed deceptive and confirmed truthful suspects. Their false negative rate was 5%, and their

Table 8.3. Percent Accuracy on Individual Questions for Original Examiners and Blind Interpreters

Confirmation	(n)	Outcomes			Correct decisions
		Correct	Wrong	Inconclusive	
Deceptive					
Original examiners	(76)	79	4	17	95
Blind interpreters	(83)	65	4	31	94
Truthful					
Original examiners	(62)	76	3	21	96
Blind interpreters	(68)	52	9	39	85

Note. From Raskin et al., 1988.

false positive rate was only 4%. The blind interpreters performed at a similar level of accuracy on confirmed deceptive subjects, but their accuracy was somewhat lower on confirmed truthful subjects.

Lens model analyses (Slovic & Lichtenstein, 1971) indicated that the superior performance of the original examiners occurred because they used other information, probably the case information and/or the subject's verbal behavior, to make more accurate numerical evaluations. The results also indicated that when subjects were truthful to one or more relevant questions and deceptive to other relevant questions in the same test, it was slightly more difficult for the original examiners to correctly identify deception and truthfulness (85% and 91%, respectively), but it was particularly difficult for the blind interpreters (84% and 63%, repectively).

The results of this recent study clearly demonstrate that polygraph techniques are capable of very high levels of accuracy when utilized in criminal investigations by properly educated and trained examiners. They also indicated that numerical evaluations by the original examiners yield the most accurate decisions. Taken as a whole, these data provide strong support for the accuracy of control question polygraph tests when properly used in criminal investigation. They also point to the need to minimize the number of issues in the tests in order to maximize the accuracy of the tests.

The field data generally indicate that the rate of false positive errors is somewhat higher than the rate of false negative errors. For the studies surveyed by the OTA (1983), the rates were 20% and 10%, respectively. A similar pattern of results occurred in the laboratory studies reviewed above, 7% false positives and 3% false negatives. Although the Secret Service data did not show such a pattern for the original examiners, a similar pattern was observed in the results from the blind interpreters, especially when there was a mixture of issues, with the subject being truthful on some and deceptive on others. It is clear that the major weakness of the traditional control question test is its susceptibility to false positive errors.

Directed Lie Control Test

Recently, the directed lie question has been proposed as a substitute to remedy some of the problems inherent in the type of control question originated by Reid (Fuse, 1982; Honts & Raskin, 1988; Horowitz, 1988). The traditional control question test is difficult to adminster. Psychological sensitivity, sophistication, and skill on the part of the examiner are crucial to obtaining an accurate outcome on the test. Unfortunately, many polygraph examiners lack adequate training in psychological methods and do not understand the basic concepts and requirements of a standardized psychological test. These problems are exacerbated when the examiner formulates and introduces the control questions to the subject, because it is very difficult to standardize the wording and discussion of the questions for all subjects. A great deal depends on how the subject perceives and responds to the control questions when they are introduced and discussed during the pretest interview.

The difficulties with traditional control questions are compounded by problems related to the characteristics of examinees. Some examinees are very anxious about the subject matter of the control questions, making it difficult for the examiner to establish effective control questions. The control questions may be personally intrusive and offensive to some subjects. For other subjects, they may encompass prior criminal behavior of a serious nature that poses problems for the subjects, some of whom may refuse to answer the questions. Also, it can be very difficult to explain the functions of control questions and their role in interpreting the outcome of the test to those who use the results of polygraph tests (investigators, lawyers, judges, and juries). They may not understand the rationale of the control question test and may interpret strong physiological reactions to control questions as indicating that the subject is dishonest and guilty. For all of these reasons, the directed lie question has been developed.

A typical directed lie question is "Before age 25, did you ever tell even one lie?" The subject is instructed to answer no to that question, and it is made clear that anyone who denied having ever lied in the past would be lying. The directed lie questions are introduced to the subject following the number test and after the review of all other questions. A typical directed lie question sequence is shown in Table 8.4. It is the same as the traditional

Table 8.4. Directed Lie Question Sequence

I. Do you understand that I will ask only the questions we have discussed? "Yes"
SR. Regarding the theft of that ring, do you intend to answer all of the questions truthfully? "Yes"
N1. Do you live in the United States? "Yes"
DL1. During the first 20 years of your life, did you ever tell even one lie? "No"
R1. Did you take that ring? "No"
N2. Is your name Rick? "Yes"
DL2. Prior to 1987, did you ever break a rule or regulation? "No"
R2. Did you take that ring from the desk? "No"
N3. Were you born in the month of November? "Yes"
DL3. Before age 21 did you ever make a mistake? "No"
R3. Did you participate in any way in the theft of that ring? "No"

control question test, except that C1, C2, and C3 are replaced by directed lie controls DL1, DL2, and DL3.

The purpose of the directed lie questions is explained to the subject as follows:

> On this test I need to ask you some questions to which I want you to lie. Just as on the number test, I need to have questions to which you and I both know you are lying. That way, I can be sure that you continue to respond appropriately when you are lying and that you remain a suitable subject throughout this test. Therefore, I am going to ask you, "Before age 25, did you ever tell even one lie?" and I want you to lie to that question. Also, I want you to think of a particular instance when you did lie in the past, and I want you to have that in mind when you answer this question on the test. Do you have a particular instance in mind? . . . All right, I do not want you to tell me what it is. When I ask you that question on the test, I want you to lie by answering no, and when you answer, I want you to think about the time when you lied. That way, you and I will be sure that you are lying when you answer that question on the test, and I can make sure that you react appropriately and that you continue to be a suitable subject.

The rationale for using directed lie questions is similar to the rationale for traditional control questions. It is assumed that the subject's concern will be focused on the questions that pose the greatest risk of failing the test. For guilty subjects, the focus will normally be on relevant questions that are answered deceptively, especially because the examiner has stated that the number test clearly demonstrated how the examinee reacts when lying. Thus, guilty subjects should show stronger reactions to the relevant questions. However, subjects who are truthful in response to the relevant questions will be most concerned that the "appropriateness" of their reactions to the directed lie questions will show that they are suitable subjects and will demonstrate that their reactions are different when they are truthful. This focus of concern should enhance the reactions of truthful subjects to the directed lie questions, making them stronger than reactions to the relevant questions.

Administration and Interpretation of the Test

The directed lie test is administered and interpreted in the same way as the traditional control question test, except for the introduction of the directed lie questions and the discussion between charts. Just prior to asking the questions, the examiner says to the subject, "Be sure that you answer every question truthfully, except those questions to which I want you to lie. Be sure that you lie to them and think about the specific incident in your past when you did lie." Following the presentation of the questions, the examiner discusses any problems the subject may raise and also asks if the subject was aware that the answers to the directed lie questions were actually lies.

The substitution of directed lies for traditional control questions makes it easier to administer the test and allows greater standardization of the pretest interview. The same directed lies can be used for any type of crime and every subject, except for adjustment in the year and the subject's age. In addition, they are not intrusive, do not embarass the subjects, do not elicit admissions that require rewording of the questions, are readily answered by all subjects, and are less likely to cause the type of problems encountered when traditional control questions encompass a past criminal act of serious magnitude. Directed lies require less psychological manipulation of the subject and less examiner skill and sophistication. From the standpoint of standardization and ease of administration, directed lie questions are clearly preferable to traditional control questions.

Validity of the Directed Lie Test

Since the directed lie test is relatively new, there are only two available studies of its validity, one extensive laboratory study (Horowitz, 1989) and one field validity study (Honts & Raskin, 1988). The Horowitz study used a mock crime that closely approximated the field situation, similar to those described above. He compared the effectiveness of the directed lie test with standard control question and relevant-irrelevant tests. Different groups received one of two types of directed lies: personally relevant directed lies using the procedures previously described, or simple directed lies to three of the neutral questions that were used in the relevant-irrelevant test. The traditional control question test and the relevant-irrelevant test were similar to those previously described.

The results of the Horowitz (1989) study indicate that compared to the other three conditions, the personally relevant directed lie test produced the highest accuracy, except for the relevant-irrelevant test with guilty subjects. The outcomes for the four types of tests are presented in Table 8.5. Among all question structures, the personal directed lie produced the highest number of correct decisions on innocent subjects, and among the three tests that employed control questions, it produced the highest number of correct decisions on guilty subjects.

The other validity study of the directed lie test is a field study by Honts and Raskin (1988). They conducted polygraph tests of criminal suspects over a 4-year period and obtained 25 confirmed tests in which one personal directed lie was included along with traditional control questions. Each of the investigators then performed blind interpretations of the charts obtained

Table 8.5. Percent Accuracy of Different Types of Polygraph Tests

	Outcomes			
Experimental group	Correct	Wrong	Inconclusive	Correct decisions
Guilty				
Personal directed lie	73	14	13	84
Trivial directed lie	53	20	27	73
Control question	53	20	27	73
Relevant-irrelevant	100	0	0	100
Innocent				
Personal directed lie	87	13	0	87
Trivial directed lie	67	13	20	84
Control question	80	13	7	86
Relevant-irrelevant	20	73	7	22

Note. From Horowitz (1989). Decisions correct was obtained by excluding inconclusive outcomes and calculating percent correct using only decisions, i.e., Correct/(Correct + Wrong).

by the other investigator, scoring them with and without the use of the directed lie question.

The field results shown in Table 8.6 indicate that inclusion of the directed lie question in the numerical evaluation of the charts had a noticeable effect on the confirmed innocent suspects, reducing the false positive rate from 20% to 0%. For the confirmed guilty suspects, it had the slight effect of changing one inconclusive outcome to a false negative. The effects of the directed lie question on the numerical scores were more dramatic. It almost doubled the size of the total numerical scores for the confirmed innocent suspects, raising the mean score from +4.7 to +9.0. It had a lesser effect on the scores of the confirmed guilty suspects, lowering them from −13.8 to −11.5. Thus, the directed lie question had the effect of raising the mean score for innocent suspects from the inconclusive range into the definite truthful area, while leaving the mean score for guilty suspects clearly in the deceptive area. The main impact of the directed lie question was a reduction in false positive errors.

The results from the laboratory and the field are consistent with the proposition that the directed lie test represents a substantial advance over the traditional control question test. It is more standardized in its structure; it is easier to administer; it requires less manipulation of the subject and creates fewer

Table 8.6. Effects of the Directed Lie in Polygraph Tests of Criminal Suspects

Confirmation group	Outcomes			% Correct decisions
	Correct	Wrong	Inconclusive	
Guilty				
With one directed lie	11	1	0	92
Without directed lie	11	0	1	100
Innocent				
With one directed lie	11	0	2	100
Without directed lie	8	2	3	80

Note. From Honts and Raskin (1988). Decisions correct was obtained by excluding inconclusive outcomes and calculating percent correct using only decisions, i.e., Correct/ (Correct + Wrong).

problems for the subject; it is more readily explained to lawyers, judges, and juries; and most important, it reduces the problem of false positive errors inherent in the traditional control question test.

INFORMATION TESTS

Detection of information comprises the other major approach to the use of physiological measures in criminal investigation. Unlike deception tests, these methods do not directly assess the credibility of denials or assertions made by the subject. Instead, they measure the relative strengths of physiological reactions to specific items of information in order to determine if the subject has direct knowledge of that information (Lykken, 1981; Raskin, 1982).

Peak of Tension Tests

The oldest form of information test is known as the peak of tension test (Barland & Raskin, 1973). It is designed to determine if the suspect knows which is the correct alternative among a set of five or more alternatives concerning a fact that only the investigators and persons involved in the incident would know. For example, if a person had been shot and the caliber of the gun had not been discussed, the examiner might ask the suspect about the caliber of gun that was used. If the suspect denied knowledge of that fact, the examiner would present a series of common and equally plausible gun calibers in an order reviewed with the suspect, such as shown in Table 8.7.

Table 8.7. Peak of Tension Question Sequence

1. Do you know if it was a .22 caliber?
2. Do you know if it was a .25 caliber?
3. Do you know if it was a .32 caliber?
*4. Do you know if it was a .38 caliber?
5. Do you know if it was a .44 caliber?
6. Do you know if it was a .45 caliber?

Note. Asterisk indicates the correct alternative.

Administration and Interpretation of the Test

The first item is never the critical or correct answer and is not included in the evaluation of the outcome. The correct item is placed near the middle of the sequence. This is a known-solution peak of tension test because the correct answer is known to the investigators. The examiner asks the questions only once at a rate of one question every 15 sec. The charts are inspected to see if the subject's physiological activity increased as the critical item was approached and declined after that point. If that "peak of tension" is observed, the examiner concludes that the subject has independent knowledge of the incident.

Peak of tension tests can also be used to determine a fact that the investigators do not know but desire to discover. These are known as searching peak of tension tests. An example would be the location of the body of a person who disappeared or of a child who was kidnapped. If the general location is known to the investigators, a map can be marked off into sections, and the suspect can be questioned about the possible sections by placing the map in front of the suspect and pointing to the various sections while asking, "Do you know if the body is in this area?" The area that produced the largest reaction is then divided into progressively smaller areas that are tested until the results indicate the area for an actual search to be conducted. The same can be done with possible locations of a kidnap victim.

Concealed Knowledge Test

The peak of tension test was modified by Lykken (1959) to provide a more standardized and effective test when several independent and protected items of information are known to the investigators. Lykken called this the "guilty knowledge test." The term *concealed knowledge test* is preferred, because information cannot be guilty, and the test is designed to determine if the suspect is attempting to conceal information.

The concealed knowledge test consists of a series of multiple-choice questions, each of which deals with an independent item of information. Each question has six equally plausible alternative answers, the first of which serves as a buffer and is not evaluated. The correct alternatives are rotated across positions two through six. Laboratory research (Iacono, Boisvenu, & Fleming, 1984) suggests that a test with five multiple-choice questions may be optimal, but it also indicates that a somewhat longer test may be better for testing actual criminal suspects.

A sequence of multiple-choice questions for a concealed knowledge test using the same situation that was previously used to illustrate control question and directed lie tests, the theft of a ring from an office (Podlesny & Raskin, 1978), is presented in Table 8.8. Note that each alternative is an equally familiar and plausible choice.

Table 8.8. Concealed Knowledge Question Sequence

Q1. Regarding the type of ring that was taken, do you know if it was a
    1. sapphire class ring   2. pearl engagement ring
    3. silver and turquoise ring   *4. gold wedding ring
    5. ruby class ring   6. diamond engagement ring

Q2. Regarding the floor of the building that the ring was on, do you know if it was the
    1. 1st floor   2. 12th floor   3. 6th floor
    4. 4th floor   *5. 8th floor   6. 10th floor

Q3. Regarding the number of the room that the ring was in, do you know if it was
    1. Room 800   *2. Room 820   3. Room 810
    4. Room 816   5. Room 814   6. Room 803

Q4. Regarding the type of envelope that the ring was in, do you know if it was
    1. an intercampus mail envelope   2. a medium-size manila envelope
    *3. a business-size white envelope   4. a small-size manila envelope
    5. a small-size white envelope   6. a large-size manila envelope

Q5. Regarding the name of the doctor that the guilty person asked for, do you know if it was
    1. Dr. Trumbull   2. Dr. Tolman   3. Dr. Palmer
    4. Dr. Jordan   5. Dr. Calvin   *6. Dr. Mitchell

Note. Asterisk indicates the correct alternative.
From Podlesny and Raskin (1978).

Administration of the Test

The subject matter of each question is discussed with the suspect, but the specific alternatives are not reviewed. The reaction of a suspect who knows the answer is likely to be enhanced when the correct alternative occurs by surprise, but surprise would play no role for a suspect who does not know the correct answer. Presenting the alternatives prior to asking them on the test would allow an innocent suspect to think about which item is most likely correct, and that could increase the likelihood of a false positive result. Each question is discussed and tested before the next question is discussed. That prevents the suspect from figuring out the answer to a question that might be suggested by another question, as illustrated by Q2 and Q3 in Table 8.8. The floor number was asked first because having first asked the room number would have provided information about the floor number.

The incident is discussed with the suspect to ascertain which items of protected information the suspect denies knowing. It is important to encourage the suspect to disclose any knowledge or information pertaining to the incident. However, the examiner must be careful not to provide any information or any hints to the suspect. If the suspect acknowledges having obtained information from the media, investigators, or others, that information should not be used for questions on the test. A number test should be performed in the manner previously described. However, the explanation should be altered to indicate that a person's body reacts when a familiar item of information is recognized, especially when the individual is attempting to conceal knowledge of that information. The concealed knowledge test is explained to the suspect in the following way:

> I am going to conduct a test that is like a multiple-choice test used in school. This test will consist of several multiple-choice questions that concern items of information about the crime. Each question has one correct choice, and all of the other choices are incorrect. If you were not involved in this crime in any way or if you have not been told about it by someone who was involved, then you will not even know the correct answer to any of the questions and your body will not react, just as it did not react to

the numbers that you had not chosen on the number test. However, if you were involved or heard about it from someone who was involved, then your body will react very strongly to every correct choice on the test. First, I am going to ask you about the type of ring that was taken. If you do not know anything about that ring, you will not react when you hear the correct ring. However, if you do know, then you will give a big reaction when you hear the correct ring mentioned.

The first question is then asked as indicated in Table 8.8, and the alternatives are presented at a rate of one every 15 sec. After that question, the second question is presented, and so on until the test is completed.

Interpretation of the Outcome

Consistently strong reactions to the correct alternatives indicates that the subject has concealed knowledge of the incident. If a question has five alternatives (not counting the first alternative), then a suspect without any knowledge has one chance in five of reacting most strongly to that alternative. However, a knowledgeable suspect has a higher probability of showing a strong reaction to the correct alternative. The more questions on which the subject showed a relatively strong reaction to the correct alternative, the more likely that the subject was attempting to conceal knowledge.

The scientific literature indicates that the electrodermal response is the most useful measure for determining the outcome of a concealed knowledge test. Podlesny and Raskin (1978) evaluated skin conductance, respiration, relative blood pressure, and vasomotor reactions (finger pulse amplitude and blood volume), and they reported that only skin conductance and vasomotor reactions discriminated between guilty and innocent subjects. Iacono, Cerri, Patrick, and Fleming (1987) examined skin conductance, respiration, and finger pulse amplitude. Skin conductance and respiration produced significant discrimination between guilty and innocent subjects, but finger pulse amplitude did not. However, skin conductance produced the highest classification accuracy, and the addition of respiration and finger pulse amplitude did not improve the accuracy of classification when compared to skin conductance alone. These studies taken together argue for the use of only electrodermal activity in determining the results of a a concealed knowledge test.

Using the simple measure of amplitude of electrodermal responses elicited by each alternative, Lykken (1959) developed a scoring system that is expected to produce only a small number of false positive errors (Iacono et al., 1987; Podlesny & Raskin, 1978). It is a very simple system that can be learned in a few minutes. The system consists of assigning to each question a score of 2 if the reaction was largest to the correct alternative, a score of 1 if it was second largest, and a 0 if it was third largest or lower. That is repeated for each question, and the total for all questions is obtained. The total is then divided by the maximum possible score (twice the number of questions on the test). If that proportion exceeds .50, it is concluded that the subject was concealing knowledge about the incident. If it is less than .50, the subject is deemed not to have concealed knowledge.

Validity of the Concealed Knowledge Test

There are many laboratory studies of the accuracy of the concealed knowledge test, but there is not a single field study of it (OTA, 1983). Of the laboratory studies, many were poorly executed. The data presented in Table 8.9 summarize the results of five studies that utilized adequate experimental designs, procedures similar to those described above, and realistic simulations of criminal incidents.

Table 8.9. Percent Accuracy of the Concealed Knowledge Test in Laboratory Experiments

Experimental group	Lykken (1959)	Davidson (1968)	Podlesny & Raskin (1978)	Iacono et al. (1984)	Iacono et al. (1987)	Weighted combined results
Guilty subjects	86	92	80	82	83	84
Innocent subjects	100	100	100	100	93	99

Laboratory studies indicate that the concealed knowledge test appears to reduce the risk of a false positive error to near zero. However, the data also indicate that the test has a relatively high risk of false negative errors. The obtained false negative rate of 16% is much higher than the false negative rates obtained in laboratory studies of control question and directed lie tests. This fact has been totally ignored by those who propose the concealed knowledge test as a substitute for the control question test (Ben-Shakhar, in press; Lykken, 1981).

The relatively frequent occurrence of false negative outcomes is probably due to the failure of guilty subjects to perceive or remember the specific information that is used to formulate the multiple-choice questions on the test. This interpretation was supported by the findings of Iacono et al., (1984). They reported that guilty subjects who remembered more details of the crime produced higher scores on the concealed knowledge test. Similar findings were reported by O'Toole (1988), who emphasized the need to construct questions to which the subject would be expected to know the correct alternative.

The total lack of field studies of the concealed knowledge test is partly due to the fact that many criminal cases do not lend themselves to the concealed knowledge test. It cannot be applied in any case in which the suspect or accused admits being present but denies having performed the criminal acts. This would exclude its use in sexual assault cases where the issue is consent; assaults, robberies, and murders in which the suspect admits being present but denies being the perpetrator; claims of having played a lesser criminal role than is alleged or suspected; claims of self-defense; and claims of witnessing the criminal event as a passerby or innocent bystander. Furthermore, many suspects are rendered unsuitable as subjects for a concealed knowledge test. During the course of interviews of the suspect, it is common practice for investigators to divulge the very information that must be kept from the suspect in order to construct the test. Also, many suspects learn the important details of the crimes from the news media or from their attorneys.

Laboratory research of the effects of memory on the detectability of guilty subjects (Iacono et al., 1984; O'Toole, 1988) clearly indicates that questions used on the test must deal with information that the subject perceived at the time of the incident and remembers at the time of the test. Unfortunately, investigators and polygraph examiners have no good method to determine which information is available in the suspect's memory at the time of the examination. Information that the examiner and/or investigator believe that a guilty suspect would know may not have been perceived or remembered by the perpetrator. If the guilty suspect does not know the information used in the test items, a false negative error would occur. In contrast, the research by O'Toole indicates that a similar problem does not exist for the control question test.

In light of the foregoing, it is not likely that the concealed knowledge test will replace the control question test in criminal investigation. Given the lack of field validation, the apparently high rate of false negatives, and the lack of suitable cases and suspects to which it can be applied, it is not likely that it will ever enjoy widespread use. However, the foregoing should not be interpreted to mean that the concealed knowledge test cannot or should not be used. If investigators would make greater efforts to gather and protect the type of information that could be used to construct concealed knowledge tests, their application could be substantially increased. The test can be extremely useful, especially when employed in conjunction with a control question or directed lie test. If the results of the two tests are consistent, then confidence in the conclusions is extremely high. If the test results conflict, their resolution will require information in addition to the polygraph results.

APPLIED ISSUES

As the uses of polygraph techniques have grown in criminal investigation and evidence, there is increasing concern about factors that may adversely affect their accuracy and their uses in administrative and judicial proceedings (Raskin, 1986). Critics have pointed to potential problems of physical and mental countermeasures, such as drugs, physical maneuvers, and mental states, as well as to personality characteristics such as psychopathy or sociopathy, and the testing of victims (OTA, 1983). Some have raised questions about the value of tests conducted confidentially by defense counsel (Orne, 1975) and the possibly prejudicial effect of polygraph evidence on jurors (Abbell, 1977). This section discusses the scientific and practical aspects of these questions.

Countermeasures

Deliberate attempts by guilty subjects to distort or defeat polygraph tests are known as countermeasures. They can be divided into two basic categories: those that change the general mental or physical state of the subject, and those that produce specific effects at particular points in the test. *General state countermeasures* include the use of drugs, relaxation techniques, hypnosis, biofeedback training, and mental dissociation from the examination context. *Specific point countermeasures* include physical or mental maneuvers during control questions to increase reactions to them, and relaxing thoughts or imagery to reduce reactions to relevant questions.

It appears that all mental and physical general state countermeasures and specific point mental countermeasures to reduce reactions to relevant questions are not effective or are only marginally effective (Barland & Raskin, 1973; Gudjonsson, 1988; Honts, 1987; OTA, 1983). However, application of specific physical and mental countermeasures during control questions may produce an increase in inconclusive and false negative outcomes. The research on these techniques and on the use of drugs will be discussed in some detail.

Effects of Drugs

Several laboratory studies have investigated the proposition that guilty suspects can use tranquilizers, beta blockers, stimulants, or alcohol to defeat polygraph tests. The earliest reported study (Waid, Orne, Cook, & Orne, 1981) claimed that a moderate dose of the common tranquilizer meprobamate (Miltown) enabled a large proportion of college student subjects to beat a concealed knowledge test. However, their study suffered from many methodological flaws, perhaps the most serious of which were the lack of a realistic crime simulation and failure to provide any motivation for the subjects to avoid detection (Iacono et al., 1984; Raskin, 1982). Their report also implied that the drug might be effective against a control question test. Interestingly, Orne (1983) acknowledged that he had performed a similar study with the control question test that failed to produce any drug effects. Furthermore, a more recent and methodologically sound study (Iacono et al., 1987) failed to find any effects of mebrobamate on the outcomes of concealed knowledge tests (see below).

Other than Waid et al. (1981), there is only one published study that reported a drug to be effective against polygraph tests (Bradley & Ainsworth, 1984). Their results indicated that laboratory subjects who were intoxicated during the commission of a mock crime were more difficult to detect with control question and concealed knowledge tests, although alcohol intoxication during the tests had no effects. However, O'Toole (1988) performed a carefully designed and executed study that failed to replicate the findings of Bradley and Ainsworth. Not only did he fail to find effects of alcohol intoxication during the commission of the mock crime, but he reanalyzed the results reported by Bradley and Ainsworth and concluded that their reported effects were due to errors in computations. There is no evidence that alcohol intoxication during a crime prevents effective detection by polygraph tests, although loss of consciousness or a blackout would raise serious doubts about the effectiveness of any type of polygraph test.

Several other studies have examined the potential effects of drugs, and none has reported them to be effective countermeasures. Iacono et al. (1984) tested the effects of the tranquilizer diazepam (Valium) and the stimulant methylphenidate (Ritalin) on the outcomes of concealed knowledge tests. They found no effects of either drug. A subsequent study by Iacono and his associates (Iacono et al., 1987) similarly found no effects of the tranquilizers meprobamate and diazepam or the beta blocker propranolol.

It is more difficult for a drug to be effective against a control question or directed lie test. To produce a truthful outcome for a guilty subject, the drug must differentially decrease the reactions to the relevant questions, leaving the reactions to control questions relatively unaffected. No known drug possesses such special properties, and the most that could be expected is an overall reduction in reactivity, which might produce an inconclusive outcome. There appears to be only one mock-crime study of the effects of drugs, other than alcohol, on the control question test (Gatchel, Smith, & Kaplan, 1983). The results indicated that use of propranolol did not increase false negatives, but it did increase the correct identification of innocent subjects. Rather than reducing the relative strength of guilty subjects' reactions to relevant questions, it decreased the reactions of innocent subjects to relevant questions. The overall conclusion from the scientific evidence is that drugs are ineffective in defeating control question or concealed knowledge tests.

Specific Physical and Mental Maneuvers

Lykken (1979) claimed that it would be very easy to teach a guilty suspect to defeat a polygraph test. He stated that "any intelligent criminal can be taught to identify the three control questions and instructed to augment his autonomic reactions to these questions in a variety of covert ways" (p. 53). In fact, Lykken (1960) had already failed in his attempts to train psychologists, psychiatrists, and medical students to defeat a concealed knowledge test by using maneuvers to augment their reactions to the incorrect alternatives. These included biting the tongue, pressing the toes against the floor, contracting muscles in the buttocks and anal sphincter, and biofeedback and various other psychological maneuvers. None was effective for even one subject. Rovner et al. (1979) also obtained negative results when they gave subjects information and instructions in these methods. However, when that information was combined with practice with a polygraph, some subjects were successful in defeating the test.

Recent research has indicated that information combined with specific training from a person knowledgeable about physical and mental countermeasures may be effective. A series of studies at the University of Utah (Honts, 1986; Honts, Raskin, & Kircher, 1987) has demonstrated that laboratory subjects recruited from the community and trained to bite their tongues, press their toes against the floor, or unobtrusively peform mental arithmetic during the control questions produced approximately 35% false negative and 30% inconclusive outcomes on control question tests. Furthermore, experienced field polygraph examiners were unable to detect these maneuvers (Honts & Hodes, 1983), but measurements of muscle potentials may provide some detection (Honts, Raskin, & Kircher, 1987).

Whether these countermeasures would be effective in the high-motivation situation of a criminal investigation is not known. Fortunately, there has been a complete lack of success among those who attempted to use such countermeasures without training by an expert (Honts, Raskin, Kircher, & Hodes, 1988). It might be very difficult for criminal suspects to obtain such training, although Lykken (Lykken, 1981; Lykken & Fay, 1983) claims to have successfully assisted a prison inmate to train guilty inmates to defeat polygraph tests conducted by prison authorities concerning crimes and infractions committed in prison.

Personality Factors

Mental status and personality are important considerations in deciding if a person is a suitable subject for a polygraph examination. The small amount of available evidence indicates that psychotic and other seriously disturbed individuals present higher risks of error (see Abrams, 1977). Fortunately, most examiners should be able to identify such problems during the pretest interview. Other types of personality factors, such as psychopathy, may not be as apparent.

It is commonly believed that poorly socialized individuals and psychopaths can defeat polygraph tests because they are adept at lying and are deficient in moral development and social conscience (Waid & Orne, 1982). Waid, Orne, and Wilson (1979) reported that three college students who scored lower in socialization than other college students were undetected in deception on a single presentation of a control question sequence. They concluded that poorly socialized individuals can beat the test; however, their study had major methodological deficiencies that rendered the results meaningless (Raskin, 1986).

Careful laboratory and field research has clearly demonstrated that poor socialization and psychopathy do not reduce the accuracy of control question tests. These studies have been conducted with college students and volunteers from the general community (Honts, Raskin, & Kircher, 1985), convicted felons and clinically diagnosed psychopaths (Patrick & Iacono, 1986; Raskin & Hare, 1978), and psychopathic criminal suspects who were given polygraph tests in actual investigations (Barland & Raskin, 1975). Other investigators have produced similar results with concealed knowledge and control question tests (see OTA, 1983). The extensive scientific literature demonstrates that polygraph techniques are highly effective in detecting deception in poorly socialized and psychopathic individuals, but highly socialized individuals and even psychopaths may be subject to false positive errors (Honts et al., 1985; Patrick & Iacono, 1986).

Confidential Tests for Defense Attorneys

A major challenge to the validity of polygraph evidence offered by the defense in criminal cases is known as the "friendly polygrapher" hypothesis (Orne, 1975, p. 114). Orne proposed that a guilty criminal defendant or accused who takes a polygraph test is more likely to pass the test if it is confidential and requested by the defense attorney than if the subject is informed that adverse as well as favorable results will be disclosed to the prosecution. Orne's argument assumes that under the confidential or privileged situation, the guilty subject has little at stake and little to fear. Therefore, the guilty subject will be more confident, the examiner will be more supportive, and the results are more likely to be favorable. Orne based this hypothesis on the results of a weak laboratory study with college students who were administered card tests in an unrealistic setting (Gustafson & Orne, 1965).

The scientific literature argues against the validity of the friendly polygrapher hypothesis (see Raskin, 1986). One study (Timm, 1982) showed no effects of increased confidence in beating the test, even when subjects were given a drug (placebo) that they were told would help them to beat the test and a number test that indicated that their lie was not detected. Field data reported by Raskin (1986) showed that substantially more criminal defendants failed confidential polygraph tests than did those who knew that the results would be reported to the prosecution.

The principles and procedures of control question polygraph tests argue against the friendly polygrapher notion. First, the advisement of rights at the outset of the examination warns the subject that the results may be used as adverse evidence in court. In addition, the subject has a great deal at stake in the outcome. A deceptive result precludes the opportunity to use the polygraph to obtain a dismissal of the case or an acquittal at trial, as well as increased legal costs and a fear of disruption of the subject's relationship with the defense attorney. In order to pass a control question test, the subject must show larger reactions to the control questions, and the friendly polygrapher hypothesis offers no explanation of how reduced concern can result in larger reactions to the control than to the relevant questions. Even law enforcement polygraph examiners do not accept the Orne hypothesis.

Testing Victims

Suspects and defendants are not the only subjects of polygraph examinations. In some jurisdictions for some types of cases (e.g., suspicious robberies, questionable sexual assaults), the complaining witness may be asked to take a polygraph examination to verify the veracity of the allegations. Because there is trauma associated with such events, actual victims are more likely than other suspects to show reactions to the relevant questions when they answer truthfully. The problem is compounded by the anger and indignation experienced by many victims who are asked to prove that they really were assaulted.

In a field study of control question polygraph examinations conducted by a law enforcement agency (Horvath, 1977), all but one of the false positive errors occurred on victims of sexual or physical assault or robbery (G. H. Barland, personal communication, September 18, 1982). Because of these problems, the American Psychological Association has raised cautions about administering polygraph tests to victims of crimes (Mervis, 1986). Such applications should be approached with great caution and only when there is a strong basis for suspicion. The alleged perpetrator is usually a more suitable and appropriate subject for a polygraph test.

Impacts on Jurors

Opponents of polygraph evidence have frequently argued that it should not be admitted at trial because it will have an undue influence on the jury due to its scientific aura (Abbell, 1977). The scientific literature and experience with the use of polygraph evidence in court argue against such a view. Jury simulation studies have shown that polygraph evidence has a relatively limited impact on decisions of guilt or innocence, and data obtained from actual cases support this conclusion. A detailed description of these findings is beyond the scope of this chapter, and a summary of the evidence is contained in a previous article (Raskin, 1986).

One point that should be explained to the trier of fact by the expert is the higher degree of confidence that should be placed in a truthful as compared to a deceptive outcome for control question tests. Conversely, it should be pointed out that for concealed knowledge tests, there is higher confidence in an outcome that indicates concealed knowledge than one that indicates lack of knowledge. These conclusions may be conditioned by a discussion of the effects of varying base rates of guilt or innocence in the population and situation represented by the suspect. That is a complex matter beyond the scope of this chapter. Detailed discussions and methods to calculate those outcomes are presented in other publications (Raskin, 1986, 1987, 1988).

It seems reasonable to conclude that no compelling data or arguments support the proposition that polygraph evidence should be treated differently than any other type of scientific evidence presented through the testimony of an expert. It should be treated just as other types of expert testimony, such as ballistics, blood tests, eyewitness evidence, or questioned documents. Many of those are similar in terms of their "scientific aura," and they often have greater error rates (see Chapter 1 and also Peterson, Fabricant, & Field, 1978; Widacki & Horvath, 1978).

SUMMARY AND CONCLUSIONS

Polygraph techniques are complex and controversial methods that are extensively employed in investigation and administrative and evidentiary proceedings. The voluminous scientific literature indicates that they can be highly accurate when properly employed in appropriate circumstances, but they are also subject to abuse and misinterpretation. There are also many myths concerning their accuracy and effectiveness and the ways in which they are employed. This chapter has attempted to describe the various methods, along with their strengths and weaknesses and the scientific evidence concerning their validity. Careful consideration of these features, combined with thorough analysis of each particular case in which they have been or might be applied, should result in judicious decisions about when and how they should be used.

ACKNOWLEDGEMENTS

A great deal of the research described in this chapter was conducted with the assistance and collaboration of John C. Kircher, Charles R. Honts, and Steven W. Horowitz, whose help is gratefully acknowledged.

REFERENCES

Abbell, M. (1977). Polygraph evidence: The case against admissibility in federal criminal trials. *American Criminal Law Review, 15,* 29–62.

Abrams, S. (1977). *A polygraph handbook for attorneys.* Lexington, MA: Lexington Books.

Barland, G. H. (1988). The polygraph test in the USA and elsewhere. In A. Gale (Ed.), *The polygraph test: Lies, truth and science* (pp. 73–95). London: Sage.

Barland, G. H., & Raskin, D. C. (1972). An experimental study of field techniques in "lie detection." *Psychophysiology, 9*, 275.

Barland, G. H., & Raskin, D. C. (1973). Detection of deception. In W. F. Prokasy & D. C. Raskin (Eds.), *Electrodermal activity in psychological research* (pp. 417–477). New York: Academic Press.

Barland, G. H., & Raskin, D. C. (1975). Psychopathy and detection of deception in criminal suspects. *Psychophysiology, 12*, 224.

Ben-Shakhar, G. (in press). Future prospects of psychphysiological detection: Replacing the CQT by the GKT. In P. K. Ackles, J. R. Jennings, & M. G. H. Coles (Eds.), *Advances in Psychophysiology* (Vol. 4). Greenwich, CT: JAI Press.

Bersh, P. J. (1969). A validation study of polygraph examiner judgments. *Journal of Applied Psychology, 53*, 399–403.

Bradley, M. T., & Ainsworth, D. (1984). Alcohol and the psychophysiological detection of deception. *Psychophysiology, 21*, 63–71.

Bradley, M. T., & Janisse, M. P. (1981). Accuracy demonstrations, threat, and the detection of deception: Cardiovascular, electrodermal, and pupillary measures. *Psychophysiology, 18*, 307–315.

Davidson, P. O. (1968). Validity of the guilty-knowledge technique: The effects of motivation. *Journal of Applied Psychology, 52*, 62–65.

Davidson, W. A. (1979). Validity and reliability of the cardio activity monitor. *Polygraph, 8*, 104–111.

Dawson, M. E. (1980). Physiological detection of deception: Measurement of responses to questions and answers during countermeasure maneuvers. *Psychophysiology, 17*, 8–17.

Furedy, J. J., & Heslegrave, R. J. (in press). The forensic use of the polygraph: A psychophysiological analysis of current trends and future prospects. In P. K. Ackles, J. R. Jennings, & M. G. H. Coles (Eds.), *Advances in psychophysiology* (Vol. 4). Greenwich, CT: JAI Press.

Fuse, L. S. (1982). *Directed lie control testing technique*. Unpublished manuscript.

Gale, A. (1988). *The polygraph test: Lies, truth and science*. London: Sage.

Gatchel, R. J., Smith, J. E., & Kaplan, N. M. (1983). *The effect of propranolol on polygraphic detection of deception*. Unpublished manuscript, University of Texas Health Science Center, Department of Psychiatry and Internal Medicine, Dallas.

Gudjonsson, G. H. (1988). How to defeat the polygraph test. In A. Gale (Ed.), *The polygraph test: Lies, truth and science* (pp. 126–136). London: Sage.

Gustafson, L. A., & Orne, M. T. (1965). Effects of perceived role and role success on the detection of deception. *Journal of Applied Psychology, 49,* 412–417.

Honts, C. R. (1986). *Countermeasures and the physiological detection of deception: A psychophysiological analysis.* Unpublished doctoral dissertation, University of Utah, Salt Lake City.

Honts, C. R. (1987). Interpreting research on polygraph measures. *Journal of Police Science and Administration, 15,* 204–209.

Honts, C. R., & Hodes, R. L. (1983). The detection of physical countermeasures. *Polygraph, 12,* 7–17.

Honts, C. R., Kircher, J. C., & Raskin, D. C. (1988). Patterns of activation and deception. *Psychophysiology, 25,* 455. (Abstract).

Honts, C. R., & Raskin, D. C. (1988). A field study of the validity of the directed lie control question. *Journal of Police Science and Administration, 16,* 56–61.

Honts, C. R., Raskin, D. C., & Kircher, J. C. (1985). Effects of socialization on the physiological detection of deception. *Journal of Research in Personality, 19,* 373–385.

Honts, C. R., Raskin, D. C., & Kircher, J. C. (1987). Effects of physical countermeasures and their electromyographic detection during polygraph tests for deception. *Journal of Psychophysiology, 1,* 241–247.

Honts, C. R., Raskin, D. C., Kircher, J. C., & Hodes, R. L. (1988). Effects of spontaneous countermeasures on the physiological detection of deception. *Journal of Police Science and Administration, 16,* 91–94.

Horowitz, S. W. (1989). *The role of the control question in physiological detection of deception.* Unpublished doctoral dissertation, University of Utah, Salt Lake City.

Horvath, F. S. (1977). The effect of selected variables on interpretation of polygraph records. *Journal of Applied Psychology, 62,* 127–136.

Horvath, F. S., & Reid, J. E. (1971). The reliability of polygraph examiner diagnosis of truth and deception. *Journal of Criminal Law, Criminology and Police Science, 62,* 276–281.

Hunter, F. L., & Ash, P. (1973). The accuracy and consistency of polygraph examiners' diagnoses. *Journal of Police Science and Administration, 1,* 370–375.

Iacono, W. G., Boisvenu, G. A., & Fleming, J. A. (1984). Effects of diazepam and methylphenidate on the electrodermal detection of guilty knowledge. *Journal of Applied Psychology, 69,* 289–299.

Iacono, W. G., Cerri, A. M., Patrick, C. J., & Fleming, J. A. E. (1987). The effect of antianxiety drugs on the detection of deception. *Psychophysiology, 24,* 594.

Keeler, L. (1933). Scientific methods of criminal detection with the polygraph. *Kansas Bar Association, 2,* 22–31.

Kircher, J. C., Horowitz, S. W., & Raskin, D. C. (1988). Meta-analysis of mock crime studies of the control question polygraph technique. *Law and Human Behavior, 12,* 79–90.

Kircher, J. C., & Raskin, D. C. (1981). Computerized decision-making in the detection of deception. *Psychophysiology, 18,* 204–205.

Kircher, J. C., & Raskin, D. C. (1982). Cross-validation of a computerized diagnostic procedure for detection of deception. *Psychophysiology, 9,* 568–569.

Kircher, J. C., & Raskin, D. C. (1983). Clinical versus statistical lie detection revisited: Through a lens sharply. *Psychophysiology, 20,* 452.

Kircher, J. C., & Raskin, D. C. (1988). Human versus computerized evaluations of polygraph data in a laboratory setting. *Journal of Applied Psychology, 73,* 291–302.

Kleinmuntz, B., & Szucko, J. (1984). A field study of the fallibility of polygraphic lie detection. *Nature, 308,* 449– 450.

Larson, J. A. (1932). *Lying and its detection.* Chicago: University of Chicago Press.

Lombroso, C. (1895). *L'Homme criminel* (2nd Ed.). Paris: Felix Alcan.

Lykken, D. T. (1959). The GSR in the detection of guilt. *Journal of Applied Psychology, 43,* 385–388.

Lykken, D. T. (1960). The validity of the guilty knowledge technique: The effects of faking. *Journal of Applied Psychology, 44,* 258–262.

Lykken, D. T. (1979). The detection of deception. *Psychological Bulletin, 86,* 47–53.

Lykken, D. T. (1981). *A tremor in the blood.* New York: McGraw- Hill.

Lykken, D. T. (1987). The validity of tests: Caveat emptor. *Jurimetrics, 27,* 263–270.

Lykken, D. T., & Fay, F. B. (1983). *Defeating the polygraphic lie test: A field study.* Unpublished manuscript.

Marston, W. M. (1917). Systolic blood pressure symptoms of deception. *Journal of Experimental Psychology, 2,* 117–163.

Mervis, J. (1986). Council Takes Stand on AIDS, Polygraph; Creates Science Post. *American Psychological Association Monitor,* March 11.

Office of Technology Assessment. (1983). *Scientific validity of polygraph testing: A research review and evaluation.* Washington, DC: U.S. Government Printing Office.

Orne, M. T. (1975). Implications of laboratory research for the detection of deception. In N. Ansley (Ed.), *Legal admissibility of the polygraph* (pp. 94-119). Springfield, IL: Charles C. Thomas.

Orne, M. T. (1983, August, *unpublished*). *Proceedings of the Polygraph Validity Advisory Panel of the Office of Technology Assessment,* Washington, DC.

O'Toole, D. M. (1988) *Crime under the influence: The effects of alcohol intoxication during a crime on subsequent physiological detection of deception.* Unpublished doctoral dissertation, University of British Columbia, Vancouver.

Patrick, C. J., & Iacono, W. G. (1986). The validity of lie detection with criminal psychopaths. *Psychophysiology, 23,* 452-453.

Peterson, J. L., Fabricant, E. L., & Field, K. S. (1978). *Laboratory proficiency testing research program* (Contract Nos. 74-NI-99-0048 and 76-NI-99-0091). Washington, DC: U.S. Department of Justice.

Podlesny, J. A., & Raskin, D. C. (1977). Physiological measures and the detection of deception. *Psychological Bulletin, 84,* 782-799.

Podlesny, J. A., & Raskin, D. C. (1978). Effectiveness of techniques and physiological measures in the detection of deception. *Psychophysiology, 15,* 344-358.

Raskin, D. C. (1979). Orienting and defensive reflexes in the detection of deception. In H. D. Kimmel, E. H. van Olst, & J. F. Orlebeke (Eds.), *The orienting reflex in humans* (pp. 587-605). Hillsdale, NJ: Erlbaum.

Raskin, D. C. (1982). The scientific basis of polygraph techniques and their uses in the judicial process. In A. Trankell (Ed.), *Reconstructing the past: The role of psychologists in criminal trials* (pp. 317-371). Stockholm: Norstedt and Soners.

Raskin, D. C. (1986). The polygraph in 1986: Scientific, professional, and legal issues sorrounding applications and acceptance of polygraph evidence. *Utah Law Review, 1986,* 29-74.

Raskin, D. C. (1987). Methodological issues in estimating polygraph accuracy in field applications. *Canadian Journal of Behavioural Science, 19,* 389-404.

Raskin, D. C. (1988). Does science support polygraph testing? In A. Gale (Ed.), *The polygraph test: Lies, truth and science* (pp. 96–110). London: Sage.
Raskin, D. C., Barland, G. H., & Podlesny, J. A. (1978). *Validity and reliability of detection of deception* (Contract 75- NI-99-0001, U.S. Department of Justice). Washington, DC: U.S. Government Printing Office.
Raskin, D. C., & Hare, R. D. (1978). Psychopathy and detection of deception in a prison population. *Psychophysiology, 15,* 126–136.
Raskin, D. C., & Kircher, J. C. (in press). Comments on Furedy and Heslegrave: Misconceptions, misdescriptions, and misdirections. In P. K. Ackles, J. R. Jennings, & M. G. H. Coles (Eds.), *Advances in psychophysiology* (Vol. 4). Greenwich, CT: JAI Press.
Raskin, D. C., Kircher, J. C., Honts, C. R., & Horowitz, S. W. (1988). *A study of the validity of polygraph examinations in criminal investigation* (Grant No. 85-IJ-CX-0040). Salt Lake City: University of Utah, Department of Psychology.
Raskin, D. C., & Podlesny, J. A. (1979). Truth and deception: A reply to Lykken. *Psychological Bulletin, 86,* 54–59.
Reid, J. E. (1947). A revised questioning technique in lie detection tests. *Journal of Criminal Law, Criminology and Police Science, 37,* 542–547.
Reid, J. E., & Inbau, F. E. (1977). *Truth and deception: The polygraph ("lie detector") technique.* Baltimore: Williams & Wilkins.
Rovner, L. I., Raskin, D. C., & Kircher, J. C. (1979). Effects of information and practice on detection of deception. *Psychophysiology, 16,* 197–198.
Slovic, P., & Lichtenstein, S. (1971). Comparison of Bayesian and regression approaches to the study of information processing in judgment. *Organizational Behavior and Human Performance, 3,* 305–309.
Slowik, S. M., & Buckley, J. P. (1975). Relative accuracy of polygraph examiner diagnosis of respiration, blood pressure, and GSR recordings. *Journal of Police Science and Administration, 3,* 305–309.
Summers, W. G. (1939). Science can get the confession. *Fordham Law Review, 5,* 334–354.
Timm, H. W. (1982). Effect of altered outcome expectancies stemming from placebo and feedback treatments on the validity of the guilty knowledge technique. *Journal of Applied Psychology, 67,* 391–400.

Trovillo, P. V. (1939). A history of lie detection. *Journal of Criminal Law, Criminology and Police Science*, (Part 1) *29*, 848–881; (Part 2) *30*, 104–119.

Waid, W. M., & Orne, M. T. (1982). The physiological detection of deception. *American Scientist, 70*, 402–409.

Waid, W. M., Orne, E. C., Cook, M. R., & Orne, M. T. (1981). Meprobamate reduces accuracy of physiological detection of deception. *Science, 212*, 71–73.

Waid, W. M., Orne, M. T., & Wilson, S. K. (1979). Effects of level of socialization on electrodermal detection of deception. *Psychophysiology, 16*, 15–22.

Weaver, R. S. (1980). The numerical evaluation of polygraph charts: Evolution and comparison of three major systems. *Polygraph, 9*, 94–108.

Weaver, R. S. (1985). Effects of differing numerical chart evaluation systems on polygraph examination results. *Polygraph, 14*, 34–41.

Wicklander, D. E., & Hunter, F. L. (1975). The influence of auxiliary sources of information in polygraph diagnoses. *Journal of Police Science and Administration, 3*, 405–409.

Widacki, J., & Horvath, F. S. (1978). An experimental investigation of the relative validity and utility of the polygraph technique and three other common methods of criminal identification. *Journal of Forensic Sciences, 23*, 596–601.

Hazards in Detecting Deceit   9

Paul Ekman and Maureen O'Sullivan

It would be ideal to have a fail-safe set of behavioral clues to use in detecting deceit; however, there are no such absolute clues. Rather, some behaviors that some people exhibit sometimes are related to some kinds of deception. These behavioral clues, moreover, must be interpreted in the social and psychological context of a specific situation. Other chapters in this book deal with verbal and physiological approaches to the detection of deception. This chapter provides a brief review of some of the nonverbal cues to deception and discusses some of the hazards that bedevil the professional lie-catcher. We distinguish between lying about feelings and feelings about lying, the differential consequences of believing a lie and disbelieving the truth, and two common kinds of errors made by lie-catchers. Finally, we provide a checklist that may help lie-catchers to organize and review their thinking before deciding that a lie has occurred.

NONVERBAL CUES TO DECEPTION

One of the more frequent findings in psychological studies of deception is a tendency for vocal pitch to increase when lying

(Ekman, Friesen, & Scherer, 1976). However, not all individuals show such a pitch increase, and some people may exhibit a decrease in vocal pitch when they lie. Recent reviews of the deception literature (DePaulo, Stone, & Lassiter, 1985; Zuckerman, DePaulo, & Rosenthal, 1981; Zuckerman & Driver, 1985) suggest that other vocal characteristics related to deception include slower latency in responding, shorter speech duration, and slower rate of speech. Many of these findings, however, are based on laboratory analogues of deception in which college students lie or tell the truth about liking or disliking friends. In many of these experiments, the incentives for successful deception are trivial. Even the experiments that employ higher incentives use relatively trivial rewards and punishments (e.g., earning $25 or fooling a group of peers). Generalizing from such experiments to law enforcement situations should be done with care.

Other nonverbal behaviors that have been found to be associated with deception are increased occurrence of manipulators (hand movements in which the deceiver touches or strokes herself; Ekman & Friesen, 1972, 1974) and increased occurrence of shrugs. Some investigators have also reported an increase in the rate of eye blinking and in the size of pupillary dilation during stressful or arousing encounters (Nunnally, Knott, Duchnowski, & Parker, 1967; Simpson & Hale, 1969). Insofar as a person is stressed or aroused while lying, these eye behaviors may be signs of deception. However, people may be emotionally aroused or fearful even when they are being truthful. In such cases, more eye blinks or dilated pupils would be misleading clues to deception.

Smiling is one of the more commonly studied facial clues to deceit. Although some investigators have reported decreased smiling during deception (DePaulo et al.,1985), others have reported just the opposite (Ekman et al., 1976). Recent research addresses this contradiction and also illustrates the complexity of research in this area. Ekman, Friesen, and O'Sullivan (1988) found that different kinds of smiles occurred during honest as compared with deceptive interviews. Smiles that are characteristic of felt or experienced positive emotion were more common during honest interviews, but smiles that "leaked" negative emotion (Ekman & Friesen, 1969) were more frequent in deceptive interviews. Unless researchers specify the kinds of smiles they are measuring, they may find different answers to the question of whether the smile is a behavioral clue to deceit. True emotional smiles are less frequent during deception, but leakage smiles are more frequent, at least when the deception involves denying negative affect.

Miscellaneous hand gestures, leg and foot movements, head movements, and postural shifts may decrease slightly during deception (DePaulo et al., 1985), but the amount of decrease is small. In any event, since the methods for defining and measuring these behaviors vary markedly from study to study, drawing overall conclusions is difficult.

Direction of gaze is a clue to deception that college students often report using; they presume that liars avoid eye contact when they are lying. In 18 studies reviewed by DePaulo and her colleagues (DePaulo et al., 1985), however, the overall tendency is for eye contact to *increase* slightly during deception. It would appear that since everyone, including liars, believes that liars avert their gaze, most liars correct for this by increasing eye contact with the target person. If this is the case, gaze direction may be misinterpreted in attempting to detect deception.

LYING ABOUT FEELINGS

Many lies fail because the deceiver does not think ahead by planning fully or rehearsing the story enough. But these are not the only mistakes people make when they attempt to deceive. Mistakes are also made because of difficulty in concealing or falsely portraying an emotion. Not every deception involves emotion, but those that do may cause special problems for the liar. When emotions occur, physiological changes happen automatically without choice or deliberation. This is a fundamental characteristic of emotional experience (Fridja, 1986). People do not actively select when they will feel an emotion; instead, they usually experience emotions as happening to them. Negative emotions, such as fear, anger, or depression, may occur despite efforts to avoid them (Swann, Griffin, Predmore, & Gaines, 1987). Not only is there little choice about when an emotion is felt, but people often do not have much control over whether or not the expressive signs of the emotion are manifested to others. It may not even be possible for most people to control their observable reactions if the felt emotion is very strong. Even Machiavelli, whose name is associated with cold, calculated cunning in achieving one's ends, could not control his expressive behavior very well. Machiavelli "could not easily rid himself of the sarcastic expression continually playing round his mouth and flashing from his eyes. . . . he was frequently ruled by his powerful imagination" (Villari, quoted in Bull, 1961, p. 17).

When an emotion begins gradually rather than suddenly, the changes in behavior may be small and relatively easy to conceal if one is aware of one's feelings. However, most people are not. When an emotion begins gradually and remains slight, it may be more noticeable to others than to the self, not registering in awareness unless it becomes more intense. Once an emotion is strong, it is much more difficult to control. Concealing the changes in face, body, and voice requires a struggle. Even when the concealment is successful and there is no leakage of the feelings, sometimes the struggle itself will be noticeable and provide a clue to deception (Ekman & Friesen, 1969).

Concealing an emotion is not easy, and creating the appearance of an unfelt emotion is also a difficult task. It requires more than merely saying, "I am angry" or "I am afraid." The deceiver must appear and sound as if he is angry or afraid, if his claim is to be believed. It is difficult to coordinate the changes in face, body, and voice that are required for successful falsification of an emotion. For example, there are muscular movements in the eye area that most people make when actually experiencing fear but that very few people can perform voluntarily. Such difficult-to-perform movements are vital to successful falsification of the appearance of distress, fear, or anger.

Falsifying an experienced emotion is more difficult when one is also attempting to conceal another emotion. Trying to look angry is not easy, but if fear is felt when the person tries to look angry, conflicting forces occur. One set of impulses, arising from fear, pulls in one direction, while the deliberate attempt to appear angry pulls in the other direction. For example, the brows are involuntarily pulled upwards and together in fear, but to falsify anger the person must pull them down (Ekman & Friesen, 1975). Often the signs of this internal struggle between the felt and the false emotion betray the deceit (Ekman et al., 1988).

FEELINGS ABOUT LYING

Although there are thousands of publications dealing with the detection of deception, there has been little theory development about lying and lie detection. Bok (1978) offered the viewpoint of a moral philosopher. Ekman (1985) provided an analysis of the feelings involved in lying based on his laboratory research and clinical observations. The discussion that follows is based largely on Ekman's earlier theorizing.

Not all deceits involve concealing or falsifying emotions. The embezzler conceals that she is stealing money. The vain middle-aged man dyes his grey hair and claims that he is 7 years younger than he is. Yet even when the deception concerns something other than emotion, emotions may become involved. The man might be embarrassed about his vanity, and so he must conceal not only his age but also his embarrassment. The embezzler might feel surprise when someone else is accused of her crime. She must conceal her surprise, or at least conceal the reason why she is surprised.

Thus, emotions often become involved in deceptions that were not undertaken for the purpose of concealing emotions. Once involved, the emotions must be concealed if the deception is to succeed. Any emotion may become a problem, but three emotions are so often intertwined with deceit that they merit separate explanation. These are fear of being caught, guilt about lying, and delight in having duped someone.

Detection Apprehension

In its milder forms, fear of being caught is not disruptive and may even help the deceiver to avoid mistakes by maintaining alertness. Moderate levels of fear can produce behavioral signs that are noticeable by the skilled lie-catcher, and high levels of detection apprehension produce just what the deceiver fears, namely, evidence of fear or apprehension. The research literature on deception detection (DePaulo, Lanier, & Davis, 1983; DePaulo et al., 1985) suggests that the behavior of highly motivated deceivers is different from that of less motivated ones. In our terminology, the behavior of deceivers with more detection apprehension is different from that of deceivers with less detection apprehension. If a deceiver could estimate beforehand the level of detection apprehension that is likely to occur, this information could inform the deceiver as to whether the attempt to deceive is worth the risk—whether it is likely to succeed. Similarly, the lie-catcher can also use this information by searching for signs of fear in a suspect likely to fear being caught.

Many factors influence the level of detection apprehension that will occur. The first determinant to consider is the deceiver's belief about the skill of the target as a lie-catcher. If the target is known to be gullible, the deceiver would not ordinarily experience much detection apprehension. On the other hand, someone known to be difficult to deceive should increase detection apprehension.

In using detection apprehension as a clue to deception, the lie-catcher must distinguish between the innocent person's fear of being disbelieved and the guilty person's fear of being caught. The difficulty in making this distinction is magnified when the lie-catcher has a reputation for being suspicious and skeptical. The reputation of the skeptical lie-catcher may be the cause of the fear that the innocent person exhibits, since the innocent person may particularly fear being disbelieved,

The second determinant of detection apprehension is the

amount of practice and previous success in deceiving. A job applicant who has lied about qualifications successfully in the past should not be overly concerned about an additional deception. Practice in deceit enables the deceiver to anticipate problems. Success in deceit gives confidence and thus reduces detection apprehension.

A third determinant of detection apprehension is fear of punishment. Criminal interrogators often seek to reduce this factor by suggesting that the punishment may be less if the suspect confesses. Although they usually cannot offer total amnesty, interrogators may offer a psychological amnesty, hoping to induce a confession by implying the suspect need not feel ashamed nor even responsible for committing the crime. An interrogator may sympathetically suggest that the acts are understandable and might have been committed by anyone in the same situation. Another variation might be to offer the suspect a face-saving explanation of the motive for the crime.

A fourth factor influencing detection apprehension is the personality of the liar. Some people find it difficult to lie, whereas others can do so with ease. More is known about people who lie with ease than those who cannot (Hood, 1982). In our research, natural liars did not differ from others in terms of their scores on an objective personality test (Ekman et al., 1976). We found nothing antisocial in their makeup. Unlike psychopaths, they did not use their ability to lie well in order to harm others. Natural liars, highly skilled in deceit but not without conscience, are natural performers who should be able to succeed as actors, salesmen, trial lawyers, negotiators, spies, diplomats, or interrogators.

Superior liars may require two very different sets of skills: those needed to plan a deceptive strategy, and those needed to mislead a target in a face-to-face situation. A liar might have both skills, but presumably one could excel at one skill and not the other. Regrettably, there has been little study of the characteristics of successful deceivers. Nor has any research asked whether the personality characteristics of successful deceivers differ as a function of the setting in which the deceit is practiced.

So far we have described several aspects of detection apprehension relating to the personality of the liar and the reputation and character of the lie-catcher. Equally important are the stakes—the perceived consequences for successful and unsuccessful attempts at deception. Although there is no empirical evidence supporting our view that relates directly to deception, research on the role of appraisal in the experience of emotion is consistent with our thinking (Lazarus, 1984). We believe there is a simple rule: The greater the stakes, the more the detection apprehension. Applying this simple rule can be complicated because it may not be easy for the lie-catcher to determine what is at stake for the deceiver. For some people, winning is everything. It does not matter whether it is pennies or dollars or simply misleading someone. For such people, the stakes are high in any competition. Alternately, what is at stake may be so idiosyncratic that no outside observer would readily know.

Detection apprehension should be greater when the perceived consequences involve avoiding punishment, not just earning a reward. When the decision to deceive is first made, the stakes usually involve obtaining rewards. The deceiver thinks primarily about what might be gained. An embezzler may think only about the monetary gain when the deceit begins. After the deceit has been under way for some time, such rewards may no longer be as important. The company may become aware of its losses and suspicious enough that the embezzler is prevented from taking more. At this point, the deceit might be maintained in order to avoid being caught, and avoiding punishment is now the only stake. On the other hand, avoiding punishment may be the motive from the outset, if the target is suspicious or the deceiver has little confidence.

Two kinds of punishment are involved in deceit: the punishment if the lie fails and the punishment for the very act of engaging in deception. We believe detection apprehension will be greater if both kinds of punishment are at stake. This hypothesis is consistent with emotion theory relating increasing stimulation with increasing emotional intensity (Young, 1961).

Even if the transgressor knows that the consequences of being caught in a lie will be greater than the consequences if the transgression is admitted, the lie may still be very tempting. Telling the truth brings immediate and certain losses, whereas deceit offers the possibility of avoiding all losses. The prospect of being spared immediate punishment may be so attractive that the deceiver may underestimate the likelihood of being caught. Realization that confession would have been a better policy may come too late, if the deceit has been maintained so long and with such elaboration that confession no longer leads to a lesser punishment.

Sometimes there is little ambiguity about the relative costs of confession or continued concealment. Some actions are so unacceptable that confessing fails to yield approval for having come forward and concealment adds little to the punishment. Such is the case if the lie conceals murder, treason, terrorism, or child abuse. Unlike the rewards possible for some repentant philanderers, forgiveness should not be expected by those who confess more serious transgressions against society. Confession accompanied by contrition and cooperation may lessen the punishment in other cases, however.

Another factor that may affect how the stakes influence detection apprehension is what is gained or lost by the target, not just by the deceiver. Usually the deceiver's gains are at the expense of the target. The embezzler gains what the employer loses. Stakes are not always equal, however. The stakes for the liar and the target may differ in kind as well as in amount. The heirloom watch stolen by a co-worker may gain little for the thief, but its loss may exact a significant emotional price from the victim. When the stakes differ for the deceiver and the target, the stakes for either may determine the deceiver's detection apprehension. It depends on whether the liar recognizes the difference and how it is evaluated.

To summarize, we hypothesize that detection apprehension will be increased when

1. the target has a reputation for being difficult to deceive;
2. the target is initially suspicious;
3. the deceiver has little practice or no prior success;
4. the deceiver is particularly vulnerable to the fear of being caught;
5. the deceiver has no special skill or talent for lying;
6. the perceived stakes or consequences are high;

7. rewards and punishments are both at stake, or at least punishment is at stake;
8. the punishment is great for being caught in a lie, or the punishment for the concealed act is so great that there is no incentive to confess;
9. the target gains no benefit from the deceiver's lie.

Deception Guilt

The second type of feeling aroused by deception is guilt *about* lying, which can be distinguished from guilt feelings about the *content* of a lie. People who do not feel guilty about stealing may experience deception guilt when lying to conceal it. A child might steal candy with little feeling other than excitement or pleasure, yet experience guilt about lying to a parent in order to conceal the theft. Of course, it could be the reverse—no deception guilt, but guilt about stealing. Some people experience guilt about both the content of the lie and the act of lying itself. However, it is not necessary to feel guilty about the content of a lie in order to feel guilty about lying.

Deception guilt can vary in strength. It may be very mild or so strong that the lie will fail because the deception guilt produces leakage or clues to deception (Ekman & Friesen, 1969). When it becomes extreme, deception guilt is a torturing experience, undermining the person's most fundamental feelings of self-worth. To obtain relief from such severe deception guilt, the deceiver may confess despite the likelihood of punishment. In fact, the punishment may be sought by the person who confesses in order to alleviate intense feelings of guilt.

When the decision to deceive is first made, deceivers do not always anticipate how much they may suffer from deception guilt. Deceivers may not realize the impact of being thanked by their victims for their apparent helpfulness, or how they will feel when they see someone else blamed for their misdeeds. Another reason why deceivers may underestimate how much deception guilt they will feel is that it is only with the passage of time that they learn that one lie rarely suffices, that the lie must be repeated again and again, often with expanding fabrications in order to conceal the original deceit (Mullaney, 1979).

Shame is closely related to guilt (Tomkins,1963), but there is a difference. No audience is needed to experience feelings of guilt; the guilty person is his own judge. Shame is different from guilt because the experience of shame requires disapproval or ridicule by others (Campos & Barrett, 1984). If the misdeed is not discovered, there will be no shame, but there still might be feelings of guilt. Of course, both may occur. The distinction between shame and guilt is important since these two emotions may pull a person in opposite directions. The desire to relieve guilt may motivate a confession, but the need to avoid the humiliation of shame may prevent it.

Some people are especially vulnerable to shame and guilt about lying, for example, those who have been very strictly brought up to believe that lying is a sin. The socialization of others may not have particularly condemned lying but may have instilled more generalized and pervasive guilt feelings. Among psychiatric patients suffering from generalized anxiety disorders or depression, such guilt feelings are common. Guilt-prone people sometimes appear to seek experiences in which they can intensify their guilt. Unfortunately, there has been little research about guilt-prone individuals. More is known about their opposite.

A failure to feel guilt or shame about one's misdeeds is a salient characteristic of psychopaths (Hare, 1970). Experts disagree about whether the lack of guilt and shame is due to environmental or biological determinants (MacMillan & Kofoed, 1984; Schmauk, 1970; Vaillant, 1975). It is clear, however, that since psychopaths rarely experience guilt about lying or fear of being caught in a lie, these emotions will not contribute clues when psychopaths deceive.

If the deceiver does not share social values with the victim, it is unlikely that deception guilt will occur. People usually experience less guilt about lying to those whom they think are wrongdoers. A disgruntled employee may feel entitled to steal company goods. A spy or assassin will not feel guilty about misleading the victim. Assassins may be afraid of being caught, but they are unlikely to feel guilty about what they have planned. A professional criminal would not feel guilt about deceiving a law enforcement officer. The same principle may explain why diplomats or spies do not feel guilty about misleading their adversaries. In all of these situations, the deceiver and the target do not share common goals or values.

Deception is authorized in most of the foregoing examples by a social norm that legitimates deceiving an opponent. There is little experience of guilt about such authorized deceits when the targets are from opposing sides and hold different values. There also may be authorization to deceive targets who are not opponents and who share values with the deceiver. The priest who conceals a criminal's confession should not feel deception guilt when the police ask him about it. His vows authorize his deceit. He does not benefit from the deceit; the benefit is to the criminal whose identity remains unknown.

Even selfish deceits may not produce deception guilt when the lie is authorized. Poker players don't feel deception guilt about bluffing. The same is true about bargaining, whether in a Middle Eastern bazaar, Wall Street, or the local lawyer's office. Because the participants expect misinformation, not the truth, bargaining and poker are not technically lies (Ekman, 1985). These situations proceed on the assumption that no one will be truthful.

Deception guilt is most likely to occur when lying is not authorized. Deception guilt should be most severe when the target does not expect to be misled, when honesty is expected between deceiver and target. In such opportunistic deceits, we hypothesize that guilt about lying will be greater if the target suffers at least as much as the liar gains. Even under these conditions, there may not be much deception guilt unless some values are shared by the target and the deceiver. The adolescent who lies about drug use to a police officer or social worker may not feel any deception guilt if adults are perceived as naïve people who are incorrect or misinformed about drugs. If, in addition, the adolescent views adults as hypocrites who drink alcohol but who do not permit the use of other drugs, there is even less chance that the deceiver will feel deception guilt. However, the deceiver who respects the target may feel shame if the lie is discovered. The experience of shame requires some respect for those who disapprove; otherwise, disapproval is likely to bring forth anger or contempt, not shame.

Deceivers experience less guilt when their targets are impersonal or anonymous. It should be easier for a criminal to lie to an arresting officer who is a stranger than to a probation officer who is liked or respected. If the target is anonymous, it is easier to indulge in the guilt-reducing fantasy that the target is not really hurt, doesn't really care, will not notice the lie, or even deserves or wants to be misled (Wolk & Henley, 1970).

Often there is an inverse relationship between deception guilt and detection apprehension. Factors that decrease guilt about deception may increase fear of being caught. When deceits are authorized and there is less deception guilt, the authorization usually raises the stakes, thereby increasing detection apprehension. The employer who deceives the employee suspected of embezzling and conceals his suspicions in order to catch the thief may experience high detection apprehension but is unlikely to experience deception guilt.

Although there are exceptions, most people find the experience of guilt so toxic that they seek ways to diminish it. Deception guilt can be diminished if the deceiver can justify the deception. There are many ways to justify deceit. It can be considered retaliation for injustice. A nasty or mean target can be said not to deserve honesty, for example, "The boss was so stingy, he didn't reward me for all the work I did, so I rewarded myself." Victims may be seen as so gullible that being misled is their fault, not the fault of the liar.

Two other justifications for lying that reduce deception guilt were mentioned earlier. A noble purpose or job requirement is one, and protection of the target is the other. If the target of the deception is a willing party to it, then the deceiver may use this willingness to justify the lie. If the target cooperated in the deceit and knew the truth all along but pretended not to, then the deceiver may rationalize that there was no lie. If there was no lie, then there need not be any deception guilt. A willing target who profits from being deceived makes it easy for the deceiver to succeed. People often cooperate in being misled, as in polite social encounters (Rosenthal & DePaulo, 1979). For example, a hostess may accept without scrutiny an excuse for a guest's early departure.

An unwilling target may become a willing one in order to avoid the costs of discovering deceit. Imagine the plight of a government official who begins to suspect that a lover who has been entrusted with sensitive information might be a spy. A job recruiter may similarly become the willing victim of a fraudulent job applicant, once the applicant is hired, rather than acknowledge a mistaken judgment.

To summarize, we hypothesize that deception guilt will be greatest when

1. the target is unwilling;
2. the deceit is totally selfish, and the target derives no benefit from being misled and loses as much or more than the liar gains;
3. the deceit is unauthorized, and the situation is one in which honesty is authorized;
4. the deceiver has not been practicing the deceit for a long time;
5. the deceiver and the target share social values;
6. the liar is personally acquainted with the target;
7. the deceiver cannot construe the target as mean or gullible;
8. there is no reason for the target to expect to be misled, and the deceiver has encouraged the target to be trusting.

Duping Delight

Detection apprehension and deception guilt are negative feelings that can be aroused by lying. Lying and deception can also produce positive feelings. The lie may be viewed as an accomplishment. The deceiver may feel excitement, either when anticipating the challenge or during the very moment of lying, when success is not yet certain. Afterward, there may be the pleasure that comes with relief, pride in the achievement, or feelings of smug contempt towards the target. Duping delight refers to all or any of these feelings, which can, if not concealed, betray the deceit. Although there is no empirical research on duping delight, John Irving (1985) described something similar in his novel *The Cider House Rules*: "A lie is . . . a vigorous enterprise, it keeps you on your toes by making you suddenly responsible for what happens because of it. You must be alert to lie, and stay alert to keep your lie a secret. When you lie, it makes you feel in charge of your life. Telling lies is very seductive. . . . I love to lie. When you lie, you feel as if you have cheated fate—your own, and everybody else's" (p. 325).

Duping delight is also exemplified by the behavior of John Walker, the Navy spy. In many aspects of his life, not only his spying for the Russians, Walker delighted in assuming roles, in duping those he interacted with. As one writer noted (Blum, 1987), "On April 28, John Walker took the stand. He declared to the world that he had recruited his friend, his son, and his brother as spies. He was smiling as he spoke, as though repressing a secret hilarity. It was as if he were trying to convey one last lesson . . . across the courtroom: Betrayal is easy, a fact of life" (p. 408).

An innocent example of duping delight occurs when kidding takes the form of misleading a gullible friend. The kidder must conceal the duping delight even though the performance may be directed to an audience of friends or bystanders who are appreciating how well the gullible person is being duped.

We believe that duping delight, like all emotions, can vary in intensity. It may be totally absent, almost insignificant compared to the amount of detection apprehension that is felt, or it may be so great that some behavioral sign of it leaks, as in the case of John Walker. People may confess their deception in order to share their delight in having put one over. Criminals have been known to reveal their crime to friends, strangers, even to the police in order to be acknowledged and appreciated as having been clever enough to pull off a particular deceit.

We speculate that there are several factors that may increase duping delight. If the person being deceived has the reputation of being difficult to fool, successfully misleading such a target should increase duping delight. The presence of others who know what is going on can also increase the likelihood of duping delight. When an audience is present and enjoying the deceiver's performance, the deceiver may have the most duping delight and the hardest time suppressing any sign of it.

Some people may be more prone to duping delight than others. No scientist has yet studied such people or even verified that they do exist. Yet, it seems obvious that some people boast more than others and that braggarts might be more likely to experience duping delight.

While lying, a person may experience duping delight, deception guilt, and detection apprehension, simultaneously or in succession. An embezzler, for example, might feel all three emotions: delight in fooling fellow employees and the employer, apprehension at moments when the deceiver thinks that there might be some suspicion, and guilt about having broken the law and violated the trust shown by the employer.

To summarize, we hypothesize that duping delight will be greatest when

1. the target poses a challenge, having a reputation for being difficult to deceive;
2. the deception is a challenge, either because of what must be concealed or what must be fabricated;
3. others are watching or know about the deception and appreciate the deceiver's skillful performance.

Guilt, fear, and delight all can be shown in the face, the voice, or the body, even when the liar is trying to conceal them. Even if there is no nonverbal leakage of emotion, the struggle to prevent such leakage may produce behavior that can serve as clues to deception (Ekman & Friesen, 1969). Next we consider some of the hazards involved in detecting deception from such behavioral clues.

COMMON MISTAKES IN DETECTING DECEPTION

Most liars can fool most people most of the time. The published evidence about professional and nonprofessional lie-catchers supports this view. Zuckerman and his colleagues (1981), in reviewing the accuracy rates for detecting deception in 21 studies, found that average accuracy was only slightly better than chance. Most of the lie-catchers in these studies were college students, so this result may not be too surprising. However, similar results have been found in studies of the lie detection ability of law enforcement personnel. Kraut and Poe (1980) found no difference between college students and customs inspectors in their ability to identify guilty travelers from videotapes. DePaulo and Pfeifer (1986) found no difference between college students and federal law enforcement officers in their accuracy in identifying deception from an audiotape test using stimulus materials from a laboratory experiment on deception. The ability to detect deception in these two studies was assessed using materials that may have been inappropriate. The videotape used in the Kraut and Poe study may not have had the technical sophistication to allow inspection of facial expressions or vocal nuances. The "lies" used in the DePaulo and Pfeifer study were statements made by college students in a laboratory concerning their liking for roommates or opinions about campus issues. Since it is unlikely that this kind of lie would stimulate either detection apprehension or deception guilt, the appropriateness of this measure as an analogue for deception in the area of law enforcement is unclear.

On the other hand, in recent research, Ekman and O'Sullivan (1988) found that some groups of law professionals can do very much better than chance. Ekman and O'Sullivan used videotapes of young women who lied or told the truth about the emotions they were feeling. The women were highly emotionally aroused and were motivated to succeed in the deception. The presence of both felt emotion and detection apprehension suggest that these materials may be more ecologically valid, more like the high-stakes lies that law enforcement professionals deal with, than other laboratory analogues. Our research involved showing 10 interviews in which young women either lied or told the truth about their feelings as they watched various films. Hundreds of law enforcement personnel, such as polygraphers, Secret Service agents, robbery investigators, lawyers, and judges, as well as hundreds of college students, middle-aged people in continuing education classes, and mental health personnel, were administered this lie-detection ability measure. Although our analyses are incomplete, at this point it appears that Secret Service agents and experienced psychiatrists do significantly better than chance in detecting deception, but that the other groups do not.

Although it is not possible to avoid all mistakes in detecting deceit, precautions can be taken to reduce them. The first precaution involves making the process of interpreting behavioral signs of deceit more explicit. Information about how the face, body, voice, and speech may betray deceit will not prevent all mistaken judgments about whether someone is lying, but it may make those mistakes more obvious and avoidable.

Another precaution is to understand better the nature of the mistakes that occur in detecting deceit (Ekman, 1981). There are two general types of mistakes that are exactly opposite in cause and consequence: In disbelieving the truth, the lie-catcher can mistakenly judge a truthful person to be lying (false positive error); or in believing a lie, the lie-catcher can mistakenly judge a liar to be truthful (false negative error). It does not matter whether lie-catchers depend on a polygraph test or the interpretation of behavior, they are vulnerable to these same two mistakes. This distinction between believing a lie and disbelieving the truth is important because it forces attention to the twin hazards for the lie-catcher. There is no way to completely avoid both mistakes; the choice is between the relative risks. The lie-catcher must evaluate when it is preferable to risk being misled and when it would be better to risk making a false accusation. What can be lost or gained by suspecting the innocent or believing the liar depends upon the nature of the lie, the liar, and the lie-catcher.

Idiosyncracy Error

Both types of mistakes in detecting deceit can occur due to the *idiosyncracy error,* the failure to take account of individual differences—how people vary in expressive behavior regardless of whether they are lying or telling the truth. This error is illustrated by a comment made by Tom Brokaw, the television reporter, who said, "I don't look at a person's face for signs that he is lying. What I'm after are convoluted answers or sophisticated evasions" (Weisman, 1977, p. 13). Although these clues might indicate that some people are deceiving, for others just the opposite may be true. Furthermore, depending on one or more behaviors as absolute clues to deception will mislead the lie-catcher. Research comparing perceived behavioral clues to deception with actual behavioral manifestations during deception illustrates this. Although people believe that liars avoid eye contact and increase postural shifts while lying, these behaviors do not change significantly in deception (DePaulo et al., 1985). Most deceivers actually increase eye contact with the target and move their bodies less. Deceivers have the same misinformation as other people. In attempting to deceive, most liars try to control those behaviors that are widely regarded as clues to deception (DePaulo et al., 1985).

No clue to deceit is foolproof, not even the autonomic nervous system activity measured by the polygraph (see Chapter 8). The mistake of believing a lie occurs because some people don't commit easily detected errors when they lie. These are not just psychopaths, but also natural performers, people who are using the Stanislavski technique, and those who by other means succeed in believing their own lies, for example, individuals who use defense mechanisms to ward off intolerable information, or public figures who may come to believe their own deceptions because they repeat them so often or so heatedly. The lie-catcher must remember that the *absence* of a sign of deceit is not evidence of truth.

The presence of a sign of deceit can also be misleading, causing the opposite mistake of disbelieving the truth. A clue to deceit may be shown deliberately by a con artist to exploit the victim's mistaken belief that she has caught the con artist in a lie. Poker players reportedly use this trick, establishing what in poker lingo is called a "false tell." "For example, a player might for many hours deliberately cough when bluffing. The opponent . . . soon recognizes this pattern of coughing and bluffing. In a crucial hand of the game when the stakes are raised, the deceiver coughs again, but this time he is not bluffing and so wins a wallet-breaking pot from his confused opponent" (Hayano, 1980, p. 117).

The poker player in this example set up and exploited the mistake of disbelieving the truth, profiting from being judged to be lying. More often when a lie-catcher makes this mistake, the person who is mistakenly identified as lying suffers. It is not only deviousness that causes some people to be judged as lying when they are truthful, but an idiosyncracy in their expressive style. What might be a clue to deceit for many people is not a clue for all people. Some people characteristically show one or more of the following behaviors, whether they are lying or telling the truth:

- indirect and circumlocutious speech
- short or long pauses between words
- many speech errors
- few hand gestures or facial expressions when speaking
- many restless hand movements
- signs of fear, distress, or anger in their facial expressions regardless of how they actually feel
- asymmetric facial expressions

There are substantial differences among individuals in all of these behaviors, and these differences may produce not only mistakes of disbelieving the truth but also mistakes of believing a lie. Disbelieving the truthful person who characteristically speaks indirectly is as much an error in lie detection as believing the smooth-talking liar.

Mistakes due to the idiosyncracy error may be reduced by basing judgments on observed *changes* in the suspect's behavior. The lie-catcher must compare the suspect's usual behavior and the behavior exhibited when the suspect is under suspicion. People are most likely to be misled during the first meeting with a deceiver because there is no basis for comparison and, therefore, no opportunity to observe changes in behavior. Absolute judgments, such as "She is making so many restless hand movements that she must be very uncomfortable," are likely to be wrong. Relative judgments, such as "She is making so many more restless hand movements than is usual for her that she must be very uncomfortable," are the best way to decrease mistakes due to individual differences in expressive style. Skilled poker players follow this practice by memorizing the idiosyncratic "tells" (clues to deceit) of their regular opponents.

If a lie-catcher must make a judgment after a first meeting, the meeting should be long enough to allow the suspect's usual behavior to be observed. For example, the lie-catcher might try to focus on topics that are less stressful. However, sometimes that won't be possible. The entire meeting might be stressful for a suspect who is resentful or fearful of being under suspicion. Under these circumstances, the lie-catcher should realize the risk of mistaken judgments due to the lack of knowledge of the characteristic behavioral peculiarities of the suspect. A number of studies indicate that in some circumstances lie-catchers perform better after increased exposure to the potential liar (Brandt, Miller, & Hocking, 1980; O'Sullivan, Ekman, & Friesen, 1988).

First meetings are especially likely to lead to errors in judgment, not only because of the lack of an appropriate baseline or anchor against which to make judgments (Zuckerman, Koestner, & Colella, 1985) but also because of individual differences in people's reactions to initial encounters. In first encounters, some people carefully control their behavior and follow well learned rules about how to act. For this reason, they provide an unrepresentative sample of their usual behavior. Others find first meetings anxiety provoking, and, for the opposite reason, their behavior also provides a poor basis for comparison. If possible, the lie-catcher should base judgments on a series of meetings, hoping to establish a better baseline as acquaintance grows. While it might seem that detecting deception is easier when people know each other intimately, that is not always the case. Lovers, family members, friends, or close colleagues may develop blind spots or preconceptions that interfere with accurate judgments of behavioral clues to deceit.

Othello Error

So far we have considered only one source of errors in detecting deceit, the failure to take account of individual differences.

Another equally important factor in disbelieving the truth is the *Othello error*. This error occurs when the lie-catcher fails to consider that a truthful person under stress may appear to be lying. As discussed above, each of the feelings about lying that can produce behavioral clues to deceit may be experienced for other reasons when truthful people know that they are suspected of lying. Truthful people may be afraid of being disbelieved, and their fear might be confused with the deceiver's detection apprehension. Some people have such strong unresolved guilt about other matters that these feelings may be aroused whenever they are suspected of any wrongdoing. Signs of those guilt feelings might be confused with a liar's deception guilt.

Truthful people also may feel scorn toward those they know are falsely accusing them, or excitement about the challenge of proving their accusers wrong, or pleasure in anticipating their vindication. The signs of these feelings may resemble a deceiver's duping delight. Other emotions also may be felt either by deceivers or by truthful people who know that they are under suspicion. Although the reasons would differ, either the liar or the truthful person might feel surprised, angry, disappointed, distressed, or disgusted by the lie-catcher's suspicions or questions.

The Othello error is named for the death scene in Shakespeare's play, since it provides such an excellent example. Othello accuses Desdemona of loving Cassio and tells her to confess, since he plans to kill her for her infidelity. Desdemona asks that Cassio be called to testify to her innocence, but Othello tells her that he has already had Cassio murdered. Desdemona realizes that she will not be able to prove her innocence and that Othello will kill her.

Othello interprets Desdemona's fear and distress as a reaction to the news of her alleged lover's death, confirming his belief in her infidelity. Othello fails to realize that if Desdemona is innocent, she might also feel and show the same emotions. Distress and despair might follow Othello's disbelieving her and her recognition that her last hope to prove her innocence is gone now that Cassio is dead. Desdemona wept for her life, for her predicament, for Othello's lack of trust, and not for the death of a lover.

Othello's error is also an example of how preconceptions can bias a lie-catcher's judgments. Othello is convinced that Desdemona is unfaithful, and he ignores the alternative explanation of Desdemona's behavior by failing to consider that her emotions are not proof one way or the other. Othello seeks to confirm rather than to test his belief that Desdemona is unfaithful. Othello is an extreme example, but preconceptions often distort judgment, causing a lie-catcher to disregard ideas, possibilities, or facts that do not fit the preconceived idea.

When the stakes are high and the costs to the lie-catcher are great if the suspect is lying, even judicious people may reach the wrong conclusion. It is easy to disbelieve the truth, because deceit is a powerful and useful explanation in a complex and baffling world. A former employee of the Central Intelligence Agency wrote,

> As a causal explanation, deception is intrinsically satisfying precisely because it is so orderly and rational. When other persuasive explanations are not available (perhaps because the phenomena we are seeking to explain were actually caused by mistakes, failures to follow orders, or other factors unknown to us), deception offers a convenient and easy explanation. It is convenient because intelligence officers are generally sensitive to the possibility of deception, and its detection is often taken as indicative of sophisticated, penetrating analysis. . . . It is easy because almost any evidence can be rationalized to fit the deception hypothesis; in fact, one might argue that once deception has been raised as a serious possibility, this hypothesis is almost immune to disconfirmation. (Heuer, 1982, p. 59)

Lie-catchers should strive to become aware of their own preconceptions about the suspect. The preconceptions may be influenced by the lie-catcher's personality, strong emotion, input from others, past experience, job pressures, or the need to reduce uncertainty. Whatever their cause, explicit recognition of preconceptions about the suspect increases the chance of discovering the truth, not merely supporting the preconceptions. The lie-catcher should at least realize when preconceptions may interfere with judgments about whether or not a suspect is lying.

The lie-catcher must consider the possibility that a sign of emotion may not be a clue to deceit but a sign of how a truthful person feels about being disbelieved. The lie-catcher should estimate which emotions a particular suspect is likely to feel not only when engaging in deception but also, just as important, when being truthful. Not all liars will have every possible feeling about lying, and not all truthful people will experience every possible feeling about being under suspicion. Let us consider how the lie-catcher can estimate which emotions a truthful person might feel about being suspected of lying.

The lie-catcher may be able to base that estimate on knowledge of the suspect's personality. Earlier, we described the need for the lie-catcher to be acquainted with the suspect in order to reduce errors based on first impressions. In dealing with a truthful person, a different type of knowledge about the suspect is needed. The lie-catcher needs to know the emotional characteristics of the suspect in order to discount the signs of certain emotions that are usually considered clues to deceit. Not everybody is likely to feel afraid, guilty, angry, and so on, when suspected of wrong-doing or lying. It depends in part upon the personality of the suspect.

A self-righteous person might feel angry when suspected of lying but have little fear of being disbelieved or no free-floating guilt. A timorous individual, who lacks confidence and often expects failure, might fear being disbelieved but is not likely to feel anger or guilt. We have already mentioned individuals who are so guilt-ridden that they feel guilty even when they are wrongly suspected of a wrongdoing. Such guilt-ridden people might not, however, be particularly fearful, angry, surprised, distressed, or excited. The lie-catcher must discount the sign of an emotion as a clue to deceit if the suspect's personality would make the suspect likely to have such a feeling even when the suspect is being truthful. The emotions to be discounted depend upon the suspect, since not every emotion will be aroused in every truthful person who is under suspicion.

The specific emotion, if any, that an innocent person may exhibit when suspected depends also upon the relationship between the suspect and the lie-catcher. People who frequently make false accusations or who repeatedly disbelieve the truth may establish a relationship that makes signs of fear ambiguous as clues to deception. A wife who has repeatedly been accused of having affairs, and subjected to verbal or physical abuse despite her innocence, has reason to be afraid regardless of whether she lies or tells the truth. Among other things, her husband has destroyed the basis for utilizing signs of fear as evidence of lying.

Not every suspect has well formed expectations about every lie-catcher, and not all that do will share the same expectations. Suppose a suspect has been observed associating with people whom the Secret Service believes to be counterfeiters. The suspect needs no actual contact with Secret Service agents to have expectations about them that should be taken into account. If the suspect believes that the Secret Service never makes mistakes and is completely trustworthy, then signs of fear need not be discounted by the interrogator but may be interpreted as detection apprehension. However, if the suspect believes that the Secret Service is either inept or prone to frame people, signs of fear must be discounted. It could be fear of being disbelieved rather than detection apprehension. The lie-catcher must discount the sign of an emotion as a clue to deceit if the suspect's expectations would make the suspect likely to have such a feeling even if the suspect were being truthful.

Although the truthful person's feelings about being suspected of lying can be confusing, such emotional reactions can also help to distinguish truthtellers from deceivers. Confusion arises when the truthful person and the deceiver have the same emotional reactions to suspicion. Clarification is possible when their reactions are likely to differ. Some people have entirely different feelings about being under suspicion when telling the truth as opposed to deceiving.

It is complicated to determine which emotions a suspect is likely to experience when telling the truth and whether these differ from emotions the suspect might feel when lying. It requires considerably more knowledge about the suspect than is usually available. Even when such knowledge exists, it may not help the lie-catcher. The knowledge may suggest that the same emotion is likely to be felt regardless of whether the suspect lies or is truthful, as was the case for Desdemona. Even when the knowledge suggests that different emotions are likely to occur if the suspect is truthful or deceiving, the behavioral clues may be ambiguous, because some behaviors are signs of more than one emotion. In each of these three instances (inadequate knowledge of the emotions felt by the suspect, knowledge that the same emotions will be felt regardless of whether the suspect is lying or truthful, and knowledge that different emotions are likely to be felt by the liar or the honest person but that the behavioral clues associated with these different emotions may be ambiguous), the lie-catcher cannot utilize the clues to deceit which involve emotion.

Only by realizing this predicament can the lie-catcher avoid disbelieving the truth and be properly wary of believing a lie. Analyzing which emotions a particular deceiver is likely to feel and which emotions a truthful person might feel about being suspected or disbelieved can help to identify a deceiver. Such an analysis may isolate unambiguous signs of honesty or deceit and may alert the lie-catcher to the behaviors that must be discovered.

Liars usually succeed because no one expends the often arduous effort necessary to catch them. Since most lies are relatively trivial, the detailed emotional analysis we have described is not usually called for. When the stakes are high, however, such as when the victim would be severely harmed if misled or when the liar would be either severely harmed if caught or greatly benefited if wrongly judged to be truthful, such efforts are necessary. Lie-checking is not a simple task that can be done quickly. Many questions must be considered in order to estimate the likelihood of mistakes, what kinds of mistakes to expect, and how to spot those mistakes. Questions must be asked about the nature of the lie itself and the characteristics of the specific liar and the specific lie-catcher. No one can be absolutely certain if a liar will fail or a truthful person will be exonerated. Lie-checking provides only an informed guess, but making such estimates should reduce mistakes in both believing lies and disbelieving the truth.

A LYING CHECKLIST

Table 9.1 contains 38 questions which should be considered in evaluating or checking a lie. Most of the questions concern issues that have been mentioned in this chapter. Others are discussed in more detail in *Telling Lies* (Ekman, 1985). There has been no research on the utility of this checklist. We provide it as a convenient reminder of factors that our research and theorizing, as well as the research of others, suggest are important in detecting deception.

To illustrate how to use the lying checklist, let us consider a case in which a truthful person was judged to be lying. Gerald Anderson (Phelan, 1982) was accused of raping and murdering Nancy Johnson, the wife of his next door neighbor. Nancy's husband had returned home from work in the middle of the night, found her body, ran over to the Andersons' house, told them that his wife was dead and that he couldn't find his son, and asked Mr. Anderson to summon the police.

A number of incidents made the police suspect Anderson. The day after the murder he had stayed home from work, drank too much at a local bar, and talked about the murder. When he was brought home, he had been overheard sobbing while saying to his wife, "I didn't want to do it, but I had to." His later claim that he was talking about getting drunk, not murder, was not believed. When the police asked him about a spot on the upholstery of his car, Anderson claimed that it had been there before he bought it. Later, he admitted that the spot came from a nosebleed that happened when he slapped his wife during an argument. He lied because he was ashamed to admit that he had slapped his wife. His interrogators repeatedly told Anderson that this incident proved that he was a violent person who could kill and that he was a liar who would deny it. During the interrogation, Anderson admitted that when he was twelve he had been involved in a minor sex offense that had not harmed the girl and that had never been repeated. Later, it came out that he was not twelve but fifteen at the time. His interrogators insisted that this was further proof that he was a liar, as well as evidence that he

Table 9.1. Lying Checklist

Questions	Hard to detect	Easy to detect
About the lie		
1. Can the liar anticipate exactly when he or she has to lie?	**Yes:** line prepared and rehearsed	**No:** line not prepared
2. Does the lie involve concealment only, without any need to falsify?	**Yes**	**No**
3. Does the lie involve emotions felt at the moment?	**No**	**Yes:** especially difficult if (a) negative emotions such as anger, fear, or distress must be concealed or falsified, or (b) liar must appear emotionless and cannot use another emotion to mask felt emotions that have to be concealed
4. Would there be amnesty if liar confessed to lying?	**No:** enhances liar's motive to succeed	**Yes:** chance to induce confession
5. Are the stakes in terms of either rewards or punishments very high?	**Difficult to predict:** while high stakes may increase detection apprehension, it should also motivate the liar to try hard.	
6. Are there severe punishments for being caught lying?	**No:** low detection apprehension, but may produce carelessness	**Yes:** enhances detection apprehension, but also fear of being disbelieved, producing false positive errors
7. Are there severe punishments for the very act of having lied, apart from the losses incurred from the deceit failing?	**No**	**Yes:** enhances detection apprehension; person may be dissuaded from embarking on lie if she or he knows that punishment for attempting to lie will be worse than the loss incurred by not lying
8. Does the target suffer no loss, or even benefit, from the lie? Is the lie altruistic, not benefiting the liar?	**Yes:** less deception guilt if liar believes this to be so	**No:** increases deception guilt

Table 9.1. *(Continued)*

Questions	Hard to detect	Easy to detect
9. Is it a situation in which the target is likely to trust the liar, not suspecting that he or she may be misled?	Yes	No
10. Has liar successfully deceived the target before?	**Yes:** decreases detection apprehension; if target would be ashamed or otherwise suffer by having to acknowledge having been fooled, she or he may become a willing victim.	No
11. Do liar and target share values?	**No:** decreases deception guilt	**Yes:** increases deception guilt
12. Is the lie authorized?	**Yes:** decreases deception guilt	**No:** increases deception guilt
13. Is the target anonymous?	**Yes:** decreases deception guilt	No
14. Are target and liar personally acquainted?	No	**Yes:** lie-catcher will be more able to avoid errors due to individual differences
15. Must lie-catcher conceal his or her suspicions from the liar?	**Yes:** lie-catcher may become enmeshed in his or her own need to conceal and fail to be as alert to liar's behavior.	No
16. Does lie-catcher have information that only a guilty, not an innocent person, would also have?	No	**Yes:** can try to use the guilty knowledge test if the suspect can be interrogated
17. Is there an audience who knows or suspects that the target is being deceived?	No	**Yes:** may enhance duping delight, detection apprehension, or deception guilt
18. Do liar and lie-catcher come from similar language, national or cultural backgrounds?	**No:** more errors in judging clues to deceit	**Yes:** better able to interpret clues to deceit

Table 9.1. *(Continued)*

Questions	Hard to detect	Easy to detect
About the liar		
19. Is the liar practiced in lying?	**Yes:** especially if practiced in this type of lie	No
20. Is the liar inventive and clever in fabricating?	Yes	No
21. Does the liar have a good memory?	Yes	No
22. Is the liar a smooth talker, with a convincing manner?	Yes	No
23. Does the liar use the reliable facial muscles as conversational emphasizers?	**Yes:** better able to conceal or falsify facial expressions	No
24. Is the liar skilled as an actor, able to use the Stanislavski method?	Yes	No
25. Is the liar likely to convince herself or himself of her or his lie, believing that what she or he says is true?	Yes	No
26. Is he or she a "natural liar" or psychopath?	Yes	No
27. Does liar's personality make liar vulnerable either to fear, guilt, or duping delight?	No	Yes
28. Is liar ashamed of what he or she is concealing?	**Difficult to predict:** while shame works to prevent confession, leakage of that shame may betray the lie.	
29. Might suspected liar feel fear, guilt, shame, or duping delight, even if suspect is innocent and not lying, or lying about something else?	**Yes:** can't interpret emotion clues	**No:** signs of these emotions are clues to deceit

Hazards in Detecting Deceit

Table 9.1. *(Continued)*

Questions	Hard to detect	Easy to detect
About the lie-catcher		
30. Does the lie-catcher have a reputation of being tough to mislead?	**No:** especially if liar has in the past been successful in fooling the lie-catcher	**Yes:** increases detection apprehension; may also increase duping delight
31. Does the lie-catcher have a reputation of being distrustful?	**Difficult to predict:** Such a reputation may decrease deception guilt; it may also increase detection apprehension.	
32. Does the lie-catcher have a reputation of being fair-minded?	**No:** liar less likely to feel guilty about deceiving the lie-catcher	**Yes:** increases deception guilt
33. Is the lie-catcher a denier who avoids problems and tends to always think the best of people?	**Yes:** probably will overlook clues to deceit, vulnerable to false negative errors	**No**
34. Is lie-catcher unusually able to accurately interpret expressive behaviors?	**No**	**Yes**
35. Does the lie-catcher have preconceptions that bias him or her against the liar?	**No**	**Yes:** although lie-catcher will be alert to clues to deceit, he or she will be liable to false positive errors.
36. Does the lie-catcher obtain any benefits from not detecting the lie?	**Yes:** lie-catcher will ignore, deliberately or unwittingly, clues to deceit	**No**
37. Is lie-catcher unable to tolerate uncertainty about whether she or he is being deceived?	**Difficult to predict:** may cause either false positive or false negative errors	
38. Is lie-catcher seized by an uncontrollable emotion?	**No**	**Yes:** liars will be caught, but innocents will be judged to be lying (false positive error).

had a sex problem, and that he could be the person who raped and then murdered his neighbor.

The police investigators believed that they had their man. They interrogated Anderson for 6 days. Anderson was worn down and finally confessed to a crime that he had not committed. Anderson proclaimed his innocence almost until the end, protesting that he could not have done it since he had no memory of killing or raping Nancy. The interrogators countered by telling him that a killer might have a blackout. They said that failure to remember the act did not prove that he had not done it. Anderson signed a confession after the interrogators told him that his wife said she knew that he had killed Nancy. His wife later denied making this statement. A few days later, Anderson repudiated his confession, and 7 months later the true killer, who was charged with another rape-murder, confessed to killing Nancy Johnson.

The Anderson case illustrates several of the points we made earlier in this chapter about emotions arising from causes other than guilt about a crime. Anderson's emotional reactions could have been generated by his fear of being disbelieved and also by feelings of shame and guilt. Even though innocent of the murder, Anderson was ashamed of two other misdeeds. His interrogators knew that he was ashamed about hitting his wife and about having committed a sex offense as an adolescent. He also felt deception guilt about his attempts to conceal or misrepresent these incidents. The interrogators used these incidents to persuade Anderson that he was the type of person who could kill and rape, but this could also have magnified his feelings of shame and guilt and could have linked those feelings with the crime he was accused of committing.

Lie-checking could have provided a reminder that any signs of fear, shame, or guilt, whether they in Anderson's facial expressions, gestures, voice, speech, or autonomic nervous system activity measured by a polygraph, would be ambiguous clues to deceit. These emotions could occur whether Anderson was innocent or guilty.

Examining this case underscores the sophistication necessary to use expressive clues to deceit effectively. Impressions of others is based, in part, upon the person's expressive behavior. Usually such impressions are formed unwittingly, and the person who makes them is often unaware of the particular behavioral clues that were used. Errors are less likely if such judgments are more explicit. To our knowledge, most police training does not emphasize behavioral clues to deceit. Since behavioral training is not emphasized, many investigators may not know the bases for their hunches about the guilt or innocence of suspects. Even when training does emphasize the importance of nonverbal clues to deceit, too little attention is given to those situation in which such clues will be useless or misleading.

It is not possible to abolish the use of behavioral clues to deceit in criminal interrogations, and justice might not be served if it were. In deadly deceits, when a truthful person could be falsely imprisoned or executed for a crime or a lying murderer could escape conviction, every legal attempt should be made to discover the truth. But the process of interpreting clues to deceit or truthfulness should be more explicit, more deliberate, and more careful.

ACKNOWLEDGMENTS

The work described was supported by a Research Scientist Award from the National Institute of Mental Health (MH 06092) and a previous grant from NIMH (MH11976).

REFERENCES

Bok, S. (1978). *Lying: Moral choice in public and private life.* New York: Pantheon Press.

Blum, H. (1987). *I pledge allegiance . . . The true story of the Walkers: An American spy family.* New York: Simon & Schuster.

Bull, G. (1961). Introduction. In N. Machiavelli, *The Prince* (G. Bull, Trans.). (pp. 1–20). Baltimore, MD: Penguin Books.

Brandt, D. R., Miller, G. R., & Hocking, J. E. (1980). The truth-deception attribution: Effects of familiarity on the ability of observers to detect deception. *Human Communication Research, 6,* 99–110.

Campos, J. J., & Barrett, K. C. (1984). Toward a new understanding of emotions and their development. In C. E. Izard, J. Kagan, & R. B. Zajonc (Eds.), *Emotions, cognition and behavior* (pp. 229–263). London: Cambridge University Press.

DePaulo, B. M., Lanier, K., & Davis, T. (1983). Detecting the deceit of the motivated liar. *Journal of Personality and Social Psychology, 45*, 1096–1103.

DePaulo, B. M., & Pfeifer, R. L. (1986). On-the-job experience and skill at detecting deception. *Journal of Applied Social Psychology, 16*, 249–267.

DePaulo, B. M., Stone, J. I., & Lassiter, G. D. (1985). Deceiving and detecting deceit. In B. R. Schlenker (Ed.), *The self in social life* (pp. 323–370). New York: McGraw-Hill.

Ekman, P. (1981). Mistakes when deceiving. *Annals of the New York Academy of Sciences, 364*, 269–278.

Ekman, P. (1985). *Telling lies*. New York: W. W. Norton.

Ekman, P., & Friesen, W. V. (1969). Nonverbal leakage and clues to deception. *Psychiatry, 32*, 88–105.

Ekman, P., & Friesen, W. V. (1972). Hand movements. *Journal of Communication, 22*, 353–374.

Ekman, P., & Friesen, W. V. (1974). Detecting deception from the body or face. *Journal of Personality and Social Psychology, 29*, 288–298.

Ekman, P., & Friesen, W. V. (1975). *Unmasking the face*. Englewood Cliffs, NJ: Prentice-Hall.

Ekman, P., Friesen, W. V., & O'Sullivan, M. (1988). Smiles when lying. *Journal of Personality and Social Psychology, 54*, 414–420.

Ekman, P., Friesen, W. V., & Scherer, K. (1976). Body movement and voice pitch in deceptive interaction. *Semiotica, 16*, 23–27.

Ekman, P., & O'Sullivan, M. (1988). [Accuracy in detecting deception in law enforcement and mental health personnel.] Unpublished raw data.

Frijda, N. H. (1986). *The emotions*. Cambridge: Cambridge University Press.

Hare, R. D. (1970). *Psychopathy: Theory and research*. New York: John Wiley.

Hayano, D. M. (1980). Communicative competence among poker players, *Journal of Communication, 30*, 113–120.

Heuer, R. J., Jr. (1982). Cognitive factors in deception and counterdeception. In D. C. Daniel & K. L. Herbig (Eds.), *Strategic military deception* (pp. 31–69). New York: Pergamon Press.

Hood, W. (1982). *Mole.* New York: W. W. Norton.
Irving, J. (1985). *The cider house rules.* New York: William Morrow.
Kraut, R. E., & Poe, D. (1980). On the line: The deception judgments of customs inspectors and laymen. *Journal of Personality and Social Psychology, 39,* 784–798.
Lazarus, R. S. (1984). On the primacy of cognition. *American Psychologist, 39,* 124–129.
MacMillan, J., & Kofoed, L. (1984). Sociobiology and antisocial personality: An alternative perspective. *Journal of Mental Disease, 172,* 701–706.
Mullaney, R. (1979). *The third way—the interroview.* Unpublished manuscript.
Nunnally, J. D., Knott, P. D., Duchnowski, A., & Parker, R. (1967). Pupillary response as a general measure of activation. *Perception and Psychophysics, 2,* 149–155.
O'Sullivan, M., Ekman, P., & Friesen, W. V. (1988). The effect of behavioral comparison in detecting deception. *Journal of Nonverbal Behavior, 12,* 203–215.
Phelan, J. (1982). *Scandals, scamps and scoundrels.* New York: Random House.
Rosenthal, R., & DePaulo, B. M. (1979). Sex differences in accommodation in nonverbal communication. In R. Rosenthal (Ed.), *Skill in nonverbal communication: Individual differences* (pp. 68–103). Cambridge, MA: Oelgeschlager.
Schmauk, F. J. (1970). Punishment, arousal, and avoidance learning in sociopaths. *Journal of Abnormal Psychology, 76,* 325–335.
Simpson, H. M., & Hale, S. M. (1969). Pupillary changes during a decision-making task. *Perceptual and Motor Skills, 29,* 495–498.
Swann, W. B. Jr., Griffin, J. J., Jr., Predmore, S. C., & Gaines, B. (1987). Cognitive-affective crossfire: When self-consistency meets self-enhancement. *Journal of Personality and Social Psychology, 52,* 881–889.
Tomkins, S. S. (1963). *Affect, imagery and consciousness: The negative affects* (Vol. 2). New York: Springer.
Vaillant, G. E. (1975). Sociopathy as a human process: A viewpoint. *Archives of General Psychiatry, 32,* 178–183.
Weisman, J. (1977 September). The truth will out. *TV Guide,* p. 13.
Wolk, R. L., & Henley, A. (1970). *The right to lie.* New York: Peter Wyden.
Young, P. T. (1961). *Motivation and emotion.* New York: John Wiley.
Zuckerman, M., DePaulo, B. M., & Rosenthal, R. (1981). Verbal and nonverbal communication of deception. In L. Berkowitz (Ed.),

Advances in Experimental Social Psychology (Vol. 14, pp. 1–59). New York: Academic Press.

Zuckerman, M., & Driver, R. E. (1985). Telling lies: Verbal and nonverbal correlates of deception. In A. W. Siegman & S. Feldstein (Eds.), *Multichannel integration of nonverbal behavior* (pp. 129–147). Hillsdale, NJ: Erlbaum.

Zuckerman, M., Koestner, R., & Colella, M. J. (1985). Learning to detect deception from three communication channels. *Journal of Nonverbal Behavior, 9*, 188–194.

The Admissibility of Evidence Derived from Hypnosis and Polygraphy

10

Roberta A. Morris

Courts in the various jurisdictions in the United States have taken several different perspectives regarding the admissibility of evidence derived from hypnosis and polygraphy. Knowledge of these positions is a critical element of case preparation for the criminal investigator because, without it, he or she may inadvertently eliminate the possibility of successfully introducing essential witnesses' testimony at trial. The purpose of this chapter is to provide an overview of the positions taken by the 50 states, the District of Columbia, the federal circuit courts of appeal, and the U.S. Supreme Court. Through an analysis of the applicable case law and statutes attempts are made to distill the commonalities in these approaches and to gauge whether all perspectives are equally viable or whether a dominant trend is emerging.

It should be kept in mind that the attempt to detect trends in the law by forcing the approaches taken by the various jurisdictions into a few general categories unavoidably strips these positions of important detail. This violence to the individual case opinion or statute is necessary because without this categorization each jurisdiction, in effect, becomes a category of one, and trends in the law across jurisdictions are rendered invisible. For this reason, however, the chapter will prove inadequate for the practitioner in need of specific advice; he or she should examine the applicable law for the appropriate jurisdiction for detailed guidance.

Similarly, it should be stressed that the emphasis on published opinions in the state and federal appellate courts is not necessarily a reflection of the incidence with which the trial courts face these admissibility issues, since trial court opinions are generally unpublished. Correspondingly, the absence of a citation to a court opinion in a particular jurisdiction in any of the Appendixes to this chapter does not mean the state trial courts have not addressed these issues. Again, the practitioner is advised to explore the nuances of judicial pronouncements in his or her state in greater depth by consulting local attorneys and judges conversant in these matters.

The chapter first addresses the admissibility issues as they pertain to hypnotically refreshed testimony and then discusses them in the context of polygraphy. The chapter concludes with Appendixes providing citations to cases and statutes governing the admissibility of hypnotically refreshed testimony and polygraphy in the different jurisdictions and annotated tables describing the categories into which the jurisdictions fall.

With respect to hypnosis, both criminal and civil cases were reviewed. There are fewer civil than criminal cases; they were included because the critical issue in the two types of cases is similar, that is, whether the testimony of a key witness should be admitted if he or she has forgotten crucial elements of an event that is the subject of a lawsuit and seeks to refresh his or her memory with hypnosis. Thus, the inclusion of these cases allows a fuller discussion of the various rationales the courts have used in determining whether hypnotically refreshed testimony should be admissible.

Conversely, with respect to polygraphy, only criminal cases are discussed, in part because there are enough criminal cases to provide a full discussion of the manner in which the courts have analyzed the admissibility issues. In addition, the fact patterns for civil cases and, accordingly, the admissibility issues, tend to differ markedly from those common in criminal cases. Specifically, the use of polygraphy in an employment setting, or more accurately, a particular employment decision stemming from this use, becomes the event that often triggers the civil lawsuit. In this instance, the polygraphy itself is the basis of the dispute. By contrast, in the criminal situation the use of polygraphy is much like the use of hypnosis; it is an aid to preparing for litigation.

HYPNOTICALLY REFRESHED TESTIMONY

The Typical Fact Pattern and the Relevant Issues

The typical fact patterns that generate interest in the use of hypnosis occur when a witness is unable to recall an event with sufficient detail to assist the police in an investigation, either because of trauma or drunkenness (or other drugged state) at the time of the event or due to the passage of time since the event occurred. This witness is then hypnotized in order to refresh his or her memory of significant details. The courts have been reluctant to admit the testimony of a previously hypnotized witness for several reasons:

1. Hypnosis subjects are anxious to please, hypersuggestible, and able to purposefully lie, confabulate, or incorrectly remember things while hypnotized.
2. Hypnosis seems to have the effect of "cementing" even erroneous memories in the witness's mind, thereby giving him or her greater confidence in these memories. This confidence may render effective cross-examination impossible and cause the jury to give undue credence to this testimony.
3. The various procedures used may have a biasing effect, such as having a police officer, often with little training in hypnosis and even less in psychology, conduct the hypnosis session. (See, e.g., *State ex rel. Collins v. Superior Court, Etc.*, 1982, and citations therein for more extensive discussions of these issues.)

Because of these concerns, the courts have often held that hypnosis, and hence the product—hypnotically refreshed memory—does not meet the jurisdiction's criteria governing the admissibility of new scientific techniques. Generally, these criteria provide that a new scientific technique must be accepted as reliable by the relevant scientific community in order to warrant its admissibility into evidence. Often the court's analysis stops once this determination has been made, however. The underlying concern, mentioned in the more thoughtful opinions, is that hypnosis forever changes or "taints" the witness's memory, such that the pre hypnosis witness is really not the same person as the post hypnosis witness in that his or her pre- and posthypnosis recollections are inextricably intertwined, confabulations and all. Moreover, such a witness, it is felt, is infinitely more certain about these recollections. If this conclusion is accurate, the argument goes, then the defendant has been denied the Sixth Amendment right under the Constitution to confront and meaningfully cross-examine adverse witnesses, and the jury has been deprived of the opportunity to watch the natural courtroom demeanor of these witnesses.

Admissibility Tests for Scientific Evidence

The courts use several standards to determine whether a scientific technique has advanced sufficiently beyond its initial stages to be admitted as evidence.

The most frequently cited standard is known as the *Frye* test, or the "general scientific acceptance test" (*Frye v. United States*, 1923). In this case the court was asked to determine whether to admit expert testimony on the results of a "systolic blood pressure deception test" that was performed upon the defendant. The court affirmed the lower court's decision denying admissibility, stating:

> Just when a scientific principle or discovery crosses the line between the experimental and demonstrable stages is difficult to define. Somewhere in this twilight zone the evidential force of the principle must be recognized, and while courts will go a long way

in admitting expert testimony deduced from a well-recognized scientific principle or discovery, the thing from which the deduction is made must be sufficiently established to have gained general acceptance in the particular field in which it belongs.

We think the systolic blood pressure deception test has not yet gained such standing and scientific recognition among physiological and psychological authorities as would justify the courts in admitting expert testimony deduced from the discovery, development, and experiments thus far made. (p. 1014)

The *Frye* test has frequently faced challenges from those who argue that it is inappropriate to apply it in the context of hypnosis because *Frye* refers to the admissibility of expert testimony, whereas here the concern is with the hypnotically refreshed testimony of a witness. Courts that have considered this argument have found it unpersuasive, and consequently, *Frye* now stands for a much broader principle than the original case opinion.

The approach taken by the Federal Rules of Evidence is to allow traditional standards of relevancy and the need for expertise to govern. This "relevancy test" is preferred over the *Frye* test by *McCormick's Handbook of the Law of Evidence* (1984), a treatise on evidentiary matters, which states:

[The relevancy test] avoids the difficult problems of defining how "general" the general acceptance must be, or discerning exactly what it is that must be accepted, and of determining the "particular field" to which the scientific evidence belongs and in which it must be accepted. "General scientific acceptance" is a proper condition for taking judicial notice of scientific facts, but it is not a suitable criterion for the admissibility of scientific evidence. Any relevant conclusions supported by a qualified expert witness should be received unless there are distinct reasons for exclusion. These reasons are the familiar ones of prejudicing or misleading the jury or consuming undue amounts of time.

This traditional approach to the evidence does not make scientific testimony admissible on the say-so of a single expert. Neither does it go to the other extreme and insist on a fully formed scientific consensus. It permits general scientific opinion of both underlying principles and particular applications to be considered in evaluating the worth of the testimony. In so treating the yeas and nays of the members of a scientific discipline as but one indication of the validity, accuracy, and reliability of the technique, the traditional balancing method focuses the court's attention where it belongs—on the actual usefulness of the evidence in light of the full record developed on the power of the scientific test. (pp. 608–609; see also Giannelli, 1980, for an excellent discussion of the standards used to determine the admissibility of novel scientific evidence.)

It is tempting to assess whether the particular conclusions a court reached about the admissibility of hypnotically refreshed testimony can be predicted from a knowledge of which test the court applied. Unfortunately, such prediction is often impossible because it is typically unclear which test a court found controlling. Often the courts cite both tests and appear to apply neither, cite *Frye* for a much broader proposition than the original case holding, or cite no test at all, saying, rather, that hypnosis is not an admissibility question for the court but a credibility question for the jury. For this reason and also because the fact patterns in these cases defy categorization, it is only possible to identify trends in the law by looking at the case conclusions, rather than by analyzing the processes by which they were derived. Stated another way, the variance in court decisions is not accounted for by the test used or, in any discernible way at this point, by patterns in case facts.

Perspectives on Admissibility: State Courts

Inadmissible to Prove the Truth of the Matter Asserted.

As an initial matter, 11 states have not had occasion to consider the issue of hypnotically refreshed testimony at all, and one of the remaining 40 has had occasion to consider hypnosis only in a different context from those that have been mentioned thus far.[1] This state, South Carolina, together with Kansas,

---

[1] Discussion of the states includes the District of Columbia; thus, the total is 51 rather than 50.

Michigan, Mississippi, North Dakota, Oklahoma, and Virginia, which have each considered hypnosis in more than one context, has determined that the testimony of the hypnotist and the subject are inadmissible to prove the truth of the matter asserted. Based on the theory that a hypnotized person is unable to purposefully lie, the defense in these criminal cases attempted to offer exculpatory evidence by having the accused hypnotized and then offering the resulting statements in court.

Representative of these cases is *State v. Conley* (1981), a murder case resulting from the shotgun killing of the defendant's roommate. Briefly, the defendant came home drunk from a party one night, assisted by a woman who had also attended the party. Because the defendant was having difficulty walking, the woman woke the roommate to have him help her. When the defendant fell to the floor, the roommate took him by the feet and began pulling him towards his bedroom. To be transported in such a fashion angered the defendant, and a fight ensued. While the woman was on the phone calling for help, she heard a shot, and when she returned to the other room the roommate was lying dead on the floor.

At trial, the defendant claimed that he was so intoxicated that he could not have formed the necessary intent to kill, or *mens rea*, proof of which must be established as a prerequisite to the attachment of criminal liability. Conflicting evidence on this issue was presented, some of which indicated that he was less intoxicated than he claimed. Thus, for instance, the defendant had apparently been capable of finding the shotgun, firing it, zipping it back into its case, and replacing it in the closet. The defense wanted to admit the defendant's statements while under hypnosis, which indicated that the roommate had taken the gun out of the closet and, with both of his hands on the barrel, had used it as a prod, and that the gun discharged during the struggle with the defendant. The appellate court, noting that "the record before us does not give [the defendant's] explanation of how the charge struck [the deceased] in the back," concurred in the trial court's estimation that the proffered evidence was properly excluded as scientifically inaccurate and too self-serving.

Per Se Inadmissible

Only Delaware has determined that a per se rule against the admissibility of hypnotically refreshed memory is mandated. In *State v. Davis* (1985) the Delaware superior court indicated that state law required proof that the results of a scientific process are reliable prior to their introduction into evidence and surmised that such proof may not yet be available, given the limitations of the scientific community's understanding of human memory.

Recollections Prior to Hypnosis Admissible

Deeming the per se inadmissibility too harsh with respect to its consequences for police investigations, 25 states have adopted a variant of the per se rule, which allows the previously hypnotized witness to testify with respect to his or her recollections prior to hypnosis. Thus, the party wishing to introduce the witness's testimony must make a record of the witness's prehypnosis account of the events.

This view accommodates the court's concern for admitting only evidence considered scientifically reliable. In addition, it allows the police to use hypnosis as a useful investigative tool, without fear of jeopardizing the ability of key witnesses to testify subsequently. However, this approach ignores the issues concerning the defendant's right to a meaningful cross-examination of adversary witnesses and the jury's interests in viewing these witnesses' natural courtroom demeanors.

Admissible with Procedural Safeguards

Another 8 states have adopted yet a third perspective in the continuing judicial efforts to accommodate all of the interests of all of the parties. This approach calls for the admissibility of hypnotically refreshed testimony as long as certain safeguards and procedures are implemented. The common thread that runs through these cases is the judicial opinion that "without underestimating the seriousness of the problems associated with hypnosis, it should be recognized that psychological research concerning the reliability of ordinary eyewitnesses reveals similar shortcomings" (*State v. Hurd*, 1981, p. 94). These courts tend to view hypnosis as simply another technique used to refresh a witness's memory, such as having them read a newspaper clipping they cut out at the time of the event, or review a memo they wrote at the time. The most comprehensive opinions laying out the particulars of this approach are *State v. Hurd* and *State v. Glebock* (1981). The *Hurd* court held as follows:

> [T]estimony enhanced through hypnosis is admissible in a criminal trial if the trial court finds that the use of hypnosis in the particular case was reasonably likely to result in recall comparable in accuracy to normal human memory. If the testimony is admissible, the opponent may still challenge the reliability of the particular procedures followed in the individual case by introducing expert testimony at trial, but the opponent may not attempt to prove the general unreliability of hypnosis. The trier of fact must then decide how much weight to accord the hypnotically refreshed testimony.
>
> Whenever a party in a criminal trial seeks to introduce a witness who has undergone hypnosis to refresh his memory, the party must inform his opponent of his intention and provide him with the recording of the session and other pertinent material. The trial court will then rule on the admissibility of the testimony either at a pretrial hearing or at a hearing out of the jury's presence. In reviewing the admissibility of hypnotically refreshed testimony, the trial court should evaluate both the kind of memory loss that hypnosis was used to restore and the specific technique employed, based on expert testimony presented by the parties. The object of this review is not to determine whether the proffered testimony is accurate, but instead whether the use of hypnosis and the procedure followed in the particular case was a reasonably reliable means of restoring the witness' memory. (p. 95)

Finally, after stating that the party seeking to introduce hypnotically refreshed testimony has the burden of establishing its admissibility by clear and convincing evidence, the court listed the oft-cited "*Hurd* standards" (*State v. Hurd*, 1981) for conducting the hypnosis session:

1. A psychiatrist or psychologist experienced in the use of hypnosis must conduct the session.
2. The professional conducting the session should be independent of and not regularly employed by the prosecutor, investigator, or defense.
3. Any information given to the hypnotist by law enforcement personnel or defense prior to the hypnotic session must be recorded, either in writing or another suitable form.
4. Before inducing hypnosis, the hypnotist should obtain a detailed description of the facts as the subject remembers them.
5. All contacts between the hypnotist and the subject must be recorded, preferably on videotape.
6. Only the hypnotist and the subject should be present during any phase of the hypnosis session.

The *Glebock* (1981) court expanded on these standards by suggesting the particular manner in which this evidence should be introduced into court:

> [I]n laying the foundation for the admission of the testimony from a witness whose memory was refreshed by hypnosis, the expert should describe the manner in which he conducted the hypnotic session without relating to the jury what the witness had told him during hypnosis. The expert witness should also be asked to testify as to whether one under hypnosis has an increased capacity for recollection, what could bring on confabulation, and whether one who is or has been hypnotized has the capacity for telling deliberate falsehoods or lies. (pp. 904-905)

Finally, the party introducing the witness ordinarily should not be able to show what the hypnotized witness told the hypnotist on direct examination; rather, the opposition should have the opportunity on cross-examination to question the witness from a transcript of the session. The idea behind this point is that, aside from informing the jury that the witness was previously hypnotized and that certain risks are attendant on hypnosis, the strategic decision of whether to use the session itself as a means of impeaching the crediblity of the witness by impugning his or her ability to remember should rest with the opponent.

Not all jurisdictions requiring standards for the administration of the hypnosis session use the *Hurd* approach. The Wisconsin Supreme Court, for example, in *State v. Armstrong* (1982), formulated the following:

> In determining whether events which occurred during the hypnosis session are such as to render any subsequent statements by the hypnotized subject unreliable, the trial court should examine the session with two tests in mind. First, there should be a determination of whether there was unnecessary suggestiveness in the hypnotic process. Second, the court should take into account the fact that some confabulation may occur during hypnosis and thus the court should determine whether, under the totality of the circumstances of the information seeking process, the post-hypnotic statements of the witness are reliable. (p. 396)

In *Armstrong* (1982), as in a number of other cases (e.g., *State v. Blanchard*, 1982), the witness's pre- and posthypnosis recollections were substantially the same. In the event the posthypnosis recollections are quite different from the witness's prehypnosis memories, it can be only a matter of speculation at this time whether courts would tend to find these recollections "unreliable" because of these differences. Corrobation of the witness's testimony by other evidence may also play a part in judicial determinations of the reliability of hypnotically refreshed testimony. For example, at the federal level, the Eighth Circuit Court of Appeals, in *Sprynczynatyk v. General Motors* (1985), has specifically indicated that the extent to which the hypnotically refreshed testimony can be corroborated by other evidence may determine whether such testimony will be admissible.

Per Se Admissible

The last approach, adhered to by 6 states, is that of per se admissibility. Deciding that the issue of hypnosis is a question of credibility for the jury to decide rather than a question of admissibility for the court to decide, these states allow almost unfettered use of hypnotically refreshed testimony, imposing almost no requirements for standardizing either the manner in which the hypnotic session is conducted or the way in which this evidence is introduced in court.

Perspectives on Admissibility: Federal Courts

Before reviewing the law in the federal courts, a brief comment is in order. The federal circuit courts have held that the admissibility issue is within the trial court's (i.e., the federal district court's) discretion. This court, in turn, will often defer to the position taken by the highest state court that has addressed the issue in the state in which it is located. Thus, for example, in *Beck v. Norris* (1986), the Sixth Circuit not only discusses the position taken by the Tennessee court of criminal appeals in *State v. Glebock* (1981) but also makes an explicit finding that the standards therein set forth were met. Because each circuit court handles appeals from trial courts located in a several-state area, several divergent opinions may come out of the same federal circuit court.

With respect to the federal circuit courts, the First, Second, Fourth, Fifth, Sixth, Seventh, Eighth, and Ninth Circuit Courts of Appeal have considered the issue thus far. The First, Second, Fourth, Fifth, Seventh, and Ninth Circuits have held that hypnotically refreshed testimony is admissible, with the credibility to be determined by the jury. The Sixth and Eighth Circuits have determined that hypnotically refreshed testimony is admissible in the event safeguards are implemented during the administration of the hypnosis session.

The Second Circuit case, *United States v. Miller* (1969) is somewhat unusual in that the issue of hypnosis was not addressed at trial but rather raised on appeal. At trial, the prosecution did not disclose to either the court or the defense that they had hypnotized a key witness until after the trial was over and the jury had rendered its verdict. The appellate court held that it was reversible error for the prosecution not to have revealed the hypnosis sessions prior to trial. Because the defense already possessed considerable impeachment material on the witness, the appellate court reasoned that this additional piece of information and the possible inferences that may have been drawn about the possible effects of hypnosis on his testimony may have meant the difference between acquittal and conviction for the defendant.

On November 10, 1986, the U.S. Supreme Court granted review in *Rock v. Arkansas* (1986) in order to examine whether the rule of per se inadmissibility of hypnotically refreshed recollection violated the Fourteenth Amendment's due process clause when applied to exclude a defendant's testimony about actions she did not remember prior to hypnosis and which were vital to her defense. The case presented a somewhat novel fact pattern in that the issues raised pertained to the hypnotically refreshed testimony of the defendant, who was standing trial for the murder of her husband, rather than the testimony of a nonparty witness. Because of the narrow issue raised, the Supreme Court's opinion did not address all the concerns surrounding the use of hypnotically refreshed testimony. In fact, the Court explicitly declined to express an opinion on the admissibility of a previously hypnotized witness's testimony, although it noted in a footnote the various positions that have been adopted in the several jurisdictions. In a split decision, in which only five justices joined in the majority opinion, the Court stated:

> Wholesale inadmissibility of a defendant's testimony is an arbitrary restriction on the right to testify in the absence of clear evidence by the State repudiating the validity of all posthypnosis recollections. The State would be well within its powers if it established guidelines to aid trial courts in the evaluation of posthypnosis testimony and it may be able to show that testimony in a particular case is so unreliable that exclusion is justified. But it has not shown that hypnotically enhanced testimony is always so untrustworthy and so immune to the traditional means of evaluating credibility that it should disable a defendant from presenting her version of the events for which she is on trial.

Trends in Admissibility

The fact that there have been recent cases in each of the above-described categories, together with the limited guidance provided by the U.S. Supreme Court, indicates that each is a viable position, although the emerging trend seems to be to allow testimony pertaining to prehypnosis recollections. There are indications in the literature of substantial research and development of alternative memory enhancement procedures, that avoid many of the drawbacks of hypnosis. Specific procedures and the results of research can be found in Chapter 6. The admissibility of hypnotically refreshed testimony remains a potential land mine for the unwary in terms of its ability to jeopardize the presentation of a case, and awareness of the applicable jurisdiction's perspective on this issue continues to be an essential aspect of case preparation.

THE POLYGRAPH EXAMINATION

The Typical Fact Pattern and the Relevant Issues

Shifting now to the polygraph, the tests used to determine scientific acceptance and reliability are the same as with hypnosis, with one crucial difference. With hypnosis the issue concerns the testimony of a witness whose mind has been "tampered with" through use of a technique that has undetermined scientific parameters; with lie detection the issue is the expert testimony on the credibility of the defendant and the fact that this assessment has traditionally been exclusively a jury function.

In addition, a key distinction exists between situations in which evidence is derived from hypnosis and those in which polygraphy is used, which may cause courts to treat polygraph evidence differently, aside from strictly scientific concerns. Specifically, whereas it is generally the prosecution that attempts to introduce the hypnotically refreshed testimony of a victim/witness (but see *Rock v. Arkansas*, 1986), it is usually the defense that tries to introduce the polygraph results of the defendant through expert testimony. Thus, the defendant's due process rights under the Constitution to offer the testimony of witnesses on his or her behalf may be implicated in this instance, and the courts may be compelled to admit this evidence.[2]

---

[2] This argument has yet to receive widespread acceptance by the courts. See Giannelli (1980) and citations therein for discussions of this "emergent Constitutional guarantee."

Perspectives on Admissibility: State Courts

As with hypnotically refreshed testimony, the states have taken a variety of positions with respect to evidence derived from the use of polygraphy. In contrast to the situation with hypnosis, however, in which only 39 states have considered the admissibility issues, fully 48 have considered them as they pertain to polygraphy.

Per Se Admissible

The first category contains only 2 states, Massachusetts and New Mexico. The law in New Mexico is that once the polygrapher's qualifications have been established and the evidence has met the requirements stated by the Supreme Court of New Mexico (see Raskin, 1986, p. 71), the evidence is admitted, leaving the jury to determine its significance.

Massachusetts has a somewhat more restrictive policy, which was articulated in *Commonwealth v. Vitello* (1978) and *Commonwealth v. Wick* (1987). On a motion by one of the parties, a court hearing must be held to determine if a polygraph test can be fairly conducted on the party to the litigation who wishes to take the test, typically the defendant. If the court decides in the affirmative, the moving party then proposes the name of the polygraph expert who will be appointed by the court to conduct the test. The moving party can then decide whether or not to conduct the test and whether or not to offer the results as evidence at trial. The polygraph evidence can be offered at trial only to corroborate or impeach the testimony of the party who took the test. The court may hold a *voir dire* concerning the admissibility of the court-ordered test to determine if it was conducted by a qualified expert, if the subject was amenable to testing, if the testing conditions were proper, and if the test questions were properly phrased and presented. The opposing party can neither prevent the test from being conducted, nor can it require that the results of a test be admitted as evidence. However, if the test was conducted and was not offered as evidence at trial and the party who took the polygraph test takes the witness stand to testify, the opposing party may introduce the polygraph results as evidence to impeach the witness.

Admissible with Binding Stipulation.

The second category, containing 18 states, allows polygraph evidence if there is a binding stipulation between the parties. Generally, courts in this category require several things for the stipulation to have force:

1. It must be entered into by all parties and be a matter of record, either by a filed written document signed by all parties or by an oral agreement of the parties in open court.
2. The stipulation, whether written or oral, has been preceded by the trial judge's informing the defendant of his or her right against self-incrimination, right to refuse to submit to the test, and right, under ordinary rules of evidence, to have the fact or outcome of a lie detector test excluded.
3. Notwithstanding the stipulation, the admissibility of the test results is subject to the discretion of the trial judge; if the trial judge is not convinced that the examiner is qualified or that the test was conducted under proper conditions, he or she may refuse to accept such evidence.
4. If the graphs or the examiner's opinion are offered in evidence, the opposing party has the right to cross-examine the examiner with respect to
   a. the examiner's qualifications and training,
   b. the conditions under which the test was administered,
   c. the limitations of and possibilities for error in the technique of polygraphic interrogation, and,
   d. at the discretion of the trial judge, any other matter deemed pertinent to the inquiry.
5. If such evidence is admitted, the trial judge instructs the jury that the examiner's testimony does not prove or disprove any element of the crime with which a defendant is charged but at most only indicates that at the time of the examination the defendant was or was not telling the truth. Further, the jury members should be instructed that it is for them to determine what corroborative weight and effect such testimony should be given.

Inadmissible, Indeterminate Basis for Ruling

In the next category, 15 states hold that evidence derived from the use of the polygraph is inadmissible. It is interesting that, although it is not difficult to find a recent case where this is the holding, it is difficult to find a case where the court has taken time to fully reconsider improvements in polygraphy instrumentation, research, and training. Instead, the tendency is for the courts to endorse the holding made 10 or 20 years ago in a previous case—such is the power of prior precedent. Another interesting thing about this category is that it is often not clear whether a court's opinion is intended to be interpreted as a per se rule of inadmissibility, since some cases contain language indicating that the outcome might have been different if the parties had entered into a prior stipulation.

Per Se Inadmissible

The final category is comprised of 13 states that have held that even the existence of a prior fair stipulation between the parties would not render this evidence admissible. The opinion of *People v. Baynes* (1981) is representative of the decisions in this group:

> If the instrument is accurate and the recording of the instrument's results reliable, then we should conclude it is acceptable. But the process has not reached a level of sophistication that makes it generally more probative than prejudicial. A stipulation does not necessarily make inadmissible evidence admissible. By what logic should stipulated polygraph evidence be admitted if the same evidence, absent a stipulation, is barred? How does the agreement lend credibility to an examination that would not otherwise be given judicial recognition? If evidence is unreliable, agreeing to its admission does not make it reliable. . . . A stipulation can admit facts but cannot change the law. The law is that polygraph evidence is not admissible in the state of Illinois. At trial, evidence of the polygraph was admitted by virtue of a stipulation. This evidence would not have been considered reliable enough for admission absent the stipulation. The stipulation attempts to change the legal standard for admissibility. This court cannot accept such a result. (p. 1077)

Perspectives on Admissibility: Federal Courts

The First, Second, Fourth, Fifth, Sixth, Seventh, Eighth, Ninth, Tenth, and Eleventh Circuit Courts of Appeal have considered the issue. The First, Fourth, Seventh, and Ninth Circuits have all ruled polygraph evidence admissible. They have done so, however, only when reviewing cases on appeal in which the trial court rejected this evidence. Although stating that this evidence is generally admissible, these circuits have gone on to indicate that it is a matter better left within the sound discretion of the trial judge and, thus, that it was not an error for the trial court to have excluded it in the case under review. The Second, Fifth, Sixth, Tenth, and Eleventh Circuits have stated that polygraphically derived evidence is inadmissible, and the Eighth Circuit has allowed such evidence only if a prior stipulation exists.

The Effect of Licensure Statutes

A final point to consider is what effect, if any, licensure/certification statutes governing the qualifications of polygraphers have on the admissibility of evidence derived from polygraphy. Perhaps the presence of licensure statutes, the purpose of which is to assure trained, competent polygraphers, is a factor the courts find conducive to admitting such testimony. These statutes generally require that the licensure candidate be 18 years old (some states mandate 19, others 21), a citizen of the United States and a state resident, have good moral character, hold some level of educational attainment (some specify high school diploma, others require either 2 years of college or a bachelor's degree from an accredited 4-year college), have completed an approved polygraph examiners' course and/or some level of internship experience, have passed an examination administered by the state Board of Polygraph Examiners, and have provided evidence of a surety bond or insurance policy in a specified sum (commonly $5,000).

Thus far, 30 states have such statutes, and the relationship between these statutes and admissibility is as follows:[3]

---

[3] The admissibility issue has been resolved by statute in California and Montana.

1. Thirteen states have statutes and admit polygraph evidence.
2. Sixteen states have statutes and do not admit polygraph evidence.
3. One state has a statute and has not expressed a view as to polygraph admissibility.
4. Seven states do not have statutes and admit polygraph evidence.
5. Twelve states do not have statutes and do not admit polygraph evidence.
6. Two states do not have statutes and have not expressed a view as to polygraph admissibility.

Examination of the judicial opinions in the 28 jurisdictions that have licensure statutes and have addressed the issue of polygraph admissibility does not reveal that these courts have found the presence of licensure statutes particularly persuasive in reaching their decisions. In fact, if the statutes are mentioned at all, it is generally after a determination has been made to admit polygraph results on other grounds, in the context of determining whether a given witness truly is an an expert in polygraphy and should accordingly be allowed to testify. The courts have not considered whether the presence of licensure statutes requiring examiners to have some minimum level of training and/or experience should be considered favorably in their determination of the admissibility issue, even though it might be argued that such training/experience may be conducive to greater interexaminer reliabiity in results, thus enhancing the scientific status of polygraphy as a technique. Because the courts have tended to sever the issue of expertise from that of admissibility in this fashion, the impact of licensure on admissibility has been negligible. Both the opinions admitting polygraph evidence and those rejecting it have based their decisions on other factors, that is, the merits of allowing the parties to determine the issue through prior stipulations, or the validity of the theory and instrumentation of polygraphy itself.

Even in the context of determining whether a particular examiner qualifies as an expert, the courts have not expressed much confidence in the ability of licensure statutes to assure competence among polygraph examiners. The courts seem rather to regard the trial process, by which the expert testifies and is asked questions regarding his or her training and experience, as a more trustworthy manner of securing evidence regarding expertise than licensure alone. Thus, by stating that the examiner's possession of a polygraph license did not necessarily establish qualifications as an expert, the Utah Supreme Court essentially relegated licensure to the status of being only one factor among several used in reaching this determination (*State v. Collins*, 1980). Similarly, analysis of opinions holding polygraph results inadmissible reveals judicial sentiment to the effect that the statutorily imposed standards for polygraph examiners are generally inadequate for assuring competent personnel (see, e.g., *People v. Barbara*, 1977). Thus, by stating that licensure is not necessarily synonymous with competence, courts that have admitted or rejected polygraph evidence have diminished its significance as a basis of determining expertise as well as admissibility.

Finally, legal commentators have noted (Giannelli, 1980) that courts have also expressed concern that experts with a "professional or commercial interest in the technique" may not be sufficiently disinterested to provide nonbiased information regarding the technique's scientific attributes. This bit of legal logic may, at first blush, seem a bit perplexing, since the impact of excluding those individuals may have the effect of eliminating almost everyone who may have real expert qualifications. On the other hand, the determination that no one is qualified to testify as an expert may perhaps be construed as an ingenious judicial maneuver for eliminating the admissibility problem once and for all.

REFERENCES

Beck v. Norris, 801 F.2d 242 (6th Cir. 1986).
Commonwealth v. Vitello, 381 N.E.2d 582 (Mass. 1978).
Commonwealth v. Wick, 506 N.E.2d 857 (Mass. 1987).
Frye v. United States, 293 F. 1013 (D.C.App. 1923).

Giannelli, P. C. (1980). The admissibility of novel scientific evidence: *Frye v. United States*, a half-century later. *Columbia Law Review, 80,* 1197–1250.
McCormick's handbook of the law of evidence (3rd ed.). (1984). St. Paul, MN: West Publishing.
People v. Barbara, 255 N.W.2d 171 (Mich. 1977).
People v. Baynes, 430 N.E.2d 1070 (Ill. 1981).
Raskin, D. C. (1986). The polygraph in 1986: Scientific, professional and legal issues surrounding application and acceptance of polygraph evidence. *Utah Law Review, 1986,* 29–74.
Rock v. Arkansas, 708 S.W.2d 78 (Ark. 1986), *vacated and remanded* 107 S.Ct. 2704 (1987).
Sprynczynatyk v. General Motors, 771 F.2d 1112 (8th Cir. 1985).
State ex rel. Collins v. Superior Court, Etc., 644 P.2d 1266 (Ariz. 1982).
State v. Armstrong, 329 N.W.2d 386 (Wis. 1982).
State v. Blanchard, 315 N.W.2d 427 (Minn. 1982).
State v. Collins, 612 P.2d 775 (Ut. 1980).
State v. Conley, 627 P.2d 1174 (Kan. 1981).
State v. Davis, 490 A.2d 601 (Del. Super. 1985).
State v. Glebock, 616 S.W.2d 897 (Tenn. Cr. App. 1981).
State v. Hurd, 432 A.2d 86 (N.J. 1981).
United States v. Miller, 411 F.2d 1 (2nd Cir. 1969).

Appendix 10A
Cases/Statutes Determining the Admissibility of Hypnotically Refreshed Testimony

Federal Courts

1st Circuit	*Clay v. Vose,* 771 F.2d 1 (1st Cir. 1985)
2nd Circuit	*United States v. Miller,* 411 F.2d 825 (2nd Cir. 1969)
4th Circuit	*McQueen v. Garrison,* 814 F.2d 951 (4th Cir. 1987)
5th Circuit	*Wicker v. McCotter,* 783 F.2d 487 (5th Cir. 1986)
	United States v. Valdez, 722 F.2d 1196 (5th Cir. 1984)
6th Circuit	*Beck v. Norris,* 801 F.2d 242 (6th Cir. 1986)
7th Circuit	*United States v. Kimberlin,* 805 F.2d 210 (7th Cir. 1986)
8th Circuit	*Sprynczynatyk v. General Motors,* 771 F.2d 1112 (8th Cir. 1985)
9th Circuit	*United States v. Awkard,* 597 F.2d 667 (9th Cir. 1979)
Supreme Court	*Rock v. Arkansas,* 107 S. Ct. 2704 (1987)

State Courts

Alabama	*Prewitt v. State,* 460 So.2d 296 (Ala. Crim. App. 1984)
Alaska	*Contreras v. State,* 718 P.2d 129 (1986)

Appendix

Arizona	*State ex rel. Collins v. Superior Court*, 644 P.2d 1269 (1982)
	State v. McMurtrey, 664 P.2d 637 (1983)
	State v. Rodriquez, 700 P.2d 855 (Ariz. App. 1984)
	State v. Superior Court, 690 P.2d 94 (Ariz. App. 1984)
	State v. Poland, 698 P.2d 183 (1985)
Arkansas	*Rock v. State*, 708 S.W.2d 78 (1986), *vacated and remanded* 107 S. Ct. 2704 (1987)
California	Cal. Evidence Code sec. 795 (West 1984)
Colorado	*People v. Romero*, 745 P.2d 1003 (1987)
Connecticut	*State v. Pollitt*, 530 A.2d 155 (1987)
Delaware	*State v. Davis*, 490 A.2d 601 (Del. Super. 1985)
DC	none
Florida	*Bundy v. State*, 471 So.2d 9, (1985)
Georgia	*Walraven v. State*, 336 S.E.2d 798 (1985)
Hawaii	*State v. Moreno*, 709 P.2d 103 (1985)
Idaho	*State v. Iwakiri*, 682 P.2d 571 (1984)
	State v. Bainbridge, 698 P.2d 335 (1984)
	State v. Joblin, 689 P.2d 767 (1984)
Illinois	*People v. Wilson*, 506 N.E.2d 571 (1987)
	People v. Smrekar, 385 N.E.2d 848 (Ill. App. 4 Dist. 1979)
	People v. Byas, 453 N.E.2d 1141 (Ill. App. 3 Dist. 1983)
	People v. Cohoon, 457 N.E.2d 998 (Ill. App. 5 Dist. 1983)
	People v. Zayas, 510 N.E.2d 1125 (Ill. App. 1 Dist. 1987)
Indiana	*Strong v. State*, 435 N.E.2d 969 (1982)
	Peterson v. State, 448 N.E.2d 673 (1983)
	Gentry v. State, 471 N.E.2d 263 (1984)
	Rowley v. State, 483 N.E.2d 1078 (1985)
Iowa	*State v. Seager*, 341 N.W.2d 420 (1983)
	State v. Groscost, 355 N.W.2d 32 (1984)

Kansas	*State v. Conley*, 627 P.2d 1174 (Kan. App. 1981)
	State v. Haislip, 701 P.2d 909 (1985)
Kentucky	none
Louisiana	*State v. Wren*, 425 So.2d 756 (1983)
	State v. Goutro, 444 So.2d 615 (1984)
	State v. Porretto, 468 So.2d 1142 (1985)
	State v. White, 498 So.2d 1100 (1986)
Maine	*State v. Commeau*, 438 A.2d 454 (1981)
Maryland	*State v. Collins*, 464 A.2d 1028 (Md. App. 1983)
	McCoy v. State, 484 A.2d 624 (1984)
	Calhoun v. State, 468 A.2d 45 (1983)
Massachusetts	*Commonwealth v. Kater*, 447 N.E.2d 1190 (1983)
Michigan	*People v. Hangsleben*, 273 N.W.2d 539 (Mich. App. 1978)
	People v. Gonzales, 329 N.W.2d 743 (1982), *as modified* 336 N.W.2d 751 (1983)
	People v. Nixon, 364 N.W.2d 593 (1984)
	People v. Centers, 377 N.W.2d 4 (1985)
	People v. McIntosh, 376 N.W.2d 653 (1985)
	People v. Reese, 385 N.W.2d 722 (Mich. App. 1986)
Minnesota	*State v. Mack*, 292 N.W.2d 764 (1980)
	State v. Koehler, 312 N.W.2d 108 (1981)
	State v. Blanchard, 315 N.W.2d 427 (1982)
	Rodriquez v. State, 345 N.W.2d 781 (Minn. App. 1984)
	Matter of J.R.D., 342 N.W.2d 162 (Minn. App. 1984)
	State v. Ture, 353 N.W.2d 502 (1984)
Mississippi	*House v. State*, 445 So.2d 815 (1984)
Missouri	*State v. Greer*, 609 S.W.2d 423 (Mo. App. 1980)
	State v. Little, 674 S.W.2d 541 (1984)
Montana	none
Nebraska	*State v. Patterson*, 331 N.W.2d 500 (1983)
	State v. Levering, 331 N.W.2d 505 (1983)
	State v. Palmer, 313 N.W.2d 648 (1981)

Nevada	none
New Hampshire	none
New Jersey	*State v. Hurd*, 432 A.2d 86 (1981)
New Mexico	*State v. Beachum*, 643 P.2d 246 (N.M. App. 1982) *State v. Hutchinson*, 661 P.2d 1315 (1983) *State v. Clark*, 722 P.2d 685 (N.M. App. 1986)
New York	*People v. Hughes*, 453 N.E.2d 484 (N.Y. App. 1983)
North Carolina	*State v. Peoples*, 319 S.E.2d 177 (1984)
North Dakota	*State v. Pusch*, 46 N.W.2d 508 (1950) *State v. Brown*, 337 N.W.2d 138 (1983)
Ohio	*State v. Maurer*, 473 N.E.2d 768 (1984) *State v. Weston*, 475 N.E.2d 805 (Ohio App. 1984)
Oklahoma	*Jones v. State*, 542 P.2d 1316 (Okla. Cr. App. 1975) *Robison v. State*, 677 P.2d 1080 (Okla. Cr. App. 1984) *Harmon v. State*, 700 P.2d 212 (Okla. Cr. App. 1985) *Standridge v. State*, 701 P.2d 761 (Okla. Cr. App. 1985) *Stafford v. State*, 731 P.2d 1372 (Okla. Cr. App. 1987)
Oregon	*State v. Jorgensen*, 492 P.2d 312 (Or. App. 1971) *State v. King*, 733 P.2d 472 (Or. App. 1987) Or. Rev. Stat. sec. 136.675 (1984)
Pennsylvania	*Commonwealth v. Nazarovitch*, 436 A.2d 170 (1981) *Commonwealth v. Taylor*, 439 A.2d 805 (Pa. Super. 1982) *Commonwealth v. Smoyer*, 476 A.2d 1304 (1984)
Rhode Island	none
South Carolina	*State v. Pierce*, 207 S.E.2d 414 (1974)
South Dakota	none
Tennessee	*State v. Glebock*, 616 S.W.2d 897 (Tenn. Cr. App. 1981)
Texas	*Zani v. State*, 679 S.W.2d 144 (Tex. App. 6 Dist. 1984)

	Walters v. State, 680 S.W.2d 60 (Tex. App. 7 Dist. 1984)
	Vester v. State, 713 S.W.2d 920 (Tex. Cr. App. 1986)
Utah	*State v. Tuttle,* No. 20068 (Utah April 12, 1989) (LEXUS, Utah library, Utah file).
Vermont	none
Virginia	*Greenfield v. Commonwealth,* 204 S.E.2d 414 (1974)
	Hopkins v. Commonwealth, 337 S.E.2d 264 (1985)
Washington	*State v. Martin,* 684 P.2d 651 (1984)
	State v. Coe, 684 P.2d 668 (1984)
	State v. Laureano, 682 P.2d 889 (1984)
	State v. Yapp, 726 P.2d 1003 (Wash. App. 1986)
West Virginia	none
Wisconsin	*State v. Armstrong,* 329 N.W.2d 386 (1982)
Wyoming	*Chapman v. State,* 638 P.2d 1280 (1982)
	Gee v. State, 662 P.2d 103 (1983)
	Pote v. State, 695 P.2d 617 (1985)
	Haselhuhn v. State, 727 P.2d 280 (1986)

Appendix 10B
Criteria for the Admissibility of Hypnotically Refreshed Testimony

Federal Courts

1st Circuit	Admissible
2nd Circuit	Admissible
4th Circuit	Admissible
5th Circuit	Admissible
6th Circuit	With safeguards
7th Circuit	Admissible
8th Circuit	With safeguards
9th Circuit	Admissible

State Courts

Alabama[a]	Prehypnosis
Alaska	Prehypnosis
Arizona	Prehypnosis
Arkansas	Prehypnosis

[a] Specifically, the *Prewitt* court held that it was not improper for the trial court to have excluded the witness's hypnotically induced recollections in the absence of proof

California	Prehypnosis
Colorado	With safeguards
Connecticut	Admissible
Delaware	Per se inadmissible
DC	No controlling rule
Florida	Prehypnosis
Georgia	Prehypnosis
Hawaii	Prehypnosis
Idaho	With safeguards
Illinois[b]	Prehypnosis
Indiana	Prehypnosis
Iowa	Prehypnosis
Kansas[c]	Prehypnosis
Kentucky	No controlling rule
Louisiana[d]	Admissible
Maine[e]	No controlling rule
Maryland	Prehypnosis

---

that such testimony either satisfied the Frye test or was generated under circumstances warranting the inference that the recollections were reliable. The court declined to address whether, as a matter of law, hypnotically refreshed testimony was admissible, stating that it had to wait until the issue was fully litigated in the trial court and presented on appeal.

[b] Although the Illinois Supreme Court held in *Wilson* that witnesses may testify concerning their prehypnosis recollections, it specifically declined to determine whether hypnotically enhanced testimony was admissible. Illinois appellate court opinions on this matter are inconsistent. See, for example, *Smrekar, Byas, Cohoon,* and *Zayas*.

[c] These state courts have held that the substance of a hypnosis session cannot be admitted to prove the truth of the matter asserted.

[d] In *Wren* the Louisiana Supreme Court indicated that the witness's testimony would be admitted, since it was no different than it would have been if his memory had not been hypnotically refreshed. This specific finding, that pre- and posthypnotic memories were the same, has been made in all subsequent cases in which the issue has been addressed (see, e.g., Goutro, Porretto, and White).

[e] In *Commeau* the Maine Supreme Court considered whether hypnotizing a victim during the police investigation of a crime rendered her identification of the defendant unnecessarily suggestive (and determined that it did not), but it has not yet addressed the issue of whether hypnotically refreshed testimony is admissible.

Appendix 361

Massachusetts	Prehypnosis
Michigan[c]	Prehypnosis
Minnesota[f]	Prehypnosis
Mississippi[c]	With safeguards
Missouri	With safeguards
Montana	No controlling rule
Nebraska	Prehypnosis
Nevada	No controlling rule
New Hampshire	No controlling rule
New Jersey	With safeguards
New Mexico	With safeguards
New York	Prehypnosis
North Carolina	Prehypnosis
North Dakota[c]	Admissible
Ohio[g]	Prehypnosis
Oklahoma[c]	Prehypnosis
Oregon[h]	Admissible
Pennsylvania[i]	Prehypnosis

[f] Although in *Ture* the Minnesota Supreme Court stated that "[t]his court has consistently adhered to the rule of general inadmissibility of hypnotically induced testimony in criminal cases" (p. 513), a statement that seems inconsistent with its holdings in *Mack, Blanchard, Koehler,* and *Ture,* the Minnesota Court of Appeals in *Rodriguez* clarified this anomaly by asserting that the supreme court's standard "is interpreted to exclude from trial only those recollections that are recalled for the first time during the hypnosis" (p. 785).

[g] The Ohio Supreme Court in *Maurer* held that the trial court properly allowed a witness to testify about matters recalled and related prior to and independent of hypnosis but declined to address whether hypnotically refreshed testimony was admissible. This court declined to review the decision in *Weston,* in which this issue had been addressed by the Ohio Court of Appeals for Clermont County, and thus left standing the appellate court's opinion that hypnotically refreshed testimony may be admissible if the *Hurd* standards are applied to the hypnosis session.

[h] Admissible by case law in 1971 and by statute (with safeguards) from 1977 on. Statute applied in *State v. Luther,* 663 P.2d 1261 (Or. App. 1983).

[i] In *Smoyer* the Pennsylvania Supreme Court extended the holdings of *Nazarovitch* and *Taylor* to provide the following guidelines under which prehypnotic memories may be admitted: "[W]henever a person previously hypnotized is offered as a witness, the

Rhode Island	No controlling rule	Totals (States):
South Carolina[c]	No controlling rule	Per se inadmissible—1
South Dakota	No controlling rule	Admissible—6
Tennessee	With safeguards	With safeguards—8
Texas	Admissible	Prehypnosis—25
Utah	Prehypnosis	No controlling rule—11
Vermont	No controlling rule	
Virginia[c,j]	Prehypnosis	
Washington	Prehypnosis	
West Virginia	No controlling rule	
Wisconsin[k]	With safeguards	
Wyoming[l]	Admissible	

---

offering party must so advise the court, and show that the testimony to be presented was established and existed previous to any hypnotic process; that the person conducting the hypnotic session must be trained in the process and is neutral of any connection with the issue or the parties; and, the trial judge shall instruct the jury that the testimony of a witness previously hypnotized should be carefully scrutinized and received with caution" (p. 1308).

[j] The Virginia Supreme Court did not address the admissibility issue of hypnotically refreshed testimony but, rather, held that the trial court did not abuse its discretion by allowing a witness to testify with respect to his prehypnotic memories.

[k] The Wisconsin safeguards are substantially different from the *Hurd* standards: "In determining whether events which occurred during the hypnosis session are such as to render any subsequent statements by the hypnotized subject unreliable, the trial court should examine the session with two tests in mind. First, there should be a determination of whether there was unnecessary suggestiveness in the hypnotic process. Second, the court should take into account the fact that some confabulation may occur during hypnosis and thus the court should determine whether, under the totality of the circumstances of the information seeking process, the post-hypnotic statements of the witness are reliable" (*Armstrong*, p. 396).

In Armstrong, the witness's pre- and posthypnosis recollections were substantially the same. The question remains whether this court would find any posthypnosis recollections unreliable simply because they differed from those prior to hypnosis.

[l] It is difficult to determine whether Wyoming belongs in this category or with those states allowing testimony pertaining to only prehypnosis memory. In *Chapman* the Wyoming Supreme Court stated that an attack on credibility is the proper method to determine the value of the testimony of a previously hypnotized witness. Rather than an attack on the competency of such testimony, a significant component of this court's determination was that the trial courts in *Gee*, *Pote*, and *Haselhuhn* did not err in allowing previously hypnotized witnesses to testify by finding that the pre- and posthypnotic recollections were the same.

Appendix 10C
Cases/Statutes Determining the Admissibility of Evidence Derived from Polygraphy

Federal Courts

1st Circuit	*United States v. Winter,* 663 F.2d 112 (1981)
4th Circuit	*United States v. Webster,* 639 F.2d 174 (1981)
5th Circuit	*United States v. Clark,* 598 F.2d 969 (1979)
6th Circuit	*United States v. Fife,* 573 F.2d 369 (1976)
7th Circuit	*McMorris v. Israel,* 643 F.2d 458 (1981)
	United States v. Black, 684 F.2d 481 (1982)
8th Circuit	*United States v. Alexander,* 526 F.2d 161 (1975)
9th Circuit[a]	*United States v. Marshall,* 526 F.2d 1349 (1975)
	United States v. Flores, 540 F.2d 432 (1976)
	United States v. McIntyre, 582 F.2d 1221 (1978)
	United States v. Glover, 596 F.2d 857 (1979)
	United States v. Estrada-Lewis, 651 F.2d 1261 (1980)
	United States v. Falsia, 724 F.2d 1339 (1983)
	Brown v. Darcy, 783 F.2d 1389 (1986)

[a] Typical of these opinions is *United States v. Marshall,* which states, in part, "The district court can consider that introduction of the polygraph evidence will inject a time-consuming, potentially prejudicial and perhaps confusing collateral issue into the trial" (p. 1360).

10th Circuit	*United States v. Hunter,* 672 F.2d 815 (1982)
11th Circuit	*United States v. Beck,* 729 F.2d 1329 (1984)
	United States v. Hilton, 772 F.2d 783 (1985)

State Courts

Alabama	*Wynn v. State,* 423 So.2d 294 (Ala. Ct. App. 1982)
	Ex parte Clements, 447 So.2d 695 (1984)
Alaska	*Pulakis v. State,* 476 P.2d 474 (1970)
	Leonard v. State, 655 P.2d 766 (Alaska Ct. App. 1982)
	Wilkie v. State, 715 P.2d 1199 (Alaska Ct. App. 1986)
Arizona	*State v. Treadaway,* 568 P.2d 1061 (1977)
	State v. Madsen, 609 P.2d 1046 (1980)
	Hyder v. Superior Court, 617 P.2d 1152 (1980)
	State v. Zuch, 658 P.2d 162 (1982)
	State v. Montes, 667 P.2d 191 (1983)
	Matter of Swartz, 686 P.2d 1236 (1984)
Arkansas	*Holcomb v. State,* 594 S.W.2d 22 (1980)
	Wilson v. State, 639 S.W.2d 45 (1982)
California	Cal. Evid. Code sec. 351.1 (West 1983 supp.)
Colorado	*People v. Anderson,* 637 P.2d 354 (1981)
	People v. Aalbu, 696 P.2d 796 (1985)
	People v. Robinson, 713 P.2d (1333 Colo. App. 1985)
Connecticut	*State v. Saia,* 372 A.2d 144 (1976)
	State v. Miller, 522 A.2d 249 (1987)
Delaware	*Thompson v. State,* 399 A.2d 194 (1979)
	Hughes v. State, 490 A.2d 1034 (1985)
DC	*Smith v. United States,* 389 A.2d 1356 (D.C. App. 1978)
Florida	*Coney v. State,* 258 So.2d 497 (Fla. App. 3 Dist. 1974)
	Moore v. State, 299 So.2d 119 (Fla. App. 3 Dist. 1974)

	Askary v. State, 294 So.2d 33 (Fla. App. 3 Dist. 1974)
	Codie v. State, 313 So.2d 754 (1975)
	State v. Cunningham, 324 So.2d 173 (Fla. App. 3 Dist. 1975)
	Young v. State, 387 So.2d 512 (Fla. App. 1 Dist. 1980)
	Waterman v. State, 406 So.2d 1250 (Fla. App. 5 Dist. 1981)
	Green v. State, 437 So.2d 784 (Fla. App. 2 Dist. 1983)
	Brown v. State, 452 So.2d 122 (Fla. App. 1 Dist. 1984)
	Howard v. State, 458 So.2d 407 (Fla. App. 4 Dist. 1984)
	Anderson v. State, 504 So.2d 1270 (Fla. App. 1 Dist. 1986)
Georgia	*State v. Chambers*, 239 So.2d 324 (1977)
	Williams v. State, 250 S.E.2d 848 (Ga. App. 1978)
	Jordan v. State, 285 S.E.2d 71 (Ga. App. 1981)
	Baxter v. State, 284 S.E.2d 649 (Ga. App. 1981)
	Golphin v. State, 288 S.E.2d 692 (Ga. App. 1982)
	Martin v. State, 292 S.E.2d 864 (Ga. App. 1982)
	Garmon v. State, 307 S.E.2d 298 (Ga. App. 1983)
	Davis v. State, 324 S.E.2d 551 (Ga. App. 1984)
	Brown v. State, 333 S.E.2d 124 (Ga. App. 1985)
	Bosworth v. State, 342 S.E.2d 22 (Ga. App. 1986)
	Williams v. State, 345 S.E.2d 59 (Ga. App. 1986)
Hawaii	*State v. Chang*, 374 P.2d 5 (1962)
	State v. Antone, 615 P.2d 101 (1980)
Idaho	none
Illinois	*People v. Baynes*, 430 N.E.2d 1070 (1981)
Indiana	*Owens v. State*, 373 N.E.2d 913 (Ind.App. 1978)
Iowa	*State v. Fisher*, 279 N.W.2d 265 (1979)
Kansas	*State v. Roach*, 576 P.2d 1082 (1978)

	State v. Crossman, 624 P.2d 461 (1981)
	State v. Crispin, 671 P.2d 502 (1983)
	State v. Wise, 697 P.2d 1295 (1985)
	State v. Martin, 699 P.2d 486 (1985)
	State v. Sanford, 699 P.2d 506 (1985)
	State v. Mason, 708 P.2d 963 (1985)
	State v. McNaught, 713 P.2d 457 (1986)
Kentucky	*Workman v. Commonwealth*, 580 S.W.2d 206 (1979)
Louisiana	*State v. Catanese*, 368 So.2d 975 (1979)
	State ex rel. Fields v. Maggio, 368 So.2d 1016 (1979)
Maine	*State v. Trafton*, 425 A.2d 1320 (1981)
Maryland	*Smith v. State*, 318 A.2d 568 (Md. Ct. Spec. App. 1974)
	Akonom v. State, 394 A.2d 1213 (Md. Ct. Spec. App. 1978)
	Kelley v. State, 418 A.2d 217 (1980)
	Guesfeird v. State, 480 A.2d 800 (1984)
	Johnson v. State, 495 A.2d 1 (1985)
Massachusetts	*Commonwealth v. A Juvenile* (No. 1), N.E.2d 120 (1974)
	Commonwealth v. Vitello, 381 N.E.2d 582 (1978)
	Commonwealth v. Wick, 506 N.E.2d 857 (Mass. 1987)
Michigan	*People v. Davis*, 72 N.W.2d 269 (1955)
	People v. Levelston, 221 N.W.2d 235 (1974)
	People v. Barbara, 255 N.W.2d 171 (1977)
	People v. Williams, 333 N.W.2d 577 (Mich. App. 1983)
	People v. Ray, 401 N.W.2d 296 (Mich. App. 1986)
	People v. Triplett, 413 N.W.2d 791 (Mich. App. 1987)
Minnesota	*State v. Goblirsch*, 246 N.W.2d 12 (1976)
	State v. Litzau, 377 N.W.2d 53 (Minn. App. 1985)
	State v. Anderson, 379 N.W.2d 70 (1985)

Mississippi	*Lee v. State*, 338 So.2d 395 (1976)
Missouri	*State v. Stowers*, 580 S.W.2d 516 (1979)
Montana	Mont. Code Ann. sec. 37-62-302 (1983)
	State v. Beachman, 616 P.2d 337 (1980)
Nebraska	*State v. Steinmark*, 239 N.W.2d 495 (1976)
Nevada	*Corbett v. State*, 584 P.2d 704 (1978)
	Aguilar v. State, 639 P.2d 533 (1982)
	Santillanes v. State, 714 P.2d 184 (1986)
New Hampshire	*State v. French*, 403 A.2d 424 (1979)
New Jersey	*State v. McDavitt*, 297 A.2d 849 (1972)
	State v. Powell, 484 A.2d 659 (1984)
	State v. Fraction, 503 A.2d 336 (N.J. Super. A.D. 1985)
	State v. Hollander, 493 A.2d 563 (N.J. Super. A.D. 1985)
	State v. McMahon, 524 A.2d 1348 (N.J. Super. L. 1986)
	State v. Capone, 522 A.2d 451 (N.J. Super. A.D. 1987)
New Mexico	*State v. Dorsey*, 539 P.2d 204 (1975)
	State v. Bell, 560 P.2d 925 (1977)
	State v. Brionez, 573 P.2d 224 (N.M. App. 1977)
	State v. Fuentes, 577 P.2d 452 (N.M. App. 1978)
	State v. Gallegos, 588 P.2d 1045 (N.M. App. 1978)
	State v. Urioste, 617 P.2d 156 (N.M. App. 1980)
	State v. Anthony, 676 P.2d 262 (1983)
	Tafoya v. Baca, 702 P.2d 1001 (1985)
	N.M. Rules of Crim. Proc., Dist. Cts. Rules 501 & 502
	N.M. Rules of Evidence, Rule 707
New York	*People v. Forte*, 18 N.E.2d 31 (1938)
North Carolina	*State v. Grier*, 300 S.E.2d 351 (1983)
North Dakota	*State v. Pusch*, 46 N.W.2d 508 (1950)
Ohio	*State v. Souel*, 372 N.E.2d 1318 (1978)

Oklahoma	*Carson v. State,* 529 P.2d 499 (Okla. Crim. App. 1974)
	Fulton v. State, 541 P.2d 871 (Okla. Crim. App. 1975)
	Craig v. State, 562 P.2d 887 (Okla. Crim. App. 1977)
	Walton v. State, 565 P.2d 716 (Okla. Crim. App. 1977)
	Birdsong v. State, 649 P.2d 786 (Okla. Crim. App. 1982)
	Young v. State, 670 P.2d 591 (Okla. Crim. App. 1983)
	Sheppard v. State, 670 P.2d 6004 (Okla. Crim. App. 1983)
	Weatherly v. State, 733 P.2d 1331 (Okla. Crim. App. 1987)
Oregon	*State v. Clifton,* 531 P.2d 256 (1975)
	State v. Green, 531 P.2d 245 (1975)
	Sandlin v. OWCC, 559 P.2d 1308 (1977)
	State v. Thompson, 567 P.2d 132 (Or. App. 1977)
	State v. Sheehan, 600 P.2d 971 (Or. App. 1979)
	State v. Skelton, 599 P.2d 1171 (Or. App. 1979)
	State v. Johnson, 615 P.2d 1181 (Or. App. 1980)
	State v. Kersting, 623 P.2d 1095 (Or. App. 1981)
	State v. Wardrip, 637 P.2d 219 (Or. App. 1981)
	State v. Bodenschatz, 662 P.2d 1 (Or. App. 1983)
	State v. Middleton, 668 P.2d 371 (1983)
	State v. Brown, 687 P.2d 751 (1984)
	State ex rel. Gerttula v. Hunnicutt, 687 P.2d 777 (1984)
	State v. LaStair, 726 P.2d 1193 (Or. App. 1986)
	State v. Tavernier, 555 P.2d 481 (Or. App. 1986)
	State v. Lyon, 733 P.2d 41 (Or. App. 1987)
Pennsylvania	*Commonwealth ex rel. Riccio v. Dilworth,* 115 A.2d 865 (Pa. Super. 1955)
	Commonwealth v. Gee, 354 A.2d 875 (1976)

	Commonwealth v. Pfender, 421 A.2d 791 (Pa. Super. 1980)
	Commonwealth v. Brockington, 455 A.2d 627 (1983)
	Commonwealth v. Nelson, 456 A.2d 1383 (Pa. Super. 1983)
	Commonwealth v. Watts, 465 A.2d 1288 (Pa. Super. 1983)
	Commonwealth v. Henderson, 472 A.2d 211 (Pa. Super. 1984)
	Commonwealth v. Rodriguez, 495 A.2d 569 (Pa. Super. 1985)
Rhode Island	none
South Carolina	*State v. Britt*, 111 S.E.2d 669 (1959)
South Dakota	*State v. O'Connor*, 194 N.W.2d 246 (1972)
	State v. Watson, 248 N.W.2d 398 (1976)
	State v. Muetze, 368 N.W.2d 575 (1985)
Tennessee	*Marable v. State*, 313 S.W.2d 451 (1958)
Texas	*Robinson v. State*, 550 S.W.2d 54 (Tex. Cr. App. 1977)
Utah	*State v. Collins*, 612 P.2d 775 (1980)
	State v. Abel, 600 P.2d 994 (1979)
	State v. Rebeterano, 681 P.2d 1265 (1984)
Vermont	none
Virginia	*Jones v. Commonwealth*, 204 S.E.2d 247 (1974)
Washington	*State v. Ross*, 497 P.2d 1343 (Wash. App. 1972)
	State v. Woo, 527 P.2d 271 (1974)
	State v. Descoteaux, 614 P.2d 179 (1980)
	State v. Sutherland, 617 P.2d 1010 (1980)
	State v. Grisby, 647 P.2d 6 (1982)
	State v. Bartholomew, 654 P.2d 1170 (1982)
	State v. Renfro, 639 P.2d 737 (1982)
	State v. Ellison, 676 P.2d 531 (Wash. App. 1984)
	State v. Rupe, 683 P.2d 571 (1984)

	State v. Fondren, 701 P.2d 810 (Wash. App. 1985)
	State v. Anderson, 702 P.2d 481 (Wash. App. 1985)
	State v. Yapp, 726 P.2d 1003 (Wash. App. 1986)
West Virginia	*State v. Frazier*, 252 S.E.2d 39 (1979)
Wisconsin	*State v. Dean*, 307 N.W.2d 628 (1981)
Wyoming	*Cullin v. State*, 565 P.2d 445 (1977)
	Hopkinson v. State, 632 P.2d 79 (1981)
	Schmunk v. State, 714 P.2d 724 (1986)

Appendix 10D
Criteria for the Admissibility of Evidence Derived from Polygraphy

Federal Courts

1st Circuit[a]	Admissible
2nd Circuit	Inadmissible
4th Circuit[a]	Admissible
5th Circuit	Inadmissible
6th Circuit	Inadmissible
7th Circuit[a]	Admissible
8th Circuit	Admissible with stipulations
9th Circuit[a]	Admissible
10th Circuit	Inadmissible
11th Circuit	Inadmissible

[a] In spite of the fact that these appellate courts have stated that evidence derived from use of the polygraph is admissible in the trial court's discretion, the trial courts in these cases have almost uniformly denied its admissibility.

State Courts

Alabama	Admissible with stipulations
Alaska	Inadmissible with stipulations
Arizona	Admissible with stipulations
Arkansas	Admissible with stipulations
California	Admissible with stipulations
Colorado	Inadmissible with stipulations
Connecticut	Inadmissible
Delaware	Admissible with stipulations
DC	Inadmissible
Florida	Admissible with stipulations
Georgia	Admissible with stipulations
Hawaii	Inadmissible
Idaho	No controlling rule
Illinois	Inadmissible with stipulations
Indiana	Admissible with stipulations
Iowa	Admissible with stipulations
Kansas	Admissible with stipulations
Kentucky	Inadmissible
Louisiana	Inadmissible with stipulations
Maine	Inadmissible
Maryland	Inadmissible with stipulations
Massachusetts	Admissible
Michigan[b]	Inadmissible with stipulations
Minnesota	Inadmissible with stipulations
Mississippi	Inadmissible
Missouri	Admissible with stipulations
Montana	Inadmissible
Nebraska	Inadmissible

[b] Polygraphy results have also been held inadmissible even with a prior written stipulation in civil cases; see *Stone v. Earp*, 50 N.W.2d 172 (1951).

Nevada	Admissible with stipulations
New Hampshire	Inadmissible
New Jersey	Admissible with stipulations
New Mexico	Admissible
New York	Inadmissible
North Carolina	Inadmissible with stipulations
North Dakota	Inadmissible
Ohio	Admissible with stipulations
Oklahoma	Inadmissible with stipulations
Oregon	Admissible with stipulations
Pennsylvania	Inadmissible with stipulations
Rhode Island	No controlling rule
South Carolina[c]	Inadmissible
South Dakota[d]	Inadmissible
Tennessee	Inadmissible
Texas	Inadmissible with stipulations
Utah	Admissible with stipulations
Vermont	No controlling rule
Virginia	Inadmissible
Washington	Admissible with stipulations
West Virginia	Inadmissible with stipulations
Wisconsin	Inadmissible with stipulations
Wyoming	Admissible with stipulations
Totals (States):	Admissible—1
	Inadmissible—16
	Admissible with stipulations—19
	Inadmissible with stipulations—12
	No controlling rule—3

[c] In civil case *Rutledge v. St. Paul Fire & Marine Ins. Co.*, 334 S.E.2d 131 (S.C. App. 1985), the polygraphy results were held inadmissible even with a prior written stipulation.

[d] Polygraphy results were held inadmissible in civil case *Sabaq v. Continental S.D.*, 374 N.W.2d 349 (1985).

Appendix 10E
State Statutory Licensure Requirements for Polygraphers

Alabama	Ala. Code sec. 34-25-1 *et seq.* (1985)
Alaska	none
Arizona	Ariz. Rev. Stat. Ann. sec. 32-2701 *et seq.* (1986)
Arkansas	Ark. Stat. Ann. sec. 71-2201 *et seq.* (1979)
California	Cal. Bus. & Prof. Code sec. 9300 *et seq.* (West 1975)
Colorado	none
Connecticut	none
Delaware	none
DC	none
Florida	Fla. Stat. Ann. sec. 493.561 *et seq.* (West 1981)
Georgia	Ga. Code Ann. sec. 43-36-1 *et seq.* (1984)
Hawaii	none
Idaho	none
Illinois	Ill. Ann. Stat. ch. 111 sec. 2401 *et seq.* (Smith-Hurd 1978)
Indiana	Ind. Code Ann. sec. 25-30-2-1 *et seq.* (Burns 1982)

Iowa	none
Kansas	Kan. Stat. Ann. sec. 75-740 *et seq.* (1984)
Kentucky	Ky. Rev. Stat. Ann. sec. 329.010 *et seq.* (Michie 1983)
Louisiana	La. Rev. Stat. Ann. sec. 37:2831 *et seq.* (West 1988)
Maine	Me. Rev. Stat. Ann. sec. tit. 32 sec. 7151 *et seq.* (1988)
Maryland	none
Massachusetts	Mass. Ann. Laws ch. 147, sec. 22–29 (Law. Co-op., 1981 & Supp. 1988)
Michigan	Mich. Comp. Laws sec. 338.1701 *et seq.* (1982)
Minnesota	none
Mississippi	Miss. Code Ann. sec. 73-29-1 *et seq.* (1972)
Missouri	none
Montana	Mont. Code Ann. sec. 37-62-101 *et seq.* (1987)
Nebraska	Neb. Rev. Stat. sec. 81-1901 *et seq.* (1981)
Nevada	Nev. Rev. Stat. sec. 648.005 *et seq.* (1986)
New Hampshire	none
New Jersey	none
New Mexico	N.M. Stat. Ann. sec. 61-26-1 *et seq.* (1978)
	N.M. Rules of Evidence, Rule 707
New York	none
North Carolina	none
North Dakota	N.D. Cent. Code sec. 43-31-01 *et seq.* (1978)
Ohio	none
Oklahoma	Okla. Stat. Ann. tit. 59 sec. 1451 *et seq.* (West 1971)
Oregon	Or. Rev. Stat. sec. 703.010 *et seq.* (1987)
Pennsylvania	none
Rhode Island	none
South Carolina	S.C. Code Ann. sec. 40-53-10 *et seq.* (Law. Co-op 1976)
South Dakota	S.D. Codified Laws Ann. sec. 36-30-1 *et seq.* (1986)

Tennessee	Tenn. Code Ann. sec. 62-27-101 *et seq.* (1986)
Texas	Tex. Rev. Civ. Stat. Ann. art. 4413 (29cc) (Vernon 1976)
Utah	Utah Code Ann. sec. 34-37-1 *et seq.* (1974)
Vermont	Vt. Stat. Ann. tit. 26 sec. 2901 *et seq.* (1975)
Virginia	Va. Code sec. 54-916 *et seq.* (1982)
Washington	none
West Virginia	W. Va. Code sec. 21-5-5c and 21-5-5d (1985)
Wisconsin	none
Wyoming	none

Author Index

Abbell, M., 283, 289, 290
Abrams, S., 286, 290
Adams, A. J., 11, 39
Ainsworth, D., 284, 291
Ainsworth, P. B., 67, 68, 87
Allen, S. N., 170, 182
Allison, H., 53, 87
Allport, 19
Alper, A., 15, 40
Amador, M., 211, 214
Aman, C., 201, 215
Amsterdam, A., 128, 146
Andriks, J. L., 22, 43
Arntzen, F., 219, 220, 221, 222, 223, 224, 225, 226, 227, 231, 233, 235, 237, 238, 239, 241, 244
Arons, H., 155, 176, 180
Ash, P., 266, 292
Augustynek, A., 163, 180
Ault, R. L., 155, 176, 180
Avetissian, I. V., 214

Baddeley, A., 4, 13, 39, 42, 164, 180
Bahrick H. 27, 39, 164, 180
Bailis, K., 85, 90
Baltes, P. B., 20, 39
Baratz, D., 56, 94

Barber, J., 160, 181
Barber, T. X., 160, 163, 181
Bard, M., 178, 181
Barland, G. H., 247, 252, 253, 259, 261, 263, 265, 266, 275, 281, 283, 287, 289, 291, 295
Barrett, K. C., 307, 330
Batten, G., 62, 91
Beidleman, W. B., 163, 190
Bekerian, D. A., 30, 38, 39, 118, 122, 199, 213
Ben-Shakhar, C., 281, 291
Benderly, H. P., 160, 167, 181
Bennett, P., 54, 64, 87
Berkun, M. M., 15, 39
Bernheim, A. M., 159, 181
Bersh, P. J., 265, 291
Bialek, H. M., 15, 39
Biederman, I., 76, 87
Bird, C., 22, 40
Blake, R., 8, 10, ll, 44
Blevins, J., 11, 41
Block, E. B., 176, 181
Blum, H., 311, 329
Boisvenu, G. A., 277, 281, 284, 293
Bok, S., 301, 329
Boone, S. M., 8, 43

Borchard, E. M., 65, 87
Bothwell, R. K., 17, 36, 40, 44, 72, 77, 80, 87, 90, 93, 121, 122
Bowers, J. M., 30, 38, 39, 199, 213,
Bowers, K. S., 167, 181
Boychuk, T., 241, 243, 244
Bradley, M. T., 257, 284, 291
Brandon, R., 65, 87
Brandt, D. R., 317, 329
Bregman, N. J., 165, 181
Brigham, J. C., 17, 36, 40, 44, 72, 74, 77, 80, 87, 90, 93, 101, 121, 122
Broadbent, D. E., 161, 181
Brown, A., 201, 214
Brown, M. R., 19, 40
Brown, R., 160, 181
Brown, R. J., 178, 181
Bruce, A., 21, 41
Brunn, A. D., 163, 181
Buckhout, R., 8, 15, 40, 71, 87, 99, 122, 164, 166, 181, 183
Buckley, J. P., 266, 295
Bull, G., 300, 329
Bull, R., 66, 78, 81, 82, 84, 85, 87, 88, 93
Burcart, J. M., 9, 44
Burns, H. J., 29, 30, 31, 42
Burns, T. E., 12, 15, 42
Butterfield, E. L., 160, 185
Byrd, M., 20, 40

Cady, H. M., 22, 40, 103, 122
Callot, R., 194, 214
Calverly, D. S., 163, 181
Campbell, D. T., 238, 244
Campos, J. J., 307, 330
Cash, W. S., 26, 40
Cattell, J. M., 9, 40
Cavender, J., 11, 39
Ceci, S. J., 19, 40
Cerri, A. M., 279, 280, 284, 293
Chance, J. E., 81, 90
Chandrasekaren, B., 60, 90
Charcot, J. M., 159, 181

Cheek, D. B., 157, 161, 162, 181
Chern, S., 15, 40
Chertok, L., 159, 181
Christianson, S. A., 13, 40
Christie, D., 55, 61, 88
Clifford, B. R., vii, 11, 22, 24, 40, 47–95, 66, 78, 81, 82, 84, 85, 86, 87, 88, 93, 99, 119, 123
Cohen, G., 198, 210, 214
Colella, M. J., 317, 332
Comish, S., 58, 88
Conn, J. H., 157, 158, 160, 182
Conover, J., 85, 90
Convis, F., 140, 146
Conway, M. A., 118, 122
Cook, M. R., 283, 284, 296
Cook, T. D., 238, 244
Cooper, L. M., 163, 182
Cooper, S. D., 72, 73, 91
Cormack, S. J., 52, 53, 63, 88
Craik, F. I. M., 20, 40, 160, 162, 171, 182
Crawford, H. J., 160, 170, 182
Cutshall, J. L., vii, 15, 16, 45, 50, 68, 95, 97–124, 100, 102, 106, 107, 108, 109, 122, 124

Darnborough, M., 54, 55, 60, 88, 91
Davidson, P. O., 291
Davidson, W. A., 266, 291
Davies, C., 65, 87
Davies, G. M., 27, 38, 40, 44, 47–95, 50, 51, 53, 54, 55, 56, 57, 58, 61, 62, 69, 81, 88, 89, 90, 91, 94, 117, 124, 177, 188
Davies, Graham, vii
Davis, T., 302, 330
Dawson, M. E., 261, 291
Deckert, G. H., 157, 190
Deffenbacher, K., 15, 36, 40, 41, 48, 80, 87, 89, 165, 182
DeLuce, S. M., 216
Denot, H., 86, 88
Dent, H., 69, 89

DePaulo, B. M., 298, 299, 302, 302, 310, 313, 315, 330, 331
DePiano, F. A., 163, 182
Deregowaski, J. B., 74, 90
Dettenborn, H., 219, 221, 224, 225, 226, 227, 228, 229, 230, 244
Devine, P. G., 38, 43, 66, 70, 72, 73, 74, 75, 76, 84, 93, 213, 215
Devlin, P., 65, 66, 79, 89
Dhanens, T. P., 163, 182
Diamond, B. L., 157, 163, 164, 165, 166, 182
Dinges, D. F., 164, 179, 183, 185, 215
Dodson, J. D., 14, 45
Domingo, F., 52, 54, 55, 89
Doob, A., 76, 89
Dorcus, R. M., 155, 161, 163, 182
Douce, R. G., 163, 176, 185
Doyle, J. M., vii, 128, 133, 135, 137, 140, 146, 147
Driver, R. E., 298, 332
Du Maurier, G., 156, 182
Duchnowski, A., 298, 331
Duncan, E. M., 20, 41
Dunn, J. G., 28, 41
Dunning, D., 82, 89, 135, 146
Duval, C., 50, 55, 59, 60, 91
Dzieszkowski, P. A., 176, 184

Eagly, A. H., 22, 41
Easterbrook, J. A., 22, 41
Ebbesen, E. B., 99, 121, 123
Ebbinghaus, H. E., 25, 26, 41, 97, 122
Edmonston, W. E., 167, 182
Edwards, J., 141, 146
Egan, D., 68, 71, 80, 81, 90
Egeth, H., 99, 123, 139, 147
Ekman, P., viii, 297-332, 298, 299, 300, 301, 303, 306, 308, 312, 313, 314, 317, 323, 330, 331
Ellis, H. D., 21, 27, 38, 40, 41, 44, 50, 51, 54, 55, 56, 58, 61, 69, 74, 80, 81, 88, 89, 90, 94, 117, 124, 177, 188

Ellison, K. W., 164, 183
Ellsworth, 135, 146
Ellsworth, P. C., 35, 44, 82, 89
Erdelyi, M. H., 164, 170, 183
Erickson, M. H., 159, 183
Esplin, P. W., 232, 241, 243, 244, 245
Estabrooks, G. H., 179, 183
Evans, F. J., 161, 163, 183, 184
Eysenck, M. W., 12, 41

Fabricant, E. L., 290, 294
Farrimond, T., 20, 41
Fay, F. B., 286, 293
Ferguson, T. J., 36, 44, 45
Fernandez, A., 38, 41
Ferrara, S. J., 176, 183
Fessler, P. K., 80, 91
Field, K. S., 290, 294
Fischer, R., 161, 167, 183
Fisher, R. P., 22, 41, 119, 122, 163, 166, 168, 169, 173, 177, 183, 191-216, 195, 197, 198, 204, 205, 208, 209, 210, 211, 214
Fisher, Ronald P., viii
Flavell, J. H., 201, 214
Fleet, M. L., 72, 80, 90
Fleming, J. A. E., 279, 280, 284, 293
Fleming, J. S., 277, 281, 284, 293
Fleming, W., 86, 88
Flin, R., 50, 55, 56, 89, 90
Flynn, M. B., 32, 41, 199, 215
Foster, T. E., 167, 188
Fowler, R., 59, 91
Frankel, F., 159, 183
Frankel, F. H., 163, 183
Frankfurter, F., 65, 90
Friesen, W. V., 298, 299, 300, 301, 303, 306, 312, 317, 330, 331
Frijda, N. H., 299, 330
Froehlich, H., 219, 221, 224, 225, 226, 227, 228, 229, 230, 244
Furedy, J. J., 253, 291
Fuse, L. S., 269, 291

Gaines, B., 300, 331
Galanter, E., 161, 185
Gale, A., 247, 291
Gansler, D. A. 163, 172, 173, 177
Gast II, R. S., 52
Gatchel, R. J., 285, 291
Geiselman, R. E., viii, 22, 41, 119, 122, 163, 164, 166, 168, 169, 172, 173, 177, 183, 191–216, 194, 195, 197, 198, 201, 204, 205, 206, 208, 209, 210, 211, 214, 215
Gerhard, D., 32, 44
Giannelli, P. C., 352, 353
Gilbert, J. N., 156, 183
Gillenson, M., 60, 90
Glenberg, A. M., 38, 41
Goetze, H. J., 202, 214
Goldstein, A., 85, 90
Goldstein, A. G., 68, 80, 81, 90
Goldstein, M. S., 167, 183
Goodman, G. S., 19, 20, 41, 201, 202, 215
Gottfredson, G. D., 158, 183
Gottschalk, L. A., 157, 183
Gray, R., 69, 89
Greene, E., ix, 32, 41, 42, 199, 215
Griffin, J. J., 300, 331
Griffin. G. R., 165, 184
Griffith, W. R., 9, 44
Griffiths, A., 51, 90
Griggs, L., 170, 188
Gross, S. R., 138, 146
Gruneberg, M. M., 98, 118, 122, 123, 202, 215
Gudjonsson, G. H., 238, 244, 283, 292
Gustafson, L. A., 287, 292
Guth, M., 43, 201, 215

Haig, N., 60, 90
Hale, S. M., 298, 331
Hall, D., 58, 71, 91
Hare, R. D., 261, 263, 287, 295, 307, 330

Hatton, K. L., 151, 184
Hayano, D. M., 315, 330
Henderson, M. D., 178, 184
Henley, A., 309, 331
Heslegrave, R. J., 253, 291
Heuer, R. J., 319. 330
Hibbard, W. S., 157, 166, 184
Hibler, N. S., 155, 184
Hiland, D. N., 176, 184
Hilgard, E. R., 152, 159, 160, 161, 166, 167, 181, 184
Hilgendorf, E. L., 72, 91
Hirschman, J., 201, 215
Hocking, J. E., 317, 329
Hodes, R. L., 286, 292
Holland, H. L., 22, 41, 119, 122, 163, 166, 168, 169, 173, 177, 183, 195, 197, 198, 204, 205, 210, 214
Hollin, C. R., 11, 40, 81, 88
Holmes, D. L., 20, 43, 201, 215
Homa, G., 52, 59, 91
Honts, C. R., 251, 261, 262, 267, 269, 272, 273, 274, 283, 286, 287, 290, 292, 295
Hood, W., 303, 331
Horney, J., 48, 89
Horowitz, I., 176, 184
Horowitz, S. W., 252, 261, 262, 264, 267, 269, 272, 273, 290, 292, 293, 295,
Horvath, F. S., 265, 266, 288, 290, 292, 296
Hosch, H. M., 72, 73, 80, 91
Hryciw, B., 59, 95
Hull, C. L., 159, 184
Hunter, F. L., 266, 292, 296
Hurd, P. D., 11, 41
Hurvich, L. M., 10, 41
Hutton, L. A., 214

Iacono, W. G., 277, 279, 280, 281, 284, 287, 293, 294
Idzikowski, C., 13, 42
Imwinkelried, E., 140, 146

Author Index

Inbau, F. E., 259, 295
Irving, B. L., 72, 91
Irving, J., 310, 331

Jacoby, L. L., 162, 182
Janet, P., 157, 184
Janisse, M. P., 257, 291
Jenkins, R., 58, 91
Jones, H. P. T., 22, 45
Jurkevich, L. M., 209, 210, 214

Kaplan, N. M., 285, 291
Kassin, S. M., 37, 42
Keating, J. F., 193, 215
Keating, J. P., 23, 39, 42
Keeler, L., 249, 293
Kern, R. P., 15, 39
Key, W. B., 161, 184
Kihlstrom, J. F., 161, 163, 184
Kim, C. K., 163, 166, 173, 177, 179, 190
King, E., 67, 68, 87
King, M. A., 19, 42, 201, 215
Kinsbourne, M., 152, 189
Kircher, J. C., 251, 254, 261, 262, 264, 267, 285, 286, 287, 290, 292, 293, 295
Kirschenbaum, H., 76, 89
Kitson, A., 54, 55, 60, 91
Kleinhauz, M., 176, 184
Kleinmuntz, B., 249, 293
Kline, D., 8, 43
Knight, P., 85, 90
Knott, P. D., 298, 331
Knox, J., 170, 186
Knox, V. J., 171, 188
Koehnken, G., ix, 217–245, 219, 231, 237, 239, 244, 245
Koestner, R., 317, 332
Kofoed, L., 307, 331
Konecni, V. J., 99, 121, 123
Kovac, P., 43, 201, 215
Kozin, M., 13, 43
Krafka, C., 38, 42, 80, 91, 101, 123

Kramer, T. H., 17, 42
Kraut, R. E., 313, 331
Kroger, W. S., 158, 159, 163, 176, 179, 185
Kuehn, L., 49, 91
Kulik, J., 160, 181
Kunen, S., 20, 41

Lachman, J. L., 160, 185
Lachman, R., 160, 185
Lanier, K., 302, 330
Larson, J. A., 249, 293
Lassiter, G. D., 298, 299, 302, 315, 330
Laughery, K., 50, 53, 55, 58, 59, 60, 62, 63, 80, 91, 92, 93, 94
Laurence, J. R., 157, 161, 164, 178, 179, 185, 186
Lavigueur, H., 77, 93
Lazarus, R. S., 304, 331
LeCron, L. M., 162, 181
Leibowitz, H. W., 6, 10, 42
Leippe, M. R., 72, 73, 74, 76, 80, 91, 92, 95
Lenorovitz, D. R., 63, 80, 91, 92
Levin, J., 201, 215
Levine, B., 125, 147
Levine, F. J., 65, 66, 92
Levine, M., 145, 147
Lichtenstein, S., 268, 295
Lindsay, R. C. L., 36, 37, 42, 44, 45, 74, 78, 80, 81, 82, 83, 84, 92, 117, 124,
Linton, M., 26, 27, 42
Lipton, J. P., 21, 34, 42, 103, 123
Littmann, E., 236, 237, 241, 245
Lloyd-Bostock, S. M. A., 99, 119, 123
Lockhart, R. S., 160, 171, 182
Loftus, E. F., ix, 8, 12, 13, 15, 16, 17, 23, 28, 29, 30, 31, 32, 35, 39, 40, 41, 42, 44, 99, 109, 120, 123, 124, 128, 133, 135, 137, 138, 140, 143, 147, 161, 165, 166, 167, 185, 191, 193, 199, 202, 215
Loftus, E. G., 22, 43

Loftus, G. R., 16, 42
Lombroso, C., 247, 293
London, P., 163, 182
Lundy, R. M., 163, 167, 182, 189
Lykken, D. T., 253, 262, 267, 275, 276, 280, 281, 285, 286, 293

Maas, A., 101, 122
Maass, A., 17, 44, 80, 87
Machlovitz, H. R., 164, 172, 173, 183
MacKeith, J. A. C., 238, 244
MacKinnon, D. P., 22, 41, 119, 122, 163, 166, 168, 169, 173, 177, 183, 195, 197, 204, 205, 206, 210, 214, 215
Mackworth, N. H., 16, 43
Macleod, M., 49, 92
MacMillan, J., 307, 331
Madigan, S. A., 97, 124
Malpass, R. S., 38, 43, 66, 70, 72, 73, 74, 75, 76, 77, 84, 93, 213, 215
Manber, M., 39, 42, 193, 215
Marchioni, P. M., 72, 73, 91
Marin, C., 201, 215
Marion, B. V., 43
Markham, R., 55, 90
Marshall, J., 8, 10, 20, 43
Marston, W. M., 249, 293
Mauldin, M., 58, 93
Mayman, M., 163, 185
McAllister, H. A., 165, 181
McCann, T., 170, 188
McCarty, M., 197, 215
McCloskey, M., 30, 38, 43, 99, 123, 139, 147
McConkey, K. M., 163, 185
McCormick. E., 139, 147
McEwan, N. H., 103, 124, 166, 168, 169, 170, 177, 190
McGaugh, J. L., 160, 185
McKenna, J., 99, 123
Mende, L., 206, 215
Menninger, K., 163, 185
Mervis, J., 265. 289, 294
Messo, J., 16, 42

Miller, D. G., 29, 30, 31, 42
Miller, G. A., 161, 185
Miller, G. R., 317, 329
Miller, M., 128, 146
Milne, A., 55, 56, 89
Monks, J., 202, 215
Morris, P. E., 98, 118, 122, 123
Morris, Roberta A., ix, 333–353
Moss, A. J., 26, 40
Mueller, P., 176, 187
Mullaney, R., 307, 331
Munsterberg, H., 77, 93, 120, 123
Murray, D. M., 36, 45, 77, 80, 95
Muscio, B., 35, 43

Naatanen, R., 12, 43
Neisser, U., 97, 123, 161, 162, 164, 167, 177, 185
Nelson, S. A., 180, 185
Newell, A., 97, 123
Nielsen, M. M., 187
Nilsson, L. G., 161, 164, 185
Nogrady, H., 163, 185
Nunnally, J. D., 298, 331

O'Brien, J. B., 62
O'Connor, J., 65, 93
Offermann, J. T., 72, 95
O'Reilly, K. E., 206, 215
Orne, E. C., 164, 179, 183, 185, 215, 283, 284, 296
Orne, M. T., 156, 157, 161, 163, 164, 165, 166, 170, 171, 179, 183, 185, 215, 283, 284, 286, 287, 292, 294, 296
Ostrom, T. M., 71, 74, 76, 91, 95
O'Sullivan, Maureen, x, 297–332, 298, 301, 313, 317, 330, 331
O'Toole, D. M., 281, 182, 284, 294
Owens, A., 6, 42

Padilla, J., 201, 205, 214
Paivio, A., 160, 186
Parker, L. C., 165, 186
Parker, R., 298, 331

Author Index

Patrick, C. J., 279, 280, 284, 287, 293, 294
Penfield, W., 161, 186
Penrod, S. D., 38, 42, 80, 91, 101, 120, 123
Perry, C. W., 157, 159, 161, 163, 164, 178, 179, 185, 186, 188
Peters, D. P., 15, 43, 101, 123
Peterson, J. L., 290, 294
Peterson, M. A., 18, 43
Pfeifer, R. L., 313, 330
Phelan, J., 323, 331
Piaget, J., 201, 215
Pigott, M. A., 77, 80, 93, 121, 122
Pittner, M., 68, 80, 81, 90
Platz, S., 80, 91
Podelsny, J. A., 251, 259, 261, 262, 265, 266, 277, 279, 280, 294, 295
Poe, D., 313, 331
Postman, I., 19, 163, 186
Poulton, E. C., 24, 44
Powers, P. A., 22, 43
Predmore, S. C., 300, 331
Pressley, M., 201, 215
Pribram, K. H., 161, 185
Pridgen, D., 66, 94
Prosk, A. L., 214
Pruyser, P., 163, 185
Putnam, W. H., 163, 165, 167, 186, 198, 215

Raginsky, B. B., 163, 176, 186
Raikov, V. L., 161, 186
Rainer, D., 165, 186
Rashid, 21
Raskin, D. C., ix, 232, 233, 241, 243, 244, 245, 247-296, 247, 248, 249, 251, 252, 253, 259, 260, 261, 262, 263, 264, 265, 266, 267, 269, 272, 273, 274, 275, 277, 282, 283, 284, 285, 286, 287, 288, 289, 291, 292, 293, 294, 295, 343, 353
Rathborn, H., 85, 88, 93
Raymond, D. S., 208, 214

Read, J., 59, 93
Ready, D. J., 74, 87, 163, 165, 166, 169, 170, 171, 177, 186
Redston, M. T., 170, 186
Reed, R. S., 19, 20, 41, 202, 215
Reid, J. E., 252, 259, 263, 266, 269, 292, 295
Reiser, M., x, 152, 153, 155, 156, 158, 159, 161, 163, 165, 166, 167, 172, 175, 176, 178, 179, 183, 186, 187, 188, 193, 196
Relinger, H., 156, 164, 165, 166, 177, 187
Rhodes, B., 62, 91
Riesman, S., 163, 172, 173, 177, 187
Rodic, R., 11, 39
Rokeach, M., 160, 187
Rosenthal, R., 298, 310, 313, 331
Ross, 135, 146
Ross, D. F., 19, 40
Ross, K., 156, 175, 187
Ross, L., 82, 89
Rossi, M. H., 159, 183
Rossi, S. I., 159, 183
Rovner, L. I., 261, 285, 295
Rubin, D. C., 13, 43, 161, 187
Rubio, R., 176, 187
Rumpel, C., 80, 92

Saks, M. J., 98, 124
Salzberg, H. C., 163, 182
Sanders, G. S., 163, 170, 172, 173, 177, 187, 191, 215
Sangrey, D., 178, 181
Sannito, T., 176, 187
Sarason, I. G., 12, 43
Saslove, H., 85, 93
Schaefer, D. W., 176, 187
Schaie, K. W., 20, 39, 44
Scherer, K., 298, 303, 330
Schmauk, F. J., 307, 331
Schneck, J. M., 156, 187
Schneider, A. L., 9, 44
Schooler, J. W., 8, 32, 43, 44, 58, 94
Scott, J., 11, 22, 40

Sears, A. B., 163, 187
Segal, B., 128, 146
Sekuler. R., 8, 10, 11, 44
Sheehan, P. W., 159, 165, 170, 188
Shepard, R. N., 26, 27, 44
Shepherd, J. W., 21, 27, 38, 40, 41, 44, 49, 50, 55, 56, 58, 61, 64, 69, 74, 80, 81, 88, 89, 90, 92, 94
Shevrin, H., 163, 189
Shields, E., 54, 55, 60, 91
Shields, I. W., 171, 188
Siegel, J. M., 17, 44
Sies, D. E., 178, 188
Silberman, C. F., 23, 44
Silverberg, G., 15, 40
Simmon, W. L., 170, 187
Simpson, H. M., 298, 331
Siprelle, C. N., 167, 183
Slater, H., 160, 182
Sloane, M. C., 163, 173, 188
Slovic, P., 268, 295
Slowik, S. M., 266, 295
Smith, J. E., 285, 291
Smith, M. C., 169, 188, 216
Smith, S., 193, 216
Smith, V., 53, 59, 92
Smith, V. L., 35, 44
Snyder, L. D., 80, 87, 101, 122
Sobel, N. R., 66, 94
Soskis, D. A., 215
Spaulding, K. D., 80, 87, 101, 122
Spear, N., 160, 188
Spector, R. G., 167, 188
Sperber, Z., 156, 188
Spiegel, D., 157, 163, 188, 189
Spiegel, H., 157, 158, 179, 189
Sporer, S. L., 77, 94, 220, 245
Stager, G., 163, 167, 189
Steller, M., x, 217–245, 232, 233, 243, 245
Stephenson, G. M., 37, 44
Stern, L. W., 77, 94, 105, 120, 124
Stomovits, M., 15, 40
Stone, A. R., 216
Stone, J. I., 298, 299, 302, 315, 330

Stratton, J. G., 175, 189
Stross, L., 163, 189
Sullivan, S. J., 214
Sumi, D. H., 9, 44
Summers, W. G., 252, 295
Surtes, L., 198, 210, 214
Swann, W. B., 300, 331
Swanson, J. M., 152, 189
Sykes, R. N., 98, 118, 122, 123
Szewczyk, H., 219, 221, 224, 225, 226, 227, 228, 229, 230, 236, 237, 241, 244, 245
Szucko, J., 266, 293

Tapp, J. L., 65, 66, 92, 125, 147
Thompson, B., 58, 94
Thompson, D. M., 68, 94
Tickner, A. H., 24, 44
Timm, H. W., 165, 168, 177, 189, 288, 295
Tobin, Y., 176, 184
Toglia, M. P., 19, 40
Tomkins, S. S., 307, 331
Tooley, V., 17, 44
Trankell, A., 21, 44, 219, 222, 226, 235, 245
Traynor (Justice), 68
Trovillo, P. V., 296
Tsegaye-Spates, C. R., 158, 183
Tulving, E., 97, 124, 160, 162, 189
Turnbull, D. G., 68, 94
Tversky, B., 56, 94
Twining, E., 65, 94

Udolf, R., 157, 163, 165, 189
Underwood, B. J., 163, 186
Undeutsch, U., 219, 221, 222, 224, 226, 227, 228, 229, 230, 233, 234, 235, 236, 238, 239, 241, 245

Vaillant, G. E., 307, 331
Vollmer, T., 152, 189
Von Bertalanffy, L. 160, 189
Von Winterfeldt, E., 141, 146

Author Index

Wade, N. L., 176, 183
Wagstaff, G. F., 167, 170, 189
Waid, W. M., 283, 284, 286, 296
Wall, P. M., 65, 66, 68, 70, 95
Wallace, B., 160, 182
Watson, D. E., 178, 190
Watzlawick, P., 160, 190
Weale, R. A., 11, 44
Weaver, R. S., 260, 296
Wegener, H., 219, 237, 239, 245
Weiner, B. J., 207
Weisman, J., 315, 331
Weldon, D. E., 77, 93
Wells, G. L., 36, 37, 44, 45, 59, 68, 74, 76, 77, 78, 80, 81, 82, 83, 84, 92, 95, 99, 117, 124
West, L. J., 157, 190
Wester, W. C., 178, 188
Whipple, G. M., 120, 124
Whitehouse, W. G., 164, 183, 185
Whitney, P., 20, 41
Wicklander, D. E., 266, 296
Widacki, J., 290, 296
Wigmore, J. H., 119, 124, 129, 147
Williams, G., 65, 95
Wilson, S. K., 286, 296
Winkler, J., 120, 123
Wogalter, M., 49, 50, 55, 58, 59, 60, 62, 91, 95

Wolk, R. L., 309, 331
Woocher, F. D., 66, 95
Woocher, J., 129, 147
Worring, M. A., 157, 166, 184

Yagi, K., 15, 39
Yarmey, A. D., 7, 21, 22, 35, 45, 85, 93, 95, 99, 124, 166, 167, 190, 191, 216
Yerkes, R. M., 14, 45
Yoblick, D. A., 80, 91
Young, P. T., 304, 331
Yount, M., 53, 92
Yuille, J. C., x, 15, 16, 24, 45, 50, 68, 95, 97–124, 102, 103, 106, 107, 108, 109, 124, 163, 166, 168, 169, 170, 177, 179, 190, 201, 215, 232, 243, 245

Zanni, G. R., 35, 43, 72, 95, 109, 123
Zaragoza, M., 30, 38, 43
Zeiner, W., 61, 62. 95
Zelig, M., 163, 190
Zima, H., 61, 62, 95
Zisman, F., 11, 39
Zuckerman, M., 298, 313, 317, 331, 332

Subject Index

Aberdeen Index to Photofit, 56
Aberdeen Police, Scotland, 49
Accuracy:
   absolute, in testimony, 167
   confidence as indication of, 36–37
Admissibility:
   new scientific techniques, 336
   relevancy test, 337–338
   tests for scientific evidence, 336–338
   system requirements, 126
   see also Evidence; Hypnosis; Polygraph
Age of witness:
   reliability of testimony, 19
Aging:
   and color vision, 11
   memory processes, 20
Aircraft accidents, 176–177
American Medical Association, 179
Amnesia, 159, 160, 161, 163
Anderson, Gerald, 323, 328
Anxiety, danger situations, 15
Apple MacIntosh, 61
Arizona Supreme Court, 142
Arousal, memory recall, 171

Ashcroft, Inspector, 87
Attention, and emotional events, 12

Backster's system, 260
Bennett, Sergeant, 87
Bias:
   expectations affecting memory, 18
   hypnotized witness, 335
   index of, 74–75
   instructional, 72
   lineup identification, 67, 70, 72–73
   postevent suggestion, 31
Blank lineups, 82–84
Braggarts, 312
British Home Office, 60
Brokaw, Tom, 314

California, 178
Car accidents, 176
Central Intelligence Agency, 319
Child witness:
   cognitive interview, 201–205
   confabulations, 205
   details beyond comprehension of, 227
   motivation, 228

387

Child witness *(cont.)*
  psychological assessment, sexual abuse cases, 217
  sexual abuse cases, xv–xvi, 232
  suggestibility, 19–20
Children:
  reliability of testimony, 19
  voice identification, 85
Choosing, social psychology, 66–68
Cognitive interview, xv, 191–216
  accuracy estimation, 212
  be complete, 193–194
  change perspectives, 193, 194
  child witnesses, 201–205
  effectiveness, 211–212
  event-interview similarity, 209
  experiments (seven), 195–212
  extensive retrieval, 209–210
  field testing, 211–212
  focused retrieval, 209
  Frye vs. United States (1923), 192
  hypnosis- and standard-police interviews compared, 196–197
  leading questions (experiment), 198–201
  license plate information, 206
  memory enhancement techniques (four), 192–193
  mnemonics, 194–195
  nonstudent population (experiment), 197–198
  persons, objects, events (experiment), 203
  recall in different orders, 193, 194, 203
  recall in revised/original interviews (table), 211
  reconstruct the circumstances, 192–193, 202
  refining, 208–211
  standard interview compared with, 207
  witness-compatible questioning, 210

Color vision, 7, 10–11
  aging affecting, 11
  causes of blindness, 11
Comphotofit, 61
Compusketch, 61
Computer-Assisted Photographic Search and Retrieval (CASPAR), 63
Computer graphics, 60–61
Computers:
  in deception tests, 261–262
  memory research, 161–162
Concealed knowledge test, 276–282
  accuracy; laboratory experiments (table), 280
  administration of test, 278–279
  electrodermal response, 279–280
  field studies, 281
  interpretation of outcome, 279–280
  question sequence (table), 277
  validity, 280–282
Concealment, of emotion, 300, 301
Cones and rods, 7
Confabulation, 165–166, 171, 172, 174, 180, 205
Confessions:
  criteria-based statement analysis, 238
  deception tests, 265
  relative cost, 305
Confidence:
  accuracy of witnesses, 36–37
  excessive; hypnosis, 172
  weight in identification, 79–80
Confidential tests, 287–288
Consciousness, 161
Context reinstatement, improving memory, 38–39
Contextual embedding, 224
Control question test, 252–269
  administration of test, 258–259
  blind interpreters; percent accuracy (table), 268
  computer interpretations, 261–262

Subject Index

design, 253
development of, 252
estimates of accuracy, 266
field studies, 264–269
global evaluation, 259
interpretation of results, 259
introducing the question, 254–255
laboratory simulations, 263–264
numerical evaluation, 260
pretest interview, 255–258
question sequence (table), 257
scientifically faulty premise, 253–254
specific lie response, 253
validity, 262–263
Conversations:
related external associations, 227
reproduction of, 225
Credibility assessment:
physiological methods, 247
polygraph tests, 262
Credibility of statements, see Criteria-based statement analysis
Criteria-based statement analysis:
accurately reported details misunderstood, 22
admitting lack of memory, 229
attribution of perpetrator's mental state, 22
classification of criteria, 219
cognitive abilities of witness, 232
confessions, 238
content criteria, 218–231; (table), 221
contextual embedding, 224
credibility of statements, 235
credible testimony: at least three reality criteria, 231
criteria for credibility of testimony (table), 220
deceptive/truthful accounts, 237
descriptions of interactions, 224–225

details characteristic of the offense, 230
details in, 240
discriminating power of criteria, 243
doubts about one's own testimony, 229
empirical basis, 241
false accusations, 228
field setting, 234, 241, 242, 243
forensic applications, 233
future research, 244
in judicial processes, 231–234
incontinence (criterion), 219, 223
length of statement, 232
logical structure (criterion 1), 222
low frequency of some criteria, 237
motivation-related contents, 228–230
number of details, 240–241
offense-specific elements, 230–231
pardoning the perpetrator, 230
peculiarities of content, 226–228
quantity of details, 223
range of application, 233
reality criteria, 218
related external associations, 227
reproduction of conversation, 225
scientific basis, 234–242
self-deprecation, 229–230
specific contents, 223–224
spontaneous corrections, 228–229
standardizing assessment procedure, 243
subjective mental state, 227–228
superfluous details, 226
unexpected complications during incident, 225
unstructured production, 222–223
unusual details, 226
validation of, 235–236
validity, 234, 239
veracity of accused persons, 233
Cross-examinations, 128–130

Cross-racial identification, 131–132
Cultural bias, affecting memory, 18

Danger, 15
Deception:
  authorization for, 308
  behavioral clues, 297
  detection, xvi
  duping delight, 310–312
  guilt feelings, 306–310
  as hypothesis, 319
  impersonal targets, 309
  justifying, 309
  mistakes people make, 299
  positive feelings from, 310
  punishment (two kinds), 304
  reward as motive, 304
  social norms, 308
  success in, 303
  vocal characteristics, 298
  willing target, 309–310
  see also Detection of deception
Deception tests:
  control question test, 252–269
  directed lie control test, 269–275
  formulation of questions, 248
  relevant questions, 249
  relevant-irrelevant test, 249–252
  traditional control questions, 269–270
Description:
  free, cued, prompted, 48, 49
Detection of deception:
  accuracy rates (21 studies), 313
  beginnings: European origins, 247
  behavior changes, 316
  behavioral clues, 314
  characteristic behaviors, 316
  common mistakes in, 312–322
  detection apprehension, 302–306
  expressive behavior, 328–329
  gain/loss as factors in, 305
  gaze direction, 299
  gestures, 299
  hand movements, 316
  hazards in, 297–332
  idiosyncracy error, 314–317
  increase of apprehension, 305–306
  law enforcement personnel, 313
  lying checklist, 323–327
  nonverbal behaviors and, 298
  smiling, 298–299
Devlin Report, 67
Differential interest hypothesis, 22
Directed lie control test, 269–275
  accuracy, 273
  criminal suspects; effects (table), 274
  purpose explained, 271
  question sequence (table), 270
  rationale, 271
  validity, 272–275
Disbelieving the truth, 302, 316
  easy to do, 319
  lie-catcher, 314, 315, 318–322
  Othello's error, 318
  signs of emotion, 320, 322
Distance, estimating, 9–10
Drugs, polygraph tests, 283–285
Duping delight, 301–312
Duration of event, 8–9
Due process of law, 133
  identification procedures, 135–138

Elderly witnesses, 20–21
Electrodermal response, 279–280
Emotional events, 12
Emotions (feelings):
  causes other than guilt, 328
  concealing, 300, 301
  duping delight, 310–312
  falsification, 300–301
  feelings about lying, 301–312
  lying about feelings, 299–301
  signs, and the lie-catcher, 320, 322
Error:
  concealed knowledge test, 281
  conviction of innocent persons, 126

Subject Index

false information in memory, 29
false negative, 252
  polygraph tests, 265, 260
  preventive approach; witnesses, 132–138
  vulnerable to, 125
Estimates of duration, 8
Evidence:
  expert testimony and, 139
  Frye vs. United States (1923), 139
  hypnosis and polygraphy, 333–353
  identification procedures, 47–95
  see also Admissibility; Eyewitness; Hypnosis; Polygraph
Expectations, and memory, 18–19
Experience:
  training and memory, 23–25
Expert witnesses, 138–145
  admissibility debate, 143
  jury attitude towards, 140
  overstated testimony, 144
  People vs. MacDonald (1987), 142
  State vs. Chapple (1983), 142
  United States vs. Addison (1974), 140
  United States vs. Downing (1985), 142
Eye contact, 299, 315
Eyewitness evidence:
  cross-examination, 128–130
  Green vs. Loggins (1980), 136
  jury trial methods, 138
  legal issues in, 125–147
  preventive approach to error, 132–138
  structuring the use of, 126
  trials, 127–132
Eyewitness research:
  accuracy criteria, 104
  accuracy of recall, 112, 116
  bank robberies (case), 114–117
  breadline shooting (case), 112–114
  distribution of errors; police and research interviews, 108
  ecological validity, 98–99
  generalizability, to real-life, 100–101
  gun store robbery and shooting (case), 106–110
  investigation of four cases, 105–117
  investigative hypnosis, 164–167
  laboratory and real world, 101
  methodology, 102–104
  misleading information, 109
  rate of false identification, 115
  rating degree of stress, 110
  real-world application, 99
  recognition memory, 101
  reconstruction of details, 104–105
  restaurant shooting (case), 110–112
  staged crimes, 100
  typical framework, 99–100
Eyewitnesses:
  accuracy related to stress, 16
  age/reliability relation, 19
  cognitive interview, 191–216
  confidence/accuracy relation, 36–37
  credibility assessment, 217
  elderly persons, 20–21
  estimation of duration, speed, distance, 8–10
  evidence; legal perspective, xiv–xv
  hypnotically refreshed testimony, 335–346
  intellectual abilities; content criteria, 232
  memory, *See* Memory
  men/women performance compared, 21–23
  psychology, 217–218
  psychology; *Ibn-Tamas vs. United States* (1970), 139
  testimony; psychology, 3–45
  violence/memory relationship, 11–13
  see also Child witness; Identification

Eysenck Personality Inventory, 121
Eye movement data, 16–17

Face: 49, 50–51, 53, 54, 56, 60, 63, 64
  deception clues, 314
  better described, better identified, 77–78
  expressions: lying or truth-telling, 316
Face Analysis, Comparison and Elimination System (FACE), 64
Face Retrieval and Matching Equipment (FRAME), 63–64
Facts, information tests, 276
False confessions, 238
Fear, 300, 301
  evidence of lying, 321
  eyewitness memory and, 13–16
  of getting caught, 302–306
  of punishment, 303
Federal Bureau of Investigation, 52
Federal Rules of Evidence, 35
Feelings, *see* Emotions
Field Identification System, 53, 58
Field studies:
  cognitive interview, 211–212
  concealed knowledge test, 281
  control question test, 264–269
  criteria-based statement analysis, 234, 241, 242, 243
  investigative hypnosis, 173–177
  memory research, 97–124
  polygraph tests, 264–269
First impressions, 317
Forgetting, 25–28, 163
  causes, 27–28
  Ebbinghaus forgetting curve, 26–27
  interval length, 27
  motivated, 28
Fourteenth Amendment, 345
Friendly polygrapher hypothesis, 287–288
Frye vs. United States, 336–338

Gaze direction, 299
Gender and memory, 21–23
Germany, xv, 217, 232, 238, 242
Gestures, during deception, 299
Glebock (1981) Court, 342
Guilt:
  deception tests, 265, 266
  detection apprehension and, 309
  feelings about lying, 306–310
  guilt-prone people, 307
  severity, 308
Gullibility, 311

Hidden observer, 152
Houston Mugfile Project, 62
Hurd standards, 341–342
Hypermnesia, 160, 161, 162–164, 171, 172
Hypnosis (including hypnotically refreshed testimony):
admissibility of evidence from, 333–353
  Beck vs. Norris (1986), 344
  bias, 335
  cases/statutes determining a. (list), 354–358
  cementing erroneous memories, 335
  criteria for a. (list), 359–362
  evaluation of posthypnosis testimony, 345
  Federal Courts, 344–345
  Hurd standards, 341–342
  lying possibility, 339
  per se admissible, 343–344
  procedural safeguards, 340–342
  recollections prior to, 340
  Rock vs. Arkansas (1986), 345
  Sprynczynatyk vs. General Motors (1985), 343
  State Courts, 338–339
  State vs. Armstrong, 343
  State vs. Blanchard, 343
  State vs. Glebock (1981), 344
  trends, 345–346

United States vs. Miller (1969), 344
all self-hypnosis, 156–157
arousal; maximizing recall, 171
coerced confessions, 157–158
danger (myth), 157
evidence from, xvi–xvii
hypnotic ability, 160
interview: cognitive interview, 196–197
mind control (myth), 156
myths, misinformation, misunderstandings, 156–160
recall and recognition errors, 171–172
suggestibility, 159, 160, 169
therapeutic, 158
trance, 159
truth-compelling (myth), 157
Hypnosis, Investigative:
building rapport, 153
cases, 151–152
controversial issues, 160–167
critiques of laboratory research, 177
decision-making ability, 166
deepening phase, 154
dehypnotization phase, 154
ecological validity, 167–173
excessive confidence hypothesis, 172
field research in, 173–177
interview guidelines, 155
legal/political issues, 178–179
memory distortions, 164
misunderstandings re police training, 159
People vs. Shirley (1982), 178
People vs. Singleton (1980), 152
phases (seven), 153
photograph lineup responses, 170
process, 153–155
recall amount related to meaningfulness, 176
recall quality, 167
research on utility of, 167–179
Rock vs. Arkansas (1987), 178
techniques for eliciting information, 154
training police; brief history, 155–156

Identification, 64–86
accuracy and confidence; weight, 79–80
accuracy assessment, 49, 50
computer-assisted searching, 62–64
confidence as factor in, 79–80
constitutional guarantees, 133
context reinstatement, 38
cross-racial, 131–132
descriptive phase, 48–61
due process of law, 135–138
elapsed time, memory strength, 80
errors in, 65
expert psychological testimony, 138–139
by eyewitnesses, xiv
facial features, 49
laboratory testing, 50
mistaken, *See* Mistaken identification
obtaining evidence; procedures, 47–95
People vs. Lutz (1982), 137
right to counsel, 133–135
search of archives/records, 61–64
Simons vs. State (1980), 137
structural perspective, 70–78
suggestiveness in, 136, 137, 138
three major phases, 48
unattractiveness of choosing, 66
United States vs. Phillips (1981), 136
United States vs. Wade (1967), 133, 135
verbal descriptions, 48–51
visual representations, 51–61
composite systems, 52–57

Identification *(cont.)*
  computerized composite systems, 60–61
  flexibility, in sketches, 60
  formal training, 55
  multidimensional scaling, 55
  police artists, 51–52
  sketches and composites, 59–60
  true likeness vs. realistic portrait, 56–57
  voice, *See* Voice identification
  witness memory aid or hinderance question, 57–59
  see also Eyewitnesses; Lineup
Identikit, 52, 56, 57, 58, 59, 60, 63, 154
Incest, criteria-based statement analysis, 231
Individual differences:
  detecting deceit, 314
  first impressions, 317
Information:
  false/new in memory, 29–30
  residing in memory, 25
Information-processing, 161–162
Information tests, 275–282
  concealed knowledge test, 276–282
  peak of tension tests, 275–276
Inglewood, Calif., 192
Innocent persons:
  fear, and the lie-catcher, 302
  Gerald Anderson case, 323, 328
  relevant-irrelevant test, 252
  polygraph tests, 265, 266
International Society for Investigative and Forensic Hypnosis Resolution, 179
International Society of Hypnosis Resolution, 179
Interrogation methods, *see* Cognitive interview
Interviewing, xv
  improved techniques through training, 212–213
  in police academies, 191
  standard form, 192
  strategy, 34–35
  see also Cognitive interview
Investigative hypnosis, *see* Hypnosis, Investigative
Investigative methods:
  effectiveness, xiii

Jury:
  correct decision-making, 129–130
  decision-making in, 127
  expert witnesses and, 140
  eyewitness reliability and, 138
  instructions to, 130–132
  polygraph evidence and, 289–290
  selection process, 128
  standard instruction (text), 130–131
  United States vs. Telfaire (1972), 131

Kennedy, Edward:
  events at Chappaquiddick, 28
Kidding, 311
Kum, Doreen, 122

Leading questions, 32, 35, 198–201
Liar; Lie; Lying:
  believing, 314
  checklist, 323–327
  eye contact, 299, 315
  fear as sign of, 321
  feelings/emotions, 299–312
  gain from, 308
  guilt feeling, 306–310
  John Irving on, 311
  justifications for, 309–310
  lying checklist, 326
  personality of, 303
  successful, 322
  superior skills, 303
  vocal pitch, 297–298
License plate information, 206

Lie-catcher, 302, 304, 314, 315, 318–322
  lying checklist, 327
  preconceptions, 319
  signs of emotion, 320, 322
Lie detection, *see* Detection of deception
Light adaptation, 7–8
Lighting conditions, 6–7
Lineup:
  biased against the suspect, 75, 76
  blacks in, 74
  blank, 82–84
  cognitive perspective, 78–84
  construction of, 76–78
  decision process, 67
  fairness, 74
  fear of reprisal, 68
  influencing factors in, 65–66
  investigative hypnosis, 170
  live vs. still, 68
  memory role, 78
  perpetrator-absent, 69, 70–72, 82–83
  positive identification, 65
  potential for suggestion in, 70, 73
  relative judgment process, 79
  resemblance, 81–82
  right to counsel, 134
  screening devices, 83
  sequential, 83–84
  size, 73, 75
  social psychology, 66–70
  videotaped, 68
Los Angeles, 192
Los Angeles County Sheriff's Department, 175–176
Los Angeles Police Department, 155, 156, 159, 175, 180
Lying, *see* Liar

Mac-A-Mug Pro, 61
Machiavelli, 300
Memory, xiv
  admitting lack of, 229

acquiring information, 6–25
  accuracy of initial perception, 24–25
  dark adaptation, 7
  duration of event, 8–9
  experience/training study, 24
  light adaptation, 7–8
  lighting conditions, 6–7
  occupational training, 23–25
  prior expectations, 18–19
  stress and fear, 13–16
  type of fact, 9
  violence of an event, 11–13
  weapon focus, 16–17
advances in scientific knowledge, 5
alteration by postevent information, 30, 31–32
alteration of recollection, 32
arousal affecting, 15
child witnesses, 19
chronic stress and, 17–18
coexistence; postevent information, 30
concealed knowledge test, 281–282
context reinstatement, 38–39
decline over time, 80–81, 120
distortions, 31–34, 164–165
eyewitness problems, 3
false information integrated into, 29
general theory of, 5–6
improving retrieval of, 37–39
investigative hypnosis, 160–162
operation; theory, 193
plasticity, 30
postevent information, 28–31
real/unreal memories, 32–34
recall and relaxation, 170
reconstruction model, 162
research; computer impact, 161–162
retaining events in, 23–34
retrieving events from, 34–39
subconscious, 161

Memory *(cont.)*
  three-stage analysis, 6
  time interval affecting, 31
  see also Forgetting; Lineup; Recall
Memory research:
  accuracy of recall (tables), 107, 111, 114, 115
  accuracy of recall, 110
  doubts about ecological validity, 97–98
  errors of estimation, 109
  factors affecting human memory, 118
  field research problems, 119
  field studies, 97–124
  forensic settings, 120–121
  initial misperceptions, 109
  laboratory/actual witnesses, 120
  laboratory eyewitnesses, 100
  long retention interval, 114
  misleading questions, 120
  nature and function; 100 years of research, 97
  real world, 98
  recognition memory, 116
  reliable analysis needed, 102
  systematic field research needed, 121
  witness's fallibility, 119
Mental health professionals, 178–179
Metro-Dade County, Florida, 192
Metro-Dade Police Department, 211
Microcomputers:
  identification-search routines, 62–63
Mistaken identification:
  cases, 4
  Donald Thomson, 4
  improper suggestion as cause, 70
  Manson vs. Braithwaite (1977), 135, 136
  variables inherent in, 5
Mock crime experiments, 261, 263, 285

Mock witnesses, 74–75, 76
Moonlight, 7
Mugshots, 62

Names, recall technique, 195
National Jury Project, 128
New information, 24
  affecting memory, 29–30
New York, 191
Night vision, 6
Nixon, Richard, 18

Occupation:
  training and memory, 23–25
Office of Technology Assessment, 283, 294
Optical Identification of Characteristics of Facial Features, 63
Othello error, 317–322
Owens, Aaron Lee, 4

Pardons, 82
Peak of tension tests, 275–276
People vs. Wright (1980), 131
Perception, xiv
  general theory of, 5–6
Performance, stress affecting, 14
Personality, signs of emotion, 320
Photoarray technique, 134
Photofit, 53, 54, 55, 56, 57, 60, 61
Photographs, 57
Photospread, 68, 69
Plea-bargain arrangements, 238
Poker players, 308, 315–316
Police:
  memory study, 24
  positive effect of training, 24
  training for witnessing, 23
  training in interviewing, 191
  use of hypnosis distrusted, 178–179
Police artists, 51–52, 57–60

Polygraph, xvi
  admissibility of evidence from, 333–353
    binding stipulation, 348
    cases/statutes determining a. (list), 363–370
    Commonwealth vs. Vitello (1978), 347
    Commonwealth vs. Wick (1987), 347
    criteria for a. (list), 371–373
    Federal Courts, 350
    inadmissible; indeterminate basis, 349
    lecensure statutes' effect on (list), 377–378
    licensure statutes, 350–352
    People vs. Barbara (1977), 352
    People vs. Baynes (1981), 349
    per se admissible, 347
    per se inadmissible, 349
    Rock vs. Arkansas (1986), 346
    State Courts, 347–349
    State vs. Collins (1980), 352
  applied issues, 282–290
  clue to deceit not foolproof, 315
  competence and licensure, 352
  countermeasures, 283–286
  criminal cases, 334
  detection of deception, 247–296
  drugs and, 283–285
  friendly polygrapher hypothesis, 287–288
  impact on jurors, 289–290
  information tests, 275–282
  levels of accuracy, 268–269
  licensure requirements (State statutes; list), 374–376
  licensure statutes, 350–352
  numerical evaluation, 260
  percent accuracy of different tests (table), 273
  personality factors, 286–287
  pretest interview, 255–258
  prisoners, 286
  psychological maneuvers, 285–286
  psychopaths, 286–287
  testing victims, 288–289
  tests of reliability, 346
Prisoners, polygraph tests, 286
Propranolol, 284–285
Psychologist(s):
  as expert witnesses, 138–145
Psychology:
  investigative effectiveness, xiii
  statistical/probabilistic information, 125–126, 141
Psychopaths:
  guilt feelings, 307
  lying, 303
  polygraph tests, 286–287, 315
Punishment, fear of, 303, 304

Quantel paintbox, 53
Questioning:
  inconsistent information affecting memory, 29
  leading questions, 32, 35, 198–201
  wording affecting memory, 31–32, 34–36

Realism, in police portraits, 56
Reality criteria, *see* Criteria-based statement analysis
Recall:
  cognitive interview, 192
  enhanced by recreation of event, 152
  errors; research in hypnosis, 171–172
  hypnotically-aided, 173
  memory refreshment, 174
  review of 35 experiments, 164
Recollection, *see* Memory
Relaxation:
  memory improvement, 170
Relevancy test, 337–338
Relevant-Irrelevant test, 249–252
  interpretation of results, 250–251
  psychophysiologically naive, 251

Relevant-Irrelevant test *(cont.)*
  rationale of, 250
  structure and administration, 249–250
  validity, 251–252
Retrieval cues, 162
Rewards:
  decision to deceive, 304
Right to counsel:
  Brewer vs. Williams (1977), 134
  identification procedures, 133–135
  Moore vs. Illinois (1977), 134
  United States vs. Jones (1973), 135
Rods and cones, 7
Royal Canadian Mounted Police, 62, 102, 106, 122

San Jose Methods Test, 12
Seattle, Washington, 49
Self-deprecation, 229–230
Sequential lineup, 83–84
Sexual abuse of children, 230, 232, 241, 242
  see also Child witness
Shakespeare, William, 318
Shame, and guilt, 307
Sixth Amendment, 133, 134
Size, and estimation of speed, 10
Sketches, 59–60
Smiling, 298–299
Society for Clinical and Experimental Hypnosis, 179
Speed, estimating, 9–10
State vs. Hurd, 341–342
Stealing, guilt feelings, 306
Stress:
  appearance of lying, 318
  degree of; research, 110
  chronic, and memory, 17–18
  eyewitness memory and, 13–16
Subconscious memory, 161
Success, in deceit, 303

Suggestibility:
  child witnesses, 19–20
  hypnosis and, 159, 169
  power of suggestion, 159–160
Suspicion:
  emotional reaction to, 321

Testimony:
  absolute accuracy in, 167
Tests, *see* Concealed knowledge test; Controlled question test; Deception tests; Directed lie control test
Thomson, Donald, 3–4
Time estimation, 8–9
Training, affecting memory, 23–25
Trance, 159, 172
Trials:
  eyewitness role in, 127–132
  see also Eyewitnesses
Trustworthiness, assessing, 218
Truth:
  absence of sign of, 315
  disbelieving, *see* Disbelieving the truth
Truthful people:
  signs of feelings, 318, 321
Truth-telling:
  reward and punishment, 304–305
Turner, Mark, 122

UCLA, 199
United States Secret Service, 267, 268, 321
United States Supreme Court, 133
Utah, 252, 260
Utah Supreme Court, 352

Vancouver City Police, 102, 122
Vancouver, skid row, 113
Victims' Bill of Rights, 178
Victims of crime:
  cognitive interview, 191–216
  polygraph tests, 288–289
Videofit, 53

Subject Index

Violence:
    affecting witness perception and memory, 11–13
    eyewitness research, 117
Vision, color, *see* Color vision
Voice identification, 84–86
    accuracy studies, 85–86
    confidence/accuracy relationship, 85
    cross-racial problems, 85
    trainability, 85
    under-researched, 86
Voir Dire, 128

Walker, John (Navy spy), 311
Warning: altering recollection, 32

Warren Court, 127, 137
Weapon focus, 16–17
West Germany, 219
Wisconsin State Police, 63
Witness, *see* Eyewitness
Women:
    performance as eyewitnesses, 21–23
Wording of questions, 35–36
Wrongdoers, lying to, 307

Yerkes-Dodson Law, 14

DATE DUE